Rethinking Asian Capitalism

Thi Anh-Dao Tran
Editor

Rethinking Asian Capitalism

The Achievements and Challenges of Vietnam Under Doi Moi

palgrave
macmillan

Editor
Thi Anh-Dao Tran
LASTA (University of Rouen Normandy)
Faculty of Law, Economics and Management
Rouen, France

IRASEC-CNRS
Bangkok, Thailand

ISBN 978-3-030-98103-7 ISBN 978-3-030-98104-4 (eBook)
https://doi.org/10.1007/978-3-030-98104-4

This Palgrave Macmillan imprint is published by the registered company Springer Nature Switzerland AG.
The registered company address is: Gewerbestrasse 11, 6330 Cham, Switzerland

In memory of my grandparents, who gave a deep meaning to my professional dreams and to the ongoing engagement I have had with Vietnam over many years

Preface

Today, Vietnam is conducting its multilateral foreign policy. It has its own cultural and philosophical identities, but its level of technology and economic management still leaves much to be desired. We intend to benefit from the valuable knowledge and experience of all countries without jeopardising our culture, our spirit of independence and autonomy, and our Vietnamese character traits.

General VO Nguyen Giap met Former US Defence Secretary Robert McNamara, 9 November 1995

Contemporary globalisation is posing new challenges in the twenty-first century. Understanding this requires reflection upon the past for useful insights in a comparative perspective. Since the end of the Cold War, the process of globalisation has resulted in a renewed diversity of socio-economic regimes and growth strategies, which have to be explored. To our knowledge, such an unorthodox view has not been deployed in Southeast Asian studies. Mainstream theory has permeated economies and societies there, including those in transition to a market economy.

In this volume, we pay particular attention to Vietnam during and after *Doi Moi*. Present-day Vietnam is in many ways similar to a large number of developing countries and is seen by many in the era of globalisation as an emerging Asian economy. Despite being written basically from an economics perspective, this edited book is, nevertheless, intended to reach a much wider readership. By unveiling various dimensions of the post-*Doi Moi* period, it attempts to reflect on the changes that Vietnam has experienced over the past 30 years, what has been achieved so far and what has still to be done. Moreover, understanding conditions in other Asian countries makes it possible to elucidate some of the features specific to the Vietnamese context.

Vietnam's story during and after *Doi Moi* is told in many different ways, keeping its essence but adding a different flavour each time a different perspective is adopted. This volume stands at the crossroads of two major fields, namely economics (political economy) and (Southeast) Asian studies. But by involving scholars with diverse backgrounds in the social sciences, it seeks to develop a multi-dimensional analysis. With the aim of highlighting context-specific changes, a diversity of approaches to the Vietnamese trajectory is provided by combining economics, anthropology, culturology, sociology, ethnography, history and political science. Being methodologically pluralist (including both theoretical and empirical studies), it aims to give a higher profile to the research of heterodox economists in comparative political economy.

The publication is an educational tool to remind young scholars and policymakers that there is much to learn from the past. We believe that it comes at a time when great changes are about to take place in Southeast Asia, where heterodox economic development strategy is rather understudied. The main thesis of this book is that the "neo-liberal moment" that followed the collapse of the Berlin Wall should be questioned in order to better face the challenges ahead. Thus one of the book's important objectives is to identify avenues for addressing some of these challenges.

Rouen, France
November 2021

Thi Anh-Dao Tran

Acknowledgements

For two years from 2018 to 2020, I had the opportunity to do my research at the Research Institute on Contemporary Southeast Asia (IRASEC-CNRS). A significant number of people have worked together with me from the very beginning, when we organised the international conference *Rethinking Asian Capitalism and Society in the 21st Century: A Comparative Overview on 30 Years of Vietnam's Achievements Under Doi Moi and Challenges Ahead*. This conference was held on 7–8 November 2019 at the Southern Institute of Social Sciences (SISS-Vietnam Academy of Social Sciences) and followed an academic workshop "Regulation theory: A lecture by Robert Boyer" on 6 November 2019 at the Ho Chi Minh City Open University (HCMC-OU).

While I will, in what follows, try to do justice to their many vital contributions, I apologise in advance for any omissions. The list is long and a complete inventory is simply not feasible, as with any project of this sort.

A profound debt is owed to my colleagues from the Southern Institute of Social Sciences and Ho Chi Minh City Open University in Vietnam, who worked directly with me during my secondment at the Research Institute on Contemporary Southeast Asia (IRASEC-CNRS). Without their tireless and effective support in organising the conference, the present volume would have been impossible. I had frequent opportunities for fruitful exchanges with Associate Professor Dr LE Thanh Sang (Director of SISS) and Associate Professor Dr NGUYEN Minh Ha (Rector of HCMC-OU). To them go my sincerest thanks.

I am sincerely grateful to IRASEC, who supported me in many ways over the period in question. The manuscript has benefited at all stages of work from the financial support provided by the Institute for copy editing and for the initial conference held in Ho Chi Minh City. This work would not have been possible without continuous professional and administrative assistance from Joe, Bertrand and Hervé. I would like to highlight my gratitude to Associate Professor Dr Thi Liên Claire Tran, the former Director of IRASEC. I personally appreciated her leadership and effective management, while she also provided most helpful advice and support. Without her involvement, the publication would never have seen the light of day.

I would like to thank all the contributors who have been actively involved from the early stages when we shared our points of views during the conference. Their profiles can be found in the list of contributors, and I wish to express my gratitude for their analytical work and encouraging research that makes up the very core of this volume. I am most grateful to Professor Robert Boyer, who encouraged me to publish this volume at a critical moment. Special thanks are also due to Nguyen Don Phuoc: more than an independent translator, he enabled me to spend a worthwhile three years in Ho Chi Minh City with fruitful and enjoyable exchanges of ideas.

Lastly, this work has benefited from the valuable help of Andrew Wilson in correcting the original manuscripts. I would like to express my deepest sense of appreciation for the valuable time he spent with us, in reading and editing the different contributions.

It is clear that I am indebted to a large number of people. I will do my utmost to ensure that the mutual collaboration we have managed to establish will continue to develop and flourish.

About This Book

The fall of the Berlin Wall has exposed the diversity (and interdependency) of socio-economic regimes and growth strategies. The existing literature on varieties of capitalism identifies broadly four important types of capitalism: Anglo-Saxon, Continental European, Nordic European and East Asian.[1] This identification of the diversity of capitalism is an original contribution of *régulation* theory, which has highlighted the different types of capitalism interacting within the global economy.[2] In the spirit of what *régulation* theory has done in Europe and East Asia, this book attempts to better understand the long-run transformation of economies and societies in Southeast Asia. More precisely, it contributes to the approach on the renewed diversity of socio-economic regimes by scrutinising the Vietnamese experience in a regional and comparative perspective. From a historical perspective, Vietnam is nowadays cited as "an economic success or miracle"[3] just as Japan was regarded in the 1980s. In some aspects, the flying geese paradigm needs to be further explored for useful insights.

At the other end of the spectrum, the literature on Vietnam reflects predominantly mainstream or conventional approaches to transition and

[1] K. Lee and H. Shin (2021): "Varieties of capitalism and East Asia: Long-term evolution, structural change, and the end of East Asian capitalism". *Structural Change and Economic Dynamics*, 56, 431–437, March.

[2] R. Boyer, H. Uemura, and A. Isogai, Eds. (2011): *Diversity and transformations of Asian Capitalisms*, London: Routledge.

[3] P. Vanham (2018): "The story of Viet Nam's economic miracle". World Economic Forum, published on 11 Sept 2018: https://www.weforum.org/agenda/2018/09/how-vietnam-became-an-economic-miracle/

development. In the early years of *Doi Moi*, however, there was a body of literature which was enriched by a focus on Vietnam's context-specific economic, social and political transformation or the "Vietnamese style". Some authors developed a unique and original perspective, where Vietnam's successful path was described as an unpredictable process with a sceptical stance to dealing with market reforms and liberalisation. To the best of our knowledge, such an unorthodox view has not so far been reinvigorated. For example, recent publications in economics have already gone a long way towards establishing the idea that there is a single model of development in Asia (illustrated by the successive waves of export-led industrialisation), not to mention the judgement that Vietnam is duplicating the Chinese strategy. But reality is far more varied than it appears, and contextualisation is in order.

This edited book aims to fill the gap by positing an alternative analysis to the current economic literature. First, we attempt to identify the diversity of socio-economic regimes in Asia by looking into Vietnam. Second, we propose a comparative perspective on Vietnam's achievements by deploying a multidisciplinary approach. Useful insights with reference to the time and space dimensions are provided to help reassess the country's future path in a contemporary international and regional context.

The rise of neoliberalism in Southeast Asia has brought about significant changes in many ways. With Asia playing an increasingly important role in the world economy, this volume makes an important contribution to our understanding of the key dynamics reshaping Asia's role. But readers wish not only to hear about the economic transformation but also to see certain hidden aspects or original evidence in order that they can perceive the other dimensions put in place in a market-oriented economy. To this end, the publication brings together scholars with diverse backgrounds in social sciences in order to take a multidimensional standpoint.

Contents

Notes on Contributors

Frédéric Boccara is a member of the *Centre d'Economie de l'Université Paris Nord* (CEPN, Sorbonne Paris Nord University and CNRS). He is an economist statistician, and his work continues the development of the systemic regulation school (Paul Boccara) on globalization and multinational enterprises, foreign direct investment, SMEs, ecology, monetary policy and theory and the construction of Europe. His PhD was on multinational firms in the informational revolution and financial globalization. Co-editor of *Economie & Politique*, a Marxist economics journal, he contributed to a bill presented to the French Parliament "For Security of Training and Employment". He co-founded the *Economistes Atterrés* ("Appalled Economists") association. He is an honorary member of the French constitutional assembly CESE (Economic, Social and Environmental Council). He has launched several citizens' appeals sustaining struggling workers or social movements and developing alternative proposals to managements' plans.

Robert Boyer is a French economist trained at the *Ecole Polytechnique*, *Sciences-Po Paris* and Paris 1 University. Previously a senior researcher at CNRS and professor at *École des Hautes Études en Sciences Sociales* (EHESS), he is a fellow of the *Institut des Amériques* (Paris). He has developed a historical and comparative analysis of the institutional transformations of capitalism, under the label of *régulation* theory. Systematic international comparisons converge toward a taxonomy of contemporary socioeconomic regimes and their growing interdependence within an unprecedented configuration of the world economy. His original publications on *régulation* theory include *La théorie de la régulation: une analyse critique* (1986), completed, with Y. Saillard, by *La théorie de la régulation: l'état des savoirs* (1995).

Homepage: https://robertboyer.org/en/new/

The Cuong Bui holds a BA in political economy from the Ha Noi National University and a doctorate in sociology from the Institute of Sociology and Social Policy (Academy of Sciences, German Democratic Republic). Recently, he was visiting professor at the Institute of Asian Studies (Brunei Darussalam University) and visiting fellow at the Center of Southeast Asian Studies (Kyoto University). He has worked for 40 years at the Vietnamese Academy of Social Sciences, including the positions of Vice-Director of the Institute of Sociology (1999–2005), Director of the Southern Institute of Social Sciences (2005–2012), and Editor-in-Chief of the Ho Chi Minh City Journal of Social Sciences (2005–2013). He is a member of the standing committee of the Vietnamese Association of Sociology. He has been teaching and studying in several fields such as social stratification, public policy, and transdisciplinary research.

Anne Cheng is a graduate of ENS Paris and has held the chair in Chinese intellectual history at the prestigious *Collège de France* since 2008. For 40 years at French National Centre for Scientific Research (CNRS), National Institute for Oriental Languages and Civilizations (INALCO) and now at the *Collège de France*, she has taught and conducted research in that field, Confucianism in particular. She is the author of a French translation of the *Confucian Analects* and of a history of Chinese thought (*Histoire de la pensée chinoise*, Seuil, latest ed. 2014), which has been translated into numerous languages (including Chinese, Japanese and soon Vietnamese). She has edited several collective volumes (notably *Uses and Abuses of the Great Learning*, Collège de France, 2015) and, since 2010, has been chief editor of a bilingual series (classical Chinese/French) at *Les Belles Lettres.*

Guillaume Duteurtre is a researcher at the French Agricultural Research Centre for International Development (CIRAD). His research relates to livestock economics and livestock development policies. He has worked for 20 years in various developing and emerging countries in Africa and Southeast Asia. He worked in Vietnam from 2009 to 2015 in collaboration with Institute of Policy and Strategy for Agriculture and Rural Development (IPSARD) and National Institute for Animal Science in

Hanoi (NIAS). He coordinated the Revalter research project devoted to assessing the sustainability of livestock development pathways in Vietnam. He has many years of experience in institutional economics and in interdisciplinary research. His work is development-oriented, seeking partnerships with policymakers.

Etienne Espagne is a senior economist at *Agence Française de Développement* (AFD), the French government's bilateral development bank. He develops and contributes to a research programme on the modelling and evaluation of climate damage, adaptation and mitigation strategies in developing and emerging economies. He holds a PhD in environmental economics from the *École des Hautes Études en Sciences Sociales* (EHESS) and is also a graduate of the French *École des Mines de Paris* and the Paris School of Economics. He has published several papers in academic journals in the field of climate change and energy economics and regularly teaches at Paris 1 University, EHESS, *Ecole Polytechnique* and *ENSTA Paristech*. He has previously worked at *France Stratégie*, CEPII and CIRED.

Elodie Mania is a lecturer (assistant professor) at Paris Dauphine University and research associate at LASTA (University of Rouen Normandy, France). With recent publications in relevant journals such as *Journal of International Development* and *Structural Change and Economic Dynamics*, her research focuses on economic issues related to trade diversification, the vulnerability of growth models in developing countries to macroeconomic instabilities and environmental issues. She is currently working from a comparative perspective on the interactions between trade performance and economic growth in developing regions.

Duy Mong Ha Nguyen is Head of the Office of Educational Testing and Quality Assurance at the University of Social Sciences & Humanities (USSH), Vietnam National University, Ho Chi Minh City (VNU-HCMC). She is a lecturer and researcher in education management and leadership, English Linguistics, literature and cultural studies. She holds a BA in English Linguistics and Literature (1994) and an MA in TESOL (2000) from VNU-HCMC. She holds a master's degree from the Technical University of Dresden (2002) and a PhD in cultural studies from VNU-HCMC (2016). She has published papers in different fields (higher education, culture and society, leadership and management, and intercultural competence) and is engaged in educational innovation projects.

Mai Huong Nguyen holds a doctoral degree in agricultural economics from the *SupAgro* Montpellier (France). She is now Deputy Director of the Rural Development Centre (RUDEC)—a research centre under the Institute of Policy and Strategy for Agriculture and Rural Development (IPSARD). Her main expertise is in the areas of public services, food systems, rural production systems, sustainable development and sector and economic modelling. Her current research interests focus on multiscale evaluations of sustainability and prospective scenario planning. Her research involves much field work, interacting with farmers and communities at grassroots level to support evidence-based and pro-poor decision making.

Minh Doi Nguyen is a lecturer in the Faculty of Economics and Public Management, Ho Chi Minh City Open University. He is currently completing his PhD at Heidelberg University (Germany). He holds a master's degree in governance and public policy from the University of Passau (Germany) and a BA in public administration from the National Academy of Public Administration in Vietnam. His academic work focuses on policy making, urban governance, and development. His recent and on-going research projects include enhancing the effectiveness of governance in public sectors (such as public services) and public-private partnerships. Prior to joining HCMC Open University, he served as an official in the municipal government of Ho Chi Minh City.

Thi Thu-Ha Nguyen is currently completing her PhD at LASTA (University of Rouen Normandy, France). She was awarded a French Excellence Scholarship 2018, enabling her to carry out doctoral research entitled "*Essays on Globalization and the Effects of Climate Change for Developing Countries: A Case Study of Vietnam*". She is working for her PhD under the umbrella of the GEMMES-VN project being undertaken by *Agence Française de Développement* (AFD). After a master's degree in development economics and project analysis at the University of Clermont-Ferrand (France), she has developed competencies in macroeconomic modelling, especially in stock-flow consistent (SFC) models. She co-published "The Three Dialectics of Adaptation Finance in Vietnam" in *Sustainability*.

Emmanuel Pannier is an anthropologist and is a research fellow at the French Research Institute for Sustainable Development (IRD). He is currently hosted by the University of Social Sciences and Humanities in Hanoi. His research areas are in the field of "economic anthropology" and deal with non-commercial flows, personal relationship networks and social change in rural areas of Vietnam. He is now involved in the GEMMES-VN (AFD) project on the socio-economic impacts of climate change in Vietnam and adaptation strategies.

Thanh Thanh Phan is a full-time researcher at the Institute of Human Studies, Vietnam Academy of Social Sciences (VASS). She is currently a PhD student at the Institute of Human Rights and Peace Studies (IHRP, Mahidol University, Thailand). She holds a master's degree in international development from the Regional Center for Social Science and Sustainable Development (RCSD, Chiang Mai University) and a bachelor's degree in sociology from the Academy of Journalism and Communication (Hanoi, Vietnam). Her interests focus on human rights, human security and development and her PhD deals with land law, agricultural land conversion and farmer resistance in Vietnam.

Arsène Rieber is Associate Professor of Economics and Research Affiliate at LASTA (University of Rouen Normandy, France). He was formerly Head of the Centre for Research in Economics Applied to Globalisation (CREAM, University of Rouen Normandy). His main research interests are macro-dynamics, development economics and post-Keynesian economics. His recent work deals with the sustainability of growth strategies based on export diversification, globalisation and climate change. He has published in major international journals such as the *Cambridge Journal of Economics*, *Journal of Post Keynesian Economics*, *Structural Change and Economic Dynamics*, *Journal of Economic Integration*, *Journal of Economic Development*, and *International Economics*.

Natedao Taotawin is Associate Professor in Anthropology and Ethnography at the Faculty of Liberal Arts (Ubon Ratchathani University, Thailand). Her research interests are in changing livelihood strategies in response to vulnerability and disaster in the Pak Panang River Basin in Southern Thailand (2007); cross-border mobility and sexual violence in Thai-Lao Border Zone (2008); livelihood strategies of Northeastern female migrants who leave the city and migrate back homes in Ubon Ratchathani Province of Thailand (2013); the boom of cash crops and the change of land uses and land ownerships in the borderland of Thai-Laos (2015); the illicit border trade: conditions, mechanisms and state agencies' management in Thai-Laos border trade (2017).

Yves Tiberghien holds PhD, Stanford University, 2002, and is Professor of Political Science, Director Emeritus of the Institute of Asian Research, and Co-Director of the Center for Japanese Research at the University of British Columbia, Vancouver, BC, Canada. He was a Harvard Academy Scholar in 2006 and a Fulbright Scholar in 1996. He is also Distinguished Fellow at the Asia-Pacific Foundation of Canada and at the University of Alberta's China Institute. In November 2017, he was made a *Chevalier de l'ordre national du mérite* by the French President.

His research focuses on comparative political economy, international political economy, global economic and environmental governance, with an empirical focus on China, Japan, Korea, Southeast Asia, and Europe. He has recently published a book entitled *The East Asian COVID-19 Paradox*.

Homepage: https://politics.ubc.ca/profile/yves-tiberghien/

Ninh Ton-Nu-Thi is the former Ambassador of Viet Nam to the European Union and Belgium, former Vice-Chair of the Foreign Affairs Committee (Viet Nam National Assembly), and current President of Ho Chi Minh City Peace and Development Foundation (HPDF). Educated in France and Europe, Madam Ninh has been a university lecturer, career diplomat and elected official.

Today she is engaged in the socio-cultural sphere, working to promote Viet Nam's sustainable development and empowerment of women and youth and contribute to Viet Nam's more effective international integration and nation branding. Through her frequent interaction with the public, especially women, young people and the media, she is known as one of the public figures with a meaningful voice in Viet Nam. She is *Doctor Honoris Causa* of Social Sciences conferred in 2017 by RMIT.

Thi Anh-Dao Tran is Associate Professor of Economics and Research Affiliate at LASTA (University of Rouen Normandy, France); she is also research associate at the Research Institute on Contemporary Southeast Asia (IRASEC-CNRS). She was seconded to the French Institute of Research for Development (DIAL-IRD) in Hanoi before being posted to IRASEC in Ho Chi Minh City. She is Vice-President (representing Europe) of the International Society of Vietnam Economists, whose mis-

sion is to build capacities and to encourage and promote research and training in economics, management and finance among Vietnamese scholars across the world.
Her main fields of interest are the issues of globalisation, trade integration and sustainable development from the perspective of dynamic emerging economies in the Global South. Whatever the topics covered, her research work analyses the issues associated with export-oriented development strategies and the related vulnerabilities. In that respect, comparative studies are developed using a structuralist approach in the emerging and developing economies. Her research work has been published in various academic journals including *Asia-Pacific Journal of Accounting and Economics*, *Cambridge Journal of Economics*, *Comparative Economic Studies*, *Journal of Development Studies*, *Journal of Post-Keynesian Economics*, and *Post-Communist Economies.*

Si Anh Truong holds a bachelor's degree in regional and economic geography (1986) from Charle's University (Prague, Czech Republic) and a master of science degree (1993) from the Asian Institute of Technology (AIT, Thailand). He has 15 years of experience as a senior researcher at the Economic Research Institute of HCM City where he was involved in a number of international joint projects with UNDP, ESCAP and UNFPA and spent five years working for the Fulbright Economics Teaching programme (FETP) as Associate Director. He is a member of the International Association of Survey Statisticians (IASS) and the Population Association of America (PAA). He joined Kantar Media VN in 2007 and has held several important positions in the company as COO and Director of Training and Insights and is now a Senior Advisor to the Managing Director with a lot of expertise and experience in media research and audience measurement methodology.

Thi Nha Truc Van is Head of the Department of American & British Culture and Literature, Faculty of English Linguistics and Literature at the University of Social Sciences & Humanities (USSH), Vietnam National University, Ho Chi Minh City (VNU-HCMC). She holds a master's degree in TESOL in 2004 and MBA in 2012. She teaches English language skills, British/American literature and culture, business English, and intercultural communication. In 2014, she was part of the faculty exchange program between USSH (VNU-HCMC) and John Carroll University (USA). She is currently a PhD student in culturology at her university. Her academic interests are intercultural communication, business/corporate culture and university education management.

Wei Zhao is an associate professor at the ESSCA School of Management, Senior Fellow at the Institute for Pearl River Delta Reform and Development at Sun Yat-Sen University, and associate researcher at the *Centre d'Economie de l'Université Paris Nord* (CEPN). Before academia, he was Marketing Director of a Hong Kong real estate company and Director of Public Affairs with Carrefour in South China. Since 2011, he has conducted empirical research on China's industrial modernization and innovation policy with the think tank established jointly by the Guangdong Provincial Government and Sun Yat-Sen University. He holds a master's degree in sociology from Sun Yat-Sen University and a PhD in Economics from Paris 3 University.

List of Figures

List of Tables

CHAPTER 1

Introduction

Thi Anh-Dao Tran

The late twentieth century was a time of major geopolitical upheaval in the world. The fall of the Communist bloc brought about the end of a bipolar world order built around the rivalry between the US and the Soviet Union. Economic and military structures such as the Council for Mutual Economic Assistance (COMECON) and the Warsaw Pact were dissolved in 1991. The events of the late 1980s also accelerated the process leading to German reunification and opened a new round in the construction of the European Union. From that moment onwards, most scholars argue that contemporary economies and societies have been entering into a new and unexplored era in the history of capitalism.

Yet, in developing a series of comparative institutional analyses of the varieties of capitalism in Europe and East Asia, the recent volume "Evolving Diversity and Interdependence of Capitalisms" concluded by rejecting the post-1989 thesis: "globalisation does not imply economic and political convergence" (Boyer et al., 2018, p. 460). This book is a milestone in the historical and comparative analysis drawing on *régulation* theory that aims to understand the long-run transformation, renewed diversity and

T. A.-D. Tran (✉)
LASTA (University of Rouen Normandy), Faculty of Law, Economics and Management, Rouen, France
e-mail: thianh-dao.tran@irasec.com

T. A.-D. Tran (ed.), *Rethinking Asian Capitalism*,
https://doi.org/10.1007/978-3-030-98104-4_1

interdependence of the varieties of capitalism. Three major lessons were drawn. First, the collapse of the Berlin Wall on 9 November 1989 allowed a remarkable and renewed diversity of socio-economic regimes and growth strategies to develop and flourish. Second, intense internationalisation has brought about an unprecedented long-range interdependency among very diverse and, sometimes, complementary socio-economic regimes. Third, regional economic integration has taken contrasting forms in Europe and East Asia, and yet in some cases at least, it has been a promising avenue to follow.

Recently, new questions have been asked, such as whether the ongoing process will yield similar end-products in Southeast Asia, with its vastly different heritages and histories, or whether we will see the emergence of variants in Asian capitalism. Thirty years after the end of the Cold War, the transition economies of Asia are on different paths compared to their counterparts in Eastern Europe and yet they face similar challenges. Turning to the Asian sub-region, first by joining the initially anti-communist "enemy" alliance the Association of Southeast Asian Nations (ASEAN) in 1995 and then in 1998 by joining the Asia Pacific Economic Coopération (APEC), Vietnam and the other countries of the so-called CLMV group (Cambodia, Laos, Myanmar) have followed their own path to "grow in light" without showing the hidden face of their success: highest GDP growth rates, alleviation of poverty, deep regional integration and progress in global business environment rankings (*Ease of Doing Business* by the World Bank, *ASEAN SME Policy Index* by the OECD or *Global Manufacturing Competitiveness Index* by Deloitte).

When the CLMV group launched their transition process from a centrally planned to a market economy in the mid-1980s, they were poor agricultural economies plagued by conflicts and instability. Today, the four economies have reached lower middle-income status and are deeply involved in the rapid rise of Asia. In addition to practically making Asia the only part of the world where the socialist regime remains, the historical "moment" of 1989 has opened up new perspectives for the organisation of a world in which Asia, communist or not, is rapidly rising as a major player (Mahbubani, 2008). What the World Bank (1993) defined as an "East Asian Miracle", initially led by Japan, is now being structured around China, leading to the emergence of a new path of development in the area.

Since the initiation of *Đổi Mới* ("renovation" in Vietnamese) in 1986, Vietnam has gone through a far-reaching transformation from a command economy to one that is globalised and market-based. Behind the story, integration into the world capitalist system has been the key driver of Vietnam's outstanding economic and social outcomes: its accession (as a non-market economy) to the World Trade Organisation (WTO) in late 2006 was the culmination of a long process that transformed what was one of the world's poorest nations into a lower middle-income country.[1] Vietnam also resisted both the collapse of the Soviet bloc and international sanctions (the US embargo was only lifted in 1994). Spurred by a policy of rapid industrialisation, economic reforms allowed the country to cope with a series of domestic and external shocks: macroeconomic turbulence during the transition process, the financial market crisis of 1997 in East Asia and then the global crisis of 2008. In 2018, the country recorded its highest growth rate (nearly 7%) since 2011 and although hit hard by the ongoing COVID-19 pandemic, GDP grew by 2.9% in 2020.

This economic vitality has allowed Vietnam to play a growing and decisive role in the region through a multilateral policy in which Asia has its rightful place (Le & Tsvetov, 2018). Following the 13th Party Congress Resolution of the Communist Party (adopted in February 2021), the country is now entering a new phase of national development with the objective of becoming a "socialist-oriented developed nation with a high-income level" by 2045. Being the third most populous ASEAN country, a million young workers enter the labour market every year and the overall population is expected to reach 120 million by 2050 (with the 65+ age group set to increase 2.5 times).

The World Bank describes Vietnam as "a model country" of liberalism and market-oriented reforms (Cling et al., 2013). Yet the country's growth record over the past years has had a heavy social and environmental impact, while the "socialist-oriented market economy" (which has never been precisely defined) has created opportunities for corruption and rent-seeking behaviours. Economic performance is widely highlighted but progress in human development has slowed sharply and lags behind when compared to prior achievements. In this respect, part of the success story is untold and significant gaps remain in renewing abilities to meet the needs of a socialist-oriented developed nation proactively involved in the major challenges to sustainability and fairness.

[1] With a per capita GDP of US $98 in current US dollars, Vietnam was the poorest country in the world in 1990, ahead of Somalia (US $130) and Sierra Leone (US $163). Between 2002 and 2018, poverty rates declined sharply from over 70% to below 6% while the vast majority of Vietnam's remaining poor (86%) are ethnic minorities.

Today, Vietnam is more than ever developing a strategic multilateralism in a context made unstable by the geopolitical and economic rivalry between the US and China. To make the best possible decisions for the future, it is therefore important to take stock of what has been achieved to date, while considering future challenges with no room for complacency. There is also much to learn from the past by adopting an approach based on comparative political economy. On the occasion of the 30th anniversary of the dissolution of the Soviet Union, it is important then to rethink Vietnam's "successful" path by viewing it critically through a multidimensional lens. Useful insights with reference to the time and space dimensions are required to help reassess the country's future path in the twenty-first century, which will be the "Asian Century".

Accordingly, the objective of this volume is twofold. First, we attempt, through the Vietnamese *Đổi Mới* experience, to identify country specificities in the "double transition" (from central planning and from underdevelopment) in Southeast Asia. Second, we seek to depict the main challenges in the ongoing process and suggest ways they can be tackled. Written basically from an economics perspective, this edited book is yet intended to reach a multidisciplinary audience by approaching the problems from the vantage point of various specialists. In an attempt to highlight context-specific economic, social and political change, the book discusses Vietnam's peculiar features in different ways by combining various disciplines in the social sciences, including economics, anthropology, culturology, sociology, ethnography, history and political science. The *Đổi Mới* "success story" has been questioned over the past decade and this book attempts to describe the real substance of these changes and their implications for Vietnam's future development. Being methodologically pluralist (including both theoretical and empirical studies), it aims to give a higher profile to the research in comparative political economy being carried on in Southeast Asia, where heterodox economic development strategies are rather understudied.

1 Stabilisation and Growth in Vietnam: The Early Experience

The Vietnam Communist Party (VCP) formally endorsed a programme of *Đổi Mới* at its Sixth National Congress in 1986, which profoundly changed the country's path. The reforms made Vietnam one of the fastest growing economies: from 1992 to 1997, GDP growth reached an average rate of 8.9% per year while inflation, starting from 400% in 1986, was brought under control so effectively that it fell to single digits during the same period. After three decades of *Đổi Mới*, the country is now entering a new phase of development and has set itself the goal of becoming a modern, industrialised, high-income economy by 2045 in accordance with the Socio-Economic Development Strategy (SEDS) 2021–2030 and accompanying Plan (SEDP) 2021–2025, which outlines the mid-term priorities (World Bank, 2020).

Unlike in Eastern Europe, Vietnam avoided the collapse in economic activity in the early years of its transition (Tran, 1998a). Even in the Visegrad group (Czech Republic, Hungary, Poland, Slovakia) which had superior economic performance, cumulative GDP decline within 1989–1994 period averaged 15.5%. Observed data for Vietnam showed negative growth rates for industrial value-added and for the state-owned enterprises (SOEs) sector in 1989 and 1990: but this had only a limited effect on GDP, since both accounted in these two years respectively for 24% and 33% of GDP while most of the real growth was driven by the agriculture and services sectors.

Several factors contributed to a one-off jump in the supply of goods and services. First, the performance of a dynamic private sector explained the positive real growth rates in Vietnam. More generally, the development of private businesses in services, handicrafts and consumer goods industries had wholly absorbed disruptions generated by the transition process in production, distribution and domestic trade. Second, observed data suggest also that the main segments of the industrial sector that performed well were those in which SOEs were predominant: notably heavy or capital-intensive industries which were not directly linked to the reforms (e.g. oil and gas) or which had excessive capacity after large-scale projects, previously financed by Soviet aid (power, cement, steel, fertilisers), had come on stream. In other words, while SOEs had often been cited as impairing the performance of transition economies in Eastern Europe, state industry had become the leading sector in Vietnam's process as fast as restructuration policy strengthened its output performance.

As regards the demand side, the Vietnamese transition is quite specific in that key reforms were first implemented in vast rural areas, fostering a broad-based growth. *Đổi Mới* unleashed farmers' and businesses' initiative away from the command economy and this helped spur demand. As in China, a one-time jump in productivity enjoyed by the rural sector improved living standards for the bulk of the population. This, in turn, fed back into the economy by demand linkages in a number of resource-based or large-scale light industries (construction and building materials, retail trade, consumer goods).

Increased labour mobility was also an important element in averting a fall in real aggregate demand, following the removal of consumption and price subsidies. Besides the fact that the country had a huge pool of labour to draw on, the vast majority of the population was employed outside the state and industrial sectors. This preponderance of workers without direct financial connection with the state facilitated labour shifts towards activities in the private sector, thereby spurring income growth.

All in all, the series of virtuous effects described above assisted Vietnam's integration into the world economy and its adjustment to the trade disruptions caused by the breakups of COMECON and the Soviet Union. It was mostly on the import side that the external shock had a major negative impact on growth; however, this shock was alleviated by the small size of the country's heavy industries, the economy's relatively low openness at that time and the already high share of external trade charged at world prices when the shock occurred.

The export performance, on the other hand, helped to ease the country's external balance constraint at the beginning of the transition; it resulted from both a shift in the country's trading partners and the diversification in exported goods. While East Asian countries replaced the former COMECON countries as major markets, export promotion policy benefited initially from the emergence of new opportunities directly marketed in the convertible area: the coming on stream of oil projects, the primary sector's supply response to reforms (rice, coffee, marine products). Handicrafts and light industrial products, which relied heavily on the COMECON markets, became a growing part of Vietnamese exports towards the convertible area (from 1.6% in 1990 to 22% in 1995).

All this brings us to the question of whether initial conditions can determine transition outcomes. In most of the comparative debates, differences in initial conditions are widely supported as explanations for the large differences in patterns of transition (Lipton & Sachs, 1990; de Melo & Gelb, 1996; de Melo et al., 2001).

An initial set of differences concerns economic conditions and structures prior to reforms. In contrast to the over-industrialised and old urbanised societies of Eastern Europe, Vietnam was characterised by a rural-based economy dominated by labour-intensive activities. Furthermore, its mode of production relied heavily on household-scale organisation and micro-enterprises, in contrast to the socially organised state sector and its prevalence of subsidised jobs in Eastern Europe. The relative lack of large-scale heavy industries and a less developed state sector also minimised supply rigidities. A general feature of Vietnamese industry was the predominance of light industries and handicrafts concentrated in small-scale enterprises that absorbed the bulk of the labour force. This very fragmented industrial sector, operating on a small scale and with simpler technologies, made it easier to introduce market forces and hard budget constraints in the state industrial sector.

Besides the high labour mobility, the demographic structure of the country also made the labour market more adaptable to the changing environment. According to population data, 68% of Vietnamese people were under the age of 30 and the median age was low (about 20.2 years in 1989). This youth-heavy population structure explains the relatively small size of the working population (about 40%).

A final set of initial differences concerns the country's administrative and organisational structures. In Vietnam, central planning had never been really consolidated because of economic and productive structures that were far less complicated and differentiated than those in Eastern Europe. Planning inefficiency was attributed to the low skills of the managerial staff, or information deficiencies. However, it was mostly the very large number of small-scale companies that explained why a large part of economic activity was excluded from the central planning process.

2 The Vietnamese Approach to Reforms

The Asian transition experiences challenge prevailing explanations in political economy and standard theories of development (Malesky & London, 2014). Besides the advantages of "backwardness", an alternative proposition to account for the wide variation in transition experiences across countries has been the approach to sequencing policy reforms (Guo, 2006). Rana and Hamid (1995) were the first to define a bottom-up approach to transition in Asia. While the Soviet Union, Eastern Europe and China were in varying degrees starting to reform their socialist economic systems, the process began in Vietnam with evidence-based practices at the microeconomic (local) level that were then applied at the macroeconomic (national) level, providing a transition path from the bottom to the top (Rama, 2008).

Firstly, most of the early *Đổi Mới* reforms consisted of experimentations at the grassroots level which subsequently created a consensus at the central state level for emulation by other parts of the country. The household responsibility system, for instance, had already been implemented in some localities by 1979, even though it went contrary to central policy direction. Equally striking, the provinces in the Mekong Delta abolished the rationing subsidy system (*bao cấp*) and opted definitively for a market-based price system in early 1980. Without such illegal or pilot practices, there is evidence that market mechanisms could never have emerged so rapidly. In fact, the Second Five-Year Plan (1976–1980) was ending in total failure, revealing the deficiencies of Vietnam's socialist system (Kimura, 1989). Although *Đổi Mới* marked a great turning point in the political process, the VCP had actually been forced to begin such reforms in 1979 under Le Duan, one of the country's leading figures.

Secondly, Vietnam started its reform process from the household-based rural sector, a vast self-sufficient economy, before extending it to the urban industrial state sector. Because agricultural production is characterised by labour-intensive technologies and by an equitable allocation of individual plots, the initial emphasis on rural reform unleashed an economy-wide adjustment and gave dramatic encouragement to the majority of the population. The earliest reforms also legitimised a private sector that had lived on since the end of the war. This whole process amounted to "privatisation at the bottom", the opposite of the massive privatisation of ownership in Eastern Europe.

At the same time, a "marketisation" process was gradually introduced in the urban industrial sector. In 1981, a triple-plan system, coupled with a dual-track pricing system similar to that employed in China, was designed to introduce price and cost sensitivity. By and large, this bottom-up approach intensified domestic competition and encouraged the rebirth of a market economy that had survived despite forced collectivisation, together with a dualism in which the socialist soft budget constraint coexisted with the new hard budget constraint (including within the state sector).

However, initially financed by Soviet aid, the two-track approach in Vietnam suffered rapidly from resource shortages. The monetary overhang widened the price gap and spurred the tendency for supply diversion: such transfers of scarce goods from the command to the liberalised economy exacerbated further chronic shortages in the former. This, in turn, further widened the price gap and contributed either to growing price subsidies from the central state or successive increases in administered prices, forcing Vietnam into greater reliance on economic assistance. These developments were the reasons why the economic reforms of the Third Five-Year Plan (1981–1985) gave rise to severe inflation and macroeconomic imbalances. They also brought about a confrontation between reformers and conservatives that went beyond economics (Kimura, 1989). Faced with a budget deficit and huge inflation rates, the government was forced in 1988 to extend the transition process to macroeconomic reforms: withdrawal of the centralised subsidy system, monetary reforms aimed at mobilising domestic resources, as well as exchange rate, trade and Foreign Direct Investment (FDI) reforms aimed at mobilising external resources (Tran, 1998a).

Although the Vietnamese experience strongly suggested an inflation-fiscal deficit-money growth linkage, there is evidence that it reflected a resource shortage within the economy rather than excessive absorption. It was something of a counterexample to the familiar argument advanced by international organisations that macroeconomic stabilisation is a precondition for the successful liberalisation of repressed sectors. First, the open inflation caused by the resource shortage had greatly facilitated the removal of subsidies by making official prices increasingly irrelevant. Second, increased competition and the development of liberalised sectors (agriculture, services, external trade) released the supply of goods and then shifted the former sellers' towards a buyers' market with market-clearing prices. To some extent, it was inversely effective growth that had created the preconditions for macroeconomic stabilisation in Vietnam.

It would appear, then, that a bottom-up approach, coupled with initial conditions that provided the context for reform, were the pillars on which political leaders built their "socialist-oriented market economy". Such a combination had stimulated a broad-based growth, in that the vast majority of the population benefited from the reforms; and even if there were losers (notably, public sector employees), the winners tended to far outnumber the former. Even though the early reforms proceeded without a well-defined blueprint (and therefore it would have been mistaken to speak of a reform "strategy"), the Asian transition countries rooted their pace of reform in the existing decentralised political, administrative and social structures. This stands in stark contrast to Eastern Europe, where the reform approach involved "building the new by destroying the old" using "big bang" or shock therapy.

Historical and political considerations broadly explain Vietnam's devolution of revenue and expenditure responsibilities to local authorities during the transition process: for example, the regionalisation of industry during the war and ineffective coordination through central planning. These distinctive features added to favourable initial conditions in spurring transition outcomes, such as the survival of a market economy in the South, despite the extension of the Soviet model to the whole country after reunification, or the geographical location of Vietnam in a dynamic area of trade and investment following the Plaza agreement signed in September 1985.

3 Vietnam's "Socialist-Oriented Market Economy" in Contemporary Capitalist Globalisation

Because no clear-cut consensus emerged on the relationship between planning and market mechanisms, numerous labels have been attached to the Asian transition process, including "socialist market economy", "socialist-oriented market economy" and "market socialism". What comes out of the process, however, is that the market is considered compatible with socialist economies, in which "the state guides the market and the market guides the enterprises" (Guo, 2006). In other words, the market mechanism is viewed as an instrument of economic development.

To some extent, Vietnam is the only country in the world, together with China, that has put in place a market economy in which a central state has, by and large, continued to conduct highly active public policies in all areas under the party rules. The one-party system gives the VCP and its affiliated organs (mass organisations) very strong control over the transmission of decisions from the national to the local level, shaping the main distinctive features of an original political economic organisation or "political settlement" (Cling et al., 2013). In the end, this combination has helped to preserve socialist ownership in accordance with a market-based system. As an illustrative example, the state was still the dominant owner of the means of production in the late 1990s while the affiliated sector was regaining its leading role as a driving force in the industrialisation process, following a short phase of restructuring under *Đổi Mới*. Albeit reduced in number, SOEs were restructured into state conglomerates in specific industries such as oil, rubber, steel, transport and cement. However, they also took advantage of new opportunities provided by reforms to expand into new areas, including real estate, banking, tourism and entertainment. It is worth mentioning that the senior managers of those business companies were already members of the VCP or the party-state organisations (Guo, 2006). And if close business-government relations are a growing feature of Vietnam, they are ruled out by the one-party state so that SOEs are institutionally embedded in the political system.

Such a market economy combined with strong government intervention shares many characteristics with the first-tier Newly Industrialising Countries (NICs) of East Asia, enabling the political theory of the "Development state" to focus on the centrality of business-government relations and, more globally, on the relationship between the state and the private sector (domestic and foreign). Vietnam is obviously observing and learning lessons from successful East Asian economies. One wonders if the country is following Japan, South Korea or Taiwan in attempting to imitate the institutional structure of industrial policy associated with the developmental state (Haggard, 2018). However, three distinctive features deserve our attention.

Firstly, in contrast to its previous dependence on Soviet aid and economic assistance which shifted the country towards the market mechanism, Vietnam today is characterised by a preponderant reliance on foreign resources. Ironically, the macroeconomic turbulence of the early part of the twenty-first century was mainly the outcome of the unprecedented volume of capital inflows the country was attracting. One of the consequences of contemporary globalisation is that strong outside influences will play a structural role in determining national growth models, wherein the Global South ("a political collectivity") represents an internal periphery and stands in a subordinate relational position to global capitalism (Malher, 2017). With regard to macroeconomics and economic policy, for example, South Korea seems closer to Vietnam in scale, but the former relied far less on inward FDI, giving the country room for manoeuvre in shaping its development. In that respect, the growth models approach, which is part of the comparative political economy literature, gives prominence to distributional conflicts in explaining systemic instability; but so far, the analysis has almost exclusively been applied to advanced economies (Stockhammer, 2021). Insofar as market liberalisation and integration are part of a set of policies that serve to undermine the capacity of governments to guide the development path, Vietnam will be less able to retain control over its own destiny in the post-*Đổi Mới* period.

Secondly, a high level of inherited decentralisation in Vietnam contrasts with the highly centralised systems that characterise the first-tier NICs such as South Korea and Taiwan (Amsden, 1989; Wade, 1990). For example, Tran (1998b) analyses grassroots initiatives by local leaders that proliferated in the pre-*Đổi Mới* period. Her analysis shows that it was regional experimentation beyond what was allowed by the rules that built up a policy consensus at party headquarters (Mio, 1989). Based on his long conversations with Vo Van Kiet, former Prime Minister of Vietnam, Rama (2008) revisits Vietnam's transition from a policy history perspective and offers valuable insights on contemporary issues and lessons for other developing countries as well. He reports that in the face of many bottlenecks in imports, the People's Committee of Ho Chi Minh City authorised lower levels of government to establish companies with names ending in "imex" to directly handle foreign trade. On the eve of *Đổi Mới*, exports by these "imexes" already exceeded the centrally controlled exports of Vietnam to market economies by a factor of ten. Over the years, Cholimex for example, a joint stock food company, has become popular in Vietnam and today occupies a leading position in Asian supplies of culinary products.

A final clear distinction between the first-tier NICs and Vietnam is in leadership mechanisms. Whereas strong personal leadership prevailed in the former, *Đổi Mới* in the latter marked a move towards balancing power distribution between regions in lead positions. In Vietnam, the principle of collective leadership (from North, Centre and South) structures the decision-making process. Under *Đổi Mới*, for example, the same person was not allowed to hold multiple positions. Yet, most of the Party leaders had earlier been leaders at the provincial level, which created feedback channels from local policy experimentation to large-scale decisions endorsed by the Politburo (Rama, 2008). The other side of the coin is that, due to less rotation than in China, Vietnamese officials are associated with their home province, making for a possible perverse system that links promotion to regional economic performance as well as giving policy making and transfers a hometown bias (Malesky & London, 2014).

As Vietnam moves into the ranks of the middle-income countries and its economy becomes more developed and sophisticated, there is considerable room for improvement in critical areas, although in the end major policy decisions still require the endorsement of the Politburo. In view of this, a set of more complex institutional arrangements needs to take shape. More than escaping from the well-known "middle income trap", institutions become decisive in this critical stage in which the central state clearly fears the potential risks of failure. But the blind copying of outside models, without making sure that they are relevant to the peculiar features of Vietnam, would be unwise.

If we apply the notion of the Asian Developmental state to Vietnam, one wonders if decentralisation now makes the decision process and policy implementation more complex to manage, thereby necessitating recentralisation. Notably, a main characteristic of Vietnam's decentralisation is that FDI is licensed by numerous state agencies at different levels (province, district and commune). It is clear that the trade-FDI *nexus* has spurred Vietnam's structural transformation since the early 1990s: this has come from export-oriented direct investment made by foreign entities through global production and trading systems, and has affected the country's trade patterns and outcomes. Against this backdrop, geography clearly matters because agglomeration effects are at play as FDI management and the implementation of FDI-attracting policies are localised and not uniform across provinces, leading to regional disparities (a matter of concern for the central state).

On the other hand, sound local governance can play a critical role in mitigating risks and uncertainty and decentralisation can be a major building block in generating change and policy innovation. This link is particularly important in Vietnam. But the institutional conditions that support local authorities in the efficient conduct of Vietnam's structural transformation call for deeper insights. Otherwise, weak or opaque mechanisms, together with a lack of clarity where competencies overlap, encourage outright corruption and the ensuing social discontent has a corrosive impact on the legitimacy of Party leadership.

According to the orthodox approach, East Asia continues to be the global exemplar of successful development achieved through a combination of outward-oriented growth, human capital development and sound economic governance (World Bank, 2019). But with this dominant model now established in Asia, a growing matter of concern for Vietnam is the heavy reliance on foreign investment and trade in capital accumulation. With the country's deep integration (both regionally and internationally) under the export-oriented growth regime, one wonders if the early success in implementing *Đổi Mới* will last in this context-specific development strategy. In contrast to the "economics of shortage" that prevailed before transition together with dilapidated infrastructure and wartime management, contemporary capitalist globalisation offers abundant resources in foreign markets. However, this new context implies that the power relationship will evolve along economic, social, political and geographic lines beyond the reach of the party, that is, conservatives and reformers.

One illustrative example is in the way in which the Socio-Economic Development Strategy (SEDS), which outlines the country's priorities, is drawn up today. The consultations held to define the long-term planning of growth policies (fixing long-term national goals) are now organised with international donors or financial institutions, which are more involved in the decision-making process than in the early periods. The sum of public and private funds from other sources (official development assistance, commercial loans, portfolio investment and FDI) is also weighing more and more heavily, implying greater constraints depending on the extent of foreign currency-denominated debt and how sensitive the country is to international financial shocks. Even before the effects of the COVID-19 shock were fully felt, Vietnam was encountering difficulties in terms of its bargaining leverage with foreign multinational firms. Given the asymmetries that exist on the global playing field, there is a fear that wide-reaching international engagement coupled with deep integration into the global economy narrows the state's capacities to construct a national growth model.

Another striking example is given by the growing number of civil society organisations or "civic organisations", non-governmental organisations and philanthropists involved in alleviating social needs and improving people's livelihoods, taking over the dominant role played by the Communist party and its affiliated organs under the subsidy system. The central state used to supply the necessary goods for production and living at very low prices. In return, the beneficiaries were paid very low wages but as long as the rationing system supported them, their minimum living needs were guaranteed (Mio, 1989). Vietnamese workers, public servants and officials received upwards of 50% of their earnings in kind along with their monetary income (Kimura, 1989).

This system of "sharing poverty" no longer exists. Instead, support is provided by other stakeholders in society, including Vietnamese overseas, who are encouraged to invest in and send remittances to the country.[2] Meanwhile, the relationship between state and society has evolved as

[2] Due to the COVID-19 pandemic in 2020, personal remittances received were estimated at 6.3% of Vietnam's GDP according to the World Bank data. See "Remittances to fall for first time in 11 years", VN Express published on 9 November 2020.

society itself has changed but is increasingly coming into conflict with socialist principles and ethics. In the past decade, there were expressions of public discontent and protests about how local and provincial officials seized farmland with minimal compensation, currying favour with investors and developers by stealing not just people's land but also their livelihood.

However, linkages across sectors are much stronger as globalisation has forged wide-range interdependency among nations. Consequently, any policy mistake or inadequate policy decision carries with it much higher social costs. Vietnam's *Đổi Mới* was initially associated with the determination to avoid losers, in the sense that nobody was made "worse off"; in the post-*Đổi Mới* period, power struggles have emerged because a multitude of interacting actors at different levels are involved. Without any form of organisation in this new era, an overlap of stratified communities weakens social cohesion, prevents voices from the grassroots being heard and increases social resentment and exclusion. In other words, policies that worked when Vietnam was poor and capital-scarce and less integrated into the world economy, are less likely to work today. For example, widening inequalities, environmental degradation and health risks (i.e. the multifaceted aspects of development sustainability) can only be overcome by well-integrated policies and strategies at different levels.

Globalisation is most visible in its economic dimension; by reshaping contemporary societies, however, the world capitalist system poses questions and leads to major disputes around inequality, social polarisation and power over the collective condition. To address these issues, additional research is needed on the CLMV countries, which are heterogeneous in terms of their heritages and history but whose trajectories are deeply interconnected. This book is published at a time when great changes are about to take place in Southeast Asia.

4 Organisation of the Volume

President Ho Chi Minh taught the Vietnamese people and leadership a lesson in pragmatic wisdom, which enabled Viet Nam to steer its way through the pitfalls of great power rivalry and tensions, especially during the Sino-Soviet antagonism i.e. ***refrain from taking sides.***

—**TON-NU-THI Ninh** (Ho Chi Minh City Peace and Development Foundation, Viet Nam)

Building trust to ensure social cohesion alongside sustainable development is a long-term challenge and requires well-integrated perspectives. By unveiling various dimensions of the post-*Đổi Mới* period, the volume seeks to develop a multi-dimensional analysis by bringing together a number of scholars who, despite their diverse disciplinary backgrounds in the social sciences, deal with common themes. To the best of our knowledge, this joint research is the first of its kind. It is composed of fifteen separate chapters, and the way in which they are framed structures what questions are asked and what factors are included in the analysis.

To set the scene, **Part I** of the book looks at the structural transformations and crises that have taken place over the last three decades. As a leading figure in the *régulation* school, **Robert Boyer** in Chap. 2 attempts to draw seven main lessons from a comparative history of capitalism in East Asia. From this retrospective analysis, he concludes that inward looking development is now on top of many national agendas, which might help in designing a development strategy for Vietnam.

The next two chapters focus on Vietnam by scrutinising agriculture, which was at stake during the initial transition stage to a market-based economy. In line with research based on social anthropology that explores the extra-economic foundations of capitalism, **Emmanuel Pannier and Guillaume Duteurtre** in Chap. 3 analyse the place and role of interpersonal arrangements by conducting two field studies in the dairy and maize sectors in Northern Vietnam. A specific entanglement of various socio-economic logics is highlighted that the authors propose to grasp through the concept of "economic hybridity".

With Nguyen Mai Huong, the same co-authors in Chap. 4 capture the new agrarian capitalism that has accompanied the renewal of the dairy sector with the emergence of mega dairy farms. This rapid change reflects the growing importance of financial capital and high technologies in the transformation of today's Vietnamese agriculture. But mega farms also constitute a challenge to the social dimension of agriculture: they provide fewer jobs per litre of milk than smallholder farms, because they substitute capital for labour. The rise of this new agrarian capitalism is constrained by the fact that the State, which formally owns the land, tends to preserve land-use rights for smallholder farmers.

A question is then posed as to whether Vietnamese traditional values are aligned with or conflict with the values that are essential in the new context, which traditional values should be made use of and which can be transformed? On the basis of an interdisciplinary framework, especially of educational management and sociocultural background, **Nguyen Duy Mong Ha & Van Thi Nha Truc** in Chap. 5 explore the key factors in Vietnam's socio-economic transformations as the country undergoes modernisation.

Part II discusses existing and emerging issues related to Vietnam's transformation from a rural to modern society. The main focus here is on institutional change and its converse, namely how the central state continues to conduct highly active public policies in all areas and enters into relationships with other actors such as peasants and citizens, local governments, ethnic minorities and other communities.

Nguyen Minh Doi in Chap. 6 examines the institutional change from urban governance under the centralised government model to new models in which Public-Private Partnerships (PPPs) have emerged as one of the potential tools. The growth of PPPs has taken place in distinct phases, reflecting the shift from "urban government" to "urban governance". By comparing Leipzig, Shanghai and Ho Chi Minh City since the 1990s, the author shows that there are various types of PPPs in post-socialist urban governance, all of which have renewed the forms of coordination among key stakeholders.

Vietnam under *Đổi Mới* also has its dark sides. **Phan Thanh Thanh** in Chap. 7 examines the progress made in implementing economic and political rights amidst the ongoing conversion of agricultural land in Vietnam. Duong Noi was chosen as a case study because farmers' resistance in the district of Ha Dong is one of the best-known cases among recent land-use conflicts reported by the Vietnamese media. Moreover, it is located in the peri-urban areas of Hanoi which are usually the targets of rural land expropriation under the growing pressure of economic development and urbanisation policies.

In Vietnam, the state holds the key responsibility for social issues; however, other actors also play an important and indispensable role. One significant challenge for sustainable development today is to recognise, valorise and promote the role and contribution of non-profit actors and society at large towards the country's social sector. **Ton-Nu-Thi Ninh** in Chap. 8 provides an overall perspective of the awareness, together with practical insights into the state and evolution of philanthropy in Vietnam (term used in the broadest sense to cover the whole spectrum of entities that seek to "do good"). The aim here is to identify the philanthropy ecosystem's main areas of strengths and weaknesses and to bring out the role of philanthropy and social entrepreneurship in developing a medium to long-term vision for Vietnam's inclusive and sustainable development.

Bui The Cuong and **Truong Si Anh** in Chap. 9 investigate social stratification in Vietnam by analysing income-based groups during the period 1998–2018. Based on data from the population living standard survey conducted by the General Statistics Office, they show that the coefficient of income disparity between social classes increased over the past two decades, albeit faster in the 2010s. There was also significant evolution in the shape of stratification: from a pyramidal form in 1998, the layered structure became diamond-shaped in 2018.

Part III directs attention to the multiple dimensions of Vietnam's place in the regional and global settings. The rise of neo-liberalism in Southeast Asia has brought about significant changes in many ways.

Over the years, Vietnam has become firmly embedded in strong trade inter-linkages within the region and between geographical areas. However, a key concern is whether such trade-led growth is sustainable in the long run and resilient to global shocks. Accordingly, **Elodie Mania**, **Arsène Rieber and Tran Thi Anh-Dao** in Chap. 10 measure the respective contributions of trading partners to Vietnam's macroeconomic resilience. By using a multi-country specification of Thirlwall's law, they analyse how and through which transmission channels the changing geography of international trade has impacted Vietnam's long-run growth rate before and after WTO accession.

As a member of the ASEAN Free Trade Agreement (AFTA), Vietnam might draw on Thailand's experience. In the context of trade liberalisation in the sub-region, **Natedao Taotawin** in Chap. 11 analyses the complexity of border trade and seeks to understand how the laws and regulations illustrate a dialectic relation between state-centred and local powers. Drawing on a case study in Ubon Ratchathani Province, a sociological approach is adopted to examine illicit cross-border trade and its effects on the local economy and livelihoods of people living in the border areas.

Any examination of the regional and global landscapes would of course be incomplete without looking at China and how the "Middle Kingdom" is prone to draw from the past in determining Asia's future path. In a historical perspective, **Anne Cheng** in Chap. 12 comes back to and challenges the self-representation of a "China-world". This universal concept is now being brought back by the Chinese leadership, not just as a nostalgic representation but much more aggressively as a unifying factor in the predominant ideology of a "Greater China".

Finally, **Part IV** presents some future challenges in a globalised world where hyper-connection and interdependence between nations prevail. Vietnam is moving forward but has to face up to growing uncertainties in a global economy. As Robert Boyer in his contribution concludes, "Vietnam has to explore a mixed strategy combining investment in infrastructures, technological improvement and prudent integration into an uncertain world system". This last part contains four chapters that examine major aspects.

The assessment of climate damage in Vietnam is rightly seen as a political emergency in a country that has two immense deltas, more than 3200 kilometres of coastline and an increase in average temperatures of up to two degrees in places. Taking stock of the trans-disciplinary knowledge and policy dialogue deployed in the Gemmes-VN project, **Etienne Espagne and Nguyen Thi Thu-Ha** in Chap. 13 analyse how the political discourse on climate change is currently being gradually institutionalised and becoming an integral component of Vietnamese social dynamics. The way adaptation and mitigation policies as well as the discourse on climate change actually shift the Vietnamese mode of development has come under particular challenge since the Glasgow Climate Pact and Vietnam's announcements at COP26.

Since the 2008 global crisis, the focus of industrial policy has shifted to manufacturing strategy in the main economies in the world. Against this backdrop, **Wei Zhao** in Chap. 14 puts the US, Germany, Japan and China into the analytical perspective of varieties of capitalism and developmental state. This perspective aims to have a better understanding of the strategy plans and implementation as a mode of regulation and their impacts on each country's mode of production and accumulation. For all four countries, while there is a superficial convergence in terms of the structure of their manufacturing strategy plans, the mechanisms for monitoring implementation still differ because each national manufacturing strategy is deeply embedded in the existing institutions and structures.

Frédéric Boccara in Chap. 15 brings another view by framing the theoretical ground. There is a need to debate advances in the common core of heterodox economics, taking seriously the "new" and the "past" challenges arising out of today's reality. Heterodoxy is being called into question by profound changes affecting multinational enterprises (MNEs), money and technology. We need to go beyond the "common core" of the past, but without regressing. If the neo-liberal theory of globalisation is unable to account for the transformation of today's capitalism, we must look at analytical alternatives. In that respect, the challenge of envisioning another kind of globalisation is also a challenge for heterodoxy to overcome the diversity and fragmentation of theoretical approaches.

Given the uncertainty surrounding its magnitude and duration, the impact of the ongoing COVID-19 pandemic is taken into account in a closing epilogue. Building on his most recent book published in 2021, **Yves Tiberghien** in Chap. 16 analyses the geopolitics of COVID-19 in East Asia. It is a global pandemic, a global economic and social shock and a geopolitical shock combined; and yet, it partially accelerates pre-existing trends. Against this backdrop, the author reviews the health and economic performance of Vietnam throughout the pandemic. However, the long duration and multiple channels of the COVID-19 shock partially wore Vietnam down over time; according to the author, this moment is also bound to increase social demands on the government and to test the governance system of Vietnam.

Although its roots are essentially in economics, this volume is inspired by the large body of social science research that has been dealing with Asian studies, but also by some critical approaches to emerging trends in Vietnam. In comparison with the latest monographs on the country, many issues or topics here are part of the ongoing debate in different social science disciplines. Since they cannot all be covered, the proposed analysis of Vietnam's achievements over the past three decades may result in shortcomings and, as editor, I must take responsibility for this.

Nevertheless, the picture that emerges from this edited book, in which various methodological approaches are deployed, is that the "neo-liberal moment" that followed the collapse of the Berlin Wall should be questioned. In the decades ahead, CLMV countries will have to face major new challenges and major demands on the socio-economic, societal, geopolitical and environmental fronts. Their future will be shaped partly by how they meet these challenges and partly by how the difficult conjuncture in the world unfolds.

There is much more to be done in analysing the diversity of socio-economic regimes in Asia; this edited book attempts to contribute to this. It is essential that we have sufficient understanding of the conditions within individual countries and the international relations of the entire region in order to plan better for the future. In the coming years, we expect the heterodox approaches to mature and flourish in this sub-region; we also hope the insights of pluralism in economics will help us to better understand the long-run transformation of the Asian transition economies.

References

Amsden, A. (1989). *Asia's next giant: South Korea and late industrialization*. Oxford University Press.

Boyer, R., Uemura, H., Yamada, T., & Song, L. (Eds.). (2018). *Evolving diversity and interdependence of capitalisms. Transformations of regional integration in EU and Asia*. Springer.

Cling, J. P., Razafindrakoto, M., & Roubaud, F. (2013). Is the World Bank compatible with the 'Socialist-oriented market economy'? A political economy approach applied to the case of Vietnam. In *Political Economy of Contemporary Asia (1)*, Special Issue, *Regulation Review*, 13, Spring.

de Melo, M., Denizer, C., Gelb, A. H., & Tenev, S. (2001). Circumstance and choice: The role of initial conditions and policies in transition economies. *The World Bank Economic Review, 15*(1), 1–31.

de Melo, M., & Gelb, A. H. (1996). A comparative analysis of twenty-eight transition economies in Europe and Asia. *Post-Soviet Geography and Economics, 37*(5), 265–285.

Guo, S. (2006). *The political economy of Asian transition from communism*. Routledge.

Haggard, S. (2018). *Developmental states* (Elements in the Politics of Development Series). Cambridge University Press.

Kimura, T. (1989). *The Vietnamese economy, 1975–1986: Reforms and international relations*. Institute of Developing Economies.

Le, H. H., & Tsvetov, A. (2018). *Vietnam's foreign policy under Doi Moi*. ISEAS Publishing.

Lipton, D., & Sachs, J. (1990). Creating a market economy in Eastern Europe: The case of Poland. *Brookings Papers on Economic Activities, 21*(1), 75–148.

Mahbubani, K. (2008). *The new Asian hemisphere. The irresistible shift of global power to the east*. Public Affairs.

Malesky, E., & London, J. (2014). The political economy of development in China and Vietnam. *Annual Review of Political Science, 17*, 395–419.

Malher, A. G. (2017). Global South. In *Oxford Bibliographies in Literary and Critical Theory*.

Mio, T. (Ed.). (1989). *Indochina in transition. Confrontation or co-prosperity*. The Japan Institute of International Affairs.

Rama, M. (2008). Making difficult choices: Vietnam in transition. *Working Paper N°40*. Commission on Growth and Development, The World Bank.

Rana, P. B., & Hamid, N. (Eds.). (1995). *From centrally planned to market economies. The Asian approach*. Oxford University Press.

Stockhammer, E. (2021). Towards a growth models analysis for the global south. A post-Keynesian approach. *Implications of Post-Keynesian Economics for the Study of Growth Models in the Global North and South: Theoretical and*

Methodological Challenges, 2nd Workshop of the Growth Models in the Global South Studies Network (9 September).
Tiberghien, Y. (2021). *The East Asian COVID-19 paradox* (Element Series). Cambridge University Press.
Tran, T. A. D. (1998a). Stabilization and growth in transition economies: The case of Vietnam. *Economic Systems, 22*(3), 310–316.
Tran, T. A. D. (1998b). Regional decentralization and transition. A comparison between China and Vietnam. *Mondes en Développement, 25*(99), 27–39.
Wade, R. (1990). *Governing the market. Economic theory and the role of government in East Asian industrialization*. Princeton University Press.
World Bank. (1993). *The East Asian miracle. Economic growth and public policy.* Oxford University Press.
World Bank. (2019). *A resurgent East Asia: Navigating a changing world.* World Bank East Asia and Pacific Regional Report. Washington, DC: World Bank.
World Bank. (2020, January). *Vietnam Development Report 2019: Connecting Vietnam for Growth and Shared Prosperity.* Washington, DC: World Bank.

PART I

Setting the Scene Over 30 Years: A "lessons learned" Inspection

CHAPTER 2

The Transformations of Contemporary Capitalisms: Seven Lessons

Robert Boyer

1 Introduction

Exploring the possible futures of the various Asian capitalisms requires some understanding of their emergence and evolution, at least since the Second World War. The findings of standard economic theory and political economy are quite different.

Modern economics basically investigates the efficiency of the allocation of scarce resources within a *market economy* that is supposed to govern product, labour and finance. Once property rights and good incentives are correctly instituted most theoreticians conclude that the economy should converge towards a structurally stable growth pattern. The efficient pooling of information by financial markets makes irrelevant or even dangerous any government intervention intended to shape the mode of development. This vision experienced a serious blow with the succession of financial crises that culminated with the 2008 American financial collapse. Conversely, the surprising long-run dynamism of the East Asian capitalisms was built upon a proactive State policy (Wade, 1990).

R. Boyer (✉)
EHESS and Institute of the Americas, Paris, France

T. A.-D. Tran (ed.), *Rethinking Asian Capitalism*,
https://doi.org/10.1007/978-3-030-98104-4_2

Furthermore, the resilience of the Chinese economy after 2008 suggests that different configurations do coexist and might deliver better outcomes than the emblematic North American capitalism (Boyer, 2011; Alary & Lafaye de Micheaux, 2015). Thus, any a-historical approach makes it quite difficult to make predictions about the prospects for market economies.

Political economy starts from the concept of *capitalism* defined by the interaction of competition among firms and the dominated status of wage earners. This sets in motion a relentless accumulation process, prone to widening inequalities and financial crises, which are cyclical but also at some specific junctures structural. This vision is essentially dynamic since the institutional forms that shape accumulation are transformed by their success until they enter a structural crisis. Capitalism is *a constantly evolving socio-economic regime* impelled by two core mechanisms (Boyer, 2015a).

Firstly, some major crises may cause a particular mode of development to become structurally unstable, triggering a search for an alternative set of institutional forms: this phenomenon has been labelled endo-metabolism, that is, the self-transformation of an autonomous system driven by endogenous forces (Lordon, 1997).

Secondly, because accumulation tends to transcend political borders, national economies become interdependent, not only through trade, foreign investment, patents and finance but also via institutional mimetic behaviours in terms of technologies, contracts, institutional arrangements and even economic policies. Nevertheless, recurring historical investigations have shown that pure imitation is rarely feasible: the legacy of different trajectories in the development of social relations and the nature of the relations between the State and the economy makes a mimetic strategy nearly impossible (Boyer et al., 1998). Basically, hybridization is the rule, complete imitation is the exception. The interactions between the United States and Japan do display the interplay of these two mechanisms, endo-metabolism and hybridization (Fig. 2.1).

Development, therefore, is an endless series of processes connecting localized socio-economic and political spheres (Boyer, 2017). This analytical framework has an important consequence for the comparative analysis of capitalisms (Hollingsworth & Boyer, 1997). Traditionally, scholars embarking on a new case study take *the US economy as the benchmark*, probably because of its role in international relations and the attractiveness of its academic system. Unfortunately, it is risky to gauge any capitalism by comparison with the exceptional American configuration. It is a large continental economy with a very diversified and advanced economic

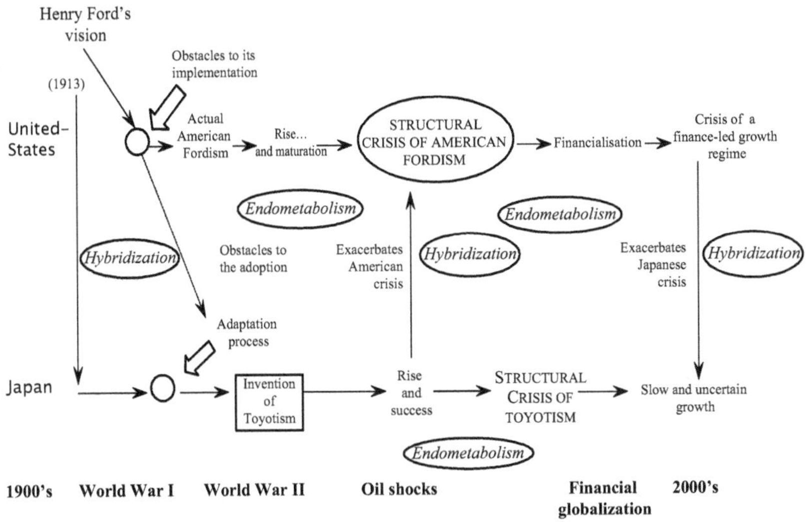

Fig. 2.1 Capitalism: a constantly evolving socio-economic regime

specialization; its government has the freedom to use the dollar as the international currency and may use the facility of extra-territorial laws to defend its competitiveness. Until recently, American governments have been at the forefront of economic deregulation, and this constitutes a major difference from the more cautious policies followed in Europe and Asia.

Comparative empirical institutional investigations of OECD countries (Amable et al., 1997; Amable, 2003) confirm that American capitalism is only one among other brands of capitalisms based upon contrasted compromises that rely on different institutional arrangements or mechanisms: not only markets but also state interventions, coordination among large corporations or negotiations between the social partners (Table 2.1). This is an important finding prior to any investigation about the future of Asian and in particular Vietnamese economic system.

This analytical framework inspired by *régulation* theory (Boyer & Saillard, 2001) has generated a succession of investigations from which seven main lessons can be derived. East Asia has shown that the inevitability of underdevelopment can be overcome under favourable circumstances and thus opened up a trajectory that is dramatically different from that of

Table 2.1 American capitalism is one brand among OECD economies

	Regulation			
	Market-oriented	*Meso-corporatist*	*Statist*	*Social-democratic*
1. Overall logic and hierarchical principle				
	Market logic is the organising principle for almost all of the institutional forms	Principle of solidarity and mobility in an economic unit that is large in size and diverse in output terms	Economic circuit shaped by public interventions in areas like production, demand and institutional codifications	Social partners negotiate rules governing most aspects of society and the economy
2. Implications for institutional forms				
Wage labour nexus	Significant decentralisation of wage bargaining, individualisation of pay and segmentation of labour market.	Wage compromise within large companies but pay hikes are synchronised	Trend towards a strong institutionalisation of rules on employment, working hours, wages and social benefits	Traditionally with a centralisation of collective negotiations, under a constraint of short and medium-term competitiveness
Competition	Concentration restricted by legislation, reshuffling from one oligopolistic type of competition to another	Relatively intense in the product markets, involving big companies with activities in many different markets	Moderate competition, channelled by public regulations or by professional associations, with high degree of capital concentration	Small number of big firms (that are also highly internationalised and thus have to compete)

(*continued*)

Table 2.1 (continued)

	Regulation			
	Market-oriented	*Meso-corporatist*	*Statist*	*Social-democratic*
Money and finance	Central bank is independent, financial market logic prevails, financial innovations proliferate, companies are tightly run by a financial logic	Role of main bank and keiretsu in funding and capital allocation. State authorities (financial regulators / Central Bank) have tight control	State has tight control over credit and monetary policies. Traditionally the Central Bank has had little autonomy to speak of, the financial sphere having played no crucial role	Most funding is by the banking sector. Monetary policy aims to enhance employment and at a later date competitiveness
The State	Fragmented into series of agencies and control entities, growth possibilities are highly restricted because of competition in the political marketplace	Ensures provision of collective services plus co-ordinations that the big firms are incapable of running. Small size but significant role	Strong quantitative and qualitative development of State interventions: nationalised companies, regulations, public spending, social benefits, etc.	Multitude of public interventions lead to financial transfers and extensive and restrictive regulations
Insertion into international system	Adhesion to free trade principles, degree of autonomy varies depending on status and size (differences US vs. UK)	Trade and finance-related choices are conditioned by imperative of technological and economic development.	Traditionally a tight State control over external relations (tariffs, norms, quotas, restrictions on financial flows).	Acceptance of competitiveness principle based on technological and organisational innovation

(*continued*)

Table 2.1 (continued)

	Regulation			
	Market-oriented	*Meso-corporatist*	*Statist*	*Social-democratic*
3. Characteristics of the mode of regulation				
	Regulation very market-oriented, controlled by sophisticated legal mechanisms	Large companies, the market and the State make adjustments at the meso-economic level	State at heart of macroeconomic adjustments, with markets and firms adapting to its rules	Tripartite bargaining (employers-unions-State) lies at the heart of institutional reforms
4. Effects on				
Innovation	Schumpeterian waves predicated on radical innovation, preponderance of a patent-based logic and individualisation of benefits derived from innovation	Aptitude to copy and adapt products and processes by operating incremental yet profitable innovations	Radical innovation supposing major investments and a long-term time frame. Adaptation of Fordist (i.e. relatively centralised) innovations	Innovations are focused on resolving social and economic problems, be they marginal or radical..
Specialisation	Sectors tied to radical innovation: IT, space, pharmacy, finance and leisure industry.	Sectors requiring major coordination efforts and mobilising a localised but cumulative type of competency: auto, electronics, robotics	Sectors involved in major public infrastructures: transportation, telecom, aeronautics, space, arms industry, etc.	Sectors tied to social demand (health, security, environment. etc.) or exploit natural resources through technological innovation

Source: Amable et al. (1997, pp. 194–195)

most Latin American countries, plagued as they are by poor economic performance (Sect. 2). Given the quite late development fuelled by the opening-up of the world economy and the mobility of foreign direct investment, the East Asian capitalisms are not mere replicas of mature industrial ones: they display distinctive institutional architectures (Sect. 3). The various brands of capitalism are frequently denominated according to the continent they belong to. This might be quite misleading, because a precise comparative analysis falsifies the hypothesis that geographical proximity implies similar capitalism brands that should converge in the long run (Sect. 4). A widely shared opinion states that the acute competition among national economies is making past capitalism brands obsolete and transforming them. This underplays the possibility that radically new configurations may also emerge and be built upon surprising complementarities between typical capitalist competition and the State's ability to monitor technological catching up and even leapfrogging: China is a key example of such a novelty (Sect. 5). The patient building of complementarities between institutional forms, the productive system and specialization are dramatically mitigating the competition among the different socio-economic regimes: each of them can deepen its trajectory provided that a stable international regime prevails and channels medium- and long-term expectations. De facto, until 2008, the evolution of the world economy was governed by the strategic interactions of US finance-led and Chinese competition-led capitalism (Sect. 6). Nowadays, the future of international relations is at stake under the converging pressures of the limits reached by global value chains, the rise of nationalist movements and governments and the diverging national interests around the design of new multipolar international institutions. This creates a radical and largely unprecedented uncertainty (Sect. 7). Consequently, almost all past development strategies have to be reassessed, especially those which used to rely upon the mobility of financial capital or direct foreign investment coupled with export-led growth: inward-looking development is now a top priority on many national agendas. Furthermore, curbing the explosion of inequalities and coping with climate change have become two key objectives for all brands of capitalism (Sect. 8). A brief conclusion derives some consequences concerning the choices ahead for Vietnam.

2 The Club of Developing Economies Was Not Closed: The Rise of East Asia

Back in the 1950s, the literature on development used to stress the barriers to self-sustaining growth, such as unfavourable terms of trade between primary resources and manufactured products and the inability to challenge the technological leadership of mature economies. Latin America and the Caribbean were good examples of this underdevelopment trap, and Sub-Saharan Africa even more so. However, two regions have given the lie to the assumption that the club of developing countries was closed, namely South Africa and East Asia and Pacific. The rate at which these two regions have been catching up is impressive indeed (Fig. 2.2).

Nevertheless, within East Asia some economies are more successful than others. For most of them, the growth rate is smooth and moderate. China, however, is a clear outlier. In the early 1980s, it was among the poorest countries; by 2015, it was nearly the most advanced in terms of real gross domestic product per capita (Fig. 2.3). The very rapid East Asian catch-up has given rise to the concept of compressed development (Whittaker et al., 2010). But, conversely, the fact that Latin America has lagged behind suggests that such a catch-up is neither automatic nor homogenous across countries. Domestic characteristics matter.

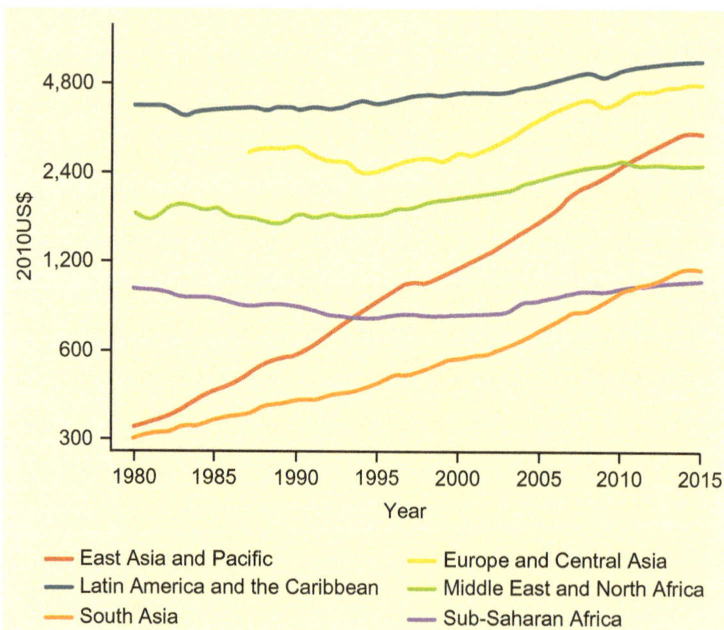

Fig. 2.2 Real gross domestic product per capita in developing regions

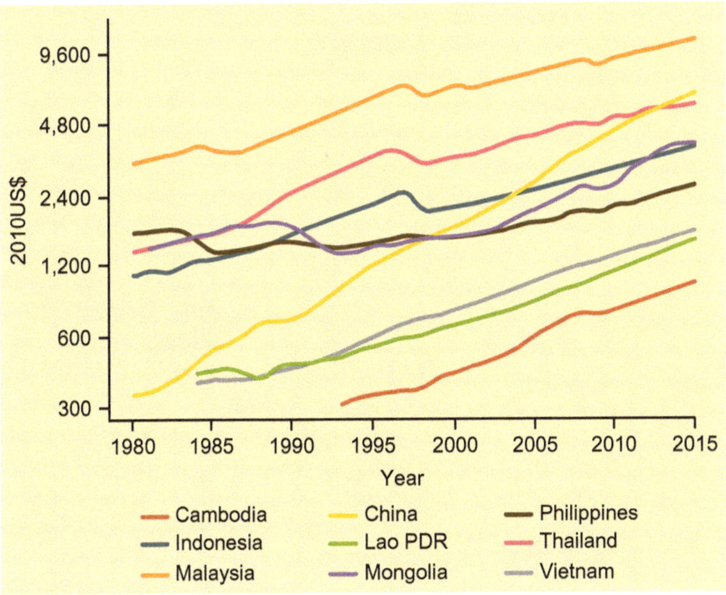

Fig. 2.3 Real gross domestic product per capita in developing East Asia and Pacific

3 The Asian Capitalisms Are Different

3.1 Not a Mere Replication of Western Capitalisms

Each national economy displays a specific configuration in terms of labour institutions, degree of competition, intensity of internationalization and style of public intervention. These features are tentatively captured by qualitative and quantitative indexes, and they help in searching for clustering among distinctive configurations (Harada & Tohyama, 2011). An interesting taxonomy can be derived from this analysis (Fig. 2.4). Actually, East Asian economies form four specific clusters:

1. *Insular Semi-Agrarian Capitalism: Indonesia and the Philippines*
   This cluster is characterized by a low level of GDP per capita, regulated product and labour markets, a lower level of social security and stricter international capital controls. Public interventions shape most institutional forms within a heavily regulated economy.

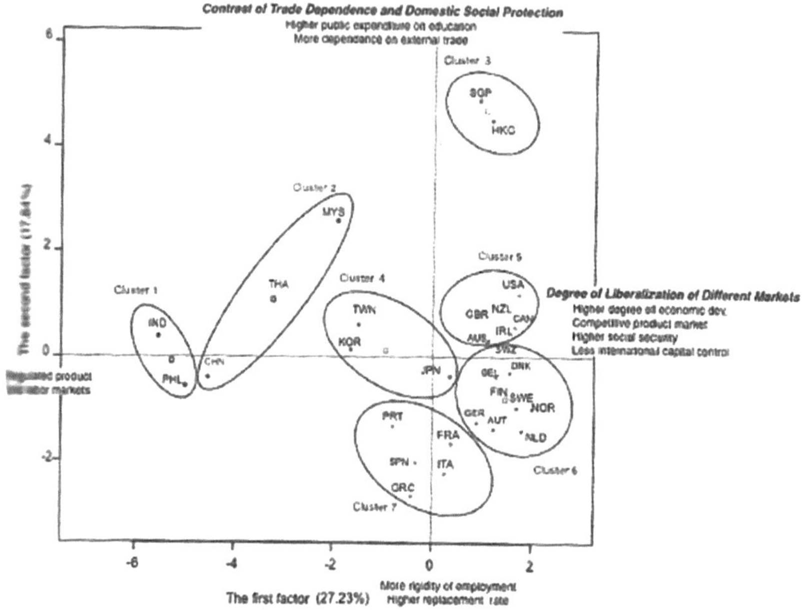

Fig. 2.4 Distinctive configurations not observed elsewhere. (Source: Harada and Tohyama (2011), p. 247)

2. *Trade-led Industrializing Capitalism: Malaysia and Thailand and China*
   These countries have common features of relatively low levels of GDP per capita, regulated product and labour markets, lower levels of social security, stricter international capital control, relatively higher public expenditure on education and higher dependence on external trade, and less rigidity of employment and hours worked. However, China has its own distinctive characteristics in terms of certain variables, such as public expenditure on education and dependence on external trade, so that it occupies a different position from the other two countries within the cluster.
3. *City Capitalism: Singapore and Hong Kong*
   They share the following common characteristics: a high level of GDP per capita, less regulated product and labour markets, less strict international capital control, higher public expenditure on education, much higher dependence on external trade, no rigidity of

employment and hours worked, and a lower replacement rate for the unemployed.

4. *Innovation-led Capitalism: Japan, Korea and Taiwan*
   They show similar characteristics with regard to high GDP per capita, levels of barriers to entry and public expenditure on education, but they have their own distinctive features in terms of other variables.

In any case, the East Asian economies are not the equivalent of other capitalisms in OECD member states, which are distributed across three other clusters:

1. *Advanced liberal capitalism* (Australia, Canada, the UK, Ireland, New Zealand and the USA).
2. *Welfare capitalism* (Austria, Belgium, Switzerland, Denmark, Germany, Finland, Netherlands, Norway and Sweden)
3. *European mixed capitalism* (Spain, France, Greece, Italy and Portugal).

3.2 No Convergence Towards a Common Asian Model

Some theoreticians, either neoclassical or neo-Schumpeterian, state that institutional configurations are ultimately selected by the competition among them: in a sense, the most efficient are bound to impose their logic on all others. Theoretically, this has to be challenged because a capitalist brand is organized around a series of complementary institutional forms that are quite difficult to replicate since they are the outcome of idiosyncratic socio-political compromises, domestically nurtured. Basically, given the dynamic nature of any capitalism, the criteria of static efficiency have to be abandoned in favour of another one, namely the structural viability of the accumulation regime shaped by the configuration of competition, capital/labour relations and the type of integration into the world economy.

Empirical comparative institutional analyses confirm the absence of convergence among these seven brands of capitalism. Firstly, as far as the developed economies are concerned, they are far from all joining the group of advanced liberal capitalist economies, in spite of the wave of deregulation. Secondly, Asia is the territory of diverging trajectories as evidenced, for example, by the opposite trajectories of city-capitalism and trade-led industrializing capitalism. More generally, institutional evolutions are far slower than economic activity, and their main features exhibit the long-run inertia typical of an economic specialization and national basic institutional compromises. Capitalism diversity is here to last and East Asia contributes to this diversity. An extension of the number of countries confirms this diversity and it even includes some rather unstable configurations (Combarnous & Rougier, 2017).

4 Geographical Proximity Does Not Mean Identical Brands of Capitalisms

This is an important remark that explains, in particular, why European integration is so difficult. Neither the single market nor, particularly, the euro has triggered convergence towards a common brand of capitalism (Boyer, 2018). The advanced liberal, welfare and mixed capitalisms have not merged into a common configuration, as Fig. 2.5 shows. The same result

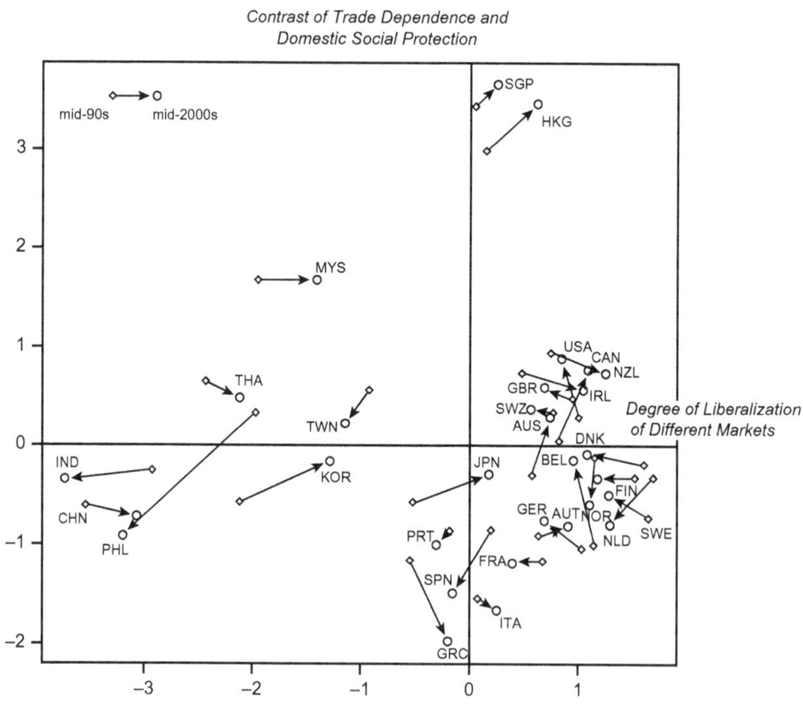

Fig. 2.5 No convergence towards a common "Asian model". (Source: Harada and Tohyama (2011), p. 252)

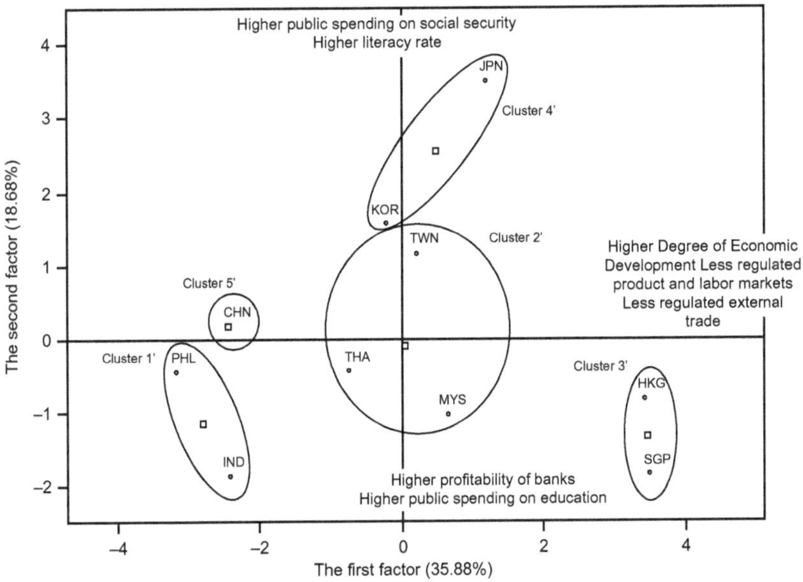

Fig. 2.6 Seen from within: at least five types. (Source: Harada and Tohyama (2011, p. 250))

is observed when the analysis is restricted to the Asian economies (Fig. 2.6). China emerges as a genuine model distinct from all the others, and this result captures the idiosyncratic feature of a continental economy. By the way, size may matter very much, since city capitalisms do not have the same constraints or opportunities as medium-sized economies. Consequently, it would be analytically misleading to label any capitalism by its geographical situation, even though Asian economies may share some common distinctive characteristics, compared to Latin American ones, in particular, an absence of abundant primary resources and an emphasis on export-led growth (see Stein and Ngok (2013) and Fig. 2.9, infra).

5 Mixing Market Mechanisms with Government Control in a Multi-Level System: China

As a new brand of capitalism, the formation and expansion of Chinese capitalism not only illustrates that divergence rather than convergence is still one of the main characteristics of modern capitalism but also reveals the mutually enhancing relationship between the progress of regional integration and the rise of a huge capitalist economy.

It is quite difficult to label Chinese capitalism by reference to conventional comparative political economy research. When Beijing began its reforms and opening-up policies about 40 years ago, many observers believed that China would adopt a brand of capitalism similar to American capitalism, European welfare capitalism or Japanese capitalism. However, 40 years later, it is obvious that Chinese capitalism is far removed from the aforementioned three kinds of capitalism and is hard to locate in the existing map of the diversity of capitalism. On the one hand, there is considerable variety even within the Chinese economy. The varieties exist in the key institutional domains and these varieties give rise to the difference of modes of production at firm level. The state-owned enterprises (SOEs), multinationals and local private enterprises are in the ascendancy in different industries and dominate different modes of production at firm level. On the other hand, Chinese capitalism is still evolving. Seen in this light, it is appropriate to call Chinese capitalism a mixed capitalism. Basically, a sophisticated variety of forms of property (Chavance, 2017) and a subtle mix of public interventions and market mechanisms (Mcnally, 2017) are generating an impressive accumulation dynamic (Revue de la regulation, 2017).

As a new brand of capitalism, the formation and expansion of Chinese capitalism not only illustrates that divergence rather than convergence is still one of the main characteristics of modern capitalism but also reveals the mutually enhancing relationship between the progress of regional integration and the rise of the huge capitalism economy. It is built upon three complementary pillars (Fig. 2.7).

At the local level, the public authorities guarantee favourable conditions for firms that cannot rely upon a clear definition of property rights, and this is the source of the dynamism of investment and productive capacity formation. Actually, this rapid growth generated by a myriad of local State corporations allows fulfilment of the society-wide compromise: the promise to the Chinese population of better standards of living goes hand in hand with implicit political support for the Chinese Communist Party. The coherence of this socio-economic regime is obtained by a third component, that is, a State-Administration arrangement in which local authorities enjoy a significant degree of autonomy in the financing of their budget by selling the right to use land and are promoted according to their ability to enhance growth, while minimizing social conflicts and

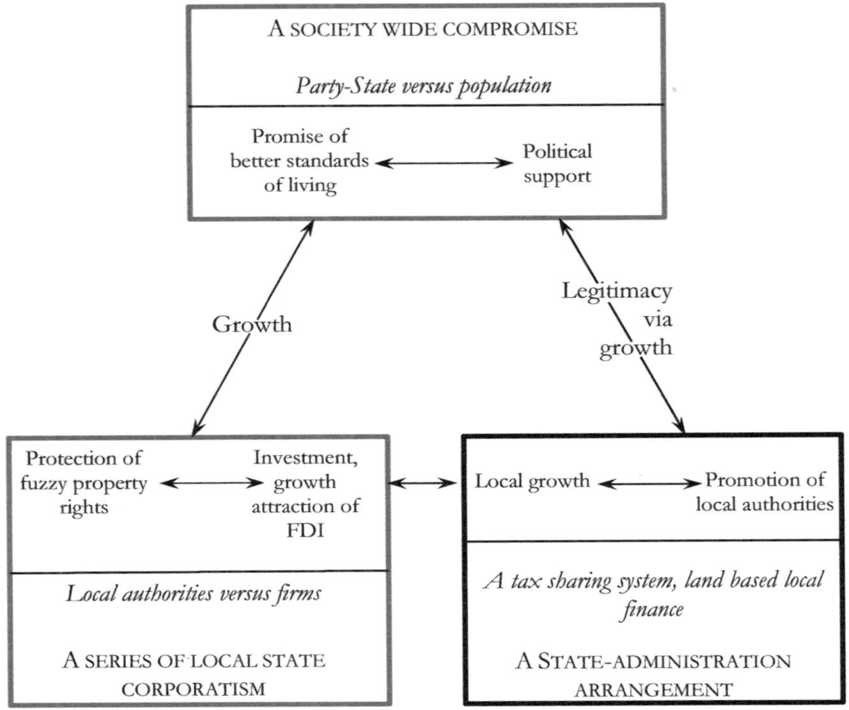

Fig. 2.7 China: a unique mix of institutional arrangements. (Source: Adapted from Lei Song and Yan Chengnan (2018), Chap. 13)

possibly reducing environmental damage. The difference between this arrangement and Soviet-type regimes should be noted. The dynamism emerges out of the incentives present at the local level and Central Government is tentatively monitoring the imbalances, thus generated by full use of the exchange rate, credit controls and periodic reforms. This distinctive brand of capitalism is the largely unintended consequence of the layering of successive piecemeal and cautious reforms, which is quite difficult to replicate elsewhere.

6 More Interdependence than Competition Among Contrasting Socio-Economic Regimes

One strand of the literature tends to extrapolate the competition among firms to the nation-states in their search for competitiveness, that is, a successful and viable integration into the world economy. Basically, all governments announce quite mimetic plans for exploring the technological frontier, but actually their economies follow quite contrasted trajectories.

6.1 A Deepening of Economic Specialization with the Opening-Up of World Trade

In accordance with most international trade theories, the distribution of revealed competitive advantages is clearly polarized (Miotti et al., 2012). The first criterion opposes economies that export mainly natural resources to those that prosper by producing and exporting manufactured products: Latin America on one side, China, South Korea, Singapore, Japan and Taiwan on the other. A second dividing line distinguishes between services and manufactured goods: the opposition is then between the United States, the United Kingdom, India and Hong Kong, on the one hand, and Germany and most East Asian countries, on the other hand.

From 2000 to 2009, Latin America diverged ever further from East Asia, with the former becoming ever more dependent on exports of primary resources and the latter confirming the dynamism and competitiveness of newly industrializing countries (Bresser-Pereira, 2009). Globally, Asia has thus acquired a precise position in the international division of labour, and a new dependency has struck most Latin American countries, with the exception of Mexico.

6.2 *Interdependent and Even Complementary Socio-Economic Regimes*

We now have an explanation as to why such contrasting socio-economic regimes are resilient and tend to persist in the long run (Boyer, 2016). Basically, their external and internal disequilibria are compensating one another and making them compatible and, in some cases, complementary (Fig. 2.8).

- Finance-led capitalism in the United States is associated with an external trade deficit, growing public debt and the rise of inequality due to the explosion of top incomes. It is the mirror image of the Chinese competition-led capitalism: the permanent oversupply finds an outlet in a structural trade surplus that is partially used to finance the American economy. This complementarity has led to a surge of inequality in China generated by the rapid modernization of the productive system. Consequently, these two capitalism brands are evolving in step with each other and thriving on their differences.

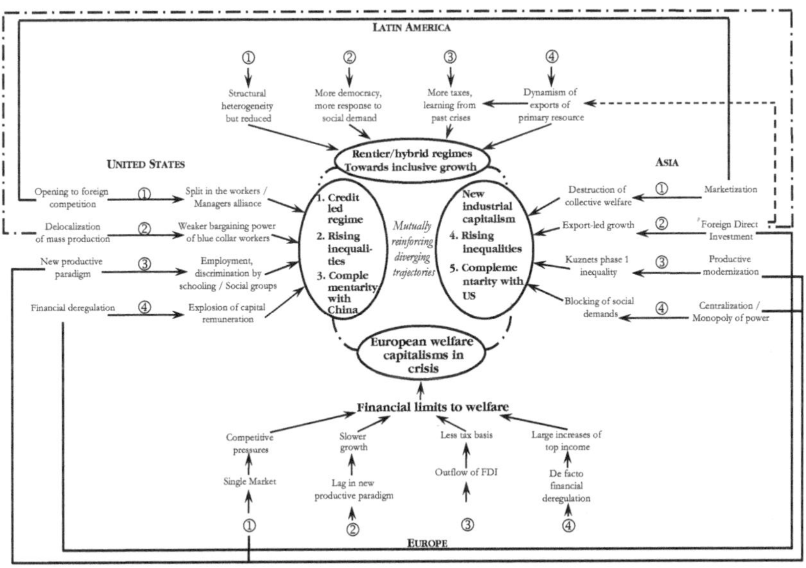

Fig. 2.8 An interdependent world, complementarity development modes and growth regimes until the early 2000s

- The euro crises of the 2010s struck another regime that could be described as welfare capitalism, with state-led or social-democratic variants. Public opinion defends the ideal of solidarity, and income inequalities remain rather moderate. But the redistributive tax system and generous public spending have come under fire from the twin pressures of the rapid Chinese catch-up in most industries and the recurring global financial crises generated by the American victory in promoting the liberalization and globalization of trade, capital and finance. The future of these welfare capitalisms is thus being partially shaped by the evolution of Chinese and North American capitalisms.
- The resource-based rentier regimes, very relevant in Latin America, either typical (Venezuela) or hybrid (Brazil), are structurally dependent on the demand from industrial and financial capitalisms. When both were booming in the early 2010s, governments celebrated the success of a new and inclusive socio-economic regime and the (modest) reduction in economic inequality, albeit from a starting point of extreme social polarization. Nevertheless, when world demand and the prices of primary resources collapse, the viability of these regimes is at stake. Again, this reversal of fortune is explained by the Latin American specialization that is complementary to that of China and the US. When economic crises erupt, the past political alliances, allowed by the transition to democracy, are challenged. A political economy approach is required to understand these episodes (Palombarini, 2001).

7 The 2010s: The International Regime Is at Risk from Converging Pressures

The relative predictability of the world economy suffered a serious blow when the great financial crisis of 2008 spiralled out from the United States to nearly all countries. Most actors realized that a historical period of internationalization and volatile financial flows was over but the search for a successor to the international regime brought opposing national interests into conflict with each other.

7.1 The Defence of National Economic Sovereignty by New Political Movements

In retrospect, the implicit acceptance of globalization appears quite surprising. Actually, many societies have been significantly transformed by stiffer competition, employment restructuring and widening inequalities in the context of a reduction in the redistributive role of the tax system and the welfare. Within a complex web of technological, economic and financial processes, it was tempting to blame the internationalization of economies as the main culprit since it actually polarized societies between a small group of winners and a far larger one of those left behind. Since in Europe, for instance, both Christian and social democrats tended to share the same vision of the potential benefits of globalization; this opened an avenue to so-called populist movements with distinctive programmes, the main objective of which was to defend those who lost out as national economies were opened up and neo-liberal policies implemented.

Nationalism, protectionism, anti-political elites and authoritarianism characterize some of the brands of populisms that have emerged in response to national political traditions (Boutin et al., 2019). At world level the number of these populisms in government has grown after each economic crisis: first after the bursting of the Internet bubble in 2000 and then after the collapse of the sub-prime speculative boom (Kyle & Gultchin, 2016). It seems that the first populist wave was a reaction to the worsening of socio-economic well-being and that the second highlighted the issue of identity and national sovereignty (Fig. 2.9). In both cases, some degree of protectionism was presented as a solution. This is specially the case in the United States. Previously a defender and promoter of free trade and globalization, the USA under Trump was at the forefront of the destruction of the rules of the game at international level. China had to respond to the extensive protectionist measures by increasing tariffs at the risk of breaking down the global value chains from which large American multinationals benefited so much. Similarly, Brexit is testimony to the diffusion of the temptation to withdraw from international cooperation.

7.2 The Open Conflict Between Economic Complementarity and Geopolitical Rivalry

Most economic theories suggest that the generalization of "beggar my neighbor" policies is a loss-loss strategy and in fact 2019 saw a notable

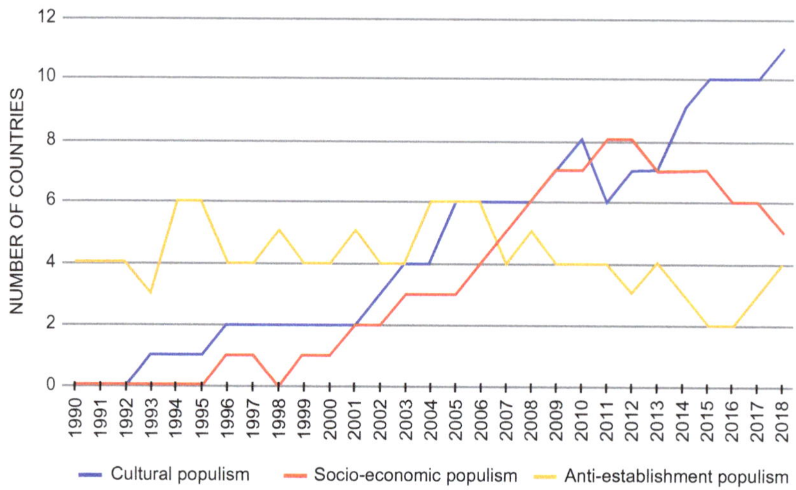

Fig. 2.9 The rise of various types of populism in power (1990–2018). (Source: Kyle Jordan and Limor Gultchin (2016), Populist power around the world, Tony Blair Institute for Global Change. https://institute.global/insight/renewing-centre/populists-power-around-world)

slowing down of world trade and ultimately growth for most national economies (Fig. 2.10).

It seems totally irrational from an economic standpoint. It is not necessarily so if the analyst takes into account domestic political and geopolitical political factors. The contemporary world is torn by an open conflict between an unprecedented level of economic interdependence between countries and the search for national sovereignty for most governments and the struggle for international hegemony by the United States and its implicit challenger, China. This tension is permeating contemporary international relations, and it is specially so with regard to the contradictory role of China within Asian integration and the world system.

In fact, China is located at the centre of the web of contradictions that operate in the contemporary world: between economic complementarity and geopolitical rivalry in Asia, especially with Japan; between reluctant cooperation and open conflict with the United States; between an alliance for rebuilding international institutions and asymmetrical integration with Latin America and Africa; between the need to maintain the euro as a currency that may compete with the dollar and the pressure to turn the yuan

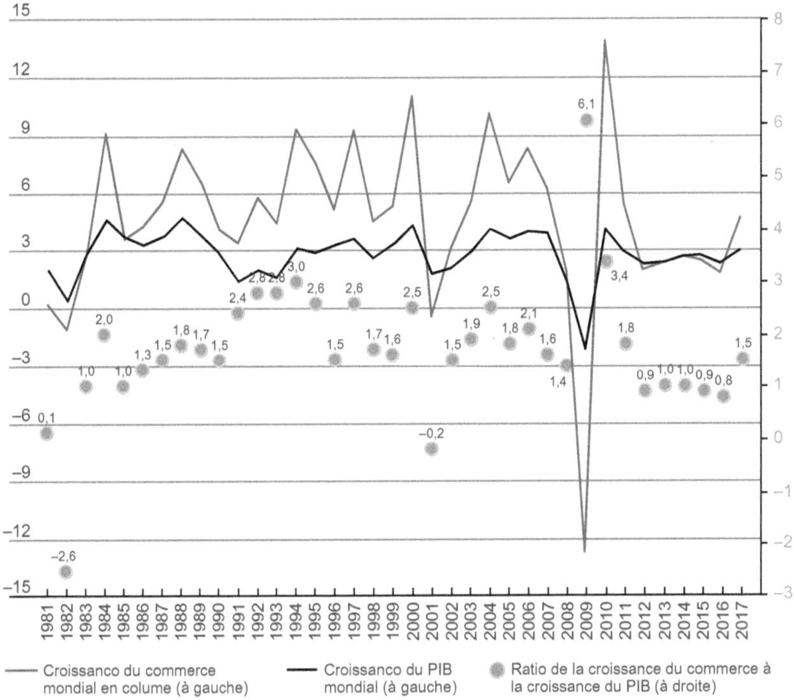

Fig. 2.10 Ratio of world trade volume growth to real-world GDP, 1981–2017 (Annual variation rate % and ratio). (Source: World Trade Organization (2018), World Trade Statistical Review, p. 32)

into an international currency, so that an independent monetary and exchange rate policy continues to be the essential tool for governing and controlling the Chinese economy. In this global game, the European Union occupies a less advantageous position than Japan: dominated by American finance and open to the winds of Asian competition, Europe is an aggregate of old nations that have given up the exercise of any geopolitical power in the reconfiguring of the coming world and the defence and diffusion of their welfare capitalism (Fig. 2.11).

This complex web of economic interdependence and geopolitical rivalry introduces considerable uncertainty into both the reconfiguration of international relations and the choice of an economic strategy, both for developed and developing nation-states.

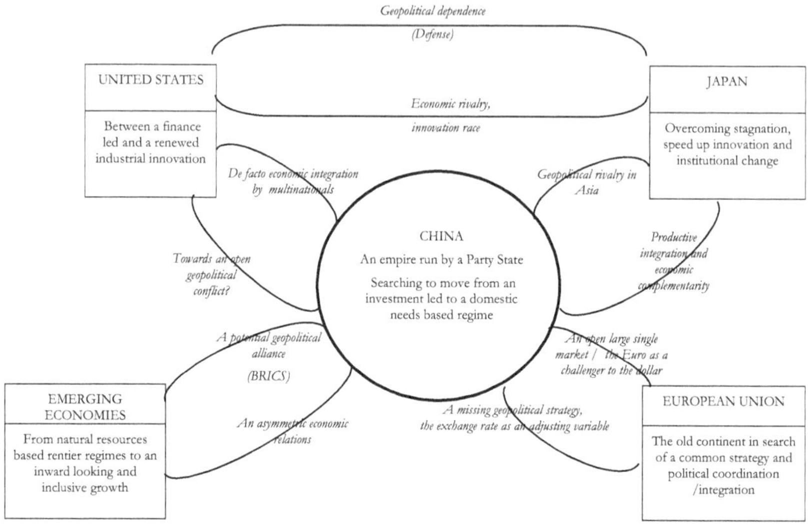

Fig. 2.11 The difficult conciliation between political rivalry and economic interdependency: the example of China

7.3 The Crisis of Post-WWII International Organizations

Can a new international system emerge from the present configuration and deliver more satisfactory outcomes for each member state? It is far from evident since the heterogeneity of national regimes, ideologies and interests raises many obstacles, the more so the more policymakers forget the dramatic near collapse of 2008.

Finance-led capitalisms require complete freedom and mobility of capital to maximize the gains from financial intermediation which, although located on Wall Street and in the City of London, has become global. The emerging industrial capitalisms base their legitimacy on rapid growth enabling job creation and rising living standards (Bresser-Pereira, 2009). By contrast, in pure rentier regimes the struggles are polarized around conflicts over rent sharing without any great concern for improving domestic production capacity (Hausmann, 1981). The capitalisms based on innovation thrive on industrial specialization in products in high demand by the emerging industrial regimes, and they require a full opening-up of the world economy. The mature industrial capitalisms are torn between strengthening their domestic markets and improving their industrial specialization, which would enable them to better integrate into the global economy. Mixed regimes—both rentier and industrial—face a similar dilemma: on the one hand, they push domestic growth in order to promote their potentially self-sufficient domestic production systems, on the other they can also benefit from the redistribution of income associated with the sector exporting raw materials and agricultural products (Table 2.2).

Clearly, the pure economic justification does imply political support for institutionalizing such public goods (Hugon, 2004). According to another theory, a common is a collective resource, the commodification of which may cause a crisis for an entire society. But the question remains the same: How do these commons emerge in the international political arena? Finally, can we mobilize the theory of commons? It is not obvious since a community has to agree upon how to implement and manage rules to maintain this common and it is easier locally than internationally (Ostrom, 2010). This is the concern that runs through this present analysis: all institutional arrangements involve political processes, and they are especially difficult to build at the international level in the absence of a benevolent hegemon.

Table 2.2 The difficult agreement on common objectives for an alternative international system: the consequence of contrasted socio-economic regimes

Socio-economic regime	*Objectives*			
	Domestic growth	*Economic specialization*	*Managing the rent*	*World financial intermediation*
Finance-led capitalism(US, UK)	**			***
Emerging industrial capitalisms(China, India)	***	**		*
Pure rentier regime(Venezuela, Saudi Arabia)	*		***	*
Capitalism based on innovation/export(Japan, Germany, South Korea)	*	***		
Mature industrial capitalisms(France, Italy)	**	**		
Mixed rentier/industrial regimes(Brazil, Argentina)	**	*	**	*

8 All Development Strategies Have To Be ReDesigned in the Face of Major International Uncertainties

The uncertainty about the redesign of international relations requires past development strategies to be updated because past successes are not a guarantee of the future and the choices open to governments might differ from one country to another.

8.1 Size Matters

Past comparative research has identified an important discriminating variable in the distribution of capitalism brands and growth regimes: integration into the world economy can be either a constraint or an opportunity and the size of the domestic economies that determines the outcome (Boyer, 2015a). Two opposing configurations can be observed.

- On the one hand, countries with a large population and potential domestic market enjoy significant autonomy in the design of their development strategy because they can mobilize the increasing returns to scale generated by a deep division of labour within the domestic territory.
- On the other hand, small economies have to rely upon international trade to satisfy domestic demand and, conversely, to sell the goods and services they are specialized in. Their governments have to nurture socio-political compromises in order to share both the benefits and the risks associated with their dependency on the evolution of international markets.

Consequently, continental economies such as the United States and China may externalize on to the world economy some of the core imbalances of their growth regime: excess consumption and low savings in the United States, overcapacity and excess savings in China. Both are so economically important that they have the power to influence the evolution of the rules governing the international order. By contrast, small economies have to comply with the forces of international competition and they have little say and influence over the rules of the game at world level.

In between these two extremes, many economies are medium-sized and they face a dilemma: being relatively small, they do not have the ability to significantly influence the evolution of the world, but they are large enough to enjoy some degree of freedom in implementing an inward-looking mode of development. Japan, South Korea, Vietnam, Germany, UK, Italy and France, for instance, belong to this category. With the process of internationalization, most mid-sized economies have become small economies. Those that used to be export-led now face a key structural weakness: the volatility and synchronization of world evolution challenge their core strategy (Japan, South Korea and probably Vietnam). Those that relied upon consumption-led growth have to identify and negotiate another socio-political compromise in order to preserve their competitiveness (Italy and France).

8.2 The Transformation of the International Regime: Four Scenarios

Given the structural incompatibility of the strategies adopted by governments, the present international relations system cannot last unchanged in the long run. A tipping point is bound to come but nobody can deterministically forecast how the world regime will be redesigned. Scenario building might be another and more realistic way of exploring a future shaped by the strategic interactions of the key actors (Table 2.3).

- *New international institutions for global cohesion*
  Coerced by the necessity to cope with climate change, concerned by the risk of a fragmenting world economy and moved by the will to prevent the repetition of a major world financial crisis, the so-called international community decides to build the supranational institutions for the twenty-first century. These institutions have to comply with the new balance of economic might and geopolitical influence across the world with the objective of creating the conditions for the coexistence of alternative and possibly divergent national trajectories.
- *A long cold economic war within a segmented world*
  Some histories of international relations suggest another scenario: a lengthy struggle between a declining hegemon that defends its geopolitical power at the cost of world stability and a rising economic power reluctant to play the role of new benevolent superpower in charge of monitoring the emerging international regime (Kindleberger, 1996). The world would experience a new divide between two coalitions built on opposing political conceptions, dif-

Table 2.3 One global world, a new international divide, incentives to regional integrations or a myriad of economic nationalisms

	One global world	*An economic cold war*	*Regional integration*	*Competing nationalisms*
Economic conditions	No more tariffs and non-tariff barriers	Two competing economic systems: US and China led	Single market generates significant economies	Primacy of national sovereignty does not bear large economic costs
	Immaterial goods abolish distances	Two sets of norms and technological systems	Still sheltered sectors	A coherent national productive system
Political configuration	Need for strong and unified world institutions	Inability to design and implement new international institutions	Acceptance of partial pooling of national sovereignty	A strong state defending national interests
Viability	Problematic self-regulation	Danger of recurring conflicts and economic trade wars.	If distribution of integration gains supporting legitimacy by social groups at the national level	Dependent on an acceptable trade-off between autonomy / well-being
Type of crisis	Incapacity to sustain global commons / public goods	Currency wars, nationalism factor of war, no solution to global commons (climate change, financial stability, peace)	National economic divergence and inability to redefine new rules of the game	Tensions around standards of living, rising costs of economic nationalism

ferent regulations of competition, distinctive technological norms and so on. This scenario assumes that economic competition between two blocks does not degenerate into an open war.

- *Regionalization as an alternative to globalization*
  The present difficulties experienced by the European integration project are frequently interpreted as evidence of the impossibility of building a supranational political entity in an age characterized by the overwhelming power of transnational firms and rising populist movements. One method based on the primacy of supranational institutions building over economic concerns has shown its limits in

the European Union. Nevertheless, de facto economic regional integration has progressed remarkably in East Asia with a minimalist codification in formal political institutions (Boyer et al., 2018). One could thus imagine genuine forms of regional integration that would temporarily mitigate the weakness of global level institutions and possibly pave the way for the negotiation of new global rules of the game by a small number of strong regional emerging powers.

- *One nationalism against another*
  This last scenario would replicate the interwar period of the last century: protectionist measures are not a bargaining tool in order to negotiate a fairer international regime but the central tool for regaining national political autonomy whatever the economic costs imposed on domestic populations. The Brexit episode is a good example of this absolute primacy of national sovereignty. If generalized, this strategy has the potential to destroy any chance of converging towards a new stable and peaceful international order.

8.3 Reconsidering the Benefits of Foreign Direct Investment and Export-Led Growth

The task then is to tentatively estimate whether the various growth strategies thrive, suffer or even enter crisis depending on the international scenario that will prevail. Clearly, there is no strategy that can guarantee good outcomes whatever the international context (Table 2.4).

- If the world order collapses, then innovation and export-led growth, which was so successful in the past, might deliver quite poor results due to the excessive specialization in response to world demands. Conversely, the inward-looking regimes will be better equipped to respond to citizens' demands even if their overall performance is mediocre.
- China's domestic investment and export model can probably be converted into another one based upon domestic consumption whatever the fate of the international regime: the size of the potential domestic market will continue to feed the increasing returns to scale typical of emerging new industries.
- Low-wage export and FDI and export models are especially vulnerable to the segmentation of the world economy, since they are either

Table 2.4 The joint evolution of international regimes and domestic development strategies

International / *Domestic*	*One global world*	*A new cold war*	*Regional integration*	*Competing nationalisms*
1. Import substitution	--	~	+	++
2. Low wages export-led	++	+	~	--
3. Innovation and export-led	++	++	~	--
4. Foreign investment and export-led	++	+	~	--
5. Domestic investment and export-led	++	++	+ (investment)	--
6. Finance-led	++	~	-	--
7. Natural resources rentier regime	++	+	-.	--

weakening their domestic demand or totally dependent on foreign technologies and expertise.

- By contrast, a segmented world is an incentive to explore again a realistic import substitution strategy whose complete and irreversible irrelevance was supposed to have been proved by the Asian miracle. It is an invitation to revisit the success of many Latin American countries from the 1930s to the 1970s (Cardoso & Faletto, 1979) and its updating after the wave of deregulation of the 1990s (CEPAL, 2012). Clearly, the international regime and national development strategies are constantly evolving in tandem with each other: if the international division of labour regresses, seemingly obsolete—but of course far from optimal—policies are again on the agenda, at least for some specific socio-political configurations.

These policymakers face difficult choices: they have to decide on a domestic strategy in an environment characterized by radical uncertainty. Depending on the odds, the same decision can turn out to have been wise and fruitful or ill-advised and wasteful. But they have also to detect the possible emergence of new opportunities not captured by traditional approaches.

8.4 *The Century of the Anthropogenetic Model?*

In the past, analysts tended to consider that improved quality of life and longer life expectancy were the result of society's enrichment, something that allowed more resources to be devoted to the healthcare sector. Today, theorists and practitioners also insist on the impact of education and healthcare on the development process (Deaton, 2001). On the one hand, they improve skills, including those involved in the healthcare provided within families by women (Esping Andersen, 2008). On the other hand, lower infant mortality and the victory over major epidemics have changed the demographic regime, allowing for an economic dividend via, for example, a younger population. At the same time, investments in general education and training yield additional benefits, thanks to the extension of the life cycle, which carries over into professional life and increases the return on education policies (Cutler & Lleras-Muney, 2006).

Thus, successful development results from a circular process and, in this case of cumulative success, it runs from business investment, which creates productive capital, to educational expenditures, which in turn contributes to social capital. The latter then enters into synergy with government-created infrastructures. On this view of things, a proactive strategy in the area of healthcare can in some cases help accelerated growth. This holds even more so for education, since it also shapes access to healthcare and generates interest in efforts to promote the well-being of children and the family (Fig. 2.12). This scenario has been studied historically (Fontvieille & Michel, 2002; Michel & Vallade, 2007), and under the surface of industrial innovations, this anthropogenetic model is significantly shaping contemporary Japan (Boyer, 2015b).

This conception of development has been combined with more orthodox analyses in terms of human capital and (more fundamentally) capacity development by way of the basic goods that are access to education and healthcare (Sen, 1997, 2000). The human development indicators that are regularly published by international organizations, among them the World Bank, testify to this modernization. They are no longer merely the results of success in accelerating growth; they can be the conditions for a better quality of development. This change of paradigm does not only hold for emergent countries; above all, it applies—perhaps especially—to the most advanced countries, where the search for prosperity might gradually be substituted for that of growth (Cassiers, 2011).

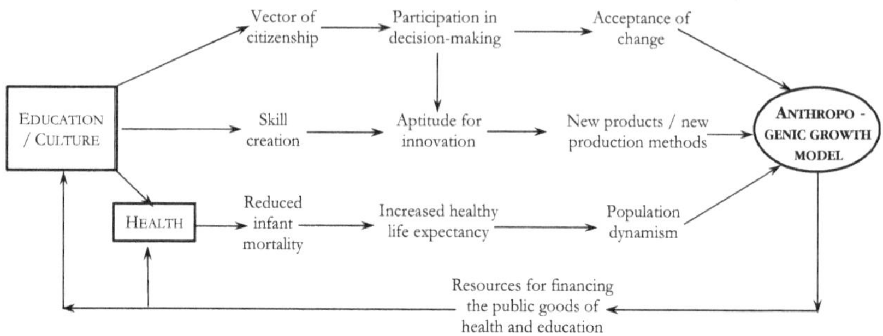

Fig. 2.12 Education, health and culture at the heart of the anthropogenetic mode of development

9 Conclusion

Some proposals for the future of Vietnam development can be derived from consideration of past developments.

1. The country probably faces *the dilemma typically faced by mid-sized economies*: they are too big to enjoy the opportunistic behaviour of a small economy but too small to engineer a purely inward-looking development. Vietnam has to explore a mixed strategy combining investment in infrastructure, technological improvement and prudent integration into an uncertain world system.
2. Can Vietnam follow a *Chinese type strategy* but with a lag given the probable long-term slowing down of world trade, FDI and the acute defence of intellectual property rights? Can the Communist Party continue to monitor market competition and local alliances between entrepreneurs and political authorities in order to sustain economic dynamism and innovation? What reforms could enhance the synergy between central and local authorities?
3. The concern for *ecological sustainability* should go along with the search for *social cohesion*, especially the well-being of the Vietnamese population. Investment in education, training, health and culture might well turn out to be the core of the next development mode for the end of this century. This anthropogenetic model suggests that these investments are facilitated not only by successful development strategy but also they are precondition and prerequisite of any of them.

References

Alary, P., & Lafaye de Micheaux, E. (2015). *Capitalismes asiatiques et puissance chinoise: Diversité des modèles, hégémonie de la Chine*. Editions Sciences-Po.

Amable, B. (2003). *The diversity of modern capitalism*. Oxford University Press.

Amable, B., Barre, R., & Boyer, R. (1997). *Les systèmes d'innovation à l'ère de la globalisation*. OST/Economica.

Boutin, C., Dard, O., & Rouvillois, F. (2019). *Le dictionnaire des populismes*. Editions du Cerf.

Boyer, R. (2011). Asian capitalism and regional integration after the subprime crisis. *Journal of Northeast Asia Development, 13* (December), 1–16. Northeast Asia Development Institute University of Incheon.

Boyer, R. (2015a). *Economie politique des capitalismes. Théorie de la régulation et des crises*, Grand Repère Manuel, La Découverte, Paris, Octobre.

Boyer, R. (2015b). Japan: The frugal production to an anthropo-genetique plan (the). In *Building the future we want, a planet for life 2015*, Part 2, Chapter 8, Teri Press.

Boyer, R. (2016). A world contrasted but interdependent inequality regimes: The Latin America paradox. *Review of Political Economy, 28*(1), 1–22.

Boyer, R. (2017). Development and régulation theory. In E. S. Reinert, J. Ghosh, & R. Kattel (Eds.), *Handbook of alternative theories of economic development* (chap. 20, pp. 352–385). Elgar Editors.

Boyer, R. (2018). Brexit: Lessons for the viability of the European Union and other regional integration. In Boyer Robert, Hiroyasu Uemura, Toshio Yamada, Lei Song (Eds.), *Evolving Diversity and Interdependence o capitalisms* (pp. 259–302). Japan: Springer Nature.

Boyer, R., & Saillard, Y. (2001). *Regulation theory: The state of the art*. Routledge.

Boyer, R., Charron, E., Jurgens, U., & Tolliday, S. (1998). *Between imitation and innovation: The transfer and hybridization of productive models in the international automobile industry?* Oxford University Press.

Boyer, R., Uemura, H., Yamada, T., & Song, L. (Eds.). (2018). *Evolving diversity and interdependence of capitalisms: Transformations of regional integration in EU and Asia*. Springer Verlag.

Bresser Pereira, L. C. (2009). *Mondialisation et compétition: Pourquoi certains pays émergents réussissent et d'autres non*. La Découverte.

Cardoso, F. H., & Faletto, E. (1979). *Dependency and development in Latin America*. University of California Press.

Cassiers, I. (Ed.). (2011). *Redéfinir la prospérité. Jalons pour un débat*. Editions de l'Aube.

CEPAL. (2012). *Cambio Estructural para la Igualdad. Una visión integrada del desarrollo*, Nations Unies, Santiago, Chile.

Chavance, B. (2017). Ownership transformation and system change in China. *Revue de la régulation* [En ligne], 21 | 1er semestre / Spring 2017, mis en ligne le 20 juin 2017, consulté le 16 février 2018. http://journals.openedition.org/regulation/12298; https://doi.org/10.4000/regulation.12298

Combarnous, F., & Rougier, E. (Eds.). (2017). *The diversity of emerging capitalisms in developing countries. Globalization, institutional convergence and experimentation.* Palgrave Macmillan.

Cutler, D., & Lleras-Muney, A. (2006). *Education and health: Evaluating theories and evidence.* Working Paper NBER 12352. http://www.nber.org/papers/w12352

Deaton, A. (2001). *Health, inequality and economic development.* Cambridge University Press.

Esping Andersen, G. (2008). Childhood investments and skill formation. *International tax and Public Finance, 15*, 14–49.

Fontvieille, L., & S. Michel (2002). Analysis of the transition between two successive social orders—Application to the relation between education and growth. *Review, 25*(1), 23–46. Fernand Braudel Centre, New York.

Harada, Y., & Tohyama, H. (2011). Asian capitalisms: Institutional con-figurations and firm heterogeneity. In R. Boyer, H. Uemura, & A. Isokai (Eds.), *Diversity and transformations of Asian capitalisms* (pp. 243–263). Routledge.

Hausmann, R. (1981). *State landed property, oil rent and accumulation in the Venezuelan economy*, Ph.D. Thesis, Cornell University.

Hollingsworth, R., & Boyer, R. (Eds.). (1997). *Contemporary capitalism: The embeddedness of institutions.* Cambridge University Press.

Hugon, P. (2004). Les biens publics mondiaux et le niveau transnational de la régulation. *La Lettre de la Régulation*, n° 48, avril.

Kindleberger, C. P. (1996). *World economic primacy: 1500 to 1990.* Oxford University Press.

Kyle, J., & Gultchin, L. (2016). *Populist power around the world.* Tony Blair Institute for Global Change. https://institute.global/insight/renewing-centre/populists-power-around-world

Lordon, F. (1997). Endogenous structural change and crisis in a multiple time-scales growth model. *Journal of Evolutionary Economics, 7*(1), 1–21.

Mcnally, Ch. A. (2017). Rebalancing the economy, refurbishing the state: The political economic logic of Sino-capitalism in contemporary China. *Revue de la régulation* [En ligne], 21 | 1er semestre / Spring, consulté le 16 janvier 2018. http://journals.openedition.org/regulation/12294

Michel, S., & Vallade, D. (2007). Une analyse de long terme des dépenses sociales: vers un indicateur synthétique de développement des hommes. *Revue de la Régulation*, | Juin / June 2007. http://regulation.revues.org/1507

Miotti, E. L., Quenan, C., & Zan, E. T. (2012). Continuités et ruptures dans l'accumulation et la régulation en Amérique latine dans les années 2000: le cas de l'Argentine, du Brésil et du Chil. *Revue de la régulation* [En ligne], 11 | 1er semestre / Spring 2012. http://journals.openedition.org/regulation/9756

Ostrom, E. (2010). *Gouvernance du bien commun. Pour une nouvelle approche des ressources naturelles*, Louvain La Neuve, De Boek.

Palombarini, S. (2001). *La rupture du compromis social italien*. CNRS Éditions.

Revue de la Regulation. (2017). Lectures institutionnalistes de la Chine, n° 21, 1er semestre / Spring. http://journals.openedition.org/regulation/12228

Sen, A. (1997). Development thinking at the beginning of the XXI century. In L. Emmerij (Ed.), *Economic and social development into the XXI century* (pp. 531–551). Inter-American Development Bank-John Hopkins University Press.

Sen, A. (2000). *Development as freedom*. Anchor Books.

Song, L., & Chengnan, Y. (2018). Dynamics of Chines-style developmentism as the mode of regulation: Formation, weakening and redesign of flexible rigidity. In R. Boyer, H. Uemura, T. Yamada, & L. Song (Eds.), *Evolving diversity and interdependence of capitalisms: Transformations of regional integration in EU and Asia* (pp. 361–378). Springer Verlag.

Stein, R., & Ngok, K. (2013), *What kind of welfare state is emerging in China?* Working Paper 2013-2, Unirisd, Geneva.

Wade, R. (1990). *Governing the market: Economic theory and the role of government in east Asian industrialization*. Princeton University Press.

Whittaker, H., Zhu, T., Sturgeon, T., Han, M., Tsai, T., & Okita, T. (2010). Compressed development. *Studies in Comparative International Development, 45*(4), 439–467.

World Trade Organization. (2018). *World trade statistical review 2018*, Geneva. Available online at www.wto.org/wtsr18

CHAPTER 3

The Hybrid Nature of the Vietnamese Market Economy: Personal Relationships and Debt in the Dairy and Maize Sectors

Emmanuel Pannier and Guillaume Duteurtre

1 Introduction

> There are no exclusively capitalist societies. (…) There are only societies that have a regime or rather—which is even more complicated—regime systems more or less arbitrarily defined by the predominance of one or other of these systems or institutions. Mauss (1997, p. 565—our translation)

In the late 1980s, Vietnam moved from a planned collectivist system to a market-oriented economy. Major institutional reforms have gradually led the country into a new socio-economic regime that promotes private

E. Pannier (✉)
IRD (UMR Paloc), Paris, France USSH (VNU), Hanoi, Vietnam
e-mail: emmanuel.pannier@ird.fr

G. Duteurtre
CIRAD, UMR Selmet (CIRAD, INRA, Mtp Supagro, University of Montpellier), Montpellier, France
e-mail: guillaume.duteurtre@cirad.fr

T. A.-D. Tran (ed.), *Rethinking Asian Capitalism*,
https://doi.org/10.1007/978-3-030-98104-4_3

entrepreneurs and companies operating in competitive markets and making use of their capital and wage labor to generate profit and wealth (Fforde & De Vylder, 1996; Duteurtre et al., 2021). This capital-based economy has been progressively opened up to international trade and foreign investment, leading Vietnam to be part of the dynamic of global capitalism. Vietnam became a member of the Association of South East Asian Nations (ASEAN) in 1995 and of the World Trade Organization (WTO) in 2007. This process has not undermined the preeminent role of the State in the economy (Gainsborough, 2010a; London, 2019) or the importance of the ritual economy and of non-commercial interpersonal exchanges (Malarney, 2002; Lantz et al., 2005; Tessier, 2009; Hy, 2016; Pannier, 2015, 2018a).

Recognizing and understanding this particular socio-economic regime requires us to analyze the types of institutional arrangements that have emerged in this context (Boyer, 2004, Boyer et al., 2012; Alary & Lafaye de Micheaux, 2013; Cornia & Popov, 2001). In parallel with the extensive literature assessing the impacts of these changes on the standard economic performance indicators (Glewwe et al., 2004; Cuong & Nguyet, 2018), some anthropologists have sought to explore the extra-economic logics that shape the Vietnamese market economy (McElwee, 2007; Lainez, 2014; Endres, 2014; Grillot, 2016; Horat, 2017; Endres & Leshkowich, 2018; Lam, 2019). This chapter aims to contribute to this body of literature. To go further in the analysis of the various social logics shaping the Vietnamese economy and its links with global capitalism, we propose to build on the concept of economic hybridity as developed by Yang (2000).

The official denomination of "socialist-oriented market economy" already indicates the hybrid nature of the Vietnamese economy, characterized as it is by a "strange mixture of seemingly free-market capitalism and yet continued talk of socialism" (Gainsborough, 2010b, p. 1). More broadly, Vietnam would be an interesting case of a hybrid economy, since its economy appears to be regulated by the entangled logics of semi-subsistence farming and pre-industrial small-scale trade, centrally planned Party-State institutions, liberal market mechanisms, transnational capitalism, interpersonal networks, and ritual economy (Kerkvliet & Selden, 1998; Kleinen, 1999; Beresford and Dang Phong, 2000; Papin, 2003; Gironde & Maurer, 2004; Hy, 2010; Gainsborough, 2010a; Sasges & Cheshier, 2012; Fforde, 2016). This is particularly true in the agri-food sector, which is structured by both small-scale household production and large capitalist-industrial firms, both connected with and regulated by the State apparatus (De Koninck, 2010; Duteurtre et al., 2016, 2021).

In describing the development of two agricultural sectors (dairy and maize) in northern Vietnam, this chapter shows how the gift and debt logics that regulate interpersonal relationships within village society pervade and shape these industrial-capitalist sectors. These social logics and practices are very close to the Chinese "*guanxi*" (personal relationship), a research field that has already been analyzed in detail, especially in relation to China's transition toward a market economy (Yang, 1989, 1994; Yan, 1996a, 1996b; Wilson, 1997; Gold et al., 2002). Nevertheless, this topic is still not sufficiently studied in Vietnam, while the logic of personal relationships (*quan hệ*) appears to be a major aspect of any attempt to understand the functioning of society in general (Hy, 2016; Pannier, 2018a, b; Nguyen & Le, 2021) and the dynamics of the Vietnamese market economy in particular (Lantz et al., 2005; McElwee, 2007).

In line with research that explores the extra-economic foundations of capitalism (Aglietta & Orlean, 1998; Boyer, 2004; Theret, 2008) and with approaches that take into account the various forms of connectedness between the economic and the social (Polanyi, 2001; Zelizer, 1994; Granovetter, 2000; Laville, 2008), our analysis illustrates how non-capitalist and non-market exchange logics characteristic of the village sociality of northern Vietnam join forces with and support the functioning of the Vietnamese market economy, while undermining the hegemony of capitalism (Tsing, 2017).

The first section will present the conceptual framework proposed by Yang (2000) in order to account for how societies reconfigure capitalism by absorbing it. The second and third sections apply this conceptual framework to two empirical case studies that illustrate which specific socio-economic logics organize the exchanges that lie at the base of agro-industrial sectors. The last section discusses how this "imbrication" or interweaving of extra-economic logics and the market economy characterizes Vietnam's hybrid economy.

2 From the Heterogeneity of Economies to Economic Hybridity

With a view to "putting global capitalism in its place" in the case of contemporary continental China, Yang (2000) proposes a useful theoretical framework that seeks to address the non-capitalist dimensions that pervade capitalism and, more broadly, "to reveal the multiplicity of economies, the tensions between them, and their differential embeddings within the larger social formation" (2000, p. 481). Starting from the empirical observation that the establishment of capitalism in a society does not always compromise or replace the other local forms of economic activity, Yang encourages us to reconsider the modalities of "encounter" between capitalism and other economic and social formations. Without denying the structural transformations brought about by the introduction into a society of wage labor, entrepreneurial profit-driven activities, and trade liberalization, Yang criticizes the Eurocentric "capitalocentrism", in line with what Gibson-Graham calls "a totalizing discourse that sees non-capitalist forms as modeled upon, complementing, imitating, or serving capitalism" (Gibson-Graham, 1996, p. 6). Rather than describing how societies are "penetrated" by capitalism, Yang proposes to reverse the perspective and to study how societies deal with and absorb capitalism.

Yang proposes two concepts to address this phenomenon. The first is "economic hybridity", which describes "the coming together of economic logics and practices from different epochs and cultural histories" (Yang: 477). The second is "imbrication", "a process in which difference is embodied internally" (Yang: 485). According to Yang, these two concepts go beyond the Marxist theory of the articulation of modes of production, "wherein modes are presented as more or less intact, distinct, and separate (…) obscuring the fact that each formation carries within it the economic logics and impulses of diverse epochs" (Yang: 478). The concept of hybridity also challenges Braudel's approach, which distinguishes the logics and practices of three different socio-economic systems that are juxtaposed and complement each other while preserving their integrity (Braudel, 2018). By adopting Yang's approach, we can grasp how they are intertwined, reconfigured, and mutually shaped to the point that their respective borders become blurred. As a matter of fact, "the organic hybridization presupposes a smooth and unproblematic blending of traits and does not encapsulate the contested and agonistic features of the process of combination". By contrast, *imbrication* does not reflect "a situation of two different entities entering into a relationship" but rather a situation where those different entities "are merging into one" (Yang: 485).

From this perspective, Yang argues that the capitalist "forces of production" can operate with non-capitalist "relations of production", such as state socialist relations or household and kinship production. Then, in order to take a step aside from the Marxist tropism on production as the central dimension in defining an economic formation, Yang calls for greater attention to be paid to other dimensions, such as consumption and distribution.

She stresses that, while relations or forces of production may be conventionally capitalist in nature, modes of consumption or distribution may take a non-capitalist form. Yang's study illustrates the hybridization process primarily through the ways in which consumption diverts the capitalist logic. In doing so, she neglects the issue of distribution. By contrast, our study focuses more on the circulation of resources and exchange relationships in order to show how extra-economic logics and practices pervade and shape a liberal market economy. Moreover, although Yang addresses the various combinations of capitalism and other forms of economic activity, she emphasizes how the latter challenge and contest capitalism and tends to focus her arguments on a binary opposition between capitalism and non-capitalist systems. Our study, on the other hand, shows that non-capitalist logics can compete with, run parallel to, or complement capitalism.

It is therefore from this perspective that we propose to rethink the Vietnamese market economy, with the objective of concretely illustrating some aspects of its hybrid character. The ambition is not to describe exhaustively its hybrid nature, but to present some aspects of this hybridization, highlighted here because they seem particularly significant in the Vietnamese economy. In order to achieve this ambition, we conducted qualitative empirical surveys in the maize and dairy sectors in northern Vietnam.

3 The Case Studies: Context and Methodology

The two case studies were chosen because they reflect the rapid changes the agricultural sector has undergone. These two sectors are strongly connected to international value chains, but their principles of operation, particularly in the production and initial marketing segments, also depend on practices and logics that diverge from those of capitalistic international value chains.

The first case study is the Ba Vi milkshed located in Hanoi province. In the Ba Vi district, dairying is an important economic activity that has a high reputation in the whole country. It is the largest milkshed in the Red River Delta. In 2014, there were 7600 head of cattle in the district, producing 20,000 tons per year or 55,000 liters per day. This dynamism relies on small-scale dairy producers as well as on large private corporations and local government authorities, which are both very proactive in supporting milk production and rural development (Duteurtre et al., 2015, 2016; Nguyen et al., 2018).

The second case study concerns the maize sector in Mai Son district, a mountainous area in northwestern Vietnam, where market development and the arrival of high-yielding hybrid varieties have fostered the transition from diversified subsistence agriculture to specialized cash crops (Friederichsen & Neef, 2010). Once supervised and supported by the State, the maize sector is now dominated by large international private companies positioned upstream and downstream of the value chain. However, at the local level, production is based on farmers from mountain ethnic groups and the transactions are organized through informal interpersonal arrangements.

The study builds on multi-site surveys (Marcus, 1995) conducted from 2014 to 2016 in both districts as part of a research project on livestock transition in Vietnam.[1] The research team comprised French and Vietnamese economists, anthropologists, geographers, agronomists, and animal scientists. We combined observation of practices with in-depth interviews with officials, villagers, collectors, agricultural input sellers, directors, or workers in different processors (industrial, semi-industrial, and cottage-type) and dairy firms. For the ethnographic survey, we conducted 46 interviews in Ba Vi and 27 in Mai Son. We were also able to consult various written sources such as collectors' registers, the accounts of advances and loans that agricultural input sellers provide to farmers, personal archives, and so on. These field data were supplemented by an extensive literature review of the development of the dairy and maize sectors within each region and nationally. In both cases, our approach considered the current situation as well as the changes that have taken place over the last 30 years.

4 The Role of Personal Relationships in Shaping the Ba Vi Milkshed

4.1 *The Superimposition of Capitalist Forces on a Collectivist State-Led Economy*

The first dairy cows were introduced into Ba Vi in the 1920s by Marius Borel, a French colonial farmer. After the collapse of French control over Vietnam in 1954, former private concessions were nationalized and the

[1] The REVALTER project, implemented with financial support from the French National Research Agency (ANR).

old Borel dairy farm became a military farm and then, a few years later, a State farm. In the new communist property rights regime that favored collective agriculture, land and animals became State property and farmers became cooperative members. From 1960 onward, and during the whole collectivist period, milk production in Ba Vi was concentrated in a single State farm, with up to 1000 cows. In this context, workers got monthly salaries, and were not recognized as independent peasants. This system, however, suffered from the economic crisis that hit Vietnam at the end of the 1970s. From 1978 to 1985, the size of the farm's herd dropped from 1100 to fewer than 300 cows (Duteurtre et al., 2015).

Starting at the end of the 1980s, the "*đổ imới*" (Renovation) period led to the distribution of land and animals of the former State farms to individual farmers, with rural households now recognized as the main units of production. The reforms also supported the development of the private sector in the agri-food value chain, the liberalization of milk prices and milk marketing systems, and the opening of national markets to foreign investment.

The liberalization and marketization of the dairy sector resulted in the setting up of a cluster of several private enterprises throughout the 1990s and into the early 2000s. Most of these private processors were small-scale enterprises, either farmers who wanted to sell their milk along the main road or individual processors who established a short milk collection network. They mostly processed fresh pasteurized milk, but also made yogurt, caramel cream, and sweet dried concentrated milk (*bá nhsũa*). All these products were made in family businesses, with few investments, and, most of the time, no need of formal recognition of their private enterprise. Some of those enterprises have remained active until the present day.

At the same time, larger dairy companies started to invest in the collection of milk in Ba Vi. The Nestlé factory was the first; it commenced operations in 1997 but was replaced in 2006 by Vinamilk and other firms. Dairy companies involved in the Ba Vi milkshed responded to the growing demand. Since *đổ imới*, dairy consumption had grown at a very high rate, resulting from urbanization, rising incomes and new consumption habits. In particular, Vietnamese consumers were keen to feed dairy products to their children. Between 1995 and 2013, average consumption of dairy products rose from 3.7 to 20 kg of milk equivalent per capita (Nguyen et al., 2017).

This emerging market created a huge demand for healthy processed products. Consequently, the dairy processing industry developed rapidly in the 2000s, when national and international companies set up in the few milksheds that had emerged (Duteurtre et al., 2021). At the end of 2006, several large dairy companies started to invest in milk collection in Ba Vi. Two of these companies established milk processing facilities in the district and began to collect milk from livestock farmers: the International Dairy Production Company (IDP) and the VinhNga Company, which became the Ba Vi Milk Company. The latter, founded by a local entrepreneur who had worked for Nestlé, became very much involved in developing milk collection centers and linkages with farmers. Throughout the 2000s, the milk business in Ba Vi resulted in a strong development of the small-scale family dairy production that might be called "peasant" dairy production (Duteurtre et al., 2021; see Fig. 3.1).

In the 2010s, the new market economy led to the gradual emergence of integrated livestock corporations and large-scale farms. A large-scale farm with a capacity of 400 cows was set up by IDP in 2013. These large-scale companies were directly connected to the national and international capitalist economy. While the Ba Vi milk company remained a local

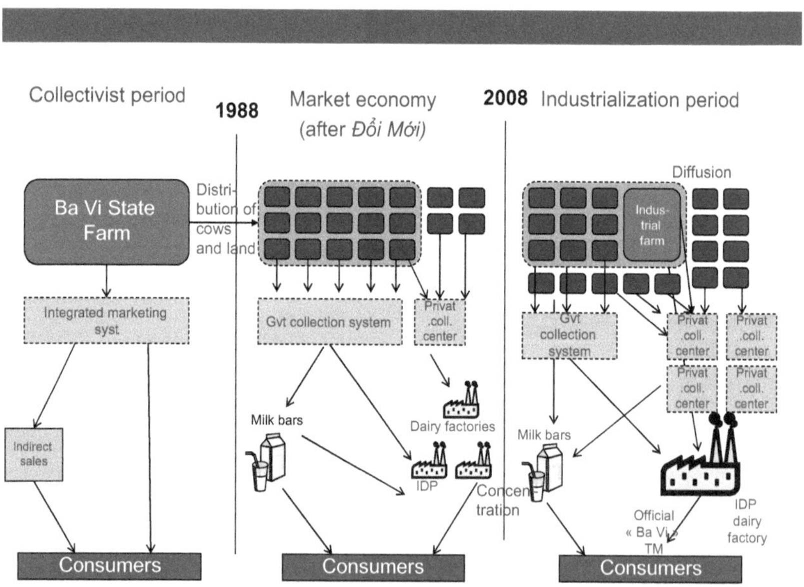

Fig. 3.1 Historical development of the milk value chain in Ba Vi

Vietnamese company, IDP was partly taken over by Japanese investors (Nguyen et al., 2017).

In three decades, the Ba Vi dairy shed has moved from a collectivist economy to a market economy integrated into the capitalist global economy but still closely supervised by the public authorities. This process led to the "formalization" of exchanges and relationships between actors within the Ba Vi dairy sector. By formalization, we mean the establishment of a social regulation regime based on mechanisms detached from individuals and governed by legal obligations, official law, rational-legal principles, and contracts. In this formal regulation regime, the rules become general and impersonal in scope, in the sense that they are applicable to all regardless of social rank, status, and relationships (Meisel & OuldAoudia, 2008, pp. 435–436).

4.2 *Toward "Formalized" Relationships Between Actors*

Since 2008, the two new large dairy companies (IDP and Ba Vi dairy company) have supported the establishment of private milk collection centers with refrigerated milk tanks installed in the villages. These collection points are managed by independent collectors under contract to one of those processing companies. The companies established hygiene controls and technical procedures for farms and for collectors. They drew up official guidelines governing the collection of milk with quality specifications (percentage of fat, protein, bacteriological quality, etc.), quality pricing, and a system of bonuses and penalties. These guidelines rely on a system of systematic sampling at each delivery, and on regular milk quality checks. The system enables the standardization and homogenization of the prices of raw milk based on the quality of the milk (and not on personal links).

This formalization process is strongly related to the registration of the certified trademark "Ba Vi cow's milk" (*sữa bò Ba vì*) in 2009. This trademark belongs to the district authorities, which are in charge of the certification. From 2009 to 2016, the public authorities restricted use of the certified trademark to these two dairy companies (which were at the time associated). In return, these companies invested a lot of money in the local dairy industry. They invested in machinery and collection infrastructures and made loans available to farmers. They also funded a large part of the technical training and information campaigns that enabled villagers to develop, improve, and formalize milk production and quality.

These changes in the Ba Vi dairy sector have had a direct impact on farmers' livelihoods. Farmers have gained access to capital, know-how, industrial inputs, and stable outlets. However, to be involved in this system, farmers have to "affiliate" with the new collectors, who act as a bridge between farmers and the new dairy companies. Indeed, one of the major institutional innovations introduced by the large private dairy companies has been the establishment of formal contracts between the farmers, collectors, and dairy company. In addition to technical specifications related to the purchasing prices of milk, the terms of the contracts are as follows: the company undertakes to buy all the milk that meets the quality criteria only if the farmer guarantees that he will sell exclusively to the company.

For farmers, the contracts with the dairy company have reduced the uncertainty around prices, since they are able to sell their production at a regular price all year round, which was not the case before. This legal bond also implies being part of an impersonal system of social regulation based on law and rational-legal principles, as well as of the capitalist system. For the company, one of the objectives of these contracts has been to assemble and stabilize a large network of raw material suppliers. For the milk collector these contracts aim to ensure the loyalty of farmers in milk delivery. Nevertheless, the establishment of lasting relationships and stable exchanges between collectors and farmers (and consequently with industries) also relies on other resources and institutional arrangements than these formal market bonds. We present those resources and arrangements in the following section.

4.3 *Financial and Moral Indebtedness as Bonds*

The contractual agreements between farmers, collectors, and dairy company are not sufficient to preserve the commercial relationship. They do not dispel all the uncertainties surrounding the delivery of milk. As all the collectors reported to us, these formal contracts reinforce the relationship but do not guarantee the "loyalty" (*trung thành*) of the farmers with whom they had signed contracts. As one interviewed collector explained to us: "We have a contract with the farmers, but it isn't enough. … They can easily break the contract or neglect to renew it. Other means are needed to gain their loyalty (*trung thành*)." More broadly, this suggests that formalization of the local transactions is not strong enough to ensure the stability of all the dairy sector's activities in the district.

Gaining the loyalty of farmers has been a central issue for collectors as they compete intensely with each other. They have to invest significant amounts to open a collection center, from 40 million ($1700)[2] to 200 million VND ($8800), depending on the number and capacity of milk tanks. All the collectors we interviewed acknowledged they had taken on debt in order to begin this new activity. As their income depends on the quantity of the collected milk and thus on the number of farmers who supply them with milk, they need to attract farmers and ensure their loyalty. They have developed a range of strategies to maintain lasting relationships of exchange with farmers in addition to the formal contracts.

Indebtedness, both financial and moral, constitutes one of the most widespread and efficient procedures for strengthening relationships between farmers and collectors. There are two main kinds of informal debts. First, interest-free advances (*ứng*) are offered to farmers at the beginning of each month and are repaid gradually delivery by delivery, day by day, until the end of the month. The amount of the advance, between 1 million VND ($45) and 3 million VND ($130), is established according to the volume of milk that the household could produce in one month, which in turn depends on the number of cows. The second type of debt bond consists of interest-free loans (*vay*) that involve higher amounts than the interest-free advances, around 20 million VND ($880) and 30 million VND ($1300). They can be repaid over a longer period of time (from a few months to 1 year). Such loans are also reimbursed little by little by daily milk deliveries. Both these kinds of loans are used to invest in livestock activities as well as to meet farmers' everyday needs or for social events (to organize a wedding, a funeral, or other ceremony). Thus, these loans are not only funds to invest in economic activities but also a form of "consumer credit" intended to cover everyday and ritual expenses.

For the collectors, the purpose of the loans is to offer interest-free loans that are reimbursable in milk in order to make sure that the farmers deliver their milk to them. They therefore obtain no direct financial advantage from these loans, but benefit from the regular milk collections, as farmers have to repay them by delivering their production. The terms used by the collectors unequivocally express the function of these loans and advances: the point is to "create an attachment" (*gắn bó, rang buộc*) and inspire "loyalty" (*trung thành*) with the farmers. In addition to the formal contracts mentioned above, these financial ties further reinforce the

[2] 1 USD = 22,700 VND (January 2022).

relationship. Nevertheless, it is still not enough to ensure lasting relationships. Farmers can repay the debt at the end of the month after delivering milk and then switch to another collector. However, the attachment and the debts are not only material. There is also a social and moral commitment.

4.4 *A Moral Agreement*

The collectors agree to make advances or loans when farmers need them, and without charging any interest. In Vietnam, interest-free loans are usually offered only to close friends or family. Even if the collector has a personal and material interest in offering such loans (the aim being to ensure the farmers' continued loyalty), they are also interpreted by farmers as a form of support (*hỗ trợ, giúp đỡ*). In return, to express their gratitude for this support, farmers are committed not only to repaying the debt but also to continuing to deliver milk in the future, even though they have already repaid the monetary debt. This moral and social commitment is a powerful factor in this local system of interpersonal exchanges where the "obligation to reciprocate" is strong (Tessier, 2009; Pannier, 2015; Hy, 2016). A farmer who borrows money from one collector but then switches to another collector would be considered unreliable and disloyal by the local community. His reputation would be affected within both the milk collection system and the local society. During interviews, collectors often explained that if a villager took advantage of the loans but "jumped" (*nhảy*) many times from one collector to another, no one would agree to take his milk or to offer him interest-free loans. While there are no legal sanctions to regulate these transactions, the moral and social sanctions enforced by the local community act as a deterrent to deviant behavior.

The stabilization of exchange relationships between farmers and collectors is an important factor in ensuring a stable supply of quality milk for the dairy companies, guaranteeing incomes for farmers and collectors and enabling local authorities to promote this activity as a driver of local development. These informal loans, which create financial, social, and moral obligations, are one of the main strategies in maintaining these exchange relationships. They illustrate how an "interpersonal regime of social regulation" (Pannier, 2021) plays a crucial role in facilitating transactions and, more broadly, in supporting the operation of the dairy sector alongside commercial and contractual processes.

4.5 *Feasts, Banquets, Gifts, and Affective Relationships*

It is not only through these debt relationships that these social and moral obligations as well as the personal bonds are built and maintained. All the collectors give their time and spend significant amounts of money in order to cultivate strong personal connections (*quan hệ* Pannier 2018b) with the farmers who deliver milk to them: they organize feasts and banquets and offer gifts to farmers during the Lunar New Year (*tết*) and on the occasion of weddings or funerals. They also organize and fund collective holiday trips for farmers. They explained to us that these gifts were related to major life-cycle ceremonies and that these convivial times (when everyone eats and drinks together) reinforced the "link". These sets of social practices related to ritual economy are indeed among the most important ways of building and reproducing what villagers call *quan hệ tình cảm*, which denotes moral and emotional personal relations based on mutual respect, trust, and obligation. These kinds of affective personal relationships occupy a very important position in northern village social order (Malarney, 2002; Pannier, 2018a). Our case shows that they are not only a glue of the village sociality: they also pervade and support the impersonal commercial system of the dairy sector. In the next section, we will see that this hybridization process in the dairy sector also occurs in the maize sector.

5 The Role of Personal Relationships Within the Maize Sector in Mai Son

5.1 *Global Agricultural Changes in Mai Sơn: The Deployment of the Forces of International Capitalism*

Since the end of the 1990s, the agricultural sector of Mai Sơn district, located in Sơn La province in Northwest Vietnam, along the Laotian border, has evolved from mainly semi-subsistence farming to commercial farming. Former agricultural practices, based on upland dry rice, glutinal-"sticky" maize (local varieties), cassava cultivation on slopes, and backyard animal rearing and using little capital investment and local market outlets, were gradually abandoned. There was a new emphasis on the cultivation of cash crops, principally sugar cane, hybrid maize, and coffee, and the raising of commercial livestock. This required the use of chemicals and other industrial inputs and greater financial investment. The major drivers of this structural agricultural transformation include the development of the private market, the increasing use of new, high-yield seeds, strong support from government (research and extension activities), and the arrival of large private companies (animal feed industry, processing factories, agricultural input companies) connected to national and international markets. In this respect, maize cultivation is the sector whose dynamic best enables us to grasp the effects and forms of these changes.

The northern highlands of Vietnam produce the largest quantities of maize in the country (Dang et al., 2004). As Friederichsen and Neefpoint out, "[H]ybrid maize has become a key production line for Vietnam's mountainous regions and is arguably the most consequential twentieth century farm innovation for the northwestern uplands. The change from maize land races to hybrid seeds resulted in massive increases in productivity and cultivated areas, higher investments and higher returns" (2010, p. 575). In the Mai Son district, maize cultivation occupied 18,860 ha in 2011,[3] giving an annual production of almost 90,000 tons,[4] which made Mai Sơn the second maize producing district in the province after MọcChâu district.[5] Mai Sơn district is today a very attractive area for maize trading companies.

Initially supervised and supported by the State, since 2007 the maize sector has been dominated by large private companies positioned upstream and downstream of the sector. Maize seeds are sold by large national and international companies (An Giang, Syngenta, Monsanto, Pioneer, CP) and most of the Mai Sơn maize production is bought by the agri-food industry within Vietnam and abroad (Dabaco, Proconco, East Hope and Cargill, CP). A large part of the maize is transported to the lowlands where it is processed into animal fodder that farmers buy to feed their pigs (Bocquillet, 2014). In other words, farmers buy hybrid seeds from large companies, produce maize for the animal feed industry, and finally buy maize-based industrial food for pigs (Fig. 3.2).

This system, which links local producers from mountain ethnic groups to global capitalism, generates rapid economic profits, but also exposes

[3] This represents about two-thirds of the lands set aside for annual crops and half the land for households (Son La Statistical Yearbook, Son La Statistics Office, June 2012).

[4] These yields rise to 46.6 quintals/ha (Son La Statistical Yearbook, Son La Statistics Office, June 2012).

[5] In the three communes studied, the number of households cultivating maize and the areas under cultivation were as follows: HátLót commune: 1324 households on 8,605,173 ha; Chiềng Mai commune: 655 households on 1,622,072 ha; Chiềng Dong commune: 323 households on 470,483 ha (Son La statistical Yearbook, Son La statistics office, June 2012).

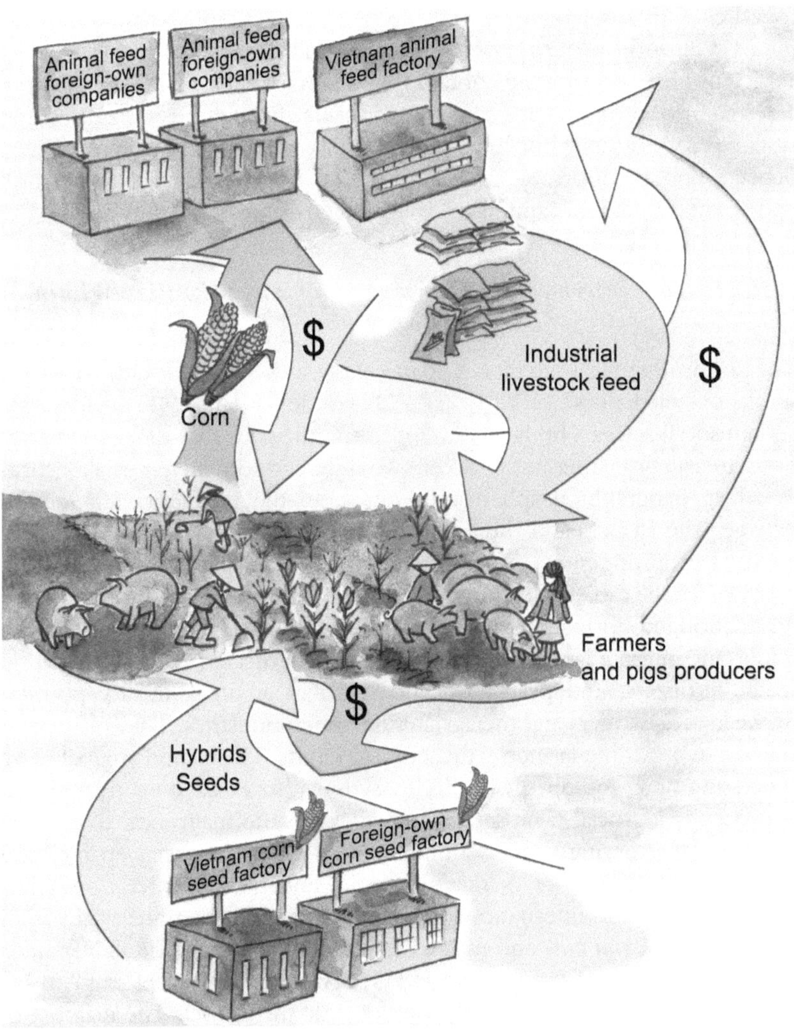

Fig. 3.2 Producers caught in the grip of big companies. (Diagram designed by Laurence Billault, graphic designer at PALOC (IRD))

producers to market and price fluctuations, and threatens the sustainability of the ecological system (Friederichsen & Neef, 2010). Because the maize is exclusively hybrid, farmers must buy new seeds every year, together with a set of industrial inputs (fertilizers, phytosanitary treatments). They therefore become dependent on the market and must hold sufficient financial capital to obtain the inputs for their maize production. The majority of inputs are sold to producers through an informal credit system, creating debt bonds as well as dependency relationships between debtors and creditors. These transactions, which illustrate the hybrid nature of Vietnamese capitalism, are outlined below.

5.2 The "Intermediaries": Actors in a Central Position Within the Network

The anthropological literature, particularly development anthropology, speaks of "mediators" or "brokers" (Olivier de Sardan, 1995) to describe certain social actors who have developed specific skills that they mobilize in order to act at the interface between two different normative, social, institutional or geographical spheres. In our case, the mediators are located between the farmers and the large companies (seed production, industrial animal feed production). They provide the inputs that enable farmers to produce for the capitalist economy and direct informal domestic agricultural production into formal capitalist channels. At the local level, there are three important intermediate actors. The first are the dealers (*đại lý*) in hybrid seeds, fertilizers, and pesticides who stand in an intermediary position between local farmers and the agricultural input industries. They play a crucial role in providing farmers with access to inputs. The second are the maize processing units equipped with drying systems (*cơ sở thu mua sấy khô*) that also occupy a crucial position because they are the main local outlets for farmers. Their drying system equipment and storage capacity enable local production to meet the market's quantity and quality criteria and thus attract national and international buying companies. The third are individual traders (*thương gia*) and maize trading companies (*doanh nghiệp nông sản*) that buy maize from farmers and processing units, transport it and sell it to large-scale animal feed companies outside the district. The majority of these intermediaries belong to the majority ethnic group (*kinh*), while their clients, the local farmers, belong mostly to the so-called minority ethnic groups from the mountainous regions.

Due to their position within the sector as the principal intermediary between local producers and outside actors, they play a central role in the flow of information, capital, and products (seeds and maize). In social network theory, this broker role is described as "betweenness centrality".

It is considered to be a structurally advantaged position (Degenne & Forsé, 1994). As other actors depend on their services (ability to isolate the actors) and as they control exchanges and information flows within the network, they can generate significant financial benefits as well as social, economic, and political power.

The exchanges between these brokers and the farmers are located at the interface of commercial relations and interpersonal relations: they illustrate well the imbrication of certain logics at work in personal relation networks within the capitalist system. As an example, we will focus now on the agricultural input dealers.

5.3 Debt Relations Between Input Retailers and Farmers

The private retailers of input provide maize seeds, rice seeds, fertilizers, pesticides, insecticides, products for protective-sanitary treatment, industrial pig feed, rice for consumption, veterinary products, and so on. Although these shops had been in the district since the end of the 1990s, they proliferated since 2007, a period that saw the arrival of hybrid seeds sold by large international firms. "Before, there were seeds sold by State-run shops", explains M. Binh, the leader of the district peasants association, "but today, the State cannot compete with private vendors, they are much more dynamic".[6] Apart from the sale of inputs, these traders are among the main providers of informal credit to farmers. The allocation of this credit and the relationships of trust on which it depends are not legally regulated and therefore play out within personal networks. Four kinds of credit can be identified.

The first, known as "credit sale", involves offering advances of agricultural products to farmers who then repay the loan at a fixed rate of interest on an agreed date, usually after the harvest. Depending on the agreement, repayment may be made in cash or farm products (usually maize or coffee). The transaction (type of product, quantity, total amount of payment, reimbursement date) is usually, but not always, registered and signed by the debtor in a register kept by the retailer. Locally, villagers use the terms *cắm* (secured loan), *cắm nợ* (secured loan-debt), *ứng* (advance), or *bán chịu* (sale without direct payment) to speak of these various kinds of payment with interest.

[6] Interview conducted on 11/06/14. All the name were coded and changed for non-disclosure information.

At the time of our research, interest rates varied between 2% and 4.5%, per month according to the loan term, type of product, and the closeness of the relationship between debtor and creditor. The amounts advanced varied between 1 million ($45) and 80 million VND ($3500). A retailer spoke of having advanced up to 200 million VND ($8800) to a single person. While all the retailers sold their products on credit, this way of operating is much more widespread among retailers located within the villages, close to farmers, who may have between 800 and 1000 debtors at any one time.

The second type of credit consists of cash loans, known locally a *vay tiền* (cash loan) or *cho bán tiền mạt* (cash selling). Interest rises by an average of 3% per month. While this kind of loan is more profitable, they are also more uncertain than advances for inputs because the cash could be used for purposes other than production, such as for day-to-day expenses or ceremonial events (wedding, funerals, ancestor commemoration, banquets, etc.). Consequently, there are less commonly used. As M. Nam, manager of a large input shop in Chiềng Mai, explained to us,

> I gain less when I sell inputs on credit than when I lend cash, but in lending inputs, I can be sure that the peasant is going to use them for cultivation and therefore I will be reimbursed, at least partially, when he harvests. If I just lend money, they might not invest it in their production so I have less guarantee of repayment.[7]

All the retailers interviewed agreed on this matter, so much so that they lend money only to clients they know very well and usually offer smaller amounts than for advances on inputs.

A third type of credit consists of the "sale of standing crops". Farmers sell their estimated production before harvest, usually at a price much lower than the market one but which provides them with funds to meet the needs of the moment and capital to invest in their production. This type of transaction, called *bán ngô non* (sell young maize) or *bán lúa non* (sell young rice), is not much favored, is not very common, and concerns either the poorest households or those temporarily in urgent need of cash.

The last type is called "to be invested" (*bị đầu tư*). It is a kind of informal "contract farming". The investor provides all the inputs as well as money and rice for daily consumption, in exchange for which the producer provides the land and the labor force. The investor then buys back

[7] Interview conducted on 19/06/14.

the entire production at a price fixed from the outset, which is much lower than the market price and is deducted from the total amount advanced. The producer undertakes to sell all his production to the investor; he cannot sell it elsewhere or repay the advance to sell his production on the market. According to our informants this practice still existed during our survey, but we did not come across any actual cases. It was more frequent 15 years previously and mainly involved vulnerable households.

5.4 *Credit and Advances: Necessary Conditions for the Sale of Agricultural Inputs*

Of the four types, the first two (credit sales and cash loans) were the most widespread at the time of our research. Retailers provide credit to their clients because they receive interest but also because they would not have any clients if they do not provide some form of credit. This comment by M. Hung, one of the retailers at Chiềng Mai we mentioned earlier, is explicit:

> If I don't sell on credit and give no loans, or if I do not align my interest rates with those of other retailers, my clients will go elsewhere. The villagers don't have the means to pay cash, I have to put up with selling on credit.[8]

Granting these kinds of credit is a condition for opening an input shop, not only because most clients cannot afford to pay cash but also because there is competition between retailers. To attract and gain the loyalty of clients in this context, it is mandatory to agree to sell on credit. The system's operating principles have a number of advantages for farmers that make these informal credits more attractive than bank credit, despite the higher interest rates.[9] While it is difficult to gain access to bank credit because of the complex administrative process, there are no administrative documents or collateral to provide to obtain these credits. The amounts granted are potentially greater than those offered by the banks, notably because the amount is calculated on the basis of productive capacity (cal-

[8] Interview conducted on 20/06/14.

[9] By comparison, at the time of our survey, official bank interest rates varied between 0.5% (Bank for Social Policies) and 1.1% per month. For the 2000–2010 period, the annual rate set by the State Bank of Vietnam varied between 7.5% and 14% (Lainez, 2014). According to article 468 of the 2015 Civil Code, the interest rate should not exceed 20% per year, but "many banks and financial companies are actually charging annual interest rates of 40–50 percent on consumer loans" (Lainez, 2019).

culated in terms of a farm's land area, its assets, and the type of product grown) and not on the value of any immovable property possessed, generally evaluated from land titles (the red book). As if to justify their activity as lenders and their high interest rates, lenders often emphasized that the conditions they offer farmers are better than those offered by the banks. For instance, M. Hung explained to us:[10]

> The Viet Nam Bank for Social Policies gives a maximum of 30 million VND, which is not enough for the peasants' needs. [...] Other banks are like pawnbrokers, but on a larger scale: they give credit according to what people are able to mortgage—if one has a house valued at 200 M VND, the bank lends only 150 M VND. It takes no risks, and does not take into account people's productive capacities, but lends according to what they have already mortgaged. They do not support production to increase. Me, I invest with a view to people's capacities.

Moreover, retailers are more flexible about repayments than banks. Delays in paying back are agreed depending on the debtor's particular circumstances. One farmer who was clearly struggling to pay back his loan (bad harvest, declining product prices, accident, health problems and funerals) had his debt reassessed without any difficulty. During our interviews, retailers distinguished between two kinds of defaulter: those who "are unable to pay back" (*không trả được do điều kiện*) and those who "are unwilling" (*không muốn trả, cố tình*). Retailers explained that they check the debtor's situation, either directly or through neighbors, in order to find out if he is really unable to pay. The following explanation provided by a retailer in Chiềng Mai describes the logic well:

> If they are unable to pay me back due to important events [marriage, funeral, new house] or an accident, I will make other advances on inputs and allow delays for unpaid debts. I know they will have the means to reimburse me later on. This is not like the banks. If people fail to pay back at the time agreed, they don't give any further loans to the debtor. In my case, if they do not repay me at the agreed time but have objective reasons, I go on lending to them. [...] The prices of coffee and maize very much determine my business since they determine my clients' ability to repay. If prices fall and people cannot repay me, I cannot force them. And if they lose their harvest because of the cold weather, I am directly affected too.[11]

[10] Interview conducted on 20/06/14.
[11] Interview conducted on 20/06/14.

The retailers show flexibility, but in return for remuneration. When debtors do not have the means to repay in the time set, the new interest is calculated on the starting sum to which is added the unpaid interest for the period just ended. This debt reassessment procedure with accumulated interest is described locally as "mother interest giving birth to baby interests" (*lãi mẹ đẻ lãi con*). As the interest accumulated, farmers could easily be drawn into a spiral of over-indebtedness. We heard of some cases of peasants who had had to sell their land in order to pay their debts to the retailers.

According to our informants, these loans are risky for the retailers. In the event of default, the seizure of goods, cattle, or even the land was often mentioned as a possible sanction but one that is rarely carried out. Such seizures are, however, preferred to official reclamations by the police, which are theoretically possible, but lengthy, complicated, and costly. These potential sanctions are nevertheless effective as all retailers attested that cases of deliberate non-payment were rare. However, all retailers pointed out that cases of default due to economic or personal problems are frequent: they are part of the risks inherent in this process of informal credit. Nevertheless, as all the interviewed retailers also told us, they are largely offset by the profits made from the interest charged. No case of a retailer going bankrupt due to non-recovery of debts was mentioned to us. One retailer spoke of four cases of retailers who had voluntarily given up their businesses because of the high risk and efforts to collect the debts. It took at least five years to recover accumulated debts and many had had to be written off.

Offering loans and advances to farmers attracts customers but, just as in the Ba Vi case study, they are also a way to "keep" them. In addition to the monetary transaction and the commitment to repay (the financial debt bond), another commitment is sealed during these transactions: the borrower undertook to repay the loan but, implicitly, he also undertook to continue to purchase inputs from the same shop.

This type of informal, financial, and moral debt relationship based on interpersonal ties also exists between farmers and maize collectors and between farmers and maize traders, that is, between all the actors at the base of the sector. These kind of transactions and relationships make possible the production of cash crops by providing agricultural inputs for farmers and, more broadly, ensuring the circulation of goods within the maize sector at local level.

6 The Imbrication of Extra-Economic Logics Within the Market Economy: Challenge or Support Capitalism?

6.1 *Financial Debts Embedded in Interpersonal Relationships*

Unlike the impersonal and contractual loans on which the development of a capitalist economy is usually based, personal relationships between the credit provider and the borrower area condition of these transactions. Personal relationship "denotes the existence of an association that goes beyond mere interaction, is sustained over time and has developed beyond one-off exchanges" (Bidart et al., 2020, p. 4). In these kind of relationships, the personal attributes, individual biographies, and singular qualities of the subjects are directly implicated (Carrier, 1991). Commercial transactions can involve personal relationships; it is even common in Southeast Asia and beyond, notably to reduce uncertainty (Steiner, 2010). However, according to the dominant individualist and legal-contractual logic of the market (in classical economics), the presence of a personal link in the interaction can occur, but is not a *condition* for the transfer to take place (Dufy & Weber, 2007). The history of global capitalism's expansion is marked by the gradual depersonalization of commercial relationships and the decoupling of exchanges from personal ties or those related to status (Polanyi, 2001). By contrast, in the case we describe here, commercial transactions cannot be separated from the interpersonal relationships in which they are embedded and through which they occur.

In Ba Vi, before agreeing to provide advances, milk collectors need to know the farmers and their circumstances personally, and in particular the number of cows they have, which determines the potential quantity of milk produced and thus the amount of the advance. As the retailers explained to us in Mai Sơn, before agreeing to sell their inputs on credit, they also needed to know the debtor's personal situation: place of residence, economic situation, farming activities, area of cultivated land, available labor force, reputation, and so on. A new and unknown customer would not have access to credit unless he had a guarantor personally known to the retailer. The amount of loans and advances, interest rates, and repayment schedule vary according to the debtor's potential production (calculated by area of grazing land in use and the number of cows), but also to the nature of the relationship (kinship, neighborhood, friend, regular customer) and the degree of proximity (degree of *tình cảm*) between the lender and the borrower. Cash loans, which are riskier than advances, are only offered to the closest customers, usually neighbors or relatives, with whom the creditors have other social and moral obligations that strengthen trust. In the event of default, the retailers mobilize personal networks in order to obtain information on the borrower's situation and assess his capacity to repay (or not). Finally, delays in repaying loans are agreed according to the particular conditions of the debtor (bad harvest, a sick cow, a funeral, accident or health problem, etc.). In contrast to the impersonal loans provided by banks, a personal relationship between the borrower and the lender plays a decisive role in the course of the transaction.

Nevertheless, although interpersonal ties are involved in both of the case study districts, the nature of the relationships varies. In Mai Son, the debt relationships (with interest) tend to produce vertical relationships, located somewhere between dependency and clientelism. Farmers sometimes became over-indebted and some retailers have recourse to pressure or even violence in order to get paid. In Ba Vi, the relationships between milk collectors and farmers are more horizontal. There is no interest charged on advances and collectors are as dependent on farmers to guarantee their income as farmers are on collectors to have regular, stable, and free access to financial capital. Moreover, transactions take place within a village or commune scale; the collectors live in the villages and are members of the local community going back several generations. By contrast, this is not always the case with the agricultural input retailers in Mai Sơn. The protagonists are not necessarily members of the same local community; transactions take place in a larger geographical context (district level) and involve more inter-ethnic relationships.

Most of the debt relationships occur on the margins of the legal framework. There are very few legal guarantees or procedures in case of infringement. In this context, in which regulation by law is minimal, even impossible in many cases, trust is regulated by other mechanisms in order to avoid the agreement being broken: the strength of the bilateral link, a bundle of social and moral obligations, and social control (reputation and face). In Ba Vi, these informal loans are provided in a world in which collectors and farmers are personally acquainted with each other, as neighbors, friends, or kinfolk. The local society monitors and sanctions any failure to respect social and moral commitments. In case of infringement, there are sanctions in terms of reputation, face, and honor. As mentioned before, a farmer who did not respect his commitments to the collectors (repay the debt and continue to deliver milk) runs the risk of being excluded from the collection networks and would therefore no longer be able to sell his milk. Social control and the sanctions associated with it are enough to prevent too frequent transgressions. In Mai Son, similar mechanisms also exist, but as the social and moral obligations between borrowers and lenders are less strong, other kinds of sanctions can be applied. The degree of pressure that lenders may use to get reimbursed varies. M. Hoang, the retailer and village leader at Chiềng Mai we mentioned earlier, was one of the strictest we met during our survey:

> People are afraid of me. I am located in the centre of the village and they often pass by here in front of me. They know that if they do not pay me even when they don't have the means, I can come and seize their goods or their motobike. But it's rare that I have to really do that. It only happens if they don't pay me for several years. If for example after two years, a household does not pay me even though they have the means, I will go and take a cow or a buffalo. But finally, I only get back 10 or 15 million VND, which does not compensate for the loss of what I advanced in inputs. I have lost a lot through non-payment of debts. Some of my debtors died before paying the whole sum, others moved house. ... In that case I have to accept it. Children are not responsible for their parents' debts.[12]

6.2 *A Part of the Gift-Giving System*

Our case studies illustrate that even if the transaction is a commercial one, extra-economic and non-commercial feature are involved. The credit providers are not obliged to agree to grant credit or advance to farmers. Agreeing to offer a loan, accepting the risk of default if the borrower faces difficulties, and thereby entrusting the customer are experienced by farmers not only as a necessary commercial strategy (customer attraction and retention) but also as a form of support (*hỗ trợ*) within an interpersonal relationship. According to the ethic of mutual aid (*giúp đỡ*) and the strong obligation to reciprocate (*có đi có lại*) around which village sociality is organized, in return for this support gesture, the recipient should express gratitude by continuing to purchase inputs from the seller, even after the debt has been repaid. As we highlighted above, these debts are financial, but also socially and morally regulated. If we analyze this situation in terms of "gift and counter-gift", an agreement to lend to a farmer constitutes

[12] Interview conducted on 20/06/2014.

the gift part (Testart, 2007). The farmer's subsequent loyalty in delivering milk or buying agricultural inputs constitutes the counter-gift.

More broadly, this transaction clearly illustrates the logics and main features of the gift-giving system that frames the sociability of northern Vietnamese villages (Pannier, 2015). Indeed, it involves the idea of aid (*giúp đỡ*), reciprocity (*có đi có lại*), and mutual obligation (*rang buộc*) based on social and moral commitment (*tình nghĩa*) or affective relations (*tình cảm*). The reputations (*uy tín*) of the protagonists are at stake, and a system of social sanctions outside the law regulates the transaction. Moreover, as in the Vietnamese ceremonial gift-giving system, while there are both mutual interests and strong material considerations in the decision to proceed with the transactions, these exchanges are based on interdependency and trust between individuals, and help to create and confirm them (Pannier, 2015; Tessier, 2009). In short, as the transaction combines interests and generosity, and involves both obligation and freedom, it falls within the definition of a typical Maussian gift system (Mauss, 2016).

6.3 The Hybrid Nature of the Vietnamese Economy

In addition to commercial and contractual processes, the logic of the personal relationship (Pannier, 2018b), between debt and gift, plays a crucial role in regulating transactions between stakeholders. We assume that an "interpersonal regime of social regulation" (Pannier, 2021) and the resources to which such a regime provides access underpins the operation of these sectors at the local level. These interpersonal relationships not only provide access to resources that are used to produce the raw material that will flow upstream. They also bind actors and reduce uncertainties in a system in which formal regulation through contracts, laws, regulations, and so on is not enough to create the trust required for sustainable exchanges.

It illustrates how the legal regulation regime associated with formal market and capitalism principles is imbricated with an interpersonal and local regulation regime based on a gift economy and the principles of village sociality. The simultaneous presence and entanglement of these two social regulation regimes constitutes one of the conditions for the functioning of these capitalist sectors and reflects the hybrid nature of the Vietnamese economy.

Yang's study of China's hybrid economy emphasizes how the logics of the ritual economy, such as extravagant expenditure, ritual exuberance, generosity, and redistribution, "undercut(s) the private accumulation of capitalist consumerism" and contest capitalism by "rechanneling its movement toward other ends" (Yang, 2000, p. 477). A similar process also occurs in Vietnam with the revival of the ritual economy since the Renovation policy of the 1990s (Kleinen, 1999; Malarney, 2002; Taylor, 2007; Hy, 2010): "a native noncapitalist logic of ritual economy made use of capitalist forms for self-renewal" (Yang, 2000, p. 481) and ultimately appropriated and consumes economic surpluses. Our case study also illustrates how resources from the liberal market economy are diverted and used for purposes that inhibit capital accumulation. This is the case, for instance, when dairy farmers use loans from milk collectors not to invest in dairy production but to fund life-cycle ceremonies. Ostentatious banquets organized by collectors in order to reinforce their relationships with farmers are another example.

However, the imbrication of extra-economic logics within a liberal market economy is not only opposed to the logic of capitalism. As Yang points out, the ritual economy also fuels economic growth and can create new employment and income opportunities. Nevertheless, she tends to overemphasize how ritual expenditures redistribute a proportion of households' economic surpluses to the wider community to the detriment of productive accumulation and reinvestment in production. By contrast, we argue that in Vietnam most of the ritual expenditure is indeed reinjected into the larger community, but mainly into the acquisition of the commodities used for rituals, banquets, or the construction of spiritual sites. Even if extravagant consumption and the ritual economy include some non-productive endeavors, it still feeds the market economy through consumption. There is a dialectic according to which market development and the integration of the national economy into global capitalism foster the development of the ritual economy as much as ritual expenditure fuels the liberal market economy.

In addition, our study points out how the gift-giving and moral debt logics not only challenge but also complement and support capitalism's expansion by building and maintaining trust and sustainable personal relationship mobilized for commercial and productive activities. The incorporation of the personal network logics of rural society into market exchanges alters the impersonal and legal-contractual logic of the liberal market economy from the inside while at the same time supporting it. Non-capitalist logics in general and the ritual economy in particular produce ambivalent effects, both feeding and hampering capitalism. In other words, "economic diversity enables capitalism but also undermines its hegemony" (Tsing, 2017, p. 131).

This being the case, it appears crucial to pay attention to the diverse possible outcomes of the intertwining of different socio-economic systems, which may lie on a continuum between the two extremes of compatibility and opposition, the different gradients of which may exist simultaneously within the same society. Thus, since the balance of power that arises when capitalism encounters other socio-economic formations does not end simply in the replacement of the latter by the former, it is necessary to study empirically the various outcomes of that confrontation and the diverse way they interrelate: absorption, merger, juxtaposition, and opposition, as well as combination, compatibility, complementarity, and hybridization.

7 Conclusion

> (…) we must deconstruct the monolithic notion of a cohesive capitalism and move toward a notion of capitalism as an open-ended, mutating process made up of disparate and conflicting elements, some of which harbor the potential to derail its forces and harness them in new directions. (Yang, 2000, p. 495)

If the Vietnamese economy is today organized around liberal market exchanges strongly connected to global capitalism, many areas of economic life are still closely controlled by the State. There is a large and strategic state-owned sector, which is the legacy of both the colonial regimes and then the centrally planned economy (Sasges & Cheshier, 2012; Fforde, 2016). Within this institutional landscape, the logic of interpersonal networks and the ritual economy continue to be the organizing principle for a large part of the resource allocation process both outside and within the market. These various socio-economic regimes are strongly intertwined. As illustrated in this chapter, the production and circulation of goods as well as access to capital in the dairy and maize sectors depend heavily on the personal connections (*quan hệ*) between actors (Pannier 2018b). In both case studies, moral and financial debts and gift logics are crucial organizing principles for transactions and relationships between actors at the interface between the informal domestic economy and the channels of capitalism. In other words, social practices and logics characteristic of northern rural sociality (Kleinen, 1999; Malarney, 2002; Pannier, 2015; Hy, 2016) are merged with market mechanisms and capitalist exchanges. These elements support the functioning of the capitalist economy while diverting some resources for non-profit purposes. The presence of non-capitalist elements in these capitalist sectors illustrates the hybrid nature of the Vietnamese economy. Gainsborough (2010a) also draws on the idea of hybridity in analyzing the Vietnamese political system since the Renovation reforms. Rejecting any interpretation in terms of "'neoliberalism incorporated', or an unmediated form of neoliberalism", he argues that "(…) we are witnessing the emergence of a hybrid state form not uninfluenced by neoliberal ideas and practices but where indigenous thinking and modes of operating remain dominant" (2010a, p. 483).

This being so, it is difficult to characterize the Vietnamese socio-economic model in a single term. If it cannot be described as an orthodox capitalist economy or standard market economy based on the Western or neo-liberal model (Gainsborough, 2010a) or "State capitalism" (Alami & Dixon, 2020) or an "informally dominated market economy" (Dibben & Colin, 2012), can we talk of "network capitalism" (Oleinik, 2004)? In our view, the concept of "interpersonal network-based capitalism" seems an appropriate one with which to characterize the Vietnamese socio-economic model.

Nevertheless, this chapter only illustrates some aspects and modalities of the hybrid nature of the Vietnamese economy. In order to open up the perspective and to analyze that phenomenon in greater depth, it would be necessary to document a large set of imbrications and connections between the different socio-economic systems that structure the Vietnamese economy and society in order to examine other forms of hybridization, in particular cases where the logic of interpersonal networks contest and undermine the capitalist system and cases where the capitalist logic intervenes and shapes the non-commercial sphere, the ritual economy, and the ceremonial gift-giving system. An historical perspective would also be useful to show that these socio-economic formations are themselves already the result of a hybridization process. This kind of approach would open up the debate on the various modes of interaction between different existing socio-economic logics, from combination to contradiction, and then enable us to better characterize the Vietnamese socio-economic system and its trajectory.

References

Aglietta, M., & Orlean, A. (1998). *La monnaie souveraine*. Odile Jacob.

Alami, I., & Dixon, A. D. (2020). State capitalism(s) redux? Theories, tensions, controversies. *Competition & Change, 24*(1), 70–94.

Alary, P., & Lafaye de Micheaux, E. (Eds.). (2013). L'économie politique de l'Asie: état des lieux et perspectives de recherche pour l'Asie du Sud-Est. *Revue de la régulation*. https://doi.org/10.4000/regulation.10266.

Beresford, M., & Dang Phong. (2000). *Economic transition in Vietnam. Trade and aid in the demise of a centrally planned economy*. Edward Elgar. Cheltenham (UK); Northampton (USA)

Bidart, C., Degenne, A., & Grossetti, M. (2020). *Living in networks. The dynamic of social relations*. Cambridge University Press.

Bocquillet Xavier (2014). "Animal feed industry in Vietnam". *Revalter working paper*. Cirad, Hanoi, 56 p. Accessible at http://www.futurelivestock.net/index.php?language=1&module=document&cateId=1290

Boyer, R. (2004). *Théorie de la Régulation, les fondamentaux*. La Découverte.

Boyer, R., Uemura, H., & Isogai, A. (2012). *Diversity and transformations of Asian capitalism*. Routledge.

Braudel, F. (2018). *La dynamique du capitalisme*. Flammarion.

Carrier, J. (1991). "Gifts, Commodities, and Social Relations: A Maussian View of Exchange". *Sociological Forum, 6*(1): 119–136.

Cornia, G. A., & Popov, V. (2001). *Transition and institutions: The experience of gradual and late reformers*. Oxford University Press.

Dang, T. H., Tran, D. T., Nguyen, T. K., Mai, X. T., Gerpacio, R. V., & Pingali, P. L. (2004). *Maize in Vietnam: Production systems, constraints, and research priorities*. CIMMYT.

De Koninck, R. (2010). La transition agraire. In S. Lagrée (Ed.), *Transitions décrétées, transitions vécues: du global au local, approches méthodologiques, transversales et critiques*, Actes de l'université d'été régionale en sciences sociales "Les journées de Tam Dao" (pp. 45–58). VASS.

Degenne, A., & Forsé, M. (1994). *Les réseaux sociaux. Une approche structurale en sociologie*. Armand Colin.

Dibben, P., & Colin, C. W. (2012). Varieties of capitalism and employment relations: Informally dominated market economies. *Industrial Relations. A Journal of Economy and Society, 51*(1), 563–582.

Dufy, C., & Weber, F. (2007). *L'ethnographie économique*. La Découverte.

Duteurtre, G., Pannier, E., Hostiou, N., Nguyen, M. H., Cesaro, J.-D., Pham, D. K., & Bonnet, P. (2021). Economic reforms and the rise of milk mega farms in Vietnam: Governing the post-socialist transition. *European Journal of Development Research*. https://doi.org/10.1057/s41287-021-00456-3

Duteurtre, G., Pham, D. K., & Cesaro, J. D. (2015). Bassin laitier de Ba Vì: Un territoire d'élevage façonné par les politiques publiques, entre logiques industrielles et soutien à la paysannerie. In M. Napoleone, C. Corniaux, & B. Leclerc (Eds.), *Voies lactées: Dynamique des bassins laitiers entre globalisation et territorialisation* (pp. 67–87). Cardère Editeur.

Duteurtre, G., Sautier, D., Pannier, E., & Nguyen, M. H. (2016). Alliances between agri-chain actors for a sustainable development of territories in Vietnam. In E. Bienabe et al. (Eds.), *Sustainable development and tropical agri-chains*. Springer. https://doi.org/10.1007/978-94-024-1016-7_5

Endres, K. W. (2014). Making law: Small-scale trade and corrupt exceptions at the Vietnam–China border. *American Anthropologist, 116*(3), 611–625.

Endres, K. W., & Leshkowich, A. M. (Eds.). (2018). *Traders in motion identities and contestations in the Vietnamese marketplace*. Cornell Southeast Asia Program.

Fforde, A. (2016). Vietnam: Economic strategy and economic reality. *Journal of Current Southeast Asian Affairs, 35*(2), 3–30.

Fforde, A., & De Vylder, S. (1996). *From plan to market: Vietnamese economic transition 1979–94*. Westview Press.

Friederichsen, R., & Neef, A. (2010). Variations of late socialist development: Integration and marginalization in the northern uplands of Vietnam and Laos. *European Journal of Development Research, 22*, 564–581.

Gainsborough, M. (2010a). Present but not powerful: Neoliberalism, the state, and development in Vietnam. *Globalizations, 7*(4), 475–488.

Gainsborough, M. (2010b). *Vietnam. Rethinking the state*. Zed Books.

Gibson-Graham, J. K. (1996). *The end of capitalism (as we knew it): A feminist critique of political economy*. Blackwell.

Gironde, C., & Maurer, J. L. (Eds.). (2004). *Le Vietnam à l'aube du XXIème siècle—Bilan et perspectives politiques, économiques et sociales*. Karthala-IUED-CRAM.

Glewwe, P., Agrawal, N., & Dollar, D. (2004). *Economic growth, poverty, and household welfare in Vietnam*. The World Bank.

Gold, T., Guthrie, D., & Wank, D. (dir). (2002). Social connections in China: Institutions, culture, and the changing nature of Guanxi. Cambridge University Press.

Granovetter, M. (2000). *Le marché autrement. Les réseaux dans l'économie*. Desclée de Brouwer.

Grillot, C. (2016). Trust facilitates business, but may also ruin it: The hazardous facets of Sino-Vietnamese border trade. *Asian Anthropology, 15*(2), 169–185.

Horat, E. (2017). *Trading in uncertainty: Entrepreneurship, morality and Trust in a Vietnamese Textile-Handling Village*. Palgrave Macmillan.

Hy, V. L. (2010). *Tradition, revolution, and market economy in a North Vietnamese Village, 1925–2006*. University of Hawaii Press.

Hy, V. L. (2016). Social relations, regional variation, and economic inequality in contemporary Vietnam: A view from two Vietnamese rural communities. In

P. Taylor (dir.), Connected and disconnected in Viet Nam: Remaking social relations in a post-socialist nation (pp. 41–72). ANU Press.

Kerkvliet, B. J. T., & Selden, M. (1998). Agrarian transformations in China and Vietnam. *China Journal, 40*, 37–58.

Kleinen, J. (1999). *Facing the future, reviving the past, a study of social change in a northern Vietnamese Village*. Institute of Southeast Asian Studies.

Lainez, N. (2014). Informal credit in Vietnam a necessity rather than an evil. *Journal of Southeast Asian Economies, 31*(1), 147–154.

Lainez, N. (2019). Debunking the Informal Credit Myths: Is Credit Liberalization the Magic Solution to Loan Sharking?. *Perspective*, n°87, Singapore: ISEAS—Yusof Ishak Institute.

Lam, M. C. (2019). Negotiating uncertainty in late-socialist Vietnam: Households and livelihoods options in the marketizing countryside. *Modern Asian Studies, 53*(6), 1701–1735.

Lantz, G., Loeb, S. G., & Lê, T. M. L. (2005). Business gift giving in Vietnam within and between organizations. *Asia Pacific Advances in Consumer Research, 6*, 286–290.

Laville, J. L. (2008). Encastrement et nouvelle sociologie économique: de Granovetter à Polanyi et Mauss. *Revue Interventions économiques, 2008*, 38.

London, J. (2019). Vietnam in 2018: Consolidating market Leninism. *Asian Survey, 59*(1), 140–146.

Malarney, K. S. (2002). *Culture, ritual, and revolution in Vietnam*. Routledge Curzon.

Marcus, G. (1995). Ethnography in/of the world system: The emergence of multi-sites ethnography. *Annual Review of Anthropology, 24*, 95–117.

Mauss, M. (1997). *Écritspolitiques*. Librairie Arthème Fayard.

Mauss, M. (2016). *The Gift*, Hau Books.

McElwee, P. (2007). From the moral economy to the world economy: Revisiting Vietnamese peasants in a globalizing era. *Journal of Vietnamese Studies, 2*(2), 57–107.

Meisel, N., & OuldAoudia, J. (2008). La gouvernance dans tous ses états. Économie politique d'un processus endogène. In S. Bellina, H. Magro, & V. De Villemeur (Eds.), *La gouvernance démocratique* (pp. 429–440). Karthala.

Nguyen Cuong, V., & Pham Nguyet, M. (2018). Economic Growth, Inequality, and Poverty in Vietnam. *Asian-Pacific Economic Literature*, 32, 45–58.

Nguyen, H. A., & Le, D. M. P. (2021). Social Capital in Vietnam: An analysis of social networks and social trust. *Journal of Mekong Societies, 17*(2), 1–27.

Nguyen, M. H., Duteurtre, G., & Moustier, P. (2017). What shapes the governance of the dairy value chain in Vietnam? Insights from Ba-Vìmilkshed (Hanoi). World Food Policy, *3*(2) & *4*(1), 57–81.

Nguyen, V. K., Hoang, T. H. Y., Tong, V. K., Linh, H. T., & Nguyen, T. D. (2018). Key analysis of the dairy value chain in Vietnam: The case of Bavi. *Journal of Agribusiness in Developing and Emerging Economies, 8*, 222–233.

Oleinik, A. (2004). A model of network capitalism: Basic ideas and post-Soviet evidence. *Journal of Economic Issues, 38*(1), 85–111.

Olivier de Sardan, J. P. (1995). *Anthropologie et développement, essai en socio-anthropologie du changement social*. Karthala.

Pannier, E. (2015). *Seule la réciprocité. Circulation non marchande et relations sociales dans un village du nord du Vietnam*. Connaissances et Savoirs.

Pannier, E. (2018a). Affects, dons cérémoniels et structures sociales: Figures et expressions des *tìnhcảm* en milieu rural au nord du Vietnam. *Tsantsa, 23*, 33–42.

Pannier, E. (2018b). Relations sociales et échanges. In Tréglodé B. de (Ed.), *Histoire du Viêt Nam de la colonisation à nos jours* (pp. 199–218). La Sorbonne.

Pannier, E. (2021). Land tenure and irrigation in North Vietnam's mountainous regions. Rights outside the law? In I. E. Frezet, M. Goetzmann, & L. Mason (Eds.), *Spaces of law and custom* (pp. 46–65). Routledge.

Papin, P. (2003). *Parcours d'une Nation*. Belin.

Polanyi, K. ([1944] 2001). The great transformation. The political and economic origins of our time. Bacon Press.

Sasges, G., & Cheshier, S. (2012). Competing legacies: Rupture and continuity in Vietnamese political economy. *South East Asia Research, 20*(1), 5–33.

Steiner, P. (2010). Marché, transaction marchande et non-marchand. In A. Hatchuel, O. Favereau, & F. Aggeri (Eds.), *L'activité marchande sans le marché?* (pp. 147–157). Presses des Mines.

Taylor, P. (Ed.). (2007). *Modernity and re-enchantment: Religion in post-Revolutionary Vietnam*. Institute of Southeast Asian Studies.

Tessier, O. (2009). 'Aide' (*giúpđỡ*) et réciprocité dans une société villageoise du Nord du Vietnam: entre solidarité et dépendance. *Moussons, 2009*(13–14), 205–242.

Testart, A. (2007). *Critique du don. Etudes sur la circulation non marchande*. Sillepse.

Theret, B. (Ed.). (2008). *La monnaie dévoilée par ses crises. Crises monétaires d'hier et d'aujourd'hui*. Editions de l'EHESS.

Tsing, A. (2017). *The mushroom at the end of the world. On the possibility of life in capitalist ruins*. Princeton University Press.

Wilson, S. (1997). The cash nexus and social networks: Mutual aid and gifts in contemporary Shanghai villages. *The China Journal, 3*, 91–112.

Yan, Y. (1996a). *The flow of gifts: Reciprocity and social networks in a Chinese Village*. Stanford University Press.

Yan, Y. (1996b). The culture of Guanxi in a North China Village. *The China Journal, 35*, 1–25.

Yang, M. M. (1989). The gift economy and state power in China. *Comparative Studies in Society and History, 31*(1), 25–54.
Yang, M. M. (1994). *Gifts, favors and banquets: The arts of social relationships in China*. Cornell University Press.
Yang, M. M. (2000). Putting global capitalism in its place. Economic hybridity, Bataille, and ritual expenditure. *Current Anthropology, 41*(4), 477–509.
Zelizer, V. A. (1994). *The social meaning of money*. Basic Books.

CHAPTER 4

The Rise of Mega Farms in the Vietnamese Dairy Sector: A Marker of a New Agrarian Capitalism in Asia

Guillaume Duteurtre, Mai Huong Nguyen, and Emmanuel Pannier

1 Introduction

This chapter is an attempt to analyze how Vietnam has been impacted by the emergence of a new agrarian capitalism, and what have been the various factors affecting this rapid transformation.

For the past 30 years, Vietnam has been engaged in a transition toward a "socialist-oriented market economy". This "post-socialist transition"

RemarkSome parts of this text have already been published in the following article: Duteurtre, G., et al. (2021) "Economic Reforms and the Rise of Milk Mega Farms in Vietnam: Governing the Post-socialist Transition". *European Journal of Development Research*. https://doi.org/10.1057/s41287-021-00456-3

G. Duteurtre (✉)
CIRAD, UMR Selmet (CIRAD, INRA, Mtp Supagro, University of Montpellier), Montpellier, France
e-mail: guillaume.duteurtre@cirad.fr

T. A.-D. Tran (ed.), *Rethinking Asian Capitalism*,
https://doi.org/10.1007/978-3-030-98104-4_4

(Fortier & Tran Thi Thu Trang, 2013) has deeply impacted the diversity of agricultural production units. How did the new forms of capitalist agriculture emerge? Is the model of "large-scale rice fields"[1] initiated at the beginning of the 2010 a sign of a new priority given to giant industrial production structures? (Vietnam News, 2016; VNA, 2017).

We propose to approach these recent changes through a study of the dairy sector. This sector is interesting due to the rapid change it has undergone. Between 1990 and 2020, Vietnamese dairy production increased by a factor of 18, the highest rate of growth of any dairy sector in this region of the world (Table 4.1). We focus particularly on the emergence of mega dairy farms, an emblematic form of the new agrarian capitalism in Southeast Asia (Vy Thao, 2015).

The first section presents the framework and method used. The two following sections describe the various time frames in which different arrangement and social relations can be identified. The last section underlines the limits of this transformation and discusses associated policy issues.

Table 4.1 Comparison of the evolution of milk production in six Asian countries (tons)

Year	*1990*	*2000*	*2010*	*2020*	*Ratio 2020/1990*
Bangladesh	1,593,503	2,430,569	3,666,086	3,578,373	**2.2**
China (mainland)	6,820,400	11,985,728	40,801,763	38,769,118	**5.7**
India	53,678,000	79,868,019	122,067,667	183,955,490	**3.4**
Indonesia	599,155	1,010,885	1,493,965	1,574,504	**2.6**
Thailand	130,278	520,155	911,000	1,200,000	**9.2**
Vietnam	60,471	81,875	338,328	1,076,243	**17.8**

Source: Faostat (2021; extracted on 31 January 2022)

[1] Also called "large-scale models" (English) or "*mô hình cánh đồng mẫu lớn*" (Vietnamese).

M. H. Nguyen
IPSARD, Hanoi, Vietnam
e-mail: maihuong.nguyen@ipsard.gov.vn

E. Pannier
IRD (UMR Paloc), Paris, France USSH (VNU), Hanoi, Vietnam
e-mail: emmanuel.pannier@ird.fr

2 Framework and Method

Understanding agrarian change in contemporary Southeast Asia requires an analysis of capitalism and its development (Bernstein, 2010). By capitalism, we understand a "system of production and reproduction based on a fundamental social relation between capital and labor (...). Capital pursues profit and accumulation, while labour has to work for capital to obtain its means of subsistence" (Bernstein, 2010).The concept of agrarian capitalism is used by analogy with that of "agrarian change", in order to considers how capitalism affects the "the social relations and dynamics of production, power relations in agrarian formations and ownership structures in the agricultural sector of an economy" (Bernstein, 2010).

As in China, where a comparable change in direction occurred with the reforms initiated by Deng Xiao Ping from 1978 onward (Zufferey, 2010), the reforms of the Vietnamese economic policies have resulted in major institutional, economic, social, environmental, and cultural consequences. The economic "transition" has therefore to be considered together with demographic, dietary, technological, and agricultural transitions, resulting in multiscale-integrated changes (Lagrée, 2010).

Grasping the multiple dimensions of a transition requires a multidisciplinary, or even transdisciplinary, approach to change pathways. The analytical framework offered by the multi-level perspective enables us to consider these pluridimensional changes as a "socio-technical transition" (Geels, 2004; Geels & Schot, 2007). This transdisciplinary analytical framework is particularly suited to consideration of long-term transitions in the agriculture sector and their impact on sustainable development (Darnhofer, 2015). The intent is "not to consider the transition uniquely as a comparison between two situations separated by an interval of time, but to grasp what is at stake during the transition: an evaluation of change[2]" (De Terssac et al., 2014).

The multi-level perspective considers three components (or analytic "levels") that determine the change dynamic: the socio-technical regime, the innovation niches, and the socio-technical landscape. The socio-technical regime is defined as a coherent set of practices, technologies, and social rules. In particular, the framework identifies six sets of factors

[2] Translated by us from original citation in French: "(...)*ne pas considérer la transition uniquement comme une comparaison entre deux situations espacées dans le temps, mais de saisir ce qui se joue pendant la transition: l'état de passage*" (de Terssac, 2014).

defining practices, technologies, and social rules: (1) market and user preferences, (2) industry, (3) policy, (4) technology, (5) culture, and (6) science. At times, reference may be made to a "dominant" regime to indicate the dominance of one type of regime at a given moment. Innovation niches are the loci of radical innovations from the dominant regime, and are found at the local level. These innovations can challenge the dominant regime. The socio-technical landscape determines the conditions outside the regime, such as overall demographic and environmental trends, policy directions, and social values. This landscape evolves under the influence of decisions or shocks, or in a gradual manner (Geels, 2004; Geels & Schot, 2007).

The multi-level perspective is used here as an open framework for the interpretation of change pathways. However, we also will try to identify the uncertain dimensions of changes that themselves depend on more contingent factors. Indeed, "the notion of a trajectory does not imply that one should conceive of it as having an evolutionary character (…), nor even that one postulates its wholeness or consistency at the risk of simplifying to the extreme the terms of the comparison. History unfolds erratically, and explanations, or to be more realistic, rationalizations, given by those deciphering the past should always take into account pure contingency" (Bayart, 1996[3]).

This chapter is a synthesis of multidisciplinary studies on the transformation of the dairy sector carried out in several regions of Vietnam between 2014 and 2016. It relies on field surveys of various stakeholders: farmers, processors, raw milk collectors, and local and national policy makers, as well as analysis of national secondary databases. The studies focused on the analysis of farm development pathways (Pham Duy Khanh et al., 2016) and on the transformation of sectors and territories (Duteurtre et al., 2015, 2016; Nguyen Mai Huong et al., 2017). These data were complemented by a recent review of newspaper articles and scientific literature on agricultural development in Vietnam.

In the following section, we use these concepts to analyze the transformations that occurred in the dairy sector from the 1980s up to 2020. During a first period, marked by the "Đổi Mới" reforms, collective farming was abandoned in favor of individual farming. During a second period, around 12 mega farms were set up throughout the country, representing in 2018 around one-third of total milk production.

[3] Translated by us from French to English.

3 Market Reforms and Support for Smallholders (1986–2008)

3.1 *The Failure of State Farms and Emergence of a Peasant Economy*

Up until the late 1980s, dairy farming in Vietnam was the exclusive domain of "state farms" (*nông lâm trường*). These large-scale farms, some of which sprang from the nationalization of former colonial farms, relied on crossbred Holstein dairy cows. However, from the late 1970s up to the mid-1980s, these state farms suffered from the crisis afflicting the collectivist economic system (Brocheux, 2009). The state farms, some of which held over 1000 cows, had encountered major management problems and lack of finance. For example, between 1977 and 1985, the number of dairy cows on the Ba Vi state farm dropped from 1113 to 265 heads (Vien Chan Nuoi, 2009 *cited in* Duteurtre et al., 2015). Following these difficulties, and as part of a complete overhaul of the economic system, the *Đổi Mới* reforms led to the gradual abandonment of this government farm model and the development of the smallholder farm model.

During the 1970s and 1980s, the persistence of family plots and home gardens contributed to the maintenance of a significant residual peasant economy. The agrarian reform in 1954–1956 notably accorded landless farmers access to micro-plots with a maximum size of 1080 m^2. Although these "micro-plots" only covered 5–20% of the cooperatives' land, they contributed more than half of household revenues between 1960 and 1975 (Brocheux, 2009). After the reunification of Vietnam in 1975, the importance of these family plots continued to increase. However, dairy farming, which previously had been carried on only on colonial farms and then on state farms, had not yet become established in this family economy (Thanh-Liêm Lâm, 1991).

The evolution of the cooperative system also was gradual. In January 1981, a system of "production contracts" (*khoán sản phẩm*) between families and cooperatives was set up by Communist Party Secretariat's Directive 100[4] in order to improve the internal efficiency of cooperatives. The regime of course remained "hostile to the free market and private enterprise". However, this contract system made it possible for an official "private" form of remuneration of family labor to emerge (Brocheux, 2009).

[4] Directive 10-CT/TW dated on 13 January 1981.

Here again, the nascent dairy sector was not affected by these developments within cooperatives. Nonetheless, Directive 100 contributed to the emergence of a family farming economy.

3.2 Smallholder Farms at the Core of the Post-Đổi Mới Dairy Economy

The official re-emergence of family farms in the Vietnamese dairy sector was made possible by the political, economic, and land reforms of *Đổi Mới*.

The change in policy was ratified at the Sixth Congress of the Communist Party of Vietnam (CPV) in 1986. In 1988, Central Committee Resolution 10[5] recognized family farming as the principal agricultural production model and authorized small farmers to directly market their production. The Land Law of 1993 established the terms of the "right to the private use of land", organized around short-term land leases. These land-use rights certificates (*giấy chứng nhận quyền sử dụng đất*), or "red books" (*sổ đỏ*), were granted for a renewable period while the land remained the property of the State. In 2006, there were 10.46 million agricultural households farming on average 0.9 ha (GSO, 2018).

In the dairy sector, these reforms led to the development of small family dairy farms within or surrounding the perimeters of former state farms. State farms were converted into research and development centers (the case of Ba Vi farm) or semi-private enterprises (the case of Moc Chau farm). The cows were given to former workers or to newly established smallholders. A small number of state farms were sold to private entities (the case of Son Dong farm).

To support this movement, the National Dairy Development Plan (NDDP), which was launched in 2001, put the growth of rural family farms at the heart of its strategy. Endorsed by Government Decision No. 167[6] put forward by the Prime Minister, this plan strengthened public farm support structures: credit for the purchase of heifers, technical training, subsidies for equipment, and inputs. In parallel, several public sector investment programs aimed to strengthen rural infrastructure.

This post-*Đổi Mới* regulatory context allowed the development of individual smallholder projects, coupled with numerous investments by private national (e.g., Vinamilk and IDP) and international (e.g., Nestlé and

[5] Resolution 10-NQ/TW dated on 5 April 1988.

[6] Decision 167/2001/QD-TTg dated on 26 October 2001.

Dutch Lady) companies. These companies purchased the milk and provided industrial feed and credit. This alliance between farmers, companies, and local authorities boosted national production. Between 1990 and 2010, dairy production increased fivefold (Table 4.2). In 2010, there were

Table 4.2 Mega farms owned by Vinamilk

Name	*Year of foundation*	*Herd capacity*	*Owner (subsidiary)*
Tuyen Quang Dairy Farm	2007	2000 head	Vietnam Dairy Cow Co. Ltd.
Binh Dinh Dairy Farm	2008	2000 head	Vietnam Dairy Cow Co. Ltd.
Nghe An Dairy Farm	2009	2600 head	Vietnam Dairy Cow Co. Ltd.
Thanh Hoa Dairy Farm	2010	1600 head	Vietnam Dairy Cow Co. Ltd.
Vinamilk Dalat Dairy Farm	2012	1600 head	Vietnam Dairy Cow Co. Ltd.
Tay Ninh Dairy Farm	2013	8000 head	Vietnam Dairy Cow Co. Ltd.
Ha Tinh Dairy Farm	2016	2000 head	Vietnam Dairy Cow Co. Ltd.
Nha Thanh Dairy Farm	2016	2000 head	Vietnam Dairy Cow Co. Ltd.
Organic Dairy Farm	2017	1000 head	Vietnam Dairy Cow Co. Ltd.
Vinamilk Da Lat Organic Dairy Farm	2018	1000 head	Vietnam Dairy Cow Co. Ltd.
Tay Ninh Dairy Resort Farm	2019	8000 head	Vietnam Dairy Cow Co. Ltd.
Total 11 farms end of 2019		**31,500 head**	
Thong Nhat Thanh Hoa 1 Dairy Farm	2018	3500 head (4000 head planned in 2018)	Thong Nhat Thanh Hoa Dairy Cow Co. Ltd.
Thong Nhat Thanh Hoa 2 Dairy Farm	2018	0 head (4000 heads to be received in 2019)	Thong Nhat Thanh Hoa Dairy Cow Co. Ltd.
Total 2 farms end of 2018		**3500 head**	
Grand Total 13 Farms (2019)		**36,000 head**	

Source: Vinamilk (2019)

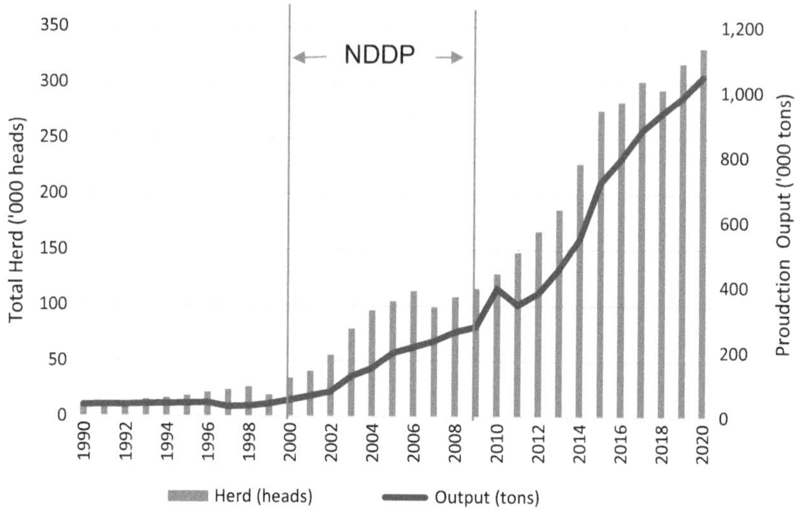

Fig. 4.1 Evolution of dairy herd and national milk production in Vietnam from 1990 to 2020. (Source: MARD (2021) (NDDP = National Dairy Development Program))

20,000 dairy farms that had on average 6 cows and produced 328,000 tons per year (Fig. 4.1).

This growth in the smallholder dairy sector was based on technical solutions adapted to the local constraints of very small farms that had under 1 ha at their disposal. This labor-intensive system was based on crossbred Holstein cows kept in tie-stall barns and trough fed with a mix of industrial concentrates and green elephant grass fodder. Through this system, high yields could be produced on very small areas. It was accompanied by the emergence of a regional network of service companies up and down the value chain that enabled this agricultural development: dairy processing units, dairy industries, concentrated feed manufacturers, raw milk collectors, and traders. The transactions between these various actors were regulated by both formal and informal arrangements. The combination of contracts, formal credits, informal debts, interpersonal trust, and moral obligation supported the circulation of resources and the establishment of the sector at the local level. The emergence of this private sector under the smallholder regime was also supported by the provision of local public services (Duteurtre et al., 2015).

The emergence of this regime over the 1990s and 2000s may also be interpreted as the consolidation of individual practices that had already emerged under the collectivist regime: the use of "family plots" starting from the 1970s and the development of "production contracts" in the early 1980s.

3.3 Conclusion on the Period

From 1990 to 2008, dairy farming in Vietnam responded to a social conception of the role of agriculture as well as to the emergence of a new demand for diversified foods (such as dairy products) that were considered synonymous with health and modernity. These changes in values were reflected in several changes in regulations and by the implementation of public policies supporting family dairy farming (liberalization of milk collection, support of public services through NDDP, etc.). This period corresponded to a "rehabilitation of the family economy" (Gironde, 2008).

The emergence of a new dairy sector was a response to a radical change in the socio-technical landscape (crisis of the collectivist economy, advent of the market economy) that spurred the emergence of new regulations and public policies supporting family farms.

Since 2008, however, the focus of public policies has shifted to the industrialization of the dairy sector. As a consequence, the dairy sector in Vietnam has undergone significant changes leading to the emergence of a new agrarian capitalism.

4 The Emergence of Mega Farms (2008–2020)

The new policy orientations that arose at the end of the 2000s involved the promotion of large farms, efforts to reduce the trade deficit, the promotion of new health standards, and a strengthening of the sector's competitiveness as it opened up to international markets. As we will see in the following sections, those policy decisions arose before and after the 2008 melamine crisis.

4.1 The "Peasant Regime" Called into Question

In the livestock sector, a new type of policy emerged progressively to meet the need to reduce the country's dependence on imports. This change in direction was endorsed by the Prime Minister's Decision No. 10/2008[7]

[7] Decision 10/2008/QD-TTg dated on 16 January 2008.

approving the "Strategy on livestock production development up to 2020". The main goal of this strategy was to create the conditions for the emergence of intensive family farms and large industrial farms.

In October 2008, when the country was importing around 618,000 tons of milk equivalent each year, or 80% of national consumption, Vietnam had to deal with imports of adulterated milk powder from China. In China, the presence of melamine in numerous batches of infant milk powder led to the hospitalization of tens of thousands of young children and caused the deaths of six infants. Vietnam reacted by ceasing to import Chinese milk and by closing certain local industries using adulterated milk powder. This crisis led to renewed industry interest in local milk production in a context in which consumer confidence in livestock farmers had been deeply damaged. Several industrial actors invested in supporting producers and in setting up specialized industrial dairy farms.

The melamine crisis occurred alongside an emerging demand for "healthy" and "safe" products (*thực phẩm sạch*) meeting industrial standards and safeguards. Following its entry into the WTO in 2007, Vietnam signed multiple bilateral and multilateral trade agreements. Directly related to these developments, Law 55 on Food Safety was ratified in 2010 and led to several decrees and implementation circulars over the years that followed. Certification mechanisms thus emerged in other sectors such as meat and "safe" vegetables. These food safety policies promoted the industrialization of the dairy sector with a greater concentration of production and the establishment of production by industrialists themselves.

4.2 *The Promotion of "Commercial Farms" (*Trang Trai*) and "Private Firms" (*Doanh nghiệp*)*

The emergence of "large-scale" individual farms was first encouraged by the certification of family farms under the label of what we will call "commercial farms" (*trang trai*). This involved defining criteria for recording the largest family farms by local authorities at the district level in order to direct some aid programs toward these farms. The criteria for certifying farms as *trang trai* were defined first in 2000 in the Inter-Ministerial Circular No. 69 issued by the Ministry of Agriculture and General Statistical Office (GSO).[8] They were revised upward in Circular No.

[8] Circular 69/2000/TTLT-BNN-TCTK dated on 23 June 2000.

27/2011[9] from the Ministry of Agriculture and Rural Development (MARD). In the livestock sector, the threshold was raised to a turnover of 1 billion VND. For a dairy farm, this represented a herd of about 25 adult dairy cows each producing 3000 liters/year. The recent MARD's Circular 02/2020[10] regulates commercial livestock farms on the basis of turnover threshold (from 2 billion VND) and livestock production scale (defined and classified by stock of livestock units).

In 2020,[11] the entire agriculture sector contained some 20,600 commercial farms as defined by this "new formula", of which 11,688 were in the livestock sector. These livestock commercial farms accounted for 56.7% of the total number of commercial farms in the country. This "commercial farm economy" (*kinh tế trang trại*) generated some 91,200 permanent jobs, of which 51% was composed of family labor and 49% of employees. During this time, the number of farming households diminished: it dropped from 10.5 million in 2006 to 9.3 million in 2016 and to 9.1 million in 2020 (GSO, 2018, 2021).

At the same time, several regulations allowed "private firms" (*doanh nghiệp*) to be set up in agriculture and agro-industry. Between 2006 and 2016, these companies doubled in number, going from 2136 to 3846 across the entire country (GSO, 2018). Since 2016, about 900 enterprises are newly established every year in the agriculture sector. By end 2019, there were 7471 agricultural enterprises, increasing by 94.2% from the figures recorded in 2016 (GSO, 2021). In the dairy sector, these companies took charge of processing, supplying inputs, and marketing dairy products.

This priority given to large farms was followed in 2014 by another sectoral policy aimed at promoting large-scale livestock farms. Decision No. 984/2014[12] by the MARD aimed to improve the value added of the livestock sector while ensuring sustainable development principles. This decision confirmed the orientation of the 2020 livestock development strategy but attempted to add some environmental safeguards. Along the same lines, Vietnam adopted a Law on Animal Husbandry (Law 32) in 2018 and a new Strategy on livestock development for the period of

[9] Circular 27/2011/TT-BNNPTNT dated on 13 April 2011.

[10] Circular 02/2020/TT-BNNPTNT dated on 28 February 2020.

[11] The statistics recorded on 1 July 2020 by GSO's rural and agriculture mid-term survey 2020.

[12] Decision 984/QD-BNN-CN dated on 09 May 2014.

2021–2025 in 2020.[13] These documents emphasized the need for cooperation between livestock sector actors, the promotion of production areas with high food safety requirements, and the continued coexistence of different livestock farming models.

In the dairy sector, this development resulted in an increase in the number of farms with over 20 head of cattle (MARD, 2019). In 2011, 9.3% of the herd was already held by farms with over 20 cows (Duteurtre et al., 2015). In 2018, this proportion was estimated to be 33%. In addition to industrial farms, there were nearly 29,000 family dairy farms in Vietnam, of which 6% had 20 cows or more (MARD, 2019).

This period also saw the growth of national dairy processing industries with international ambitions. Following the gradual privatization of part of the capital of a former state dairy the "Vietnam Dairy Company", established in 2003, Vinamilk became a major player in the sector. In 2017, the company became the third largest private company in Vietnam, with half of the market share in the dairy sector. In 2018, the State Capital Investment Corporation (SCIC), a public fund, held 36% of the company's shares alongside several private shareholders. Mention also should be made of the flotation on the stock market of TH True milk (166th largest private company in Vietnam in 2018), the takeover of the IDP dairy company by a Japanese investment fund in 2015, and the complete privatization of the Moc Chau Dairy Company in 2018.

The development of the industrial milk processing sector led to the adoption of private milk quality standards and quality control procedures that were implemented by processors and collectors. In 2017, the government published the standards QCVN 01–151:2017/BNNPTNT on "National technical regulation on milking and milk collecting establishment—Requirements for food safety". This regulation made most quality control procedures mandatory, though most farms "had not yet announced conformity with those standards" (MARD, 2019).

It was, however, the emergence of giant dairy "mega-farms" that played a key role in transforming the structure of the dairy sector in Vietnam.

4.3 *The Emergence of the "Mega Farm" Model*

Consumer enthusiasm for products made from local milk (following the melamine crisis), government support for this type of project, and the

[13] Decision 1520/QD-TTg dated on 06 October 2020.

gains expected from an integrated industrial organization led to the emergence of numerous mega farms.

Between 2007 and 2017, the private Vinamilk group, which mainly collected milk from small farms, set up ten industrial farms scattered across the entire country. In 2018, those industrial farms held a total of 23,500 cows. The same year, Vinamilk launched a new mega farm with 4000 cows in Thanh Hoa. In 2019, the company announced the launch of a new 8000 head mega farm project in Tay Ninh and another in Laos. In all, 35,000 pure dairy cows were raised in those mega farms in 2019 (Table 4.2).

In 2009, the TH Milk company founded what would become the largest private mega farm in Vietnam. Set up in Nghe An province, this farm cluster grew to hold 45,000 cows in 2014 and 49,895 four years later, including 26,231 milkers (MARD, 2019). In 2017, the firm announced the launch of a new mega farm project with 10,000 cows in Ha Giang province, and then another with 5000 head in Phu Yen. The same company said that in 2019 it planned to set up a farm with 10,000 cows in Thanh Hoa and another with 20,000 cows in Soc Trang.

Other recently established private mega farms include the 1000-head Future-Milk farm installed in 2008 on the former Son Dong state farm, and the three relatively smaller industrial farms set up between 2010 and 2015 by the Chau Moc Company.

In 2014, the mega farms held 25% of the national herd, compared to less than 5% in 2008. The rest remained in the hands of family farms (Nguyen Mai Huong et al., 2016). In 2018, that share rose to 32% (Table 4.3).

These mega farms constituted an innovation niche that generated renewed interest in high-tech and capital-intensive systems to the detriment of more labor-intensive family systems. In these production units, pure Holstein cows are raised in barn stalls and fed on a mix of silage and industrial feed via an automated feed system. To supplement forage produced on farms, whole plant corn is bought from surrounding smallholders and dry alfalfa hay is imported. Water filtration systems provide the herd with sufficient water. Animal health, milking, and breeding procedures are managed through individual animal monitoring software based on digital technologies. The cultivation of fodder crops on large areas, trough feeding, and milking activities are all mechanized, resulting in higher labor productivity than on family dairy farms. Milk is processed in large processing factories.

The units are also based on the provision of large land holdings, mostly once part of former state farms, contracted by local government. Mega

Table 4.3 Dairy herd in Vietnam per type of farm (2018)

Company	*Farm structure*	*Number of dairy cattle*	*Share of total herd*
Total large-scale farms		**93,441**	**32.08**
• TH Milk	1 mega farm	49,800	16.92
• Vinamilk	12 mega farms	27,000	9.17
• Nutifood/Hoàng Anh Gia Lai (HAGL)	1 mega farm	5000	1.70
• Moc Chau Breeding Center	3 mega farms	1800[a]	0.61
• Others	Large-scale farms	9841[a]	3.68
Households	**29,000 small farms**	**199,941**	**67.92**
• Delivering to Vinamilk	6000 small farms[a]	(Est.) 80,000	
• Delivering to FrieslandCampina	2500 small farms[a]	(Est.) 31,000	
• Delivering to Moc Chau	548 small farms	25,496	
• Delivering to others companies	16,952 small farms[a]	(Est.) 43,445	
Total		**294,382**	**100.00**

Source: MARD (2019)

[a]Our estimation from companies 2018 data

farms are therefore mostly located in rural areas, whereas family farms tend to be concentrated in periurban regions (Nguyen Mai Huong et al., 2016). According to Võ Trường Sơn (1989), there were several hundred former state farms throughout the country, which represented an important land lever for developing large capitalist production units throughout the 2000s and 2010s.

4.4 *Conclusion of the Section*

This period was dominated by large private firms (corporations) that invested in processing factories and industrial mega farms. This new regime aimed to promote productive investments in agro-industry and private firms at the expense of the complementary relationship between firms and smallholders that had previously prevailed. If this new arrangement has not entirely replaced the former regime, it seems to be becoming more and more dominant.

This transformation appears both as a change in the development model and as a strategic adaptation by actors to a new socio-technical landscape. The support of mega farm projects by the public authorities relies on several justifications that include using digital technologies, investing in the mechanization of production chains, increasing international competitiveness, and promoting international quality standards. The position adopted by the public authorities is illustrated in the following article (VnEconomy, 2021): "The dairy industry of our country has progressed very rapidly in recent years and is gradually approaching the developed dairy countries in the world. Many businesses have invested in raising dairy cows in very large numbers, such as: TH Milk currently has 63,000 cows, Vinamilk has 60,000 cows,[14] Nutifood has 7000 cows, etc."

The largest family farms are seizing the opportunities offered by the market to expand thanks to loans obtained from firms. But many smallholders are facing difficulties trying to reach those new standards. Firms are deciding to invest where there are the most promising opportunities, whether this involves access to land or raw milk collection. Furthermore, local authorities are encouraging the establishment of industrial processing plants to generate local jobs and revenues for their districts and to respond to the strong growth in domestic demand for milk.

These strategic decisions are leading to a reconfiguration of value chains that acknowledge the "co-existence" between smallholder farms and mega farms. The entire domestic milk production sector now contributes 34% of the country's consumption (Table 4.4). And average milk consumption rose from 18 to 27.5 kg per capita within a period of five years (Table 4.5).

This coexistence of production structures based on different models relies on local "compromises" between smallholder producers, industries, and local authorities, which are discussed in the final section.

5 Permanence and Resistance in the Dynamics of Capitalism

The emergence of mega farms has not led to the disappearance of smallholder farmers (Table 4.6). Rather, peasant farms have been competing (or interacting) with large commercial farms and industrial megafarms for access to resources and markets. And the public authorities have managed this

[14] The journalist mixes up the company's dairy animals (raised in mega farms) and the dairy animals owned by contract farmers (who deliver their milk to the company).

Table 4.4 The Vietnamese dairy market in 2018

Source	*Total (in tons of milk equiv.)*	*Share of total supply (%)*
Domestic production	936,000 t	34
Imports	1,764,000 t	66
Total supply	2,700,000 t	100

Source: MARD (2019)

Table 4.5 Milk consumption in Vietnam in 2018

Year	*Consumption (in kg/hab./year)*	*Production(in tons of milk/year)*	*Self-sufficiency*
2013	18	456,000	28
2015	21	660,000	35
2016	23.5	795,000	38
2017	24	881,000	40
2018	27.5	936,000	34

Source: MARD (2019)

Table 4.6 Size of smallholder dairy farms (household farms) in Vietnam (2016)

Size of households	*Number of households*	*Share of total number (%)*
Fewer than 5 cows	17,792	62.0
5–10 cows	5622	19.6
10–20 cows	3564	12.4
More than 20 cows	1716	6.0
Total	**28,694**	**100.0**

Source: 2016 GSO census, cited in MARD (2019)

coexistence through different local pragmatic compromises. The trade-offs made by the authorities in managing the transition are particularly evident in two important areas of public action: land management and the promotion of local partnerships. These two levers have played a key role in the evolution of different forms of livestock farming and in the level of coexistence between different development models observed in the field.

5.1 *Control of the Land: A Prerogative of the State in Steering the Transition*

Since *Đổi Mới*, land has appeared to be a critical element in the socio-technical landscape. Its control by government services greatly empowered the State to guide the outcome of the transition. Beginning in the early 1990s, "land distributions" to smallholder families after the reforms promoted a model of smallholder farming. This sharing of resources was particularly equitable with on average 0.9 ha of land made available to each household. This redistribution, which was enshrined in the allocation of "red books" to smallholder families, engendered the growth of diversified farming systems that were very land and labor intensive (Pham Duy Khanh et al., 2016).

However, from 2008 onward, the authorities favored the consolidation of land in order to allow the gradual emergence of larger farms able to meet the needs noted in the livestock development strategy. More recently, the 2013 land law reform encouraged land consolidation and the 12th CPV Congress in 2016 recognized land concentration as a priority (Phuc To et al., 2019). The number of "commercial farms" increased while the number of farming households decreased. At the same time, local authorities promoted land transactions that encouraged the emergence of agro-industries by attributing rights over land that had remained under direct State management. This trend was particularly clear in the dairy sector with the emergence of the mega farms mentioned above. The attribution of rights over land held by former state farms played a significant role in this land transition.

As a result, land has been gradually changing hands: new corporations (mega farms) have emerged as the owners of land rights in place of the former state farms. And large-scale farmers have replaced former smallholders, reflecting the emergence of "differentiated classes of small-scale capitalist farmers, relatively successful petty commodity producers, and wage labour" (Bernstein, 2010, p. 4).

5.2 *Local Partnerships: A Factor Structuring the Dairy Milk Sheds*

The importance of local authorities in the management of national policy priorities was also reflected in the emergence of local partnerships to support the creation of dairy milk sheds. When the mega farm projects were established in areas where smallholder dairy production already existed, partnerships that had been set up between local authorities, private investors, and smallholder farmers led to compromises. Mega farms were then presented either as "demonstration farms" (in the case of the Ba Vi industrial farm) or as "offspring production units" that could supply quality heifers to the surrounding farms. The mega farms also offered the creation of local jobs, the purchase of maize fodder from smallholder farmers in the area, and the sale of manure to arable farms.

In the midst of these adjustments, the local authorities acted to ensure this coexistence. For example, the adjustments led to the establishment of agreements between companies and local authorities, such as the MOU signed in 2012 between IDP and Bavi District authorities. Local authorities also encouraged the establishment of local certifications promoting the collection of raw milk, such as in Moc Chau and Ba Vi. In Ha Nam province, the Friesland Company set up a partnership with 189 dairy farmers, each with 17 cows on average. With the support of the local authorities, they intended to promote the setting up of 50 "professional farms" of 80–100 cows on 65 hectares of land given over to this project in the Moc Bac Commune (Duy Tien District) (MARD, 2019).

In 2017, MARD published Circular 14/2017[15] to encourage the establishment of public-private partnerships (PPP) to guide investments in agriculture. This circular was intended to support investment by private firms while at the same time promoting partnerships with public authorities and smallholder farmers. In order to implement this new strategy, the MARD's Decision 1322/2019 set up a PPP task force in the livestock sector. This taskforce, however, had not yet been very active up to September 2019 (MARD, 2019).

In these local partnerships, sector rationales sometimes outweighed the pursuit of coexistence, resulting in competition and exclusion. Coexistence and complementarity between smallholder farms and mega farms did not always appear to be possible.

5.3 *The Limits of the Sector Rationale: The Risks of Farmers' Exclusion*

In 2015, for example, the milk crisis in the Hanoi region, caused by a drop in milk prices, led many companies to concentrate on collecting milk from large farmers in order to reduce their procurement costs. Smaller farmers were forced to stop dairy production and to engage in alternative activities. In the south of the country, during the 2016 milk price crisis, the district authorities in Cu Chi wanted to develop a local certification trademark for products made from milk produced in Cu Chi. However, the

[15] Circular 14/2017/TT-BNNPTNT dated on 05 July 2017.

district's identity was not sufficiently renowned to support the development of a distinct market niche for products with this label.

The absence of compromise has sometimes led to local tensions. This was the case, for example, in 2014 around the Nghia Dan TH farm after surrounding villages were polluted by manure. In these situations, the authorities tried to encourage companies to adopt more sustainable strategies. This led to companies investing in local community support projects or in scholarship programs, with varying degrees of success. These experiences show that the change dynamic in dairy milk sheds in Vietnam is playing out within a collaborative relationship (between the State, companies, and smallholder farmers). Due to the contingency of local trade-offs, the outcome of the transition remains uncertain.

This calls for more territorial strategies, in which the coexistence of firms and smallholder farmers could be promoted in order to develop more balanced and sustainable dairy development pathways (Duteurtre et al., 2016).

6 Conclusion

The emergence of mega farms represents a return to a concentrated form of production that closely resembles the state farms that were set up during the collectivist period. What is different is the growing importance of financial capital and high technology in the transformation of these economies. As De Koninck (2010) notes with regard to the agrarian transition, we are witnessing a "changeover from a society characterized by accumulation in agriculture to a society where accumulation takes place within the industrial sector". The new regime also relies on the social construction of new food models concerned with "health safety". And it gives little consideration to environmental issues.

Our observations of the livestock transition in Vietnam emphasize the multi-dimensional character of the socio-technical change. The transition appears to be a gradual process in which individual, collective, and cognitive dimensions are interacting to produce differentiated pathways (De Terssac et al., 2014). Rather than replacing some forms by others, the transition is resulting in parallel pathways, or, in other words, in the superimposition of several regimes whose importance varies depending on the trade-offs made at the local level. Ultimately, the trade-offs made by the public authorities appear to be "pragmatic" to the extent that they reflect adjustments to socio-economic contexts undergoing radical change.

In Vietnam, agrarian capitalism appears to be in favor of large-scale farms and mega farms that compete directly with smallholder production in the market for raw milk. Furthermore, the emergence of the mega farm model contributes to family producers' loss of legitimacy in the eyes of consumers and decision makers. This economic and cultural competition does not, however, appear to be as clear-cut in local-level trade-offs, where the coexistence, superimposition, and entanglement of different forms of production can be observed.

Acknowledgment The authors are grateful to ANR and AIRD who funded this research as part of the Revalter project.

References

Bayart, J. F. (1996). L'historicité de l'Etat importé. *Les Cahiers du CERI*, no. 15, 44 p.

Bernstein, H. (2010). *Class dynamics of agrarian change*. Agrarian change and peasant studies series. Fernwood Publishing, Halifax and Winnipeg, Kumarian Press, Sterling, 142 p.

Brocheux. (2009). *Une histoire économique du Viet Nam: 1850–2007: la palanche et le camion, Les Indes savantes* (P. 257). Paris.

Darnhofer, I. (2015). Socio-technical transitions in farming: Key concepts. In Sutherland et al. (Eds.), *Transition pathways towards sustainability in European agriculture. Case studies from Europe* (pp. 17–31). CAB International.

De Koninck, R. (2010). *La transition agraire* (S. Lagrée, Ed.), pp. 45–58.

De Terssac, G., Truong An Quoc, & Catlla, M. (Dir.). (2014). *Viêt-Nam en transitions*, ENS Editions, 295 p.

Duteurtre, G., Pham Duy Khanh, & Cesaro, J. D. (2015). Bassin laitier de Ba Vì: Un territoire d'élevage façonné par les politiques publiques, entre logiques industrielles et soutien à la paysannerie. In Napoleone, Corniaux, Leclerc (Eds.), *Voies lactées: Dynamique des bassins laitiers entre globalisation et territorialisation* (pp. 67–87). Cardère Editeur.

Duteurtre, G., Sautier, D., Pannier, E., & Nguyen Mai Huong. (2016). Alliances between agri-chain actors for a sustainable development of territories in Vietnam. In Bienabe et al. (Eds.), *Sustainable development and tropical agri-chains*, Quae, 16 p. https://doi.org/10.1007/978-94-024-1016-7_5

Faostat. (2021). Data uploaded from www.faostat.org

Fortier, F., & Tran Thi Thu Trang. (2013). Agricultural modernization and climate change in Vietnam post-socialist transition. *Development and Change, 44*(1), 81–99.

Geels, F. W. (2004). From sectoral systems of innovation to socio-technical systems: Insights about dynamics and change from sociology and institutional theory. *Research Policy, 33*, 897–920.

Geels, F. W., & Schot, J. (2007). Typology of sociotechnical transition pathways. *Research Policy, 36*, 399–417.

Gironde, C. (2008). Grandes réformes et petits arrangements dans les campagnes vietnamiennes. *Autrepart* (48), 113–128. http://horizon.documentation.ird.fr/exl-doc/pleins_textes/divers18-07/010045228.pdf

GSO. (2018). *Results of the rural, agricultural and fishery census 2016*. General Statistical Office (GSO) (Statistical Publishing House, Ed.), 680 p.

GSO. (2021). *Results of the mid-term rural and agricultural survey 2020*. General Statistical Office (GSO). https://www.gso.gov.vn/du-lieu-va-so-lieu-thong-ke/2021/06/thong-cao-bao-chi-ve-ket-qua-dieu-tra-nong-thon-nong-nghiep-giua-ky-nam-2020/

Lagrée, S. (Ed.). (2010). Transitions décrétées, transitions vécues: du global au local, approches méthodologiques, transversales et critiques, Actes de l'université dété régionale en sciences sociales. *Les journées de Tam Dao* (Vietnam), 411 p.

MARD. (2019). Report of a Workshop on '*Livestock Outlook and PPP dialogue: Challenges and potential to develop dairy farming and dairy products*' held on 24th September, 2019 in Pan Pacific Hotel, Hanoi, organized by Partnership for Sustainable Agriculture in Vietnam (PSAV) Secretariat, Ministry of Agriculture and Rural Development (MARD), Hanoi.

MARD. (2021). Annual report on the Vietnamese dairy sector, ministry of Agriculture and Rural Development, Livestock Department, Hanoi, with tables.

Nguyen Mai Huong, Cesaro, J. D., Pham Duy Khanh, Hong Vu Quang, & Duteurtre, G. (2016). Hướng đi nào bền vững cho phát triên chăn nuôi bò sữa ở Việt Nam: sản xuất nông hộ hay đầu tư qui mô lớn? *Bài báo nộp cho Tạp chí Khoa học và Công nghệ Chăn nuôi*; Hà Nội, tháng 3 năm 2016, [Tendancy for sustainable development in Vietnam: Family farming versus large-scale investments? *Journal of Livestock Science and Technologies*, Hanoi, March 2016, pp. 12–21].

Nguyen Mai Huong, Duteurtre, G., & Moustier, P. (2017). What shapes the governance of the dairy value chain in Vietnam? Insights from Ba-Vì milkshed (Hanoi). *World Food Policy, 3*(2)/*4*(1), 57–81. https://doi.org/10.18278/wfp.3.2.4.1.4

Pham Duy Khanh, Duteurtre, G., Cournut, S., Messad, S., & Hostiou, N. (2016). Caractérisation de la diversité et de la durabilité des exploitations laitières familiales au Vietnam: une étude de cas en zone péri-urbaine de Hanoï. *Rev. d'élev. Méd. vét. Pays trop., 69*(4), 131–141.

Phuc To, Mahanty, S., & Wells-Dang, A. (2019). From 'land to the tiller' to the 'new landlords'? The debate over Vietnam's latest land reforms. *Land, 8*(120). https://doi.org/10.3390/land8080120

Thanh-Liêm Lâm. (1991). L'économie rurale vietnamienne: bilan du IVe plan quinquennal (1986–1990). *Annales de Géographie, 100*(560), 438–454. https://doi.org/10.3406/geo.1991.21055

Vietnam News. (2016, July 2). Large-scale rice fields booming. https://vietnamnews.vn/society/298963/large-scale-rice-fields-booming.html#UV3kPbdgydz0S47V.97

Vinamilk. (2019). Annual report 2018. https://www.vinamilk.com.vn

VNA. (2017). Tien Giang to expand large-scale fields. Published in Vietnam +, https://en.vietnamplus.vn/tien-giang-to-expand-largescale-fields/105269.vnp

VnEconomy. (2021, June 16). Chăn nuôi bò sữa Việt Nam vươn tầm thế giới. https://vneconomy.vn/chan-nuoi-bo-sua-viet-nam-vuon-tam-the-gioi.htm

Võ Trường Sơn. (1989). *Lịch Sử Cuộc Chiến Đấu Của Tộc Việt*. http://www.truclamyentu.info/tlls_lichsuvietnamcandai/lichsucaicachruongdat36.htm

Vy Thao. (2015, July 2). TH true Milk-A leading brand in Vietnam's fresh milk market. *Báo Ảnh Việtnam*. https://vietnam.vnanet.vn/english/th-true-milk-a-leading-brand-in-vietnams-fresh-milk-market/190058.html

Zufferey, N. (2010). La transition: réflexions épistémologiques à partir du cas chinois. *Lagrée*, pp. 29–44.

CHAPTER 5

Core Values in Educating Human Resources for Socio-economic Transformations in Viet Nam

Duy Mong Ha Nguyen and Thi Nha Truc Van

1 Introduction

Various scholars have done lots of research on cultural dimensions/values, including Storti (1998), Hofstede et al. (2010), and Tran Ngoc Them (2016). During its history of nearly 3000 years, Viet Nam has been influenced by various cultures in different periods of time. Some traditional cultural values are still beneficial to Vietnamese people while some others may hinder the sustainable development in the new era and some may have both positive and negative impacts on human adaptability. Since human resources as an intangible asset are crucial for the development of any organization, investments in human capital via human resources trainings of all kinds are always taken into consideration. Meanwhile, a question is posed as to whether the Vietnamese traditional values are in

D. M. H. Nguyen (✉) • T. N. T. Van
University of Social Sciences and Humanities, Viet Nam National University Ho Chi Minh City, Ho Chi Minh City, Vietnam
e-mail: ndmongha@hcmussh.edu.vn; vanthinhatruc@hcmussh.edu.vn

T. A.-D. Tran (ed.), *Rethinking Asian Capitalism*,
https://doi.org/10.1007/978-3-030-98104-4_5

alignment with or in conflict with the essential values in the new context. Which traditional values should be made use of and which can be transformed in the human resource training in order to produce the qualified workforce that can meet the requirements of the twenty-first-century skills like the 4Cs (Communication, Collaboration, Critical thinking, Creativity) or 5Cs (the 4Cs plus Continuous learning)?

2 Some Typical Cultural Values of Vietnamese People

2.1 Vietnamese Cultural Dimensions by Geert Hofstede

Geert Hofstede and his associates conducted comprehensive studies of how values in the workplace are influenced by culture and then came up with the framework of national culture consisting of six dimensions: Power Distance Index (PDI), Individualism (IDV) versus Collectivism, Masculinity (MAS) versus Femininity, Uncertainty Avoidance Index (UAI), Long-term Orientation (LTO) versus Short-term Orientation, and finally Indulgence (IND) versus Restraint. Among these cultural dimensions, UAI is closely related to the attitude toward risks and risk management. Uncertainty Avoidance (UA) is defined by Hofstede as "the extent to which the members of a culture feel threatened by ambiguous or unknown situations. This feeling is, among other manifestations, expressed through nervous stress and in a need for predictability: a need for written and unwritten rules" (Hofstede et al., 2010, p. 191). While high UAI is noted in Mediterranean countries, Japan, and South Korea (around 90 or more), Viet Nam's UAI is quite low, only 30. This can be understood as Vietnamese people have low preference for avoiding uncertainties or they are flexible in dealing with ambiguity. In addition, Viet Nam's high PDI, low IDV, and low MAS mean that the Vietnamese in general appreciate the values of hierarchy, collectivism, and harmony or good relationship as shown below (Fig. 5.1).

Hofstede et al. (2010) emphasizes that uncertainty avoidance should not be confused with risk avoidance:

> Risk is often expressed as a percentage of probability that a particular event will happen. ... As soon as uncertainty is expressed as risk, it ceases to be a source of anxiety. It may become a source of fear, but it may also be accepted as routine. ... Rather than leading to reducing risk, uncertainty avoidance leads to a reduction of ambiguity. Uncertainty-avoiding cultures shun

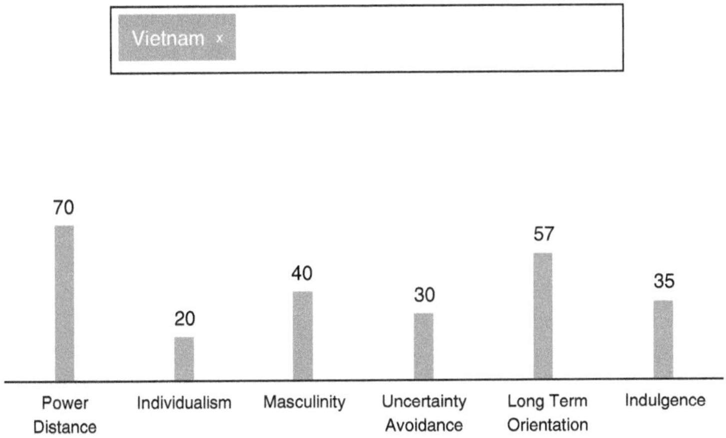

Fig. 5.1 Viet Nam's cultural dimensions by Hofstede (https://www.hofstede-insights.com/country-comparison/vietnam/)

> ambiguous situations. People in such cultures look for structure in their organizations, institutions, and relationships that makes events clearly interpretable and predictable. (pp. 197–198)

It should also be noted that countries with low uncertainty avoidance accept different kinds of risks while in countries with high uncertainty avoidance "laws, rules, and regulations were ways to prevent uncertainties in the behavior of people. … They also have more internal regulations controlling the work process" (Hofstede et al., 2010, p. 209).

A risk-averse culture such as Japan or Germany will produce great caution, and an aversion to taking high levels of risk is not conducive to the promotion of entrepreneurship. Other cultures produce managers that are willing to take high risks, such as in America, Finland, or mainland China. Then there are many shades in between, including such countries as Britain, France, or Italy that exercise risk taking and the promotion of innovation but show more caution, as in the case of Britain, or tend to support high risk, as in the case of Italy (Taplin, 2005, p. 14). Viet Nam dreams to become a "Start-up Nation" and in this context, its low UAI can be an advantage for the spirit of adventure in business on the one hand. On the other, it can be a disadvantage, that is, without effective preventive measures and timely measures to deal with various predictable crises on the basis of risk classification. Leaders should be more prepared for risks with high probability and great impact, especially familiar risks, in order to avoid bad consequences which would cost more due to damages and compensations.

With the values of hierarchy, harmony, and collectivism, both top-down and bottom-up approaches can be applied in decision-making in the Vietnamese context. Viet Nam has been influenced by Confucianism and the leader plays a significant role in setting up objectives as people tend to trust the institutions and their leaders.

2.2 *Vietnamese Dimensions Among Southeast Asian Cultural Ones by Storti*

Storti (1998) developed the four building blocks of cultures for intercultural communication: Collectivism versus Individualism, Particularism versus Universalism, Polychronic time versus Monochronic time (attitudes toward time), and Internal locus of control versus External locus of control (beliefs in internal or external forces). Viet Nam is among the Southeast Asian countries and thus, based on Storti's framework, its culture can be categorized as collectivist, particularist, polychronic, and external with the following characteristics:

- Collectivism: The survival and the success of the group (immediate family is the smallest unit) ensure the well-being of the individual. Harmony and the interdependence of the group members are stressed and valued. To Vietnamese people, groups, especially families, bear a strong emotional attachment. However, they do make a distinction between ingroups and outgroups.
- Particularism: How people behave in a given situation or what is right depends on the circumstances. Accordingly, Vietnamese people tend to treat their family, their friends, and their ingroups the best they can. There must always be exceptions to every rule. Personal feelings should be relied upon and few people expect life to be fair.
- Polychronic time: For many Vietnamese people, time is adjusted to suit the needs of people. Schedules and deadlines are subject to changes. People may have to do several things simultaneously as required by circumstances. Therefore, efficiency is not an important core value to many Vietnamese people.

- External locus of control: Viet Nam belongs to the fatalist culture and Vietnamese people tend to believe more in external forces than in internal ones. To them, some things in life are pre-determined and there are limits beyond which one cannot go and thus must be accepted; their success is usually attributed to both their effort and good fortune. This characteristic is quite aligned with their low-index IND.

Obviously, both alternatives can be relevant to many people in each pair of extremes, but in most cases, Vietnamese people tend to behave in a certain way that reflects their values. In general, the Vietnamese possess the following typical characteristics: Collectivism, particularism, polychronic time, and belief in external locus of control.

2.3 Vietnamese Traditional and Core-Oriented Values by Tran Ngoc Them

Succeeding his significant findings in 1996 and 1999, Tran Ngoc Them (2016) gives a reflection on the six Vietnamese cultural identities that have been formed in the geographical, historical, demographic/ethnographic, and social contexts after many centuries. He also discusses both pleasant and unpleasant aspects of those core traditional values and their changes, based on the results of the nation-wide survey carried out in 2014.

Firstly, the Vietnamese traditional value of village-based collectivism was shaped mainly from the traditional agricultural lifestyle. Moreover, the wet-rice farming culture has led the Vietnamese people to take emotion, love and/or hatred, as a rule of conduct like "When in love, love each other's every way, when in hatred, hate each other's relatives" or "Love is blind to errors". On the one hand, Vietnamese people have concerns for others; they find themselves responsible for paying attention to others as well as learning about others' interests and circumstances. Consequently, harmonious relationships among people (especially in terms of favor of ingroups and saving face) are appreciated; so is the harmony with the nature. Other values derived from village-based collectivism are also identified such as sense of community, solidarity, gratitude, and village-based democracy. On the other hand, the village-based collectivism can induce bad habits or behaviors in the Vietnamese contemporary life such as dependence on others, herd mentality, and individual-averse inclination.

Secondly, femininity is a typical feature of Vietnamese culture, which originates from the country's geographic location and wet-rice farming culture. Associated values like favor of stability, forgiveness, leniency, sentimentality, and hospitality are still influential today while another, respect for women, becomes less obvious. Nevertheless, femininity results in negative characteristics, noticeably passivity, conservativeness, shortsightedness, lack of resilience, and coping behavior.

Thirdly, harmony, another noteworthy quality of Vietnamese culture, is prevalent in many aspects of social and cultural life. Its manifestations are duality, moderateness and equilibrium, leisure manner, optimism, and practicality, the first three of which are said to be on the decline. Sadly, harmony is also attributed to negative habits and behaviors like indefiniteness or indecisiveness, unreasonable tolerance, and medium orientation (i.e., contentment on something at a middle level).

Fourthly, holistic view[1] or integrated thinking and acting on a large scale is an important element of Vietnamese cultural identity. Vietnamese people are open-minded and tolerant, accepting all kinds or religions, for instance. Holistic view can be considered a strength in building up relationships and a weakness too as networking can be opportunistic. Moreover, the lack of analytical and critical thinking may lead to a lack of meticulousness and risk management. Vietnamese people find it easier to accept ambiguity, and as a result, the UAI is quite low.

Fifthly, flexibility is necessary for Vietnamese people's adaptation to the environment. This characteristic is comparable to particularism, that is, there is no absolute fairness but it is important to treat people uniquely, or to polychronic time, that is, Vietnamese people accept possible changes in schedules and deadlines. Another value derived from flexibility is creativity or improvisation to be more exact. It must be noted that flexibility also leads to undesirable traits, namely spontaneity or carelessness, lack of law compliance, and mischief.

Finally, the integrated values include patriotism/nationalism and philanthropy/benevolence, which are said to result from the village-based collectivism and femininity.

Tran Ngoc Them (2016) goes on to suggest an alliance of those six traditional values and the six new ones, specifically universal values,

[1] This term is used by Tran Ngoc Them in his later works, in place of the term "synthetic thinking" used in his previous works (1996, 1999).

societal collectivism, masculinity-oriented harmony, modern holistic view, dynamism, and integrated values. These six new values are then rendered into fifteen "elite" values, which should be promoted or added. All in all, thirty-five values, both old and new, are put forth as a comprehensive system of core-oriented values for the long-term sustainable development. For the period from 2015 to 2030, the author recommends a model of shortlisted core-oriented values (Fig. 5.2).

As can be seen from the figure, the values are grouped into two broad categories: *Social values* and *Personal values*. The social values include two universal ones: Democracy and Rule of law. The personal values consist of two typical traditional identities: Patriotism and Philanthropy; two qualities for the era of international integration, namely, Honesty and Resilience; two values for interpersonal relationships, specifically, Responsibility and Collaboration; and two merits for the age of industrialization and knowledge-based economy, that is, Scientificity (scientific or critical thinking) and Creativity.

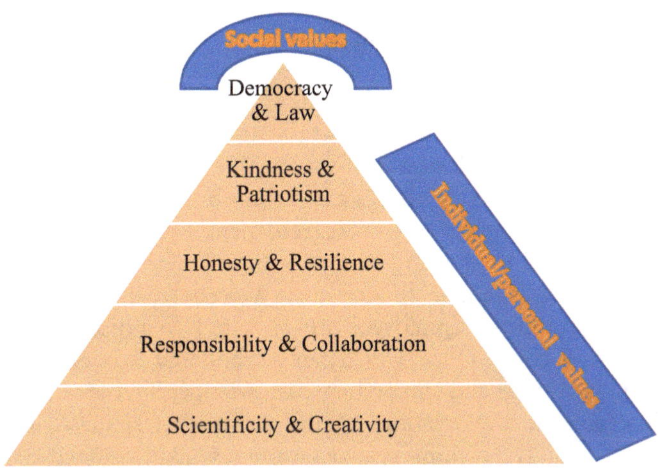

Fig. 5.2 System of core-oriented values for 2015–2030 (Tran Ngoc Them, 2016, p. 470)

3 The Twenty-First-Century Skills and the Reality of Vietnamese Human Resources

3.1 The Twenty-First-Century Skills Needed for Sustainable Development

The 4Cs stands for Collaboration, Communication, Critical thinking, and Creativity and the 5Cs refers to the above 4Cs plus Continuous improvement. These are important to prepare students for the increasingly complex life and working environment of the twenty-first century.

As for Collaboration, people in this century are required to work in the multicultural teams. They need to learn to work effectively with different groups of people, to have compromise and responsibility to reach a shared common goal. This can be a challenge to Vietnamese people who are used to working with the ingroup members instead of various groups. Interpersonal relationships among outgroups would be improved if Vietnamese people could shift from what is called "village-based collectivism" to "societal collectivism", so that the four core-oriented values "collaboration", "responsibility", "individual resilience", and "self-respect" as suggested by Tran Ngoc Them (2016, pp. 465–470) will be likely empowered.

Communication skill not only requires the clear presentation of the ideas, thoughts, and feelings but also the ability to give instructions and empower others through powerful speech. The Vietnamese have an indirect communication style and this can be an obstacle for them in the new era when time efficiency is emphasized, hence "going straight to the point" is preferred to "beating about the bush". The ability to use digital media is also significant in this century. Moreover, in the multicultural working environment, employees are expected to possess intercultural communicative competence, which can be rendered as cognitive capacity ([factual] knowledge and [procedural] knowledge: discovery and interaction, interpreting and relating; critical cultural awareness), behavioral capacity (flexibility; communicative awareness), and affective capacity (acknowledgment of identities of others; respect for otherness; tolerance for ambiguity; empathy) (Byram, 2006). In this sense, some Vietnamese cultural traits such as femininity (Hofstede et al., 2010; Tran Ngoc Them, 2016), flexibility (Tran Ngoc Them, 2016), and low uncertainty avoidance (Hofstede et al., 2010) seem to facilitate intercultural communicative competence in terms of interpersonal relationship development, adaptability, uncertainty acceptance, and empathy. Based on Tran Ngoc Them (2016, p. 465), it should be noted that a combination of femininity and masculinity with more focus on the latter would enhance the spirit of adventure; a link of flexibility and dynamism would create self-discipline; modern holistic view would result in professionalism, scientificity, and transparency; and a synthesis of several old and new values would effect integrity and directness. All of these qualities are necessary for the global citizens.

Creativity is the ability to produce new, diverse, and unique ideas. Thinking creatively means looking at things from a different perspective and not being restricted by rules, customs, or norms. Highly qualified human resource should use a wide range of idea creation techniques to create new ideas or new ways of doing things or to solve certain problems with all efforts. It is closely related to not only problem-solving but also resilience, self-confidence, and curiosity for learning. Creativity enables us to think outside the box and look at a problem from multiple perspectives. As Tran Ngoc Them (2016) points out, the flexibility of Vietnamese people results in their creativity; however, that kind of creativity is prone to impromptu behaviors or activities. It should be kept in mind that in the business context, not only contingency plans and improvisations should be made but also initiatives should be taken in order to survive and thrive. Furthermore, flexibility must be in accordance with law-abiding sense, fairness, and time management. Those are among the requirements for global workers and leaders.

Last but not least, critical thinking involves logical thinking and reasoning including skills such as comparison, classification, sequencing, cause/effect, patterning, webbing, analogies, deductive and inductive reasoning, forecasting, planning, hypothesizing, and critiquing. Data-based decision-making and information skills are integrated skills for critical thinking. In addition, a well-balanced practice of synthetic and analytical minds would help develop critical thinking, which is a vital quality for citizens in the internet age, when herd mentality is likely to occur if individuals do not have critical minds.

The requirements of the labor market today include these 4Cs (and the awareness of Continuous improvement also). The age of Industry 4.0 is apparently favorable in certain ways but simultaneously poses lots of challenges to the labor workforce. Workers need to ceaselessly enhance their 4Cs and other soft skills so that they will not be replaced by machines or Artificial Intelligence.

3.2 *The Reality of Vietnamese Human Resources*

Many papers from the proceedings "Link Between Universities and Enterprises in Solving Employability for the Graduates" (University of Economics of Ho Chi Minh City (HCMC), 2019) mention the following weaknesses of the graduates in HCMC in particular and in Viet Nam in general: (1) Lack of soft skills, initiatives, and creativity; (2) lack of resilience; and (3) lack of team work and collaboration skills. Multiple intelligence is also a topic of great concern, including EQ (emotional intelligence/ quotient), SQ (social intelligence/quotient), and AQ (Adversity Quotient).

The feedback from the employers and alumni of the University of Social Sciences and Humanities (USSH), Viet Nam National University Ho Chi Minh City (VNU-HCM) in 2017 and 2018 addresses the following weaknesses of the graduates compared with the increasingly high requirements of the employers: (1) Planning and time management skill, (2) Problem-solving skills, (3) Teamwork and Collaboration skill, (4) Communication skills, (5) Creativity and Logic thinking.

The requirements of the employers and the labor market in the modern time, especially in the era of Industry 4.0, place a pressure on the efforts of the higher education institutions (HEIs) to make changes in training the human resources, especially through closer and constant relationships between the HEIs and the enterprises. Therefore, it is found that the Vietnamese human resources need to do more to improve their 4Cs as well as many other skills and competences to satisfy the needs of the labor market. As a result, the values of responsibility, collaboration, creativity, efficiency, resilience, and sustainable development need to be added in Vietnamese HEIs.

3.3 *Awareness of Developing New Core Values in Higher Education*

The core values in a HEI are those that must be shared and supported by all the staff and learners of the institution which help them strive for the common goals. A survey was conducted at Viet Nam National University Ho Chi Minh City (VNU-HCM) in 2017, aiming to find out the core values that most people would share in developing the institutional culture. The academic (153) and non-academic staff (157) gave their feedback on the importance and necessity of the values with the means shown in Table 5.1.

Table 5.1 Feedback on the importance/necessity of the values of the HEI

The importance/necessity of the core values of the HEI	*Feedback by academic staff (mean)*	*Feedback by non-academic staff (mean)*
Excellence	4.26	4.44
Commitment/Responsibility	4.61	4.65
Innovation/Creativity	4.49	4.60
Integrity/Honesty	4.57	4.40
Collaboration/Synergy	4.57	4.48
Student-centeredness	4.52	4.54
Academic freedom	4.37	4.24
Lifelong learning	4.40	4.20

Source: Report on the Research Project about Quality Culture in USSH, VNU-HCM, 2017 (Nguyen, 2017)

The data shows that both academic and non-academic staff share many core values that they highly appreciate, including: Commitment/Responsibility (highest score in both groups), Innovation/Creativity (second highest in non-academic group and the fourth highest in academic group), Student-centeredness (nearly the same score in both groups), Integrity/Honesty and Collaboration/Synergy are also highly valued, especially among academic group. In short, higher education staff are increasingly aware of the importance of the values related to the 4Cs in the current context and era and strive for real transformations in training human resources.

VNU-HCM has also made a lot of innovations in its study programs and staff development, embedding these core values and educational philosophies. The training workshops for defining and integrating these values in all learning outcomes at different levels as well as in teaching-learning activities have been conducted annually, although there are still challenges to further overcome.

4 Implications for Improving the Human Resource Training Programs

From the research and case study above, it can be inferred that the human resource training programs in Viet Nam can take advantage of the Vietnamese core traditional values in combination with supplementary core values of the twenty-first century for an optimal balance as there are two sides to almost all values. As a result, the human resources' strengths can be maximized, the weaknesses can be overcome, and their negative impacts can be minimized, specifically as follows:

1. The Vietnamese traditional values of harmony, flexibility, and tolerance can be maintained but should be wisely utilized in balance with the other newly added values. Anything in an extreme should be avoided; otherwise, negative consequences may occur as a result. Those values also depend on each job, context, and professional discipline. For instance, the jobs related to health care, engineering, architecture, and so on require higher degree of accuracy and higher UAI than some other jobs do.
2. The core values of the 4Cs (Collaboration, Communication, Critical thinking, and Creativity) should be developed in all educational institutions, especially in the HEIs. The Vietnamese collectivism should go together with collaboration, including collaboration with those in the outgroups/from other groups sometimes. Critical thinking and creativity require a questioning mind and decision-making skill, which is a must for human resources in all fields; otherwise, they could be replaced by hi-tech robots in the era of Industry 4.0. In addition, the values of commitment, transparency, and sense of self-discipline should be further developed. These values are necessary in all disciplines and careers in the era of Industry 4.0 for survival and success. Human resources especially should be better aware and capable of continuous learning and improvement in the lifelong learning tendency.
3. These core values of the 4Cs should be embedded into all educational and training programs and in all teaching and learning activities, including extra-curricular activities. Problem-solving skills can be developed through PBL (problem-based/project-based learning), which also requires collaboration in groups. Reality shows that an individual may not be able to solve complex global problems on their own, but groups or teams, including multi-national/multicultural teams, can. Students must also improve their intercultural communication competence to become effective global citizens. Case studies, role plays, simulations, group discussions, debates, field trips, and so on are among the active teaching methods and techniques that academic staff can apply to develop students' collaboration, critical thinking, intercultural communication competence, and creativity. Rubrics for assessing these competences and

values should be designed and revised in alignment with the expected learning outcomes.

4. These core values should be transformed into KPIs which are applied to evaluate both academic and non-academic human resources of the HEIs, in terms of their teaching and management performance. Incentive measures and awarding systems should be set up to promote these core values too.

References

Byram, M. (2006). *Language teaching for intercultural citizenship: The European situation*. University of Auckland.

Hofstede, G., Hofstede, G. J., & Minkov, M. (2010). *Cultures and organizations. Software of the mind*. McGraw Hill.

Nguyen, Duy Mong Ha. (2017). *Report on the Research Project about Quality Culture in VNU-HCM. USSH, VNUHCM.*

Storti, C. (1998). *Figuring foreigners out*. World Trade Press.

Taplin, R. (2005). *Risk management and innovation in Japan, Britain and the United States*. Routledge.

Tran, Ngoc Them. (1996). *Tìm về bản sắc văn hóa Việt Nam*. Publishing House of Ho Chi Minh City.

Tran, Ngoc Them. (1999). *Cơ sở văn hóa Việt Nam*. Publishing House of Education.

Tran, Ngoc Them. (2016). *Hệ giá trị Việt Nam từ truyền thống đến hiện đại và con đường tới tương lai*. Publishing House of Culture-Literature and Arts.

PART II

Existing and Emerging Issues in the Modern Society

CHAPTER 6

Public-Private Partnerships in Post-socialist Urban Governance: Comparative Institutional Change in Leipzig, Shanghai, and Ho Chi Minh City

Minh Doi Nguyen

1 Introduction

The collapse of the Soviet Union and the Eastern Bloc, together with the growth of globalization, has had a powerful effect on those cities embedded in the old-style socialist regime. In the new context, the disappearance and decline of centralized socialist forms and the expansion of free markets and privatization have led to a dramatic shift in the running of post-socialist cities (Diener & Hagen, 2015; Drummond & Young, 2020). This transformation has emerged concomitantly with a growing interest in governance as a 'buzzword' to describe new forms, such as public-private partnerships and networks, in which power is shared not only between

M. D. Nguyen (✉)
Ho Chi Minh City Open University, Ho Chi Minh City, Vietnam

Heidelberg, Germany
e-mail: doi.nm@ou.edu.vn

T. A.-D. Tran (ed.), *Rethinking Asian Capitalism*,
https://doi.org/10.1007/978-3-030-98104-4_6

central and local government but also between the state and non-state sectors (Kooiman, 1993; Rhodes, 1996; Jessop, 2020). In this shift from government to governance, institutional changes take place as a means of implementing governance at different levels and for different purposes (John, 2001). Thus, a comparative study of such processes in these cities can serve as a basis for rethinking their reform capacity in the post-socialist context.

Leipzig, Shanghai, and Ho Chi Minh City (HCMC) are typical examples of post-socialist cities. They all played essential roles in the economy, society, and culture of their respective countries during the period of Soviet-type socialism. After the promise of blooming landscapes[1] in Eastern Germany, the opening of China,[2] and the *Doi Moi*[3] in Vietnam, these cities have focused on improving their devastated economies by developing private enterprise and engaging in international and regional competition. This integration has led to the introduction of more advanced forms of urban governance amid the lingering legacy of the past (Garcia-Zamor, 2005; Bergère, 2009; Harms, 2016). Within these forms of urban governance, public-private partnerships (PPPs) have emerged as one of the potential tools for good urban governance. Many studies have shown that their success depends on the institutional environment (Hodge & Greve, 2007; Mouraviev & Kakabadse, 2017). However, there are various types of institutions associated with PPPs. Moreover, PPPs advance in distinct phases, reflecting the shift from urban government to urban governance in these cities. Accordingly, the purpose of this chapter is twofold: firstly, to explore the differences in the institutional changes linked to the growing use of PPPs in the urban governance processes of Leipzig, Shanghai, and HCMC and then to describe and profile the causes of such differences.

Apart from this introduction, the chapter consists of four parts. First, the conceptual framework for analyzing the institutional changes in post-socialist urban governance linked to PPPs is presented. The stages in the development of PPPs are then outlined, together with the methods of

[1] During the process of German reunification in 1991, the then-chancellor Helmut Kohl used the term *blühende Landschaften* (blooming landscapes) to promise a rapid improvement in East Germany's economy.

[2] This is another way of describing the Chinese economic reform in 1978, which encouraged the opening of China's economy to the outside world.

[3] The term *Doi Moi* (renovation) denotes the reforms in Vietnam in 1986 that sought to shift its economy toward a 'socialist-oriented market economy'.

urban governance and the integrated approach to explaining institutional changes. In the second part, an analysis of case studies of PPPs in Leipzig, Shanghai, and HCMC provides arguments to explore the differences in the institutional changes associated with PPPs. Next, the integrated framework drawing on the structural, cultural, and rational actor approaches is used to explain the institutional changes in the urban governance of the three cities. Finally, the connection of the findings to collaborative governance and some policy implications are discussed.

A qualitative method, based on case studies of PPPs in Leipzig, Shanghai, and HCMC, is adopted in this chapter. The data used are drawn from the literature and empirical analysis of formal institutions from the 1990s to 2018, including legal, regulatory, and policy documents, enabling institutions, such as PPP units and other relevant organizations, and informal institutions, such as traditions and customs and practices adopted by stakeholders and their cultural aspects.

2 Conceptual Framework

2.1 *Institutional Change in Post-socialist Urban Governance*

In institutional theory, the term 'institution' refers not only to structures and organizations but also to the norms, values, rules, and practices that shape and constrain social behaviors. More precisely, institutions structure the activities of daily life and serve as mechanisms of social order that define the 'rules of the game' in a given society (Huntington, 2006; North, 1990). In the urban context, governance is based on the combined efforts of various forms of institutions that structure the actions and interactions among stakeholders in running a city, such as the state, the private sector, and civil society (John, 2001; Pierre, 2011). It is undeniable that institutions are constantly being changed by the processes of centralization and collective action, conflict, and the bargaining between stakeholders in an organization or society as they seek to control 'the rules of game' for their benefit. If they are able to assemble a 'minimum coalition', agreement can be reached and institutional change can occur. Accordingly, institutional change will take a significant time because of the impact of internal and external factors arising out of fluctuations in the external environment (DiGaetano & Strom, 2003).

Institutional change interrelates with governance dialectically. It relates to the second-order of governance in Kooiman's sense of the term

(Kooiman, 2003), which cannot solve first-order practical problems and needs to include a meta-governance consistent with the overarching structure, normative criteria, and rhetorical requirements of governance (Haus, 2010). Jessop (2016, 2020) emphasizes institutional fixes related to actors' responses and adaptations as strategic selectivities in the face of meta-governance failures. Accordingly, institutional change can act as a self-reflexive means of governance to design governance modes, improve them through meta-governance, and orchestrate them via 'collibration'. Indeed, both perspectives imply that institutional change in urban governance reflects the urban process and relational logic, which should be observed through an adequate social-spatial-temporal context.

In Western European and North American cities, private-sector principles were referenced in urban government practices from the 1980s, which later facilitated the transition to good urban governance (John, 2001; Pierre, 2011). While this process in post-socialist cities is characterized by many conflicts, multi-directional and hybrid, and can be observed through three periods corresponding to three governance systems. First, the crisis and collapse of Soviet politics in the 1990s triggered the shift from a Soviet-type to a more democratic political regime and from a centrally planned to a market economy in post-socialist urban governance (Andrusz et al., 1996). The systems embedded in this context tended toward closed governance because of the unique aspects of post-socialist urban regimes, such as the concentration of power through hierarchical management and master planning. In this governance system, many actors try to delay PPPs through the use of in-house sourcing and closed information systems whose main purpose is to achieve the outcome before the political leaders' period of office comes to an end.

Second, under the pressure of extended democracy, global competitiveness, and fiscal austerity since the mid-1990s, governance systems in post-socialist cities seem to have adopted open decision-making and institutional responsiveness in an attempt to fix the failures of the closed governance system (Tsenkova & Nedovic-Budic, 2006). Accordingly, the actors have mobilized more resources from the market and society in order to develop the city, leading to strategic planning requirements and the development of more modes of governance based on matrix management and oriented toward long-term outcomes and shared values. In the open governance system, the state still plays an essential steering role, guaranteeing community engagement, coordinated decision-making, and shared information systems.

Finally, under the impact of the 2008 global financial crisis and the subsequent failure of rigid governance systems, some post-socialist cities have sought to develop a new system of governance in order to adapt to the trends in international and global governance. One of the options under discussion is collaborative governance. This form of governance is based on complex interactive management involving a series of learning processes between authority and community stakeholders. In such a system, the actors are co-partners or co-collaborators engaged in generating new ideas and integrating strategic planning and policies in order to solve the 'wicked problems' standing in the way of achieving urban communities' sustainable values (Torfing & Ansell, 2017). Institutionalizing the partnership between the state and non-state partners fully and equitably has led to collaborative governance becoming a more widely accepted governance mechanism; however, the implementation of collaborative governance also requires an essential foundation of democracy and stakeholder competence (Bianchi et al., 2021).

With a vision of becoming global cities and constantly competing with each other, most post-socialist cities have experienced the institutional change associated with the transformation from closed to open governance systems (and some cities can implement collaborative governance) in different ways. In other words, there are differences in the level of change in each city and field based on institutional legacies, leadership, and community participation. Such variations can be investigated by means of a comparative analysis based on management forms, planning, engagement, decision-making, and information systems and outcomes.

2.2 PPPs and Urban Governance

PPPs have demonstrated their strengths when implemented in many countries as a form or instrument of urban governance. However, the concept of PPPs is defined in various ways and has a different scope depending on the practice in a specific country (Osborne, 2000). Looking through an institutional lens, PPPs involve long-term cooperation between a public agency and the private sector in order jointly to implement investment projects with a view to developing products and services based on contracts, with an explicit division of responsibilities, benefits, and risks (Van Ham & Koppenjan, 2001). Three critical characteristics of PPPs should be emphasized. First, PPPs are a form of long-term service provision. Second, PPPs involve the transfer of risk from the public to the private sector. Finally, different forms of long-term contracts are drawn up between legal entities and public authorities (Grimsey & Lewis, 2007; Page et al., 2008).

From an economic perspective, PPPs help to optimize the strengths and resources of the public and private sectors and encourage innovative and effective ways of designing, implementing, operating, and managing. In PPP projects, private enterprises are usually the capital investors, providing technology and commercial exploitation. The government may provide a one-off capital grant to make the project economically viable or, in other cases, support the project by providing revenue subsidies or tax breaks for a fixed period. The government contributions can also take the form of public assets such as land and natural resources. From a political perspective, PPP is an adaptive form developed to deal with the failure of the state and the market to provide services to the people. PPP projects reduce the burden on the state budget and create incentives for the private sector to engage in the public sphere, which is less profitable in the market. In many cases, the cost of using the services produced by PPP projects is transferred from taxpayers to consumers, creating more equity in society. Governments sometimes see PPPs as an important part of their commitment to public sector reform. They provide opportunities for the public sector to apply private-sector competence, experience, and technology to public management.

Because of the above characteristics and mechanisms, understanding PPPs requires an approach based more on governance than public management and urban regimes. In other words, a democratic and progressive governance environment optimizes and makes transparent the risks and benefits of PPP projects. Accordingly, the state plays the role of 'steering' rather than 'rowing' in PPPs. In the absence of a political commitment, PPP projects cannot balance economic benefits with public value. Conversely, when the state intervenes excessively in the PPPs, it will make this form lose its dynamism. Therefore, a good institutional framework can facilitate its advantages and limit its disadvantages.

Over time, governments have begun to understand that effective institutions have to be developed alongside PPPs in order to serve the interests of stakeholders and benefit the public (OECD, 2012). According to the United Nations Economic Commission for Europe (2008), PPPs develop in three stages. The first stage involves defining the basic institutional structures required in order to define the policy framework, test legal viability, identify a project pipeline, develop foundation concepts, apply lessons from earlier deals to other sectors, and build a marketplace. In the second stage, there are more institutional arrangements concerning the reform of legislative and publishing policy and practice guidelines, establishing dedicated PPP units, fostering the marketplace, expanding the project pipeline and extending to new sectors, and leveraging new sources of funds. The third phase sees the full development of the required institutions, such as fully functional PPP units, capital markets, a high level of collaborative governance, and more sophisticated financial arrangements.

2.3 An Integrated Approach to Comparing and Explaining the Institutional Change Associated with PPPs in Urban Governance

Studies in comparative politics usually revolve around the rational choice, cultural and structural theory. However, the problems of comparative urban research fall into the gaps between each of these theoretical strands. In 2003, DiGaetano and Strom developed an integrated framework using the structural, cultural, and rational actor approaches to cross-national comparison in order to explain the institutional changes in urban governance. The authors present an integrated framework based on three intersecting propositions: (1) the 'institutional intermediation of structural context and political actors', (2) the 'cultural intermediation of structural context and institutional milieu', and (3) the 'institutional intermediation of culture and political actors'. According to the authors, the intermediations between the different spheres are best grasped when considering institutional change because causal relationships become visible during changes. Three propositions provide a framework for comparing and explaining the institutional change in urban governance. Firstly, the source of institutional change in urban governance lies in changes in the structural context caused by, for example, the effects of globalization, transition, and the decentralization of political and administrative competencies. Secondly, political culture mediates and filters the effects of the political and economic changes in the institutional milieu. Thirdly, on the agency level, political actors try either to take advantage of these changes or to defy them.

DiGaetano and Strom (2003) also extend the integrated approach to modes of urban governance by distinguishing four essential criteria: 'governing relations', that is, the modes of interaction between different stakeholders; 'governing logic', that is, means or method by which decisions are made; 'key decision-maker'; and 'political objectives'. The authors present five modes of urban governance. The clientelist mode is characterized by personalized political patronage of favored interest groups by politicians who insist upon reciprocity, resulting in selective material benefits and political support. The corporatist mode describes a programmatic approach to governing relations based on exclusionary negotiation and consensus-building between governmental and powerful civic elites with regard to governing tasks and forming interest coalitions. The managerial mode is characterized by formal and contractual relationships between politicians and civil servants and the private sector in order to achieve effective or efficient implementation of governance programs. The pluralist mode is concerned with conflict management among contending interests in a competitive environment in which the government acts as broker or mediator. The populist mode, finally, emphasizes inclusionary negotiation and the mobilization of popular support by politicians and community movement leaders in order to bring 'social intelligence' to bear in the governing process. These five modes of urban governance are ideal types and tend to exist in more hybrid forms in actual governance systems.

The integrated approach thus proposed provides a potential model in comparative urban governance research that can be used to uncover the causal mechanisms and drivers of political, economic, and social change in cities (Pierre, 2005). Moreover, this framework is a sufficiently wide and flexible theoretical approach to be applied not only to the Western context but also to some case studies in China (Zielke & Waibel, 2014; Wang, 2018). Thus, this framework can facilitate a comprehensive understanding and comparison of institutional change associated with PPPs in and across post-socialist cities.

3 Differences in the Institutional Change Associated with PPPs in Post-socialist Urban Governance

3.1 *Institutional Change Associated with PPPs in Leipzig*

The collapse of the socialist regime led Leipzig to apply privatization directly and immediately. Accordingly, the PPP projects were very rapidly developed in Leipzig over a short period of time. The increasing number and scale of PPP projects has required Germany to make regular improvements to the institutional framework and amend the existing laws hindering the development of PPPs (Table 6.1). Moreover, the institutional change associated with the development of PPPs in Leipzig is embedded in the institutional system of the Federal Republic of Germany and the European Union (EU), which seeks to expand and promote the role of urban governance through a strong hierarchical system of decentralization, ensuring autonomy for local government and a clear and transparent framework for PPPs in public service delivery (Jacob et al., 2014).

Two urban regeneration pilot projects, the *International Quarter (IQ)-Ost* and *Gründerzeit Erleben*, have been selected as case studies to illustrate the trend in PPP governance in Leipzig. These pilot projects are described as 'micro-interventions in urban restructuring' and were aimed at re-establishing, at a district level, a dynamic economic structure and improving the attractiveness and social vitality of the districts through intervention (refurbishment/rebuilding) in the building stock, attracting 'small' businesses as well as marketing/communications and community involvement strategies. The urban 'units', considered to be the project's focal targets, are the tower blocks and their inner courtyards; some of these spaces are privately owned, while others are the property of the Municipality Housing Association. The interventions aimed to reinforce the attractiveness of the blocks (and of the districts as a whole) and improve their retail potential (development of ethical and other retailers/artisan activities in the courtyards). From 2000 to 2006, more than 19 million euros were invested in these pilot projects (10.5 in urban renewal projects, 7.5 in economic and employment projects, 1.15 in social projects, and 0.062 in information participation and management). The project drew on various sources of financing, including the European Regional Development Fund (ERDF) and various national support funds (Weidner et al., 2011).

The experimental pilot projects showed that Leipzig had developed a set of management tools based on the principle of collaborative governance that enabled it to standardize the development of PPP projects through institutional changes, such as the development of integrated open information systems and civic engagement (Weidner et al., 2011). Moreover, drawing on experience at the national and EU level, with the development of PPPs and the associated institutional arrangements, risk management, contract supervision, and stakeholder participation (Guo et al., 2017), the institutional changes in Leipzig tend toward the managerial mode, with certain elements of the pluralist mode taken from the city's

Table 6.1 The stages of PPP development in Leipzig, Shanghai, and HCMC (1990–2018)

	Elements	*Leipzig (Germany)*	*Shanghai (China)*	*HCMC (Vietnam)*
Stage One	Define policy framework	• Private law relevant to PPP contracts 1990 • The Federal Private Road Financing Act 1994	• No. 89 policy paper of 1994 • No. 208 policy paper on foreign investment 1995	• Decision No. 71/2010/ QD-TTg • A chapter in Investment Act 2014
	Test of legal viability	• Evaluation of the first PPP project in operation in 2009	• Lack of grounded evaluations (Thieriot & Dominguez, 2015)	• Expert rating: 'not optimal' (ADB, 2012)
	Identify project pipeline	• Many projects were in the pipeline in 2012 and 2013 (Jacob et al., 2014)	• The announcement of a robust project pipeline since 2005 (HM Treasury, 2015)	• The government lacks a credible PPP project pipeline (ADB, 2012)
	Develop foundation concepts	• Construction and City Development from FMT in 2003	• Opinions and rules to PPPs (Beh, 2010)	• Article 2. Decision No. 71/2010/ QD-TTg
	Apply lessons from earliest deals to other sectors	• In 2003, Warnow Tunnel was the first PPP project with many lessons to be learned (Jacob et al., 2014)	• Mid-1980s to 1990, power and water sectors projects led to PPP policy frameworks (Beh, 2015)	• Unclear
	Start to build marketplace	• Since 2003, PPP market has been built	• China's PPP market is in the early emerging stage	• PPP market is primitive (ADB, 2012)

(*continued*)

Table 6.1 (continued)

	Elements	*Leipzig (Germany)*	*Shanghai (China)*	*HCMC (Vietnam)*
Stage Two	Introduce legislative reform	• The PPP Acceleration Act 2005	• Regulations on PPP (draft) • Circular on Deepening Reform of PPP	• The Decree 15/2005/ ND-CP on PPP Investment
	Publish policy and practice guidelines	• The European Union Green Paper on PPPs • Federal Budget Code 2013	• *Cai Jin* [2016] No. 32 • Guiding Opinions, Measures in 2014, 2015	• Decree No. 30/2015/ ND-CP • Circular No. 06 & 21 in 2016
	Establish dedicated PPP units	• Consultancies, 'Partnerships' + Small PPP Secretariat in the central ministry	• PPP unit (PPP center) under the MOF	• PPP offices under MPI, MOIT, and PPP office DPI of HCMC
	Refine PPP delivery models	• I, M, K, L, G, and E models (Guo et al., 2017)	• Pilot entrusted management; franchise model	• Not yet
	Continue to foster marketplace	• German PPP market was subject to considerable changes in 2017 (Bonhage & Roberts, 2018)	• Bidding project but lack of transparency (ADB, 2010)	• Unclear
	Expand project pipeline, extend to new sectors	• PPP Projects on Federal highways; higher education sector	• Not yet	• Not yet
	Leverage new sources of funds	• Municipal loan; objection-free forfeiting (Jacob et al., 2014)	• Limited financing diversity (Thieriot & Dominguez, 2015)	• Not yet

(*continued*)

Table 6.1 (continued)

	Elements	*Leipzig (Germany)*	*Shanghai (China)*	*HCMC (Vietnam)*
Stage Three	Fully defined, comprehensive 'system'	• Some specific legislation; driven by EU legislation	• Some specific legislation	• Not yet
	Legal impediments removed	• PPP Acceleration Act 2005 remove obstacles and barriers	• Not yet	• Not yet
	PPP models refined and reproduced	• F model (Guo et al., 2017)	• Not yet	• Not yet
	Sophisticated risk allocation	• Certain risks transferred to the private contractor (Daube et al., 2008)	• The private contractors are at major risk	• The private contractors are at major risk
	Committed deal flow	• Unclear	• Unclear	• Unclear
	Long-term political consensus	• Political parties stated clearly that they would continue to use the PPP model (CDU, CSU, and SPD in 2013).	• Unclear	• Unclear
	Use of full-range of funding sources	• Not yet	• Not yet	• Not yet
	Thriving infrastructure investment market	• Not yet	• Not yet	• Not yet
	Well-trained civil service utilizes experiences	• Unclear	• Weak	• Weak

Source: Author-collected data

urban governance, which is characterized by cooperation between public sector managers and the private sector as well as with civil society, reflecting changing investment patterns and new social demands. The city government seeks greater efficiency by contracting out complex tasks. It also acts as broker or mediator for private interests that form competing coalitions in order to set the city's policy agenda.

3.2 *Institutional Change Associated with PPPs in Shanghai*

Many urban development projects in Shanghai have been implemented using PPPs. The success of some projects is ensured by the institutional framework developed based on reasonable risk allocation and rigorous project management. However, the economic and financial benefits have not been sufficient to attract investment in public projects. Additionally, significant government interference and corruption, inadequate legal regulations, weak surveillance systems, and a lack of transparency in the decision-making process are the biggest obstacles to the success of the PPP projects in China (Li & Song, 2017; Jones & Bloomfield, 2020).

There has been a massive proliferation of PPPs in Shanghai's water supply sector since the 1990s because of economic reform leading the price of water to be determined by the market. In the early stages, the Shanghai government approached transnational water corporations (TNCs), intending to upgrade the water supply and sewage treatment because they have extensive experience and the advantage of being state corporations. Consequently, domestic private enterprises in the water industry won just a few contracts because of their fuzzy relationship with the government bureau that used to own the enterprises. This relationship between domestic private enterprises and government agencies has led to a management style that relies on subsidies, which has deterred more profit-oriented corporate activities. Subsequently, however, Shanghai became one of the cities to have water supply projects funded by the World Bank and implemented through private enterprises. In this context, the local private enterprises have been involved in a large number of water management facilities by working as subcontractors for water TNCs. This enabled these enterprises to gain the necessary experience to become the main contractors in the Shanghai water sector (Lee, 2007).

The case of PPPs in Shanghai's water services serves to demonstrate the obverse of the political culture of deference to hierarchy and the concentration of state power in China. However, in some cases, the local government can flexibly implement the central government's principles through local negotiations between local government agencies and private enterprises. In the case of the Shanghai Zhuyuan Greenfield project, the local government transferred its traditional responsibilities for investment, construction, operation, and maintenance to a private water supply company, together with subsidies and preferential policies (Zhong et al., 2008). Although the evidence suggests a gradual shift from a closed to an open governance system, the state is still characterized by very centrist monopolies, while non-state actors in PPPs remain relatively weak. Government functions have not been synchronized with and adapted to the requirements of collaborative governance. Nevertheless, the central government has adopted certain important strategic measures that have given Shanghai a certain autonomy which, together with a powerful local government apparatus, was the foundation for developing the institutions required for PPPs.

PPPs in Shanghai involve hybrid modes of urban governance that are both clientelistic and managerialistic. While formal PPP institutions were being established at national level, the city authorities implemented PPPs projects according to their circumstances. Although the process of designing, bidding, implementing, and appraising projects is based on contractual relations between the city government and private-sector organizations, the interrelationships between the actors in decision-making in specific projects seem to be marked by particular, personalized exchanges. This hybridity can lead to a lack of competition in PPPs, with politicians and civil servants and administrative employees able to exploit individual and group interests.

3.3 Institutional Change Associated with PPPs in Ho Chi Minh City

Although Vietnam has had a temporary definition of 'investment in the form of PPPs' as a form of 'socialization' since 2010, there is a lack of an adequate institutional framework for PPPs (ADB, 2012). In HCMC, PPPs account for a small proportion of total public investment; however, their development is essential given the city's limited budget. These projects mainly focus on infrastructure development. However, calls for investment in these projects face many challenges regarding budget capital, support mechanisms, and political determination. The regulations governing PPPs are still inconsistent and the associated legal documents are complex and unclear. Most PPP projects in the form of BOT (Build–Operate–Transfer) and BT (Build–Transfer) are proposed by investors, and the authorities nominate or designate the investor.

The Phu My Bridge project is a well-known example of the city's PPPs. This project was to be implemented as a BOT agreement between the People's Committee of HCMC and JSC Phu My Bridge BOT (the joint investor in this project has links with the corporation under the Ministry of Transportation). According to the conclusion notice No. 2242/TB-TTCP of 2017 issued by the Government Inspectorate, this project has many problems. During the investment process, the People's Committee of HCMC did not comply with the order and procedures for investment; for instance, they assigned an incompetent investor to organize the investment for a BT project without any calls for tender, either domestically or internationally. Moreover, project management was fragile, leading to a dramatic rise in the total cost compared to original estimates, many delays, an unclear division of responsibility among stakeholders when incidents occurred, and no guarantee of any eventual benefits.

This case study indicates that the limitations created by the ambiguity of the concept, policy, and legislation in this area could lead to cronyism in PPP projects. The lessons from this project indicate that the BOT and BT forms have many shortcomings, so it is necessary to transition gradually to a proper form of PPPs. Moreover, developing a good PPP strategy is a path to improving PPP institutions and to focus on capacities, not only in the private sector but also in related government agencies in order to avoid failures in future PPP projects. Nevertheless, recommendations in government documents focus more on overcoming the risk gap that causes disadvantages for the state than on the risk-sharing mechanism with private-sector investors.

The institutional change associated with PPPs in HCMC has focused more on reforming government than governance. The changes still have many limitations regarding decentralization and participation and have led to a closed governance system for PPPs, although efforts are being made to help the private sector become real partners with the state in the urban governance process. Consequently, this change has been characterized by a dual trend. On the one hand, the aim has been to adapt to globalization and marketization and, on the other hand, to strengthen state control and management in order to maintain state dominance. Furthermore, the case study also shows that PPPs in HCMC tend to be clientelist in nature, characterized by personalized and specific interrelationships between policymakers and preferred stakeholders or clients as crucial decision-makers within a weak institutional framework. In this mode, the informal institutional relationship between private companies and political actors or administrative agencies is the obstacle to the effectiveness of urban governance in HCMC.

3.4 *Differences in Institutional Change Associated with PPPs*

The institutional changes associated with PPPs in Leipzig, Shanghai, and HCMC are similar but at the same time different. They share the same starting point and the common purpose of achieving the most significant benefits from the use of PPPs in their urban governance processes. However, the diversity in the stages of the development of PPPs, the transformation of urban governance from closed to collaborative governance, and urban governance modes show that the three cities are pursuing different paths (Fig 6.1).

All three cities have approached the decline of centralized socialist forms by expanding the free market and privatization. This, in turn, has led to decentralization and power-sharing between the state and non-state sectors in urban governance, as highlighted by PPPs. The 'maturity curves' show that the development of PPPs in all three cities has been gradual. However, they are currently at different stages of development, and the governance methods vary. To begin with, HCMC is in the initial stage, in which PPPs based on a fundamental legal framework account for BOT and BT projects. Next, Shanghai has reached the intermediate stage two, in which the institutional framework for PPPs is constantly being improved, and numerous projects serve to demonstrate its effectiveness in urban governance. Finally, Leipzig is currently embarking on phase three, in which

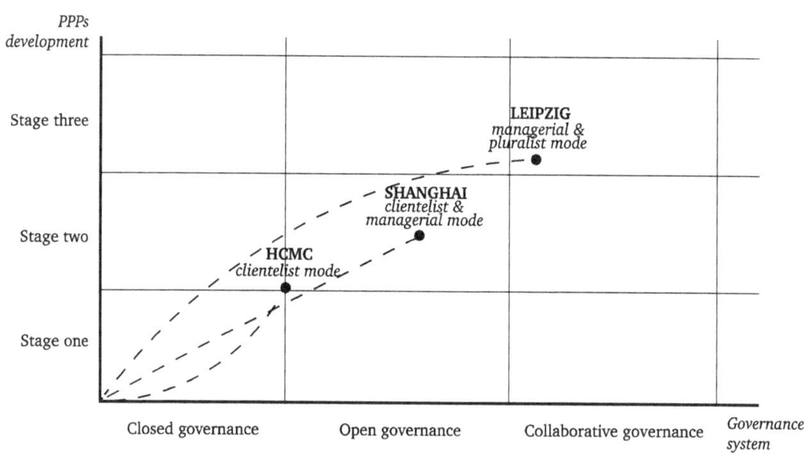

Fig. 6.1 Different pathways of institutional change associated with PPPs in Leipzig, Shanghai, and HCMC (1990–2018)

PPP projects are playing a significant role based on high-performing institutions.

From the perspective of institutional governance systems, it can be seen that weak PPPs are often formed in closed urban governance systems, as in HCMC, with harmful side effects such as corruption and group interests working to gain advantages for their members. In contrast, in a system of collaborative urban governance, strong PPPs can be formed. This is the case in Leipzig, which has some of the fundamental elements of collaborative governance, in which PPPs are guaranteed by the joint efforts of the public and private sectors and civil society. The system in Shanghai is a hybrid between open and some of the fundamental elements of collaborative urban governance, in which PPPs can be the result of coordinated decision-making in an environment characterized by asymmetries between the actors.

In the urban governance modes, while PPPs in Leipzig tend to be hybrids of the managerial mode with some aspects of the pluralist mode, in Shanghai they tend to be a mix of the clientelist and managerial modes. In addition, the case study of PPPs in HCMC proves that its urban governance institutions are still in the clientelist mode.

4 The Differences in Institutional Change Associated with PPPs in the Three Cities Described and Profiled

4.1 *The Institutional Intermediation of Structural Context and Political Actors*

Economically speaking, all three cities were important industrial centers during the Soviet-style regimes. At that time, all three countries had centrally planned economics, although some actors still tried to retain certain elements of the free market economy. This helped them to adapt the urban governance of the three cities quickly after leaving the central planning mechanism. However, the economic transition in Shanghai and HCMC differed from that in Leipzig. In East Germany, the direct transformation from a planned economy to a market economy caused increasing unemployment and population shrinkage in the 1990s, while the change in China and Vietnam was slower and more stable. The aim was to gradually establish a market-oriented economy based on pragmatic experiences, beginning with microeconomic reform before turning subsequently to macroeconomic reforms. In both countries, however, it is clear that extensive economic reform was accompanied by only limited political reform. On the other hand, the institutional change associated with PPPs in Leipzig has been more radical than in Shanghai and HCMC because the institutional framework associated with PPPs in Leipzig demonstrates that the free market has been harnessed for the benefit of the urban governance process. The institutional frameworks that have been developed for PPPs in China and Vietnam have tended, conversely, to maintain state power. Consequently, a pluralist and managerial mode of PPP is necessary for Leipzig to facilitate collaboration with private actors in the free market. In contrast, the more hybrid form combining the managerial and clientelist modes that characterize the PPPs of Shanghai has led to a more open but not collaborative governance system based on cooperation among a limited range of stakeholders. In developing a clientelist mode of governance, HCMC has tended to retain a closed governance system.

State restructuring after the transition from a Soviet-style to a more market economy also affected the institutional changes associated with PPPs, which depend on the extent to which authority and practice shifted from centralization to decentralization in the political, administrative, and fiscal spheres in the three cities. Firstly, in the case of Leipzig, the state restructuring was driven by the need to adapt to the federal-state-city system of government, with its high degree of local autonomy and self-government within local PPP projects. Moreover, this process also relates to upscaling the state structure to supranational levels because the EU has influenced urban governance in its member states (DiGaetano & Strom, 2003), encouraging a shift toward greater transparency, competitiveness, and efficiency. Moreover, the financial support from the EU and national bodies is declining, leading to increased demand for PPPs. Secondly, the central government in China has transferred some of its decision-making power to the local government in Shanghai in order to strengthen the latter's control over local PPP projects. The local government is clearly defined as a municipal government with a typical hierarchical organization for PPP projects. Moreover, the Shanghai municipal government has also transferred some of the relevant decision-making power to the district or county level. In their governance modes, there is some evidence of institutional change to support the private partners as their 'clients', in combination with managerialist modes. In the case of HCMC, the decentralization process associated with PPPs seems to be limited. The central government has retained its institutional power, and local autonomy is constrained by decisions taken by senior personnel in the central authorities when the annual budget is drawn up and allocated. In addition, the functions and tasks of the municipal government are not yet clearly defined. Consequently, against the background of a highly centralized state, institutional weaknesses are constraining the development of PPPs.

4.2 Cultural Intermediation of Structural Context and Institutional Milieu

As DiGaetano and Strom (2003) argue, political culture mediates or filters the effects of economic and political change on the institutional milieu of urban governance. The political cultures of these three cities are still influenced by the post-socialist legacy, characterized by the conflict between the hybrid political cultures of statism and privatism. However, there are differences in the continuum and level of hybridity between statism and privatism in the three cities; the extent and nature of their institutional change also vary. Since German reunification, after a period affected by statism, privatist political cultures have returned and thrived, which has facilitated the use of PPPs in Leipzig. Conversely, the contradiction between weak privatism and strong statism in the early stages of reform in China and Vietnam blunted or diluted the development of institutions conducive to the use of PPPs.

Different combinations of structural aspects and cultural settings can create different environments for the development of local political institutions and modes of governance (DiGaetano & Strom, 2003). Germany's highly devolved statist culture is more conducive to the institutional shift toward the decentralization required for PPPs to flourish in Leipzig. In contrast, the centralist cultures of China and Vietnam, steeped in the deep-rooted patriarchal tradition and the Communist system, hamper the institutional change in the direction of decentralization and local empowerment and thereby prevent PPPs from flourishing in those countries.

In fact, lacking a tradition or identity of local government, it is doubtful that cities will be able to achieve 'synergy effects' in their governance process, which means that process outcomes and benefits will not be balanced but skewed toward the private sector. All three cities have their own traditional political cultures that have affected the institutional change that has taken place in the process of developing public-private partnerships. More specifically, the tradition of transparency in Leipzig's political culture has made possible the institutional changes required to balance the interests of the various stakeholders in PPP projects. On the other hand, the tradition of irresponsibility and ambiguity in management in HCMC has facilitated institutional change that favors self-seeking interest groups wishing to take advantage of PPP projects.

4.3 Institutional Intermediation of Culture and Political Actor

According to DiGaetano and Strom (2003), political actors play a role either as agents of institutional change or as resistors to that change. In all three cities, institutional change can be explained as responses by both political actors and citizens in the context of broader socio-economic transformations following the failures of the Soviet model and the globalization process.

In the first period of the transition process, the leaders in all three cities played an essential role as agents of institutional change, effecting the shift toward urban governance. They promoted institutional change through negotiation with the government, drawing on their practical experience and political skills. This can be clearly observed in the cases of Shanghai and HCMC in the first stage of the reform process. However, other political actors also sought to resist institutional change. Because of the strong effect of traditional institutional socialism, the political actors in Shanghai and HCMC tended to remain state-centric rather than private-centric in PPP projects. The complementarity between leadership and participation was the case in Leipzig, where PPP projects become arenas of competition among stakeholders, and the city authorities act as a conductor to accommodate the PPPs within the managerial and pluralist modes of governance.

Moreover, structural change in economics and politics has also greatly influenced the coalitions that political actors construct in implementing PPPs. The local election in Leipzig in May 1990 marked the beginning of the transition from a totalitarian state to democracy and led to the construction of political coalitions. The expansion of the free market and integration into the EU has affected the sorts of coalitions that political actors construct to improve voters' interests. This effect has led to greater transparency and efficiency in PPPs. In contrast, in the case of the political systems in China and Vietnam, instead of forming formal coalitions, the changes in structure have generated informal coalitions of interests in PPP projects. Thus, such coalitions pose significant challenges for Shanghai and HCMC regarding transparency and fighting corruption in PPPs.

5 Conclusion

This chapter compares the institutional changes associated with PPPs in Leipzig, Shanghai, and Ho Chi Minh City and seeks to describe and profile distinctions. The differences between the three cities in the institutional changes associated with PPPs are related to variations in the transformation of urban governance from closed to collaborative governance systems and the stages of PPP development. Leipzig is on the highest hierarchical level of all comparative elements of the three cities, while HCMC is on the lowest.

Based on DiGaetano and Strom's integrated approach, there are three main results that point to the reasons for the differences in the institutional changes associated with PPPs in the three cities. Firstly, the institutional change in Leipzig fully exploited market values, leading to a strengthening of the trend toward the managerial and pluralist modes of governance. In the other two cities, on the other hand, the persistence of clientelism and managerialism in Shanghai and of clientelism in HCMC tended to delay the development of alternative modes of governance and to maintain state power. Secondly, because of a strong privatist political culture, institutional change in Leipzig encouraged the development of PPPs based on mixing managerial and pluralist modes of governance while persistent statism weakened privatism and led to the clientelism that characterizes PPPs in Shanghai and HCMC. Thirdly, structural change has also greatly affected the sorts of coalitions that political actors construct. Accordingly, institutional change in Leipzig ensures transparency. At the same time, the political systems in China and Vietnam and the institutions in Shanghai and HCMC favor the construction of coalitions based on self-serving group interests in PPP projects.

Collaborative governance is currently emerging as a potential paradigm for the management of PPPs in post-socialist urban governance, regardless of the current stage of PPP implementation. However, Leipzig is the only city of the three that has achieved anything like collaborative governance on a fundamental level. In order to gain more benefit from PPPs in post-socialist urban governance, the following recommendations can be made:

- It should be determined whether collaborative governance is better suited than other forms of governance to managing PPPs in post-socialist cities. This will require further research and pilot experiments based on pluralist approaches to be applied in different contexts and cultures and with different stakeholders.
- Approaches to collaborative governance are not 'one size fits all' but depend on the priorities of the individual city as part of a rational and comprehensive strategy. Thus, the complementary way, such as leadership associated with community engagement, can be used depending on the situation.
- To ensure positive outcomes from collaborative urban governance, cities should pay attention to the conditions and capacity under which institutional co-design and co-arrangements are formed in order to build trust and capacity for all stakeholders.
- The implementation of collaborative governance needs to avoid 'good ideas turning bad' because of ritualistic behaviors that effectively mask underlying political processes.

References

Andrusz, G., Harloe, M., & Szelenyi, I. (Eds.). (1996). *Cities after socialism: Urban and regional change and conflict in post-socialist societies*. Blackwell.

Asian Development Bank. (2010). *Wastewater treatment: Case study of public-private partnership in Shanghai*. Retrieved September 10, 2018, from https://www.adb.org/sites/default/files/publication/27862/urbandev-prc-nov2010-wastewater.pdf

Asian Development Bank. (2012). *Assessment of public–private partnerships in Viet Nam constraints and opportunities*. Retrieved September 10, 2018, from http://hdl.handle.net/11540/885

Beh, L. (2010). Public-private partnerships in China: A responsive participation. *Journal of US-China Administration, 7*(9), 30–35.

Beh, L. (2015). Managing across public-private partnerships: A review of implementation in China and Australia. *Contemporary Chinese Political Economy and Strategic Relations, 1*(3), 663–698.

Bergère, M. (2009). *Shanghai: China's gateway to modernity*. Stanford University Press.

Bianchi, C., Nasi, G., & Rivenbark, W. C. (2021). Implementing collaborative governance: Models, experiences, and challenges. *Public Management Review*, 1–9. https://doi.org/10.1080/14719037.2021.1878777

Bonhage, J., & Roberts, M. (2018). The public-private partnerships law review-edition 4: Germany. *The Law Reviews.* Retrieved August 28, 2019, from https://thelawreviews.co.uk/title/the-public-private-partnership-law-review/germany

Daube, D., Vollrath, S., & Alfen, H. W. (2008). A comparison of project finance and the forfeiting model as financing forms for PPP projects in Germany. *International Journal of Project Management, 26*(4), 376–387.

Diener, A. C., & Hagen, J. (Eds.). (2015). *From socialist to post-socialist cities: Cultural politics of architecture, urban planning, and identity in Eurasia.* Routledge.

DiGaetano, A., & Strom, E. (2003). Comparative urban governance: An integrated approach. *Urban Affairs Review, 38*(3), 356–395.

Drummond, L. B., & Young, D. (Eds.). (2020). *Socialist and post-socialist urbanisms: Critical reflections from a global perspective.* University of Toronto Press.

Garcia-Zamor, J. C. (2005). The city of Leipzig as a European success story in economic development. *International Public Management Journal, 8*(1), 23–37.

Grimsey, D., & Lewis, M. (2007). *Public private partnerships: The worldwide revolution in infrastructure provision and project finance.* Edward Elgar Publishing.

Guo, S., et al. (2017). The experience and reference on PPP development in Germany. *International Journal of Economics, Finance and Management Sciences, 5*(6), 327–333.

Harms, E. (2016). *Luxury and rubble: Civility and dispossession in the New Saigon.* University of California Press.

Haus, M. (2010). *Transformation des Regierens und Herausforderungen der Institutionenpolitik.* Nomos Verlagsgesellschaft.

HM Treasury. (2015). *Supporting the development of PPPs in the People's Republic of China: An international perspective.* Retrieved September 15, 2018, from https://www.gov.uk/government/publications/supporting-the-development-of-ppps-in-the-peoples-republic-of-china-an-international-perspective

Hodge, G. A., & Greve, C. (2007). Public-private partnerships: An international performance review. *Public Administration Review, 67*(3), 545–558.

Huntington, S. P. (2006). *Political order in changing societies.* Yale University Press.

Jacob, D., Kochendörfer, B., von Drygalski, M., & Hilbig, C. (2014). Ten years of PPP in Germany: Experiences and perspectives. *Proceedings of the Institution of Civil Engineers-Management, Procurement and Law, 167*(4), 180–188.

Jessop, B. (2016). *The state: Past, present, future.* Polity Press.

Jessop, B. (2020). *Putting civil society in its place: Governance, metagovernance and subjectivity.* Polity Press.

John, P. (2001). *Local governance in Western Europe.* Sage Publications.

Jones, L., & Bloomfield, M. J. (2020). PPPs in China: Does the growth in Chinese PPPs signal a liberalising economy? *New Political Economy, 25*(5), 829–847.
Kooiman, J. (Ed.). (1993). *Modern governance: New government-society interactions*. Sage Publications.
Kooiman, J. (2003). *Governing as governance*. Sage Publications.
Lee, S. (2007). Private sector participation in the Shanghai water sector. *Water Policy, 9*(4), 405–423.
Li, N., & Song, Q. (2017). Public–private partnership in developing China: Evolution, institutionalization and risks. In J. Leitão, E. M. Sarmento, & J. Aleluia (Eds.), *The Emerald handbook of public-private partnerships in developing and emerging economies: Perspectives on public policy, entrepreneurship and poverty* (pp. 113–139). Emerald Publishing Limited.
Mouraviev, N., & Kakabadse, N. (Eds.). (2017). *Public-private partnerships in transitional nations: Policy, governance and praxis*. Cambridge Scholars Publishing.
North, D. (1990). *Institutions, institutional change and economic performance (Political economy of institutions and decisions)*. Cambridge University Press.
OECD. (2012). *Recommendation of the council on principles for public governance of public-private partnerships*. OECD Publishing.
Osborne, S. P. (Ed.). (2000). *Public-private partnerships: Theory and practice in international perspective*. Routledge.
Page, S., Ankner, W., Jones, C., & Fetterman, R. (2008). The risks and rewards of private equity in infrastructure. *Public Works Management & Policy, 13*(2), 110–113.
Pierre, J. (2005). Comparative urban governance: Uncovering complex causalities. *Urban Affairs Review, 40*(4), 446–462.
Pierre, J. (2011). *The politics of urban governance*. Palgrave Macmillan.
Rhodes, R. A. W. (1996). The new governance: Governing without government. *Political Studies, 44*(4), 652–667.
Thieriot, H., & Dominguez, C. (2015). *Public-private partnerships in China*. The International Institute for Sustainable Development. Retrieved September 25, 2018, from https://www.iisd.org/system/files/publications/public-private-partnerships-china.pdf
Torfing, J., & Ansell, C. (2017). Strengthening political leadership and policy innovation through the expansion of collaborative forms of governance. *Public Management Review, 19*(1), 37–54.
Tsenkova, S., & Nedovic-Budic, Z. (Eds.). (2006). *The urban mosaic of post-socialist Europe: Space, institutions and policy*. Physica-Verlag.
United Nations Economic Commission for Europe. (2008). *Guidebook on promoting good governance in public-private partnerships*. United Nations Publications.
Van Ham, H., & Koppenjan, J. (2001). Building public-private partnerships: Assessing and managing risks in port development. *Public Management Review, 3*(4), 593–616.

Wang, L. (2018). *Changing spatial elements in Chinese socio-economic five-year plan: From project layout to spatial planning*. Springer.

Weidner, S., Gerhardt, J., Schaaf, J., & Riedel, N. (2011). PPP in urban development in Germany illustrated using two pilot projects in Leipzig. In R. Dalla Longa (Ed.), *Urban models and public-private partnership* (pp. 213–264). Springer.

Zhong, L., Mol, A. P., & Fu, T. (2008). Public-private partnerships in China's urban water sector. *Environmental Management, 41*(6), 863–877.

Zielke, P., & Waibel, M. (2014). Comparative urban governance of developing creative spaces in China. *Habitat International, 41*, 99–107.

CHAPTER 7

Agricultural Land Conversion and Land Rights in Vietnam: A Case Study of Farmers' Resistance in the Peri-Urban Areas of Hanoi

Thanh Thanh Phan

1 Introduction

Since Doi Moi in 1986, Vietnam has moved from a centrally planned economy to a socialist-oriented market economy. Alongside its social and economic achievements, land conversion has emerged as a painful problem for farmers. Agricultural land is being lost as it is converted for economic and social development projects. Moreover, land management in Vietnam is still based on the principle that land is owned by the people as a whole and is managed by the state. Consequently, when agricultural land is acquired for national defense and security purposes or for

T. T. Phan (✉)
Institute of Human Rights and Peace Studies, Mahidol University, Nakhon Pathom, Thailand

Institute of Human Studies, Vietnam Academy of Social Sciences, Hanoi, Vietnam
e-mail: phanthanhcmu@gmail.com

T. A.-D. Tran (ed.), *Rethinking Asian Capitalism*,
https://doi.org/10.1007/978-3-030-98104-4_7

socio-economic developments for the benefit of the nation and the public, the state can determine when, where, and how the land is to be converted.

The Vietnamese state's ideology lies somewhere between the social and the market economy. This gives rise to various conflicts around land use. The first of these is that between the allocation of land for development or for agricultural use. The second concerns the compensation paid for land purchased for conversion. There are two compensation systems: the government price system and the market price system, which are used depending on whether the land is being disposed of voluntarily or compulsorily. According to the latest Land Act of 2013, land is acquired and purchased compulsorily for the purposes of national security, defense, and socio-economic development for the benefits of the nation and the public (not for the benefit of enterprises or private individuals). Land acquired by domestic investors for commercial purposes should be acquired through voluntary exchange. However, the distinction between socio-economic development for the sake of the nation and the public and development that benefits private individuals is not clearly defined in the 2013 Land Act. The ambiguity in the definition as well as the indeterminate boundaries of the public and private benefits ensuing from compulsory purchase have been exploited in cases of land acquisition for the purposes of national security, defense, socio-economic development for the benefits of the nation and the public, and in many cases of domestic private investment for commercial purposes. Moreover, the cozy relationship between local governments and private investors has consolidated this practice (Nguyen et al., 2015; Sumera, 2017).

Because of such aberrations in land acquisition, rural households are deeply dissatisfied, which has created many tensions and conflicts in Vietnam. These grievances come mainly from land acquisition by domestic investors which are not compulsory land conversions. In the decade after the 2003 Land Act came into force, about 70 to 90 per cent of complaints in the whole country were related to land disputes (Anderson & Davidsen, 2011). Between 2004 and 2009, a total of some 750,000 ha (80 per cent of its agricultural land) was acquired for 29,000 investment projects (Ingalls et al., 2018). The repurposing of agricultural land is most prevalent in suburban areas of big cities such as Hanoi (in the north) and Ho Chi Minh City (in the south) where economic growth is rapid and urbanization has resulted in numerous land disputes (Ingalls et al., 2018).

This chapter will explore the case of farmers' resistance to agricultural land acquisition in Duong Noi—a peri-urban area in Hanoi, Vietnam.

Duong Noi is one of the most prominent cases reported by the Vietnamese media and is well known to the public. To be able to understand the resistance of farmers, theories of rightful resistance, social movement, and citizenship rights will be applied in the context of agricultural land conversion. After describing the data and methodology, research findings will be discussed in the rest of the chapter. The first part will provide an analysis of current land law in Vietnam. The second part will discuss farmers' justification for their resistance. The third part will discuss farmers' resistance strategies and the formal and informal methods adopted. The fourth part will discuss the remaining agricultural land claim as farmers' rights claims. Lastly, conclusions follow.

2 Methodology and Data Collection

The research was conducted in Duong Noi, a peri-urban area of Hanoi. There are several reasons for this. Firstly, the farmers' resistance to the conversion of agricultural land in Duong Noi is one of the most well-known cases among recent agricultural land conflicts reported by the Vietnamese media. The case has drawn a lot of attention from both the public and the government due to their prolonged and active resistance to the local government to protect their land. The case of Duong Noi is among the most well-known cases of agricultural land conversion for development (building new urban areas).

Secondly, Duong Noi is a peri-urban area of Hanoi. It is important to study the case because Hanoi is the capital of the country and has a relatively small area of land available for development, which makes remaining agricultural land attractive to investors. The land value and price after the conversion can be increased many times and significantly. Consequently, its peri-urban areas are usually the targets for rural land conversion due to the pressures of "economic development" and "urbanization and industrialization" policies together with the increasing need for housing for Hanoi's expanding population.

Thirdly, Duong Noi is undergoing rapid urbanization; massive quantities of its agricultural land have been taken for development in a short time. Its local authorities have supported enterprises eager to convert land quickly, since it has contributed to the growth of local budgets and the general economy of the country. It has also changed the face of the city through the construction of modern buildings and the installation of modern infrastructure. However, the creation of alternative jobs has not kept pace with the speed of land acquisition. Farmers losing land lose their livelihoods.

Finally, the compensation price is low compared to the market price. This is an important factor that needs to be explored to understand the farmers' extreme resistance, their social movement, and their rights claims.

To complete this research, data were collected from both secondary and primary sources. The secondary sources used in this study include academic books, journal articles, government reports, governmental and non-governmental statistics, and online media on land dispute cases due to the conversion of agricultural land in peri-urban areas in the whole country in general and in Duong Noi over the last ten years. The information was crosschecked with primary data collection sources via interviews and legal analysis to verify the accuracy and reliability of the information. Those documents were downloaded from the Internet, collected in libraries, or provided by local authorities, government agencies, and local people.

Regarding the primary sources, the data collection process was divided into two stages. The first involved textual analysis of land law, while the second focused on the farmers' resistance and strategies through a case study carried out in Duong Noi in 2019. The case study was conducted by means of in-depth qualitative interviews with key informants. By using **key informant interviews**, researchers can receive different responses from experts (ten people including human rights lawyers, and academics) based on their own understanding and perspectives. The **in-depth interviews** with 30 local people in Duong Noi served to ascertain how farmers resisted the conversion of agricultural land, why there were different forms of resistance, and how the resistance turned into rights claim by the farmers. All names of the informants in this chapter are changed to protect their identities.

3 Land Law in Vietnam and Its Implications in the Case of Duong Noi

3.1 An Analysis of Current Land Law in Vietnam

Land rights in Vietnam have traditionally been divided into three categories—land ownership, land management, and land use—that define different rights and responsibilities (Suu, 2009). All citizens have right of ownership, while the right of management falls to the state; right of use is granted to individuals, households, and organizations for a certain period of time, depending on the type of land (Suu, 2009).

As the economy grows, the demand for land for industrialization, modernization, and urbanization grows rapidly, and the value of land increases rapidly, especially in rural and suburban areas. In accordance with the Land Law of 2003, compensation on land pricing causes disagreement between compensated individuals and the state not only because of the unsatisfied compensation of land compared to the market price but also because of the intangible values such as livelihood, lifestyle, and culture of people in land conversion. The Land Law in 2003 allows the state to confiscate land, including agricultural land, for economic development purposes. While this provision is intended to encourage industrial and urban development, it also raises many land disputes. Farmers do not voluntarily lose their land but receive very low compensation.

Under the latest land law in 2013, there are still two cases of land acquisition: the first for national security and defense in Article 61 and the second for the economic, social development for public purposes in Article 62. In the first case, the government directly plans the area, location, and level of compensation and implementation of the project without consulting individuals and households owning land use rights. In the law, compulsory land acquisition in Vietnam is applicable only for purposes of security, national defense, and foreign investment; commercial and private projects of investors are not subject to compulsory land acquisition and investors must negotiate with households with land use right certificates for land compensation based on market mechanisms. Although the limitation of land acquisition "for public purposes" has been restricted by law, in practice, terms such as "public interest' and "national interest" are vague, and it cannot restrict state decisions on land acquisition for economic and social purposes. In practice, local governments often engage in land confiscation process for real estate projects in the name of land use planning or new city development. The compensation level is lower than the land market value and often leads to disagreements and conflicts.

In addition, the land law of 2013 also allowed local governments to purchase land for the purpose of socio-economic development and urban development. Accordingly, state-owned constructions such as high-tech zones, industrial parks, and new urban areas serve "public interests." Under current land law, the government can recover land based on the land use planning which allocates to different levels of government. The land use planning represents the "public interests" for urban development. The land use plan reflected the idea of state intervention in the land market, and it became an important tool for state-owned development projects. Moreover, land use planning in Vietnam demonstrates the will of the government in local development rather than market demand and becomes the legal basis for local investment. The existing planning system in Vietnam has abused the centralized power so that there is a lack of community participation in the planning and approval process. Land use planning is therefore thought to be a tool for the state to manage land use rather than to represent "public purposes."

The 2013 Land Act also made some modest improvements. Firstly, in Article 126, it extended rights of use for agricultural and forestry land of individuals, organizations, and enterprises from 20 years to 50 years. The term of land use for production and business in economic zones is not over 70 years according to Article 151. Secondly, investors who acquire land must provide two plans: the first being a compensation assistance and the second a resettlement plan as stipulated in Article 53. Thirdly, the same Article 53 stipulates that the compensation must be paid before the land is cleared. Fourthly, if the previous rights holder still argues that the compensation price is too low, an independent land appraisal will be carried out, if necessary, as stipulated in Articles 115.1.b and 115.3.

However, there are no dramatic differences between the 2003 Land Act and the current act. The basic problems that give rise to land disputes remain largely unresolved. The old challenges remain. First, the government retains absolute power. It retains all the rights to manage and allocate land. Private land rights remain subordinate to the absolute power of the state over land management, allocation, and acquisition Second, there are the continuing challenges of differentiating between the public and private spheres and between public and private benefits. For example, for whose benefit are the new urban areas being built? Third, there are parallel compensation systems for loss of land. One is based on the governmental land price compensation system for compulsory purchases and the other on the market price of land in the event of voluntary transactions. Finally, the national strategy on promoting industrialization, modernization, and urbanization still plays a role in land conversion and is reflected in both land law and policies. By promoting economic development, the local authorities are empowered in land management issues while central government still plays the key role in national land planning.

3.2 *The Implications of Land Law in the Case of Duong Noi*

There were conflicts around land rights before the 2013 Land Act, mainly due to land acquisition for socio-economic purposes. Conflicts and complaints about land arise because, firstly, land compensation prices are not satisfactory. One of the sources of conflict is the difference in land compensation prices for the same type of land. There is a gap in state policy in determining the land price framework. For example, land in other areas close to Duong Noi was acquired at higher prices. Moreover, in the areas of high economic value land in Duong Noi (e.g., land for planting peach trees), farmers also have a lot of concerns about the compensation price for land because, in their opinion, the compensation price for agricultural land is too low compared to the market price. The second is the difference in the land clearance process. The compensation price for agricultural land under the state framework is very low. Even in this case of recovery for socio-economic purposes, the land is still subject to the state price rather than the market price as prescribed. Besides, even the inconsistent compensation price in the community itself is also causing conflict. Exemplary households (e.g., people or families having children working as government officials, Party members, those working in government agencies or people with meritorious services to the Revolution [together with the Communist Party]) are usually the leaders in the implementation of state policies and guidelines. They accepted early clearance and handed over their agricultural land early and received lower compensation prices than those who delayed land conversion. This has given rise to discontent and these exemplary households have complained about the lower compensation they received compared with those who dragged their feet, even though they are supposed to be "exemplary" households. However, in the areas where households switched from farming to operating small businesses before the time of the land conversion and where young people tend to work in the city, attachment to the land is weaker and people are less likely to struggle than the elderly, women, and middle-aged people who are unlikely to change their current livelihoods.

Secondly, the change of land use from agricultural to residential led to an excessive increase in the price differential. In the past, when the land was used for agricultural purposes only, farmers lost their land for a very low price as determined by the state framework. But after development, the value of that land rose by many hundreds of percent, making farmers who lost land feel very annoyed while their current jobs are not guaranteed.

Thirdly, the whole process of land acquisition has some problems. In many cases, the local authorities acquired farmers' land on behalf of businesses. This is unreasonable because the business buyers must work directly with the farmer-owners as negotiators, not through local government intermediaries. Moreover, they did not consult the farmers on the impacts on the farmers' cultural, economic, and social life before acquiring the land.

Fourthly, the way that local government deals with people's requests, proposals, and suggestions leaves much to be desired, leading to many years of unresolved complaints. Moreover, large swathes of agricultural land have been converted to commercial use, but many projects are still suspended because much real estate cannot be sold. That is, the land has been acquired for development but left unused for many years. People lose their livelihood, and the development project has not yet been started.

Finally, and most importantly, conflicts arise because people are not actively and meaningfully consulted on land valuation, planning, acquisition, resettlement, and career change. Participation should be a right for all people, with all decisions relating to planning, compensation, support, and implementation having to be approved by the people.

4 Conditions for Resistance in Duong Noi

Studies of the nature of farmers and the conditions for their resistance and various political actions in Vietnam as well as in Southeast Asia in colonial times have drawn on several theories.

Scott's moral economy theory is based on the principles of fairness, equality, and justice and developed from his study of farmers' movements in Southeast Asia in 1976. The moral economy was established in the closed context of traditional villages, where patron-client relations between farmers and landlords were close and interdependent. Scott concluded that this relationship was strong because poor farmers often had to resort to asking wealthier people in the village for assistance during difficult times while the richer were obliged to provide and protect the most basic and essential needs of the poor in the village. In addition, poor farmers often had limited financial resources and consequently had to bear higher risks when participating in an open market economy. Thus, the top priority for poor farmers was the right to subsistence. Once the traditional relationship was broken, poor farmers' right to subsistence was no longer guaranteed and resistance became inevitable (Scott, 1976). The recurrent economic problem of peasant life is the ecological precariousness of the food supply; therefore, those who control the scarce resources of the society are responsible for the basic material requirements of their subordinates. Here the norm of reciprocity and the right to subsistence are firmly joined. It is the right to subsistence that defines the key reciprocal duty of elites, the minimal obligation that they owe to those from whom they claim labor and gain. (Scott, 1976, p. 182)

However, in the case of Duong Noi, the argument has some limits. The village of Duong Noi is geographically closer to the center of Hanoi. In addition, the lifestyle of the people in this area has also changed more due to rapid urbanization from land acquisition for construction of commercial infrastructure such as new urban areas and shopping centers. Specifically, in the struggle for compensation for agricultural land in Duong Noi, there are two separate groups of farmers, with different forms of struggle emerging.

> Unlike Duong Noi's Can Thi Theu farmers group, who chose the collective suing method by writing a collective petition to claim back their lost agricultural land so the farmers can continue to work the land, the Duong Thi Khue group have gone down the route of individual petitions but joined together to demand an increase in the land compensation rate. (Mrs. Huong, Duong Noi, interviewed in February 2019 in Hanoi, Vietnam)

Since they no longer live in a closed village and agricultural environment, some Duong Noi farmers groups are not fighting to reclaim agricultural land but demanding compensation in accordance with the law.

> Now we cannot ask them to return our land as they have built apartments already. Now we only claim 10% service land for us to do business. (Mrs. Huong, Duong Noi, interviewed in February 2019 in Hanoi, Vietnam)

In contrast to Scott, Popkin advanced a new theory of political economy in 1979, arguing that every farmer was a rational individual. Peasants could adapt to the new market economy and maximize its benefits. Popkin further argued that farmers were not forced to enter the market economy but would do so if they could see economic opportunities within it (Popkin, 1979). Thus, Popin's argument is better suited to the Duong Noi farmers' struggle than Scott's subsistence argument.

Kerkvliet, in his research in 2014, agreed with Scott's argument, in the sense that for farmers in Vietnam the right to subsistence is still important. However, he argues that they protest not only because of "subsistence" or because they cannot depend on the village structure, or the other wealthy farmers. By emphasizing the right to equal negotiation of land acquisition prices, these farmers have entered the market economy (compensation should be based not on the state price but on the market price) (Kerkvliet, 2014). He further argued that those farmers who have family members who shed blood for the country use "fairness" and "justice" as arguments to support their claims to keep the agricultural land for the tillers and not to be grabbed for any other reason (Kerkvliet, 2014).

However, rather than simply drawing on a moral economy or political argument to explain the nature of farmers' resistance, Suu argues further that these conflicts of beliefs, views, values, and benefits are the main causes of moral and political conflicts in Vietnam (Suu, 2007). Policies that overlap or are compatible with people's views can be implemented. On the contrary, policies that go against their views and interests will face more opposition and stronger resistance, ranging from peaceful protests to more public and violent protests. And the evidence is that these farmers' protests contributed to a change in government decision-making processes and the behavior and attitudes of local officials toward the villagers (Suu, 2007). In the context of Duong Noi, I agree with Suu on these points. However, I also argue that the lack of farmers' political participation in the land conversion process is the main reason why the different views and values cannot be reconciled.

Based on my research on Duong Noi, I will propose the following conditions for the farmers' resistance about land conversion:

(1) A rising awareness of unjust and unfair situations among farmers. People's repeated frustration with complaints that remain unresolved for lengthy periods, and the government's concessions and conclusions that adversely affect people's land rights and are a potential risk for both the government and the farmers.

(2) The lack of right to participation in all matters related to farmers' lives, including land management, led to the conflict between the people and local authorities in the Duong Noi incident. Grievances about this lack of right to participate came to a head on 17 March 2008 at the People's Committee of Duong Noi Commune, Ha Dong, when a completely spontaneous protest by local people

broke out because the farmers were completely surprised by the local authority's announcement of its policy to compulsorily purchase almost 100% of the agricultural land.

(3) Leaders play an important role in the land movement in Duong Noi. They are sharp people, reasoning, arguing, being brave, and displaying a great deal of spirit in fighting for what they consider to be righteous and fair. The characteristics of the leaders of the land movement of the farmers are (a) their ability to communicate farmers' concerns verbally, to connect sources of information and to dialogue with the government. (b) At the same time, they must also be the ones with strong personalities, with a certain awareness, able to influence and persuade and be attractive to others. In the case of Mrs. Huong in Duong Noi with her verbal fluency, strong spirit, and understanding of the law, even though her educational background is only secondary school level, she became the leader of the movement in Duong Noi. Often farmers who hold leadership roles have a strong personality and a certain economic potential and a certain legal knowledge, which stands them in good stead in dealing with the authorities and the risks they may encounter in resisting the acquisition of their land for development. In the case of Duong Noi, the leaders of the protests in the disputed area are located near the center of the capital, have relatively high intellectual levels, and have access to the Internet and to technologies such as mobile phones and social networks. Those leaders use all these available resources to exercise their political rights. (c) The motivation of the leaders is to fight for the rights of all (fight for righteousness, for justice to repel social injustice), not personal gain, thereby gaining the trust of their followers.

(4) A peak conflict event escalates the resistance as participants become more and more excited, engaged, and connected.

In 2007, a part of the commune's agricultural land was acquired for land clearance on Le Trong Tan Street, although the price paid was thought to be lower than in other areas (compared to La Khe) but there was no significant counter-reaction. At the same time, people began to see local government officials measuring land in the commune's fields and rumors spread that all the agricultural land was to be taken; however, not many people were paying attention. In July 2007, when the Nam Cuong Company was building a concrete mixing station on Duong Noi fields and built houses for their workers, people spilled into the fields to destroy those (a concrete mixing station and houses for their workers to build new apartments), but the Commune People's Committee remained silent.

In 2008, at the beginning of the year, the whole village was still peaceful, the festival was cheerful and bustling, but the news spread that the local authority was to acquire more than 400 hectares of Duong Noi commune land with the following compensation policy: compensation (multiple amounts together including compensation for land, crops, trainings) at 97 million VND or around 4000 USD/1sao or 360 m2, the local government also promised to allow farmers to retain 10% of the conversion land, calling it "service land" for farmers to use for their new livelihood. At village meetings, people began to complain about the compensation value as it was low compared to the economic value of agricultural land. Psychologically, people were confused because agricultural land is the village's most important source of livelihood.

In March 2008, farmers gathered in many places in villages and communes and unanimously agreed not to dispose of land; in the whole of La Ca village, there were only about three or four people who intended to dispose of their land. People were increasingly coming to the commune to question the local authorities. Local government representatives had to answer these questions, but they were unable to satisfy the people and the commune authorities were paralyzed for about two to three weeks. The oppositional atmosphere grew ever more intense: "it felt like at that time it was never possible to get the land of the people" (Mr. Quang, leader of the residential group in Duong Noi Ward, interviewed in February 2019 in Hanoi, Vietnam).

Every unsatisfactory response from the local government representatives made people angry (Mr. Lich, the commune secretary, accidentally broke the picture of Uncle Ho of the fighters; a local radio officer rushed to a demonstrator, then to a group of angry people, eager to seek "criminals" immediately). Across the village, gongs sounded continuously, groups of people gathered in the village's public areas, such as under the banyan tree, in front of the commune cultural house, at road junctions and at people's houses; the atmosphere was lively, nobody was sleeping. Village and commune officials were under great pressure, many officials did not dare to leave their houses for fear of being insulted or having bricks thrown at them. At night, people banged gongs and drums outside the houses of commune officials, preventing them from sleeping. Those drums were banged so much they eventually had to be replaced. Mr.

Son–acting commune president whose house was pelted with stones and even bricks and whose water tank and gate house were covered with excrement. People planted banana trees in front of his gate to curse him to die quickly, the bananas were brought to the gate, and incense sticks were lit. Mr. Son's mother had to go to the gate house to beg the villagers to forgive her son. (Mr. Quang, leader of the residential group in Duong Noi Ward, interviewed in February 2019 in Hanoi, Vietnam)

People in the villages all agreed not to sign the documents allocating the land to the authorities, who feared the agreement would have severe consequences, not only alienation and estrangement from the entire village but that they would also be subjected to the most severe spiritual punishment: when their parents died, there would be no one (in the village) to carry and bury them.

April 2008 was peak stress time for Mr. Le Hong Thang, chairman of Ha Dong District People's Committee, who had to stand explaining the matter to the people the whole afternoon. However, his audience remained unsatisfied with his answers. People encircled the Commune People's Committee. More and more groups of people came, and Mr. Thang could not return home and had to stay in the Duong Noi Commune People's Committee building during the night of April 30 to May 1. The people agreed to disperse only when he promised to acquire the land only when more than 50% of the people had agreed to the reallocation.

Between 2008 and 2009, the atmosphere was calmer; some people were talking about taking compensation, and conflict began to form in each family where there were many conflicting opinions around consent to land acquisition. But in general, the movement against land acquisition still attracted most people in the village; each group of petitioners persisted in the provincial People's Committee for many days. Some people were arrested, some fled away, some temporarily sheltered. The movement started to fade away and gradually the number of people fighting was not as large as before. By December 31, 2009, majority of opponents were forced to give up their land, marking the end of the struggle against the reallocation of agricultural land in the whole village. There were only about 400 households still involved in the movement after that with the leads of two groups named "Duong Thi Khue" and "Can Thi Thue".

5 Farmers' Resistance Strategies: Lawful Resistance and Beyond

5.1 Peaceful Forms of Resistance

Resistance plays out in a context of unequal power relations and social change and may constitute an organized threat to a nation's instituted form of governance. However, according to Scott in one of his studies in Malaysia, the term "resistance" here has a weaker meaning because people in subordinate positions have little choice in the forms of resistance available to them for fear of being overwhelmed. They choose various forms of "everyday resistance" as the "weapons of the weak"; they include various forms of non-compliance, pilfering, desertion, feigned ignorance, slander, arson, sabotage, etc. (Scott, 1985).

O'Brien and Li's concept of "rightful resistance" closely resembles Scott's concept of "everyday resistance". While Scott describes the concept of "everyday resistance" as the weapon of the weak, O'Brien and Li argue that "rightful resistance" relies on noisy and public challenges. However, just like "everyday resistance," "rightful resistance" also avoids risks by stepping away from actions and discourse that go against and challenge the core political values of ruling institutions (O'Brien & Li, 1996). Although "everyday resistance" is characterized by its silent and less-organized factors, Scott in 1985 argued that those forms of resistance are preconditions for the more direct, public, and open forms of resistance, such as public protests and organized petitions (Scott, 1985, Kerkvliet 2009). Moreover, the active roles taken by the local protesters also influence the other local farmers who are less active to get involved in the resistance and make use of collective action as well as strengthening the resisters' networks (Schneider, 2011). At this point, the resistance has been transformed into a social movement where people are more organized in their collective action to address the change. However, certain conditions must be met if the resistance is to become a social movement. First, the resisters need to adopt a more open approach to allow more people to participate and to share their opinions (Nguyen et al., 2015). Second, the resistance needs a leader to bring people together (Nguyen et al., 2015).

The cases of Duong Noi have factors of everyday resistance and rightful resistance. (1) When it comes to everyday resistance, farmers have ways to show their disagreement in everyday life. In the case of Duong Noi, farmers use strong language to protest and convey the message to express themselves (insulting authorities on FB, in public, and with slogans on banners). They also call for the participation of a wide range of people and intellectuals in society. (2) The leaders in Duong Noi are brave people and have a certain understanding of the current laws (procedural law, land law).

The notion of "rightful resistance" is based on more public and noisy protests. The concept "rightful resistance" was first coined by O'Brien in 1996 in his article on the context of land conflicts in rural China (O'Brien & Li, 1996). The term was re-applied in the studies by Gillespie et al., 2014, Kerkvliet and Benedict in 2014, Labbe in 2011, and Steur and Das in 2009, which discussed the struggle for land rights in rural Vietnam. Rightful resistance is a popular, institutionalized form of dispute directed at the government due to the grievances that it creates in society (O'Brien & Li, 1996). Rightful resistance has two main characteristics. First, it takes advantage of existing laws, policies, or discourses of the nation state to form the basis for protests and resistance (O'Brien & Li, 1996). However, it does not challenge the legitimacy of the ruler. On the contrary, it accepts the legitimacy of the laws, policies, and core political values of the State but opposes it only when the government fails to fulfill its promises or has defied laws or widely accepted values for certain purposes. Second, rightful resisters accept the principle of non-violence and make use of peaceful protests, petitions, complaints, other legal channels, and dissent as weapons for dialogue with the authorities. Their purpose is to actively seek the attention of elites and influence public opinion by means of open and widespread protests (O'Brien & Li, 1996).

In the case of Duong Noi, firstly, they made use of state laws and regulations to claim their rightful benefits and rights. Their resistance strategy was based on the right to complain and denounce, as recognized by the state. Duong Thi Khue's farmers group in Duong Noi emphasized the mistakes in land conversion procedures and administrative lawsuits. In the process of appealing, the group made reference to the National Assembly's law on complaints, the law of denunciation, land law, and the regulations on clearance. It was because their complaint was based on decision No. 18 on the clearance of the Hanoi People's Committee, signed on September 29, 2008, that they achieved the following results. On May 4, 2012, their households received the conclusion of the government inspector signed by Mr. Nguyen Van Thanh, deputy general inspector of the government. On the same day, Mr. Nguyen Van Thanh signed document number 1080, which contained the general content of both the delegation of Mrs. Can

Thi Theu and Mrs. Duong Thi Khue (Ms. Huong's delegation) but was clearly divided into two parts. Due to the conclusions of the government inspector, Duong Noi people benefited from the land service allocation policy (land for small businesses for new livelihood in the local area). However, they received only 6.2% of service land instead of 10% as promised in accordance with Decree 84. In terms of their achievement, the amount of 22,607,592,480 VND (equal to 974,274.20 USD) was the compensation gained for the farmers.

However, the framework of rightful resistance still could not fully explain methods of the resistance in Duong Noi. The protesters in the case even challenged the current limited rights recognized by the law and demanded more rights in the name of justice and fairness. Protestors are not always peaceful; they are sometimes aggressive in asserting their land rights which include political rights: the right to participation, negotiation, information, and association.

5.2 *Contesting Resistance: Challenging the Current Values and Laws*

There is no single definition of what constitutes a social movement. For Shannon, it is "persistent, organized, and collective efforts to resist existing power structures, cultural repertoires, and practices and elite dominance and oppression or to introduce changes in them" (Glasberg & Shannon, 2010, p. 150). For John McCarthy and Mayer Zald, it is "a set of opinions and beliefs in a population which represents preferences for changing some elements of the social structure and/or reward distribution of a society" (McCarthy & Zald, 1977, pp. 1217–1218). For Sidney Tarrow, it is defined as "collective challenges, based on common purposes and social solidarities, in sustained interaction with elites, opponents, and authorities" (Tarrow, 2011, p. 9). In sum, social movements are characterized by (1) commonality of purpose; (2) collective action via series of contentious events, displays, and campaigns; (3) some degree of organization; and (4) an organized effort over a period to promote or resist change in society.

As far as theories of social movements are concerned, three relevant theories will be applied here, namely (1) the theory of relative deprivation and political process to answer the question of why farmers resist and (2) resource mobilization theory to answer the question of how farmers resist.

Deprivation theory argues that people of less powerful groups who often find themselves deprived of goods and resources are more likely to organize or join a social movement to defend and claim their rights (Morrison, 1978). This relative deprivation means that, when the group feels that they are worst off or have not received a "fair share" of available resources compared to others around them, then social conflicts arise. According to Morrison, a certain structural condition also increases the probability of a social movement emerging. It is when many people experience a similar kind of situation of relative deprivation.

Social movements are seen as arenas in which the processes of organizing, mobilizing, and making strategic choices educate participants about their rights. These processes create the means for people to exercise their rights. An awareness among farmers of the need to protect their land rights in the cases of land conversion led to struggles to claim other rights and to operationalize the legal content of citizenship via public contest and demands for rights. It is clear that "the waves of protest" in this context motivated the struggle for rights (land rights and other rights by extension) and disseminated the sense of individual rights (rights to participation, information, and association) via forms of collective action.

However, deprivation theory cannot fully explain the social movement/farmers' resistance in Duong Noi because, firstly, it cannot explain why some farmers groups experience deprivation and form social movements to resist while others do not. This leads to the second problem, which is the question of whether deprivation is the sole necessary condition for the emergence of farmers' resistance.

To fill this gap in the theory, I also apply the theory of resource mobilization. Resources for a social movement are knowledge, money, media, labor, solidarity, legitimacy, and internal and external support from powerful elites. Those resources explain why some groups suffering deprivation cannot form a protest while others can (McCarthy & Zald, 1977). Therefore, instead of arguing that discontent in society is the motive for the formation of a social movement, this theory argues that there is always enough discontent in any society to supply the grass-roots support for a movement if the movement is effectively organized and has at its disposal the power and resources of some established elite groups (Turner, 1986).

In the case of agricultural land conflict in Duong Noi, the local resisters did not receive any support from politicians, the resisters were also labeled as "public order disruptor," and "against people on duty." Four protest leaders were convicted from ten to twenty months in prison. As the weaker, they were creating resources such as symbols and identities for resistance. In this case, farmers used symbols accepted by the government and the Communist Party, such as the Vietnamese flag, the Communist flag, and pictures of Ho Chi Minh as strategies to protest and establish their identities as farmers (attached to agriculture and traditional livelihoods and culture) and part of the nation-building process (those who shed blood for the nation's independence in times of war) in support of their claim for land rights.

To fill this gap, the theory of political process also helps to further explore the conditions for farmers' resistance. This theory focuses on (1) insurgent consciousness, (2) organizational strength, and (3) political opportunities for developing social movements. Insurgent consciousness is shaped by deprivation and grievances, similarly to the first theory. The insurgent consciousness is the collective sense of injustice that precipitates a social movement. Organizational strength is like resource mobilization theory in the sense that it emphasizes the importance of leadership and resources in forming a social movement. The only added point is political opportunity. Its main argument is that, even if both the above conditions are satisfied, a social movement can develop only within a favorable political environment, such as a political culture of pluralism, supported by opposition elites/politicians. Consequently, a social movement cannot develop successfully in a political environment that offers few, if any, opportunities.

One of the advantages of the political process theory is that it addresses the issue of timing or emergence of social movements. Some groups may have the insurgent consciousness and resources to mobilize, but because there are no political opportunities, they will not have any chance of success. The theory, then, argues that all three of these components are equally important.

However, the theory also argues that people tend to participate in protests when they find that the risks are minimized while the benefits/results could be great (for themselves and/or the society as a whole). However, in a confined public political space/authoritarian society, the theory cannot fully explain the emergence of social movements. Events in Vietnam shows that even in a closed context, the farmers' movement has achieved some successes, as is argued in Suu's, 2007 article, even though their demands might not have been completely fulfilled. For other political debates (related to public land acquired for development), public opinions have also been considered by the Party according to Andrew-Well Dang's argument in the case of Hanoi Reunion Park (Wells-Dang, 2010).

In the case of Duong Noi, the farmers' strategy was, firstly, to use unwritten norms and codes of ethics and justice to claim the rights they deserved, including the villagers' dedication to the protection of the country in the past. Secondly, they counted on protesters joining them in large numbers and made use of collective actions (persuading many families in the village to join, including their relatives and neighbors). When the movement disintegrated, the key pillars of the movement used sharp speeches and powerful words to confront and attack the government and regularly streamed on social networks to inform more people about their movement. Thirdly, as their numbers declined and the village itself began to disintegrate, the active fighters in this village linked up with other land movements throughout the country to learn from each other and share experiences, to improve their legal knowledge and combat skills and to seek outside support in their pursuit of justice. However, one of the things that the activist families had in common was that their economic situation became more difficult than that of other households in the village because they had spent so much time, money, and effort in claiming their rights and benefits but had not received expected results.

6 Remaining Agricultural Land Claim as Rights Claim: Citizenship Rights

As I have argued above, the resistance to land conversion has moved beyond a claim for land rights to become a fight for the extension of rights. In the economic sphere, the rights in question are those to sustainable livelihoods and to equal and fair agricultural land compensation. Politically, they are the rights to participation, information, and association. However, without citizenship rights, it is impossible for farmers to form their social movement successfully.

To articulate my argument, I use the argument by Borras and France in 2010 that due to the economic and symbolic values embedded in land, the land distribution process has become a process of raising political rights. According to Bottazzi and Rist, "Tenure reforms are closely related to the recognition of stakeholders' political rights, and political issues related to various groups' struggles for territorial autonomy" (Bottazzi & Rist, 2012). The resistance on the land has moved beyond the issues of claiming land rights to become a campaign for a political restructuring between the central and the local levels and between the local authorities and the farmers. Farmers groups protesting against the government built their own parallel structure for integrating multiple levels of governance and challenged the government's current strategy and policies on land conversion (Bottazzi & Rist, 2012). Therefore, the fight for land rights accidentally or deliberately also became a fight for political rights. More importantly, the result of the farmer's land conversion movement in Vietnam led to more political empowerment for them as well as to a decentralization process from the central to the local level, improving their resistance skills and legal knowledge as well as diversifying their strategies for negotiation with different levels (from local to central authorities, from local policemen to national court staff). Again, from the resistance on the ground, land claims should be considered as a political process involving institutional diversity, political rights, and individual rights rather than being considered simply as a means of implementing economic rights.

Achieving true citizenship is a political process that needs certain conditions to be fulfilled. These conditions include the existence of constitutional forms, political practices, and campaigning social movements (Foweraker & Landman, 1997). More importantly, citizenship must be understood in terms of rights won through social struggle by subordinate groups (Tarrow, 1990). The general rights of citizenship are freedom of speech, expression, belief, information, as well as freedom of association, etc. Because citizenship rights have a great impact on "political rights and obligation", social inclusion and participation are "inevitably about the rights of citizenship" (Turner, 1986, p. 92). In other words, citizenship is the result of "the way in which different groups, classes, and movements have struggled to gain degrees of autonomy and control over their lives in the face of various forms of stratification, hierarchy and political oppression" (Held, 1989, p. 199). However, there is a huge gap between theoretical rights and actual rights. There are rights that only can be achieved through struggle (Barbalet 1988, p. 16). These rights are freedom of thought, freedom of speech, and freedom of assembly through which "citizens have to organize in defense of their own interests and identities" (Fox, 1994, p. 152). During their campaign to save their agricultural land, protesters in Duong Noi used political rights (right to sue, petition, participate) to demand their land rights.

7 Conclusion

The ambiguity of Vietnam's 2013 Land Act means that there is a lack of clarity about the ability of many subjects to claim their rights and interests over an asset with overlapping rights and interests. Moreover, the law still emphasizes the overall role of the state while focusing less on the participation of other stakeholders in land use and management. Article 62 of the Act shows that its political intention is more important than its legal content. Here, politics is the decisive factor, in that it can quickly change economic and social policies to ensure significant economic development without any risk of political instability. For those decision makers, the tragedies of farmers caused by land acquisition are temporary and necessary if they benefit the nation's development. Because these tragic decisions are made for the national and public benefit, they are still politically, morally, and legally accepted. Moreover, land acquisition for the purpose of national defense and security as stated in Article 61 of the 2013 Act shows its biased nature by the fact that it values the right of the state higher than the right of the ordinary people. Hence, in the case of agricultural land acquisition, land becomes an important source of income as well as power for the state while farmers' rights and their land rights are of secondary importance. Above all, land is managed by the state and land acquisition is considered reasonable if it serves national interests and public interests as defined by the state.

Farmers' strategies are varied and both formal and informal in character as they seek to influence public opinion as well as political and legal decisions taken by the Party and the state. The case of Duong Noi shows the vibrant roles of leaders in their resistance as well as the important role of citizenship rights that they are exercising to claim for the farmers' rights.

The case of Duong Noi shows that public resistance here emerged because of the conflicts of perceptions, views, and profits on land rights. The justification of farmers is based on the grounds of "fairness," "equality," and "the fight against corruption" as they blame the misconduct of the local cadre and lack of popular participation in the implementation of the land conversion process.

References

Anderson, J., & Davidsen, S. (2011). *Recognizing and reducing corruption risks in land management in Vietnam*. National Political Publishing House.

Foweraker, J., & Landman, T. (1997). *Citizenship rights and social movements: A comparative and statistical analysis*. Oxford University Press.

Fox, J. (1994). The difficult transition from clientelism to citizenship. *World Politics, 46*, 151–184.

Gillespie, J., Fu, H., & Nghia, P. D. (2014). *Land-Taking Disputes in East Asia: A Comparative Analysis and Implications for Vietnam*. Report prepared for UNDP Vietnam 2014, May.

Glasberg, D. S., & Shannon, D. (2010). *Political sociology: Oppression, resistance, and the state*. SAGE Publications.

Held, D. (1989). *Citizenship: And autonomy in political theory and the modern state*. Polity Press.

Kerkvliet, B. (2014). Protests over land in Vietnam: Rightful resistance and more. Journal of Vietnamese Studies 9, no. 3: 19–54.

McCarthy, J., & Zald, M. N. (1977). Resource mobilization and social movements: A partial theory. *The American Journal of Sociology, 82*(6), 1217–1218.

Ingalls, M. L., Diepart, J. C., Truong, N., Hayward, D., Niel, T., Sem, T., Phomphakdy, M., Bernhard, R., Fogarizzu, S. and Epprecht, M. (2018). *The Mekong state of land. Centre for development and environment, University of Bern and Mekong Region Land Governance*. Bern Open Publishing (BOP).

Nguyen, Q. P., Zoomers, A., & Van Westen, A. C. M. (2015). Compulsory land acquisition for urban expansion : A study of farmer's protest in peri-urban Hue, Central Vietnam. In *Land grabbing, conflict and agrarian-environmental transformations: Perspectives from East and Southeast Asia* (pp. 1–19). BRICS Initiatives for Critical Agrarian Studies (BICAS); MOSAIC Research Project; Land Deal politics Initiative (LDPI); RCSD Chiang Mai University; Transnational Institute.

O'Brien, K. J., & Li, L. (1996). Rightful resistance in rural China. *World Politics, 49*(1), 31–55.

Popkin, S. L. (1979). *The rational peasant: The political economy of rural society in Vietnam*. University of California Press.

Schneider, A. E. (2011). What shall we do without our land? Land grabs and resistance in Rural Cambodia. Paper presented at the international conference on Global land grabbing organized by the Land Deals Politics Initiative (LDPI), 6-8 April.

Scott, J. C. (1985). *Weapons of the weak: Everyday forms of peasant resistance*. Yale University Press.

Scott, J. C. (1976). *The moral economy of the peasant: Rebellion and subsistence in Southeast Asia*. Yale University Press.

Sumera, C. V. (2017). Hanoi Vietnam's Peri-urban Space and Its Impact on People's Livelihoods. International Development, Community and Environment (IDCE).

Suu, N. V. (2009). Agricultural land conversion and its effects on farmers in contemporary Vietnam. *Focaal-European Journal of Anthropology, 2009*(54), 106–113.

Suu, N. V. (2007). Contending views and conflicts over land in Vietnam's Red River Delta. *Journal of Southeast Asian Studies, 38*(2), 309–334.

Tarrow, S. G. (2011). *Power in movement: Social movements and contentious politics.* Cambridge University Press.

Tarrow, S. G. (1990). *Struggle, politics and reform: Collective action, social movements, and cycles of protest.* Cornell Studies in International Affairs, Western Societies Program.

Tria Kerkvliet, B. J. (2009). Everyday politics in peasant societies (and ours). *The Journal of Peasant Studies, 36*(1), 227–243.

Turner, B. S. (1986). *Citizenship and capitalism: The debate over reformism.* Allen and Unwin.

Wells-Dang, A. (2010). Political space in Vietnam: A view from the "rice-roots". *Pacific Review, 23*(1), 93–112.

CHAPTER 8

Philanthropy in Việt Nam: A Field Study

Ninh Ton-Nu-Thi

Abbreviations

CSR	Corporate Social Responsibility
ESG	Environmental, Social, and Governance
HNWI	High Net Worth Individuals
HNWF	High Net Worth Families
INGO	International Non-governmental Organization
NGO	Non-governmental Organization
NPO	Nonprofit Organization
SDO	Social Delivery Organization
SPO	Social Purpose Organization
VWU	Việt Nam Women's Union

1 Introduction

The Hồ Chí Minh City Peace and Development Foundation's (HPDF) mission is to promote necessary societal awareness of emerging, pressing issues. Việt Nam has declared its resolve to become a developed country

N. Ton-Nu-Thi (✉)
Ho Chi Minh City Peace and Development Foundation,
Ho Chi Minh City, Vietnam

T. A.-D. Tran (ed.), *Rethinking Asian Capitalism*,
https://doi.org/10.1007/978-3-030-98104-4_8

by 2045. Việt Nam has indeed moved into the lower ranks of the middle-income countries (MIC) group since 2010. However, if Việt Nam is to aim at inclusive and sustainable development, avoid the middle-income trap, and achieve this ambitious goal, it will have to tackle the daunting challenges of income disparities and other social inequalities and tensions, and to fully and adequately integrate the social dimension and the social sector in the overall development strategy for 2045. One significant challenge for Việt Nam's sustainable development today is to recognize and valorize the role and contribution of nonprofit, philanthropy, and other actors to the country's social sector and society at large.

In view of this, HPDF has conducted a field study of the philanthropy ecosystem in Việt Nam through 68 in-depth face-to-face interviews with founders and leaders of nonprofit organizations as well as a number of corporate philanthropists and other influencers, along with 5 focus group discussions involving over 90 participants from the philanthropy community.

2 The Philanthropy Community and Space in Việt Nam

To answer the questions whether there is a philanthropy ecosystem in Việt Nam and in the affirmative, what its characteristics are, and how it contributes to the social sector here, we need to look from different angles or perspectives.

If we adopt the traditional definition of philanthropy as voluntary action for the public good, then we can indeed assert that doing good practices have existed for a long time in Việt Nam, and over time, a community has emerged of charity—philanthropy actors increasingly aware of and opening up the philanthropy space of action and impact.

These actors, members and stakeholders of the philanthropy community, whether organizations or individuals, share to different degrees and in various forms such broadly recognized criteria as (1) intentionality (desire to do good) or purpose (social purpose), (2) explicit target community (e.g., the underserved; the vulnerable), (3) not for profit rather than non-profit, (4) voluntary (vs. mandatory), (5) private (in terms of funding).

The philanthropy sector is often called the nonprofit sector but might in fact be more suitably called not-for-profit sector: if social enterprises are to be considered part of the philanthropy space, the latter can only be labeled not-for-profit, meaning that social enterprises fit the intentionality as well as the not-for-profit criterion, that is, they need to generate revenue and even profit but without a profit first approach, rather generate profit or revenue for income generation to support their operations and thus their sustainability.

To qualify as philanthropy the voluntary and the private dimensions are traditionally emphasized. Thus, social services delivered not for profit by public agencies would not qualify as within the philanthropy sub-sector because they are mandatory in nature, not voluntary. They can belong only to the broader social sector.

The organizations within the philanthropy community may be micro-scale to very large (by Vietnamese standards) as illustrated by Vingroup conglomerate Vinif's (Vingroup Innovation Foundation) 2019–2020 disbursement of some 20 million USD or its Thiện Tâm/Kind Heart Foundation's yearly budget of some 30 million USD.

They may be very loose—operating generally like more or less formalized networks, such as VMHDS/For a livable Hà Nội, to highly structured, with clear corporate governance, such as the two foundations mentioned above.

In terms of donor members of the philanthropy community one observes the prevalence of international public and private donors and grantmakers as well as of corporate—both international and domestic—sponsors. Artists and celebrities will generally act as intermediaries channeling incognito donations through crowd fundraising appeals. Only a few give their own money. In Việt Nam state administrations will organize giving days when employees and staff contribute one-day salary worth to the Flood Relief Fund or to the Fund for the Poor.

It can be stated that the full spectrum of doing good from traditional charity or relief to various forms of organized philanthropy and borderline types of social impact investment and corporate social engagement does exist in Việt Nam, although at varying scales of deployment and levels of sophistication. Perhaps the form of philanthropy that is not as much developed in Việt Nam as it may be in other countries of Asia is HNWI and HNWF philanthropy, although the case of the late businessman Phạm Văn Bên with his Cỏ Mây Student Hostel can be pointed out as such an instance (see Case Profile 1 in Appendix).On the other hand, the five-million strong Vietnamese diaspora's giving over the years has been cumulating into a quite sizable monetary or in-kind contribution, mostly for short-term relief but increasingly also for longer-term projects or programs.

To better understand and assess the philanthropy space in Việt Nam, one has to factor in culture—broadly conceived to encompass historical aspects as well as sets of values, customs, and traditions together with contemporary realities such as increased international contacts and exchanges. Although less preponderant due to the urbanization process, the neighborhood and village spirit of mutual help and solidarity in rural and small town Việt Nam is conducive to practices of relief and charity in times of hardship. The life values and philosophy of Buddhism, the major faith in Việt Nam, are similarly conducive. Additionally, one observes a diversity of community clustering beyond the village and into cities, for example, broad genealogical or geographical clans ("bộ tộc," "đồng hương"), alumni associations or clubs, and so on. For example, the Association of people from Huế (Central Việt Nam) in Hà Nội moved speedily to send relief assistance to their hometown during the catastrophic floods of 2010.

A more recent practice since Việt Nam's reunification is the joining of hands between the State (mostly through the mass organizations such as the Youth Union or the Confederation of Labor Unions, as Kind Heart Foundation does) and the people—what is known as "nhà nước và nhân dân cùng làm," that is, the State and the people joining hands—which major foundations such as Hope Foundation are relying on, in part for considerations of effectiveness, in the implementation of their rural bridge construction program. Conversely, in order to garner enough funds to buy needed vaccines to immunize the vast majority of the population against Covid-19, the Vietnamese government launched a broad appeal for citizens' and organizations' donations to complement public resources.

Thus, *hybridity* may characterize the community, and *fluidity*, the space of philanthropy in Việt Nam. Hybridity in membership because organizations such as the VWU do meet criteria 1, 2, and 3 mentioned above but not criteria 4 (voluntary) or 5 (private) since they operate on a public budget and their staff's work is mandatory like any civil servant's. On the other hand, they also benefit from project or program grants from international government agencies or INGOs, and thus, may be included at the intersection of the philanthropy sub-sector and the social sector. The same applies to such other commonly called mass organizations including the Red Cross and the Fatherland Front—the two main officially recognized channels for relief aid. According to a long-time international practitioner cum scholar of philanthropy in Việt Nam, VWU can be considered part of the philanthropy community also because it is membership-based.

Fluidity characterizes the philanthropy space in Việt Nam because delimitation lines are often blurred and/or in flux, for example, between social enterprises and impact enterprises; or because of the grey zone of NPOs' legal status; or due to the number of domestic NPOs graduating to Foundation or Fund status.

The community of philanthropy actors and stakeholders in Việt Nam is quite broad and diverse, cutting across social or professional stratification, age groups, gender, and so on. The philanthropy community is characterized by great diversity in its constituent members, their legal incorporation, types of organizations and degree of formal institutionalization, their sizes (HR, financial resources), level of professionalism, community impact, and so on.

This is not a clearly delineated space but rather a continuum with blurred lines between the various entities and groups of entities.

2.1 Some Salient Features, Strengths, and Limitations of Philanthropy Actors and Stakeholders in Việt Nam

The philanthropy community in Việt Nam is diverse and fluid as it continues evolving and maturing, from institutional or corporate to individual donors, NPOs, corporate philanthropies or philanthropy programs, mass organizations to individuals ranging from one-time donors to celebrity fundraisers and to dedicated philanthropists.

As mentioned earlier, Vietnamese culture, customs, and traditions have a clear imprint on the motivation and certain modalities of doing good in the country. This is a positive stimulus factor. On the other hand, it may result in conservatism, a tendency to remain within a reactive charity mode of thinking and delivery, not conducive to moving toward more proactive, strategic, impactful giving.

By definition, actors, voluntary agents of public good, are core stakeholders of the philanthropic process together with the target beneficiary groups. In this process donors, be they institutional or individual philanthropists or even unidentified contributors responding to a crowdfunding call, also qualify as stakeholders.

It is worth noting that although the vast number of individual contributors may sometimes, in certain instances, make an aggregate donation for a relief cause many times larger than a grantmaking foundation would or could make, they wield no influence commensurate with their monetary donation due to their incognito and fragmented character. In contrast, regular donors do enjoy a degree of say or influence, if they so wish, in setting the direction, goals, and objectives and sometimes even the modalities of implementation of programs or projects. Practice shows that not infrequently grantees tend to, of themselves and without express donor request, be overly reliant on what they perceive as donor priorities or preferences rather than making more independent decisions in the program/project implementation.

Another feature is that most Vietnamese foundations tend toward delivery, carrying out projects and programs themselves, rather than grantmaking: this shows that maturation of foundations away from operating roughly like large or wealthier NGOs/NPOs toward a seeding role through grantmaking is still at an early stage. Vinif's provision of doctoral and postdoctoral research and innovation grants is a clear step in that direction.

Reality on the ground shows two main strengths in philanthropy practice in Việt Nam:

- Widespread readiness among the Vietnamese, including the less well-off alongside the business community and the diaspora, to donate and provide other forms of solidarity and support, especially in times of emergency and disaster.
- Dynamic civil initiative and inventiveness in the face of disaster and dire need.

On the other hand, a number of weaknesses can be identified in philanthropy in Việt Nam as a whole:

- The limited or uneven degree of understanding about and consideration for philanthropy and its role and contribution among the State, the business sector, the social and even the non-profit sector as well as public opinion. Especially both the overlapping and the difference between charity or relief work and philanthropy with its developmental dimension are still vaguely, if at all, understood in public opinion and in State agencies.
- A tendency toward impulsive, reactive modes of action, closer to short-term charity than sustainable philanthropy. This can be illustrated by the astonishingly huge and extremely fast response from

many thousands of individual donors to the fundraising call by a celebrity for donations to help people affected by the catastrophic floods of October 2020.
- The level of efficiency and effectiveness in operation and use of funds.
- The degree of demonstrated accountability to donors and other stakeholders in the use of donations, especially those obtained through crowdfunding.
- A perceived still limited professionalism among nonprofit personnel.

2.2 *The Question Arises as to Whether the Philanthropy Community and Space in Việt Nam Can Be Considered an Ecosystem?*

We believe that a philanthropy ecosystem has emerged in Việt Nam in view of:

- The existence and growth of a critical mass of diverse, committed, and enterprising actors and stakeholders.
- The mutual engagement, interaction, cooperation, partnerships, and synergies within and between each group of actors and stakeholders, domestic and international, as a result of which human resources in the nonprofit subsector benefit from increasingly effective capacity building in the whole range of knowledge, especially experiential, and skills related to delivery, monitoring and oversight, fundraising, mentoring and advising, training and coaching, networking, and so on.

Some evidence of this learning, growing, and maturing process among members of the community can be found in the diversification and greater sophistication of the community's outputs away from and above simple relief and humanitarian modes toward more development-oriented forms of action, insisting, for instance, on beneficiaries' active commitment through match-funding.

The deciding factor supporting the assertion of the emergence of a philanthropy ecosystem in Việt Nam is the increasing mutual awareness of actors and stakeholders of their respective operations and of opportunities for exchange of information, experience, and support and for cooperation or even partnerships (e.g., between domestic NPO Change—https://changevn.org/and international NPO WWLF—https://www.wwlf.org/). Thus, one witnesses extents and forms of synergy, meshing, and coalescing that qualify the philanthropy community and space in Việt Nam as an ecosystem.

This ecosystem's development stands at an early stage but is well-grounded and growing, maturing relatively fast (Graph 8.1).

A number of *limitations and constraints*, most of them more specific to Việt Nam, still hamper the ecosystem's development:

- The legal and regulatory environment tends to be more constraining than conducive, especially for domestic NPOs (e.g., in obtention of permits). On the other hand, certain lacunae in that environment may hamper due observance and oversight of transparency and accountability principles, especially in regard to charity/relief fund-raising and delivery.
- The lack of proper enabling conditions, including regulatory and tax related, fails to incentivize the growth of social enterprises.
- The need for stable funding and access to networks, the still modest level of professionalism among NPOs and limited public opinion understanding, all resulting in heightening the *central issue of trust*: between donors and implementers, between implementers and target communities, between authorities at various levels and NPOs both domestic and international.

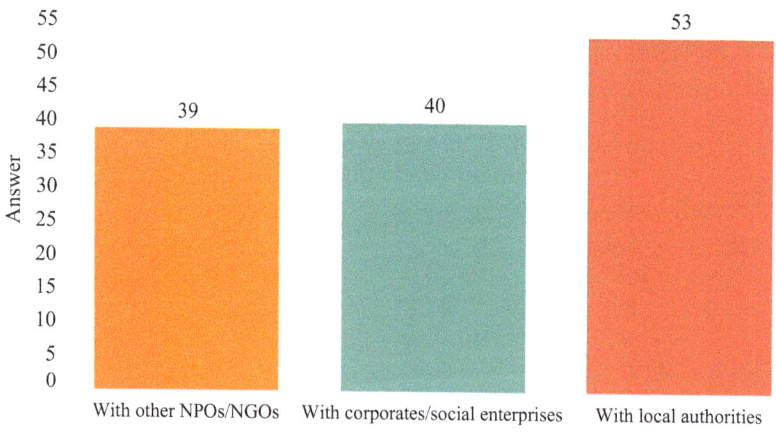

Graph 8.1 Levels of interactions of Philanthropy Ecosystem (PE) actors with other stakeholders

- It has been mentioned that state agencies tend to pay more attention to and hold in higher regard international NGOs than domestic NGOs. Another reality is that large corporate philanthropies enjoy better recognition and support from state agencies, probably because they are linked to major corporate groups such as Vingroup, Vinamilk or TH True Milk, and also because they partner up with mass organizations such as the Confederation of Labor Unions (Vingroup) or the Việt Nam Support Fund for Children (Vinamilk) in the delivery of their CSR programs.

An essential dimension to gauge the role and contribution of philanthropy toward Việt Nam's inclusive and sustainable development would be to assess its impact in related fields, aspects and issues, and ultimately for the target community. This highly worthwhile task, however, lies beyond the purview of this limited field study.

3 Emerging Trends in Philanthropy in Việt Nam

It has been asserted in the previous section that the philanthropy ecosystem in Việt Nam is diverse and fluid, growing, and gradually maturing. Therefore, the question arises as to what trends are emerging and how they impact on this ecosystem and the social sector at large.

3.1 Factors Stimulating Change in and Evolution of the PE in Việt Nam

Given the widespread desire to do good and traditional Vietnamese culture of compassion and sharing, the rise in income levels and the emergence of a growing middle class, more financial means become available to individuals and organizations who wish to support philanthropy.

Additionally, with Việt Nam's increasing and broadening international integration with contacts, exchanges and cooperation at diverse levels and among different entities, including non-profit and CSR related, members and stakeholders in the PE in Việt Nam become aware of and learn from other countries' successful practices and commonly accepted principles and standards. Thus, they recognize the need to adapt and to modernize the approach to and the practice of philanthropy in Việt Nam.

A third factor coming into play is the urbanization process and growing penetration of technology in people's daily and professional lives. This, for instance, facilitates improvement in education delivery among ethnic minority students. A striking illustration is provided by Mường ethnic minority teacher Hà Ánh Phượng being among the winners of the Top 10 Global Teacher Prize sponsored by the Varkey Foundation: her feat is, via the Internet, periodically connecting her 85% ethnic minority class in Phú Thọ Province with classes in Africa and South Asia for live exchange sessions. Thanks to technology, Việt Nam's remote, mountainous areas mostly inhabited by poorer, disadvantaged ethnic minorities can better be reached and served.

A fourth factor plays a significant role in stimulating the evolution of the PE: the mass media and social media, public opinion in general. They can have a facilitating, positive impact in several ways: alerting public opinion to cases, situations of distress in need of relief and assistance, for example, abandoned newborns, severely battered children or women; encouraging donations to natural disaster or vaccine fundraising drives; highlighting timely innovative and effective relief initiatives especially during the Covid-19 pandemic; or questioning the apparent lack of transparency, accountability, aid delivery timeliness and effectiveness in recent celebrities' relief fundraising campaigns, thus exercising a measure of civil oversight role.

A fifth aspect which contributes to energizing and enhancing greater dynamism in the PE is the steadily growing attraction among young people toward social and environmental responsibility through volunteering for non-profit causes and organizations as well as through interest in ESG ventures and startups.

3.2 *What Main Trends Are Emerging in the PE in Việt Nam?*

(a) The corporate sector's involvement with philanthropy and the PE shows definite diversification and progress:

- Enterprises in Việt Nam, especially international and larger domestic ones, increasingly consider it good for business and a condition for their own sustainability to incorporate a CSR program and even unit in the overall enterprise structure and in their communication strategy, which for them is part of a risk and opportunity management approach; especially for so-called impact businesses, ESG impact measurement is viewed as a sound risk evaluation tool.

- A growing number of enterprises declare themselves *ESG businesses*, which integrate consideration of these three dimensions in their business operations. How close to the intersection of the corporate sector with the social sector at large and the philanthropy sub-sector more specifically these ESG businesses are depends on how effectively proactive and systematic the ESG dimension's integration is, and how it translates into recognizable outcomes. In this respect, some businesses such as Saitex (https://www.sai-tex.com) have consistently planned and endeavored in that direction, and thus achieved B-Corp Certification. Another corporation such as EZLand (https://ezland.group) demonstrates an even more ambitious commitment to achieve Edge Green Building Certification for all its projects and to strive toward what they call corporate citizenship. This exemplifies the deepening of corporate awareness of and growing engagement with the PE as members of the corporate sector pay growing attention not just to outward-looking impact on the community or stakeholder base but also to inward-looking impact on corporate governance.
- It is to be noted that while a sizable number of Vietnamese youths are attracted to the concept of *social enterprise* (SE) when they think of launching their own startups (see Case profile 2 in Appendix), few of them stay the course of social entrepreneurship due to insufficient public incentives, including in terms of regulations, taxation, and financial support, in contrast with other governments in the region such as Singapore, Korea, or India. Illustrative examples of government support for social entrepreneurship in other Asian countries are Korea's 2010 Law on social enterprises stipulating that 5% of municipal budgets should be earmarked for social enterprises support, and the existence in Seoul of 24 Social Enterprise hubs; or the existence in Thailand since 2010 of a dedicated Office of Social Enterprises and the adoption in 2019 of a Thai Law on Social Enterprises.

  Many of those who attempted to move from a non-profit mode of operation to a SE having to generate profit or at least revenue could not succeed to do so as they lacked the necessary acumen, skills, and experience, and thus often failed to attract investors. As a result, after short trial runs they will move to ESG or impact ventures, or will set up a non-profit, or return to operating as a non-profit. On the other hand, a mature business like TMTM social enterprise company endeavored to submit a proposal in response to the LIFT (Livelihoods and Food Security Fund) Call for Proposals for the Chin[1] Programme 2019–2023.

- Young socially minded investors are showing increasing interest in *impact investing and venture philanthropy*,[2] which Bloomberg News underlined in February 2021:

  Rich Asian Families Are Pouring Millions Into Impact Investing
  "A lot of impact investment is driven by younger generations who want to live more sustainably."
  A recent study of 1,700 impact investors found that assets under management grew from $502 billion in 2019 to $715 billion last year, despite the Covid-19 pandemic, according to the Global Impact Investing Network (GIN). Impact funds and companies are now turning to Asia, to attract new socially conscious investors and as a place to invest. East and Southeast Asia is emerging as the second-fastest-growing region for impact fund allocations, after Europe, according to the GIN survey. And the strategy has become increasingly attractive to the region's younger or second-generation wealthy.
  A recent example is Eddie Thai, a young Vietnamese-American who moved back to Việt Nam as the co-founder of venture capital fund 500 Startups Viet Nam, and this year (2021) co-founded the higher-tier Ascend Viet Nam Ventures.

(b) The growth and diversification of the PE in turn stimulates *the continued emergence of* a particular group of actors cum stakeholders, that is, the *enablers/capacity builders*, who arise from the specific needs—objective and subjective, primary and secondary—of members of that community.

Active across Asia but also in Việt Nam are connector entities such as APPC (Asia Pacific Philanthropy Consortium), an informal network of grantmaking institutions coordinated out of Manila, which back in 2008 held a conference in Hà Nội on Diaspora Giving; or AVPN (Asian Venture Philanthropy Network) which projects itself as a "unique funders' network," a leading ecosystem builder, an advocate, capacity builder and

[1] Chin State, Myanmar.

[2] Venture philanthropy is a type of impact investment that takes concepts and techniques from venture capital finance and business management and applies them to achieving philanthropic goals.

platform that cuts across private, public and social sectors, embracing all types of engagement.

Among those active in Việt Nam to different extents, one could mention APCO Worldwide, a US entity which presents itself as an "independent global public affairs and strategic communication consultancy; or WISE Philanthropy Advisors, which accompanies donors who "seek to give strategically in order to create change," more particularly by providing access to networks and impact measurement; or SEAF (https://www.seaf.com), which "hopes" to realize both attractive returns for investors and a measurable development impact in local communities.

With a broadly recognized local community footprint (both with the business and the nonprofit sectors) is LIN Center for Community Development, which many local NPOs turn to for assistance in capacity building, especially training, networking, and most of all for fundraising. CSIP (https://csip.vn)focuses on encouraging and supporting social enterprises. Most recently Wishare (https://wishare.com) is providing an online platform for members of the community to network and explore funding or partnership opportunities.

These philanthropy and social impact investment enablers catalyze the maturation process of Việt Nam's philanthropy ecosystem by encouraging awareness of and adherence to international standards in the not-for-profit sector.

(c) Within this dynamically evolving and increasingly interconnected philanthropy community and space, these internal dynamics and synergies catalyze a coalescence process away from the scattered, fragmented status of earlier decades. In this context *NPO/SPO/SDO* entities are becoming more sophisticated and professional, and better able to find and seize opportunities. A case in point is Huynh Tan Phat Scholarship Fund (HTPSF), which through the recommendation of LIN Center was able to access Irish Aid support: this was due, to an important extent, to HTPSF's adoption of professional financial auditing for its operations.

One can also observe a trend toward *growing ownership of projects and programs by implementers* (NPOs, foundations, philanthropists) *and beneficiaries*, and thus, to greater maturation of the philanthropy ecosystem in Việt Nam. An eloquent illustration is Project Renew (https://landmines.org.vn), a NGO dedicated to UXO (unexploded ordnance) demining, explosive risk education and UXO victims support in Quang Tri province,

Việt Nam's most heavily bombed area, engaging victims and their families to work in their staff, and boasting two all-female demining teams.

Other examples of non-corporate related NGOs which have ostensibly grown in strength, capacity, and reputation can be highlighted: Sống Foundation (see Case profile 3 in Appendix), Change, or LIN Center itself. These entities succeeded in the arduous process to gain lawful status, fundraise consistently to sustain their operations and programs, and are well known among the public and media as well as relevant authorities, enjoying definite trust among their stakeholders.

(d) A fourth trend relates to *individual giving*, which has been on the rise, in response to crowdfunding calls by well-meaning citizens, resulting in modest to larger aggregate response from often anonymous individual donors. This stands in contrast with the incredibly fast and vast number of donations responding crowdfunding calls by showbiz celebrities and influencers. A popular singer's call for donations to help people affected by the catastrophic floods of October 2020 collected, in a matter of days, 178 billion VND (roughly equivalent to nearly 8 million USD), much more than, say, an international NGO's donation of 300,000 USD. This speaks to kind-hearted readiness to give of untold numbers of individual Vietnamese. It also demonstrates how powerful and effective a charity-relief facilitator information technology and social media can be. On the other hand, the generally anonymous character of crowdfunding donations and, in the case of Việt Nam, the relative absence or limited scope of existing regulations regarding calls for voluntary donations and their lawful disbursement (evidenced in related Decree 64 of 2008) have often led to lack of transparency, rigor and accountability in both collection and disbursement of funds. Recent public opinion outcry around questionable crowdfunding drives by several artists has induced the government to replace Decree 64 with Decree 93 issued in October 2021 with a twofold direction: (1) opening up the legal framework for individuals and public media to undertake crowdfunding; (2) tightening the regulations on receipt and lawful disbursement of donations.

Regarding donations by *HNWIs* in Việt Nam, the tendency is for them to contribute through their corporate brands, mostly in response to major calls by the government to such public interest causes as the Anti-Covid

Vaccine Fund, the Flood Relief Fund, and the Fund for the Poor. A recent occurrence which provoked—mostly sarcastic—commentaries has been the first Vietnamese female billionaire's donation of some 150 million pound sterling to an Oxford college in exchange for the said college to change its name to that of the Vietnamese billionairess.

A mention should be made of the *Vietnamese diaspora*'s steadily increasing remittance flow, which this year (2021) reached a record 18 billion USD (close to 5% of GDP). It may be assumed that part of this vast amount of money has flown to charitable or philanthropic causes as fundraisers today also explicitly target overseas Vietnamese.

(e) Other noticeable shifts within the PE include:

- A growing interest, especially among young activists, in causes related to environment, biodiversity, climate change, green lifestyle.
- Over the 2020–2021 period of coping with the unprecedented severe challenges to individual lives as well as to Việt Nam's economic and social life, civil society has risen to the existential challenge, particularly in Hồ Chí Minh City—the pandemic hotspot in Việt Nam—with scores of citizens' relief initiatives often coordinated with local authorities and mass organizations, sometimes even with business associations. All media provided timely daily coverage of such initiatives (e.g., Free Rice ATMs, Free Oxygen ATMs, Zero-Dong [Việt Nam currency] Minimarts, Free Hot Meals for frontline workers, 24-hour hotlines staffed by medical volunteers). It has been clear to all that without the third sector and the charity—philanthropy ecosystem's pro-active and close-to-needs strength—the central and local authorities' pandemic response would have been less effective. One may venture to assume that as a result of the Covid-19 pandemic crisis the third sector as a whole and the nonprofit ecosystem more particularly have gained higher trust from the State, eventually opening up an interesting path for tripartite partnerships between the three sectors against the background of the worldwide phenomenon of the third sector's growing importance.

4 Conclusion

In order to put the evolution of philanthropy in Việt Nam in a broad regional perspective, we shall refer to the Doing Good Index 2020 (see References), which underlines the unsustainable reality of Asia concentrating one-third of the world's wealth together with two-thirds of the world's poor, and emphasizes that "Amid these trends and challenges, the social sector in Asia has been in dramatic flux (…). The sector's increasingly evident role as a partner in sustainable development is a clarion call for governments, companies and philanthropists to support its growth."

Of the 18 Asian countries surveyed for the Doing Good Index 2020, Việt Nam ranked in Tier 2 (Doing better) alongside Hong Kong, Japan, Korea, Pakistan, the Philippines above Tier 3 (Doing OK) and 4 (Not doing enough). Above Việt Nam are Tier 1 (Doing well) Singapore and Taiwan (China).

In other words, Việt Nam's Philanthropy Ecosystem is trending positively and maturing. With the maturation of the domestic business community, a growing understanding of and readiness to engage in corporate-related forms of responsibility and contribution toward the social sector becomes discernible. The modernization of Việt Nam's social space through growing bottom-up empowerment of its citizens and grassroots entities works as a complement to the top-down systemwide and regulatory policy role of the State toward greater facilitation of all stakeholders' voice and engagement.

HPDF's qualitative inquiry does illustrate a significant dimension of Việt Nam's development which has received insufficient and inadequate attention, namely the emergence and gradual expansion, diversification, and maturation of a philanthropy ecosystem in Việt Nam, with local and international synergies, combining the traditional Vietnamese culture of giving and community solidarity with forward-looking broadly recognized principles and methods of modern philanthropy, especially among Việt Nam's very socially active youth.

Appendix

Case Profile 1

Entrepreneur Phạm Văn Bên and Cỏ May Student Hall

Family Business Philanthropy Started as Single Individual Initiative

The late Phạm Văn Bên was the founder and owner of Cỏ May Group—a leading business in the Mekong Delta specializing in the production and trading of animal feed, grain foods, and tourism with offices and factories in Đồng Tháp and Kiên Giang provinces, Hồ Chí Minh City, and Singapore. He was also the founder of Cỏ May Student Hall ("the Hall" or "the hostel")—an unprecedented philanthropic model in support of higher education in Việt Nam. From the 2016–2017 school year, the Hall has offered not only free accommodation, but free tuition and soft skills training to more than 600 low-income students.

An Entrepreneur with a Philanthropist's Vision

It was Mr. Phạm Văn Bên's belief that "The root cause of poverty is the lack of education, of scientific and technological foundation, of knowledge and virtue. Only education, science, and moral commitment can create the impulse to do good and combat meanness on a large scale." His motivation for supporting young people today stemmed from the days when he himself had to depend on an orphanage for shelter, food, regular schooling, and vocational training.

Phạm Văn Bên was a shrewd businessman and a true believer in education who demonstrated practical and effective thinking in the pursuit of both talent and virtue. Prior to the Hall, he had established a scholarship fund for his employees' children as well as needy children outside the company. To widen the scope of beneficiaries, he chose to build the hostel in Hồ Chí Minh City within reach of students in need beyond the Mekong Delta.

Looking long-term, Mr. Bên signed a 20-year cooperative agreement with the Hồ Chí Minh City University of Agriculture and Forestry (NLU). To ensure that the hostel would operate according to its purpose and objectives, Mr. Bên from the outset earmarked 14 billion VND (roughly 600,000 USD) to be disbursed annually to cover expenses. To this day, the annual allocation is still maintained by his family to keep the hostel in operation. He also recruited people of kindred spirit to help manage the hostel, providing them with adequate compensation so they did not have to take up additional work.

A Philanthropic Model Unique in Building and Operation

The four concepts at the core of the company's business philosophy were applied to the building and operation of the hostel. They emphasize the value of: People (good people make good products and deliver good services); Products (products truly benefitting customers will keep them loyal); Morality (in business, the real winners are the righteous); and Cỏ May Culture (respect for everyone). Mr. Bên thus taught his children: "As long as we still have the trust and support of the public, we'll be able to take care of students in need. This is our responsibility to society. After I'm gone, all of you and then your children must continue to live by the same principles so that my initiative can live on."

Some Cỏ May Philanthropy Highlights

- Being the only private hostel located on the campus of a Vietnamese public university.
- Offering dual support: free accommodation and scholarships (monthly stipends for tuition and meals, as well as for personal development through physical and soft skills learning at 10 special interest clubs).
- Being part of a business group (Cỏ May) in terms of organization, finances, and operation. As part of NLU's dormitory network, the hostel also has the university's support in legal and academic matters.
- Creating an effective study and educational environment thanks to its autonomous status: the hostel's daily operation is handled by the students themselves in line with the motto: respect, self-awareness, and responsibility.
- Mrs. Nguyen Ngoc Oanh (Mr. Bên's spouse) and their five children continue to support fully his aspirations, philosophy, and approach in operating Cỏ May, the business as well as the Student Hall. The family does not receive any remuneration for their contribution to the project.

This is an outstanding instance of a philanthropic initiative started by a sole individual and subsequently supported by his family, deriving from the Vietnamese people's traditional values of compassion and respect for education.

Case Profile 2

KOTO Social Enterprise and Foundation

The First Social Enterprise to Be Certified in Việt Nam

KOTO (**K**now **O**ne, Teach **ONE**) was founded as a nonprofit organization in 1999, a charity vocational training center with its own restaurants in Hà Nội and Hồ Chí Minh City (HCMC). Seventeen years later, after the adoption of the 2014 Amended Business Law, KOTO was finally certified as the country's first social enterprise.

KOTO's story is one of unwavering commitment to its mission for the last twenty years. KOTO offers vocational training to marginalized, impoverished youth, enabling them to make a living for themselves and their family and become productive members of society. Every year, 40 to 45 street children or homeless youth are awarded KOTO's 24-month scholarships to fund their vocational training in hospitality services and a variety of social, business and life skills. In over 20 years, nearly 1,000 KOTO scholarship recipients have graduated from these programs and found employment, sometimes at five-star hotels and restaurants.

From "Giving the Fish" to "Giving the Fishing Rod" and "Teaching How to Fish"

Jimmy Phạm, KOTO's founder and director, is a Vietnamese Australian. On a visit to Việt Nam in 1996, he felt that something should be done for the down-and-out youth he saw in the streets. Drawing inspiration from the precept "Be the change you want to see," Jimmy started his journey of good will. At first he simply gave shelter and food to the street youth he met in HCMC, but very soon realized that he was just "feeding them a fish day by day." Jimmy resolved to invest more in his protégés' education. With savings from his tour guide job, he supported them to take English lessons.

In 1999, noting the high demand for hospitality workers, Jimmy thought of sending the teenagers to Hoa Sữa Center for vocational training, but the homeless youth were not accepted for lack of documentation. He attempted to found a NGO, but that plan also failed. Jimmy then asked a friend to open a bakery starting with a staff of nine. Thus KOTO was established in 1999 as a home, a center where children and adolescents were taken care of and given skills for a better future, a place where they were given "fishing rods" and "taught how to fish."

KOTO's Training Culture: Building Self-esteem and Community Values

KOTO's philosophy lies in its motto, "Know one, Teach one," which embodies the spirit of leading, guiding, helping, and treating one another with kindness and respect. True to this ideal, graduates of KOTO mentor new recruits, and all who cross the home's threshold are taught about sharing and caring for one another. Personalities and characters are honed through building self-confidence, promoting community values, developing positivity, and gaining motivation for self-development.

The *criteria for admission* are that applicants must come from difficult circumstances and be willing to do what it takes to change their lives. A KOTO scholarship is worth almost 200 million VND in vocational training, topped off with an internationally recognized credential. Not everyone can withstand the industry's strict discipline and 16-hour workday regimen, but the current annual graduation rate is 92%. The last four months of the course present special challenges to strike home the evident reality that success takes hard work. Thanks to this rigorous training, KOTO graduates have a clear vision of what they want in life and what they have to do to achieve their goals.

As Jimmy shared with us, with the pandemic and ensuing lockdowns in 2020 KOTO's revenues dropped by nearly 90%. Yet their hundreds of trainees still had three meals a day and stayed healthy and positive. "Believe me, it would have been impossible to achieve if you weren't driven by focus and passion," Jimmy confided. They survived in large part thanks to KOTO's graduates, who in just two weeks raised more than 300 million VND for the operation.

Next Step for Achieving Sustainability

KOTO has two entities: the Foundation and the social enterprise (SE). While KOTO SE looks for solutions to social problems by doing business, KOTO Foundation combines fundraising from philanthropists and donors with revenues from KOTO SE to cover operating costs. KOTO's long-term objective is sustainability through system and partnership restructuring, as well as customer base expansion. KOTO hopes to create its own ecosystem where students can take initiative and realize their full potential. KOTO is grooming its next team of leaders and hopes their hard work will be recognized by the State and the people of Việt Nam.

In spite of its social enterprise status, KOTO is still operating under ordinary business laws without special treatment or incentives. In Jimmy's opinion, *SEs can survive only if the community supports them through fair, appropriate treatment. It's not just because they're doing good things that they deserve to be treated well.* Jimmy reflects that "Many gave up on the idea of a SE for lack of support. They felt alone, abandoned in this journey." Jimmy confided:

The story of KOTO shows that for philanthropic or social interventions to have real and lasting impact, the organization involved must be absolutely committed and focused. In spite of an overall environment not truly conducive to social enterprises, KOTO is upholding its original values and living up to its ideals through persistent advocacy and cooperative work. Due to its family values and sharing philosophy, KOTO today has an extensive network of loyal graduates. If put to good use, these alumni could be a reliable resource and an effective engine driving the enterprise's long-term sustainability. Jimmy Pham and KOTO's story are living proof that "Việt Kiều" (overseas Vietnamese) doing philanthropy in Việt Nam can prevail, with passion, perseverance, and professionalism.

Case Profile 3

Sống Foundation for Support and Development of Sustainable Living Community and Flood-Resilient Housing Program

Philanthropy: Consistency and Professionalism in the Support and Development of Sustainable Living Community

The Foundation for the Support and Development of Sustainable Living Community ("Sống Foundation" or "the Foundation") is a nonprofit organization that helps people in regions affected by natural disasters and climate change and aims to develop sustainable communities. Officially licensed as a nonprofit organization in 2018, the Foundation has in fact been operating since 2013 with the launch of its "Nhà Chống Lũ" (*Flood Resilient Home*) initiative to build safe houses for populations at risk. By the end of 2020, the initiative had supported 799 households in 8 provinces and cities (Quảng Ninh, Hà Tĩnh, Quảng Bình, Quảng Nam, Khánh Hòa, Bến Tre, Hậu Giang, and Sóc Trăng) in the building and renovation of their houses, as well as 122 ethnic minority households in Nam Trà My and Bắc Trà My districts, Quảng Nam province, under the "Làng Hạnh Phúc" (*Happy Village*) project. When a series of tropical storms and floods struck in 2020, people living in those houses were safe and able to face the disasters with minimal loss of property.

The Foundation's Nhà Chống Lũ program (the Program) was selected to illustrate the successful application of philanthropy in development projects, for its immediate but also sustainable results as well as for its lasting and increasing impacts in the community and society. The program's *modus operandi* (MO) of 'joining hands' and its astute leadership are invaluable assets embodying the professionalism of a modern development approach attuned to local contexts.

Practical Values of the Nhà Chống Lũ/Flood-Resilient Housing Program

- **Motivation for Creation and Long-Term Goals**

The Program was a response to the reality that Việt Nam is one of the five countries most affected by natural disasters and climate change. The poor are the most vulnerable group in times of natural disasters due to their scant resources for self-recovery. To minimize human loss and equip the poor in affected areas with better response capacities, the Program has supported the construction of safe houses based on thorough research and customized design to suit natural disasters specific to each region (e.g., mud floods, tube floods, slope flash floods, river floods).

The Foundation works on sustainability at three levels: the people, the community, and the environment. This approach is reflected in its goals: to enable people to ensure a safe life for themselves; to enhance the local populations' and authorities' capacity to cope with natural disasters and climate change; and to instill a culture of respect for nature and promote a nature-friendly lifestyle.

- **Sustainable Community Development: Professional and Based on Participatory Engagement**

The program calls for "joining hands" in implementation (the *participatory* method)—an approach in community development involving active and dynamic participation from all stakeholders. Architects and local staff conduct feasibility studies and site location assessments, develop housing designs that ensure safety, allow for future expanded functionality, minimize construction costs, and fit with the local culture to promote its preservation. The beneficiary family plays a central role throughout the entire process—from home design to construction and completion. In addition to supporting the design of the most suitable, cost-effective, and safe house models, the Program pays part of the costs (35–50 million VND) up to 50% of construction cost while the family supplies the remaining cost through cash, reciprocating labor costs or using materials from their old houses. The local government assists in surveying, overseeing, and motivating the families during the construction. Other donors provide additional funds or construction materials at large discounts.

- **Spreading the Culture of Sustainable Living and Community Development**

The "joining hands" approach helps eliminate the "one-way giving" charity tradition that often leads to overreliance and dependence on the beneficiary's part and is not a long-term solution. With the family's material contribution and active participation throughout the building process, the completed home will truly belong to the family and not the project. The goal is for this accomplishment to help all members of the family change the way they think, continue to take greater initiative, and feel proud, self-confident, and happy.

The Program also promotes the goal of "having the community come together in fostering and spreading humanistic values" with the participation of experts and sponsors (organizations, businesses, individuals). It is worth noting that members of families having completed their own house have volunteered to help other families build safe houses, or have offered to take project staff to flooded areas accessible only by rowboats. Local authorities have become more aware of the ways to develop sustainable communities; learned to enhance their capacity to connect, combine, and coordinate community projects; and begun to look for additional ways to access other sources of social support. *The Program's success has increasingly attracted donations from domestic and foreign organizations, businesses, and individuals, making it possible for the Foundation to continue and expand the Program's impact.*

- **Fundraising: Diverse, Modern, and Effective**

The Foundation raises funds online (e.g., crowd fundraising), through direct auction of donated art works, and organizing music concerts. Organizations and individuals from various fields (arts, culture, business, technology, social activities, civil servants) contribute with sponsorships, donations in cash and kind, artworks for auctions, cultural fundraisers, design and R&D skills, or time, expertise, consultancy, and connections—free of charge or at minimal rates.

The smooth operation and achievements of the Sống Foundation and the Nhà Chống Lũ program highlight the importance of the founders and their authority since they can bring into play the kind of experience and social capital that such endeavors need. The imperative now is to ensure the sustainability of both Organization and Program by building the next team of "project builders."

Giving material things is also helping, but to create real change we need to affect the way society thinks. People who need help also need to feel self-pride, self-worth, self-sufficiency, and independence. Only when people experience those feelings will life truly change for them and for the generations to come.

Phạm Thị Hương Giang, Founding Board Member and Chairperson of Management Council Foundation for Support and Development of Sustainable Living Community

CHAPTER 9

Income-Based Social Stratification in Vietnam, 1998–2018

The Cuong Bui and Si Anh Truong

1 Introduction

Social structure and social stratification have been a vibrant area of research in Vietnam for decades (Bui The Cuong, 2015c, 2016, 2019). In this field, many authors have suggested classifications of social classes and social strata in order to identify the core framework of the social structure.

This chapter proposes a framework that classifies social classes on the basis of income. Using data from three household living standards surveys conducted in 1998, 2008 and 2018 by the General Statistics Office of Vietnam, it aims to configure the social class structure in Vietnam during the period of 1998–2018.

The chapter consists of the five sections. After the introduction, the data sources and the analytical methods are described in the second

T. C. Bui (✉)
Southern Institute of Social Sciences, Vietnam Academy of Social Sciences, Ho Chi Minh City, Vietnam

S. A. Truong
Kantar Media, Ho Chi Minh City, Vietnam

T. A.-D. Tran (ed.), *Rethinking Asian Capitalism*,
https://doi.org/10.1007/978-3-030-98104-4_9

section. This is followed by a brief literature review. Finally, our key findings and main conclusions are presented.

2 Data and Methodology

The main method of this study is the second analysis of data from three Vietnam Household Living Standards Surveys carried out by the General Statistics Office of Vietnam in 1998, 2008 and 2018.

In this research, we use k-means clustering technique, by which the households in the survey samples are classified into clusters based on monthly per capita income, from no income to the highest income level. The number of clusters is given by researchers and the households with different monthly per capita income are allocated to each cluster by SPSS software through an algorithm, so that the households with the smallest difference in monthly per capita income are grouped into the same cluster and the households with the largest difference in monthly per capita income should be grouped in the different clusters (details about k-means technique, see MacQueen, 1967).

We chose a framework of six classes based on monthly per capita income and label them as: upper, upper-middle, middle, lower-middle, upper-lower and lower class. In the analysis process, these six social classes are grouped into three social strata: the upper stratum (including upper and upper-middle classes), the middle stratum (consisting of the middle and lower-middle classes), and lower stratum (comprising of the upper-lower and lower classes). The term "middle classes" is sometimes used for the middle categories (that is, upper-middle, middle and lower-middle classes).

3 Literature Review

Social classes, or standings, strata, categories and groups? These terms have a long history in international sociology and also in social research in Vietnam. Depending on the authors, nations and historical phases, those terms are either considered as distinctly different from each other or, conversely, accepted as easily interchangeable. Noll (1997, p. 105) remarked:

Whereas the concepts "class" and "strata" are frequently used as equivalents in the American literature, in Germany the distinction between "Klassen" and "Schichten" is significant both in sociology as well as in everyday life. In general it can be said that the term "Schicht" has a more neutral, even affirmative meaning compared to the term "Klasse" which is usually related to a more critical, conflict-oriented perspective of society. In everyday life too the notion of the term "class" is usually associated with its Marxist origin and meaning.

In our chapter, the term "income-based social class" is used as a working concept for statistical analysis, temporarily setting aside the theoretical aspect of the matter.

Any review of social stratification research in contemporary Vietnam would fill many pages. Such studies are only briefly referred to here, especially those focusing on class classifications by income which is the topic of our chapter.

Many attempts to offer theoretical or empirical classifications of social structure have been made in Vietnam from 1975 to the present day. In the 1980s, some sociologists constructed classifications based on the Marxist concept of ownership of the means of production; they included Hong Giao, Thanh-Giang, Tran Huu Quang, Le Minh Ngoc and Do Thai Dong (Bui The Cuong, 2019). In the following decades, some authors offered analytical frameworks combining the criteria of ownership of the means of production and occupations (Do Nguyen Phuong, 1993, 1994; Ta Ngoc Tan, 2013).

Several other researchers employed occupation-based classifications (Do Thien Kinh, 2012, 2015, 2018; Le Thanh Sang & Nguyen Thi Minh Chau, 2013; Bui The Cuong, 2015a; Bui The Cuong & Pham Thi Dung, 2016; Bui The Cuong, 2017; Bui The Cuong & Vu Manh Loi, 2017a, 2017b).

There are also classifications based on living standards (income or expenditure). In the 1980s, Pham Van Phu, To Duy Hop and Chu Huu Quy adopted such an approach (Bui The Cuong, 2019). In the early 1990s, Trinh Duy Luan (1992) made use of living standards to survey social stratification in Hanoi. Do Thien Kinh in many of his works in the second half of the 1990s and early 2000s stratified social classes by living standards (Do Thien Kinh, 1995a, 1995b, 1995c, 1996, 1999, 2000, 2003). Luu Hong Minh (2001) constructed a system of social stratification for the Red River Delta based on living standards.

Undertaking the first Vietnam Living Standards Survey in Vietnam in 1992–1993 in collaboration with the General Statistics Office, the World Bank introduced for the first time in Vietnam the quintile technique to analyse socio-economic differences between the social groupings based on income and expenditure (World Bank, 1995). From then to the end of the 2000s, the World Bank frequently used quintile technique as the key tool in all reports on living standards surveys in Vietnam (World Bank, 1999, 2003, 2007). Meanwhile, the General Statistics Office of Vietnam had been adopting it as the key classification technique in all reports on household living standards surveys up to the present (General Statistics Office, 1994, 1999, 2000, 2004, 2006, 2007, 2010, 2011, 2014, 2016, 2018). Following the World Bank's initiative, many writers have also taken advantage of the quintile technique as the analytical framework, among them Do Thien Kinh (2003), Le Huu Nghia et al. (2010), Le Van Toan (2012) and Nguyen Tran Lam and Nguyen Viet Cuong (2017).

As Vietnam successfully stepped up to lower-middle-income status from the low-income country category in 2009, the World Bank constructed two new classifications in order to investigate the recent changes in the country in timely fashion. In "Vietnam 2035 Towards Prosperity, Creativity, Equity, and Democracy" (World Bank Group and Vietnam Ministry of Planning and Investment, 2016, pp. 301–302), the World Bank adopted a four-class analysis: the global middle class (consuming more than US$15.00/person/day according to purchasing power parity, abb. PPP), the emerging consumer (spending between US$5.51 and 15.00 PPP/person/day), the near poor (spending between US$3.10 and 5.50 PPP/person/day) and the global poor (living on less than US$3.10 PPP/person/day). In "Viet Nam Development Report 2019—Connecting Vietnam for Growth and Shared Prosperity", the World Bank (2019, p. 53) constructed a framework with five economic classes based on their daily consumption per capita in 2011 in PPP dollars consisting of "the extremely poor, who live on less than US$1.90 per day; the moderately poor, whose per capita consumption ranges from US$1.90 to US$3.20 per day; the economically vulnerable, who consume US$3.20 to US$5.50 per person per day; the economically secure, consuming US$5.50 to US$15 per person per day; and the global middle class, who live on more than US$15 per person per day". Using the quintile technique less frequently for reports on Vietnam after "upgrading" the nation's status in the World Bank's country classifications by income level, the World Bank possibly discreetly suggested that it may indeed be time to give close and careful attention to other more sociologically oriented, income-based classifications rather than the quintile technique's statistical method of dividing the population into five equal groups.

Ly Chu (2018) criticises the situation of social stratification research in Vietnam because it focuses solely on economic aspects, namely living standards or income. Ly Chu urges Vietnamese scholars to see the benefits of applying Pierre Bourdieu's theory to a study of the cultural aspects of social stratification. It is our inclination to agree partially with her criticism. However, there are two points related to her argument to which we should give further consideration.

Firstly, there have actually been quite a number of Vietnamese authors who have set out to examine cultural differences among the social classes in the contemporary Vietnamese society. To give an example of such academics, as early as the mid-1990s, Pham Bich San (1992) raised awareness of cultural reproduction among the middle classes in Hanoi. Some others also took steps to address educational and cultural differences between social classes or categories; they included Do Thien Kinh (2005), Le Huu Nghia et al. (2010), Ta Ngoc Tan (2013) and Bui The Cuong (2015b). Nonetheless, it is undeniable that Vietnamese researchers, when carrying out cultural surveys and analyses, rarely refer to the cultural variables in their empirical explorations using Bourdieu's cultural capital framework. This is the point in Ly Chu's suggestion that Vietnamese researchers should take into consideration.

Secondly, analyses of differences in economic assets in general or, more narrowly, in income have always had a prominent position in the field of social stratification and inequality research in the world. Wright (2005, pp. 25–27) distinguishes three major models of class analysis: simple gradational, Weberian and Marxian class analysis. Therein he defines: "simple gradational accounts of class in which class is itself directly identified within inequalities in income" (Wright, 2005, p. 26). The economic or even income dimension still plays a significant role in social stratification research in Vietnam as well as in other nations. The World Bank and governmental statistical agencies around the world still regularly use income classifications to produce effective analyses. Many recent international studies do not ignore economic capitals in their social stratification frameworks (Savage et al., 2013, 2015). Recently, Nguyen Tran Lam and Nguyen Viet Cuong (2017) and Oxfam (2018) have sought to explore intra- and intergenerational income mobility in Vietnam.

4 Findings

This section begins with a description of the quantitative contours of six income-based social classes. The six social classes are also further grouped into three social strata. Subsequently, income differences among these

Table 9.1 The percentage of the six income-based classes and the three social strata by rural-urban areas, Vietnam, 1998–2018, weighted

No.	*Social stratification*	*Urban*			*Rural*			*Total*		
		1998	*2008*	*2018*	*1998*	*2008*	*2018*	*1998*	*2008*	*2018*
A	Six social classes									
1	Upper	2.3	2.8	2.4	0.1	0.5	0.8	0.6	1.1	1.4
2	Upper middle	2.5	9.8	18.6	0.2	1.5	4.5	0.7	3.8	9.2
3	Middle	40.3	46.8	43.1	14.0	18.5	23.4	20.3	26.4	30.0
4	Lower middle	8.9	19.4	28.4	6.2	17.3	39.0	6.9	17.9	35.4
5	Upper lower	29.7	16.0	6.7	34.8	34.2	24.3	33.6	29.1	18.4
6	Lower	16.2	5.2	0.8	44.7	28.0	8.0	37.8	21.6	5.6
	Total	100.0	100.0	100.0	100.0	100.0	100.0	100.0	100.0	100.0
B	Three social strata									
1	Upper (A1+2)	4.8	12.6	21.0	0.3	2.0	5.3	1.3	4.9	10.6
2	Middle (A3+4)	49.2	66.2	71.5	20.2	35.8	62.4	27.2	44.3	65.4
3	Lower (A5+6)	45.9	21.2	7.5	79.5	62.2	32.3	71.4	50.7	24.0
	Total	100.0	100.0	100.0	100.0	100.0	100.0	100.0	100.0	100.0
	N (HH)	1730	6837	2748	4269	2352	6420	5999	9189	9168

Source: Vietnam Household Living Standards Surveys conducted by the General Statistics Office of Vietnam in 1998, 2008 and 2018. Analysed by the authors

classes and strata are demonstrated. Those variables are analysed by urban-rural area and over time.

Table 9.1 shows the quantitative distribution of six social classes and three social strata of Vietnam in the period 1998–2018. There is a considerable change in the shape of stratification over three key points in time. In 1998, the ratios between six classes and between three strata still formed a pyramid. By 2008, the pyramid had begun to budge at the top level as well as in the middle and started to shrink at the base. Then, in 2018, it completely changed to a rhombus, with the upper layer accounting for 10.6%, the middle layer 65.4% and the lower layer 24.0%. Yet 20 years before that, these three figures were 1.3%, 27.2% and 71.4%. This means the upper tier increased by a factor of more than eight and the middle tier by a factor of 2.4, while the lower tier decreased by a factor of three.

All three middle classes grew remarkedly over the period. In 20 years, the proportion of the upper middle category soared by a factor of more than 13 and the middle by a factor of 1.5, while the lower middle increased more than fivefold. During the same period, the upper lower class decreased by a factor of 1.8 and the lower group plummeted by a factor of no less than 6.8. It appears that over the period of two decades, numerous households from the middle and lower middle classes moved up to the upper-middle bracket as many others from the upper-lower group have advanced into the lower middle class.

There are a number of similarities and differences between urban and rural areas. As early as 1998, the social strata formation in urban areas was already diamond-shaped, although its base was still almost as large as its middle. At the time, the figures were as follows: upper strata 4.8%, middle 49.2% and lower 45.9%. Ten years later, the rhombus could be seen much more clearly, with the lower layer being only one-third as big as the middle (21.2% compared to 66.2%), though its base was still 1.7 times larger than the top. The next ten years showed the bottom to be only a third of the top and its central layer to be 71.5%.

The social strata configuration of rural areas had evolved more slowly, yet in the 2010s its transformation took a climacteric turn. In 1998, this structure was a pyramid with the base accounting for nearly 80%. One decade later, it was still pyramid-formed, but its base had shrunk by 17 percentage points. It took ten more years to become truly rhombic, when its bottom was half the size of its body (32.3% versus 62.3%). Even so, in 2018, the proportion of the upper tier of that structure in rural areas was only one-quarter of that in urban areas (5.3% compared with 21.0%) while the portion of its lower layer was four times bigger (32.3% compared with 7.5%).

Table 9.2 displays the average income of different social classes and social strata in urban and rural areas as well as their income-difference coefficients during the period 1998–2018. The average income of the entire survey sample is approximately at the point of division between three higher classes and three lower classes. In 1998, the sample's average monthly income per capita was VND265,000, while that of the lower middle class was slightly higher (VND308,000). Nevertheless, in 2008, these two figures were VND1,117,000 and VND919,000 respectively. By 2018, they had risen to VND3,837,000 and VND2,702,000. In Tan Ern Ser's classification, the middle classes are those whose household income per capita is above the average household income per capita of the survey sample (Tan Ern Ser, 2015, pp. 18–19). Le Kim Sa and his research group use the poverty line to define the middle classes. Accordingly, the middle-class households are those whose average income per capita is twice the average income per capita of households at the poverty line (Le Kim Sa & Vu Hoang Dat, 2014, p. 71; Le Kim Sa, 2016, pp. 26–27). Kochhar

Table 9.2 Average income and income-difference coefficient of the six income-based classes by rural-urban areas, Vietnam, 1998–2018, weighted

No.	*Social classes*	*Urban*		*Rural*		*Total*	
		Average income	*Coefficient*	*Average income*	*Coefficient*	*Average income*	*Coefficient*
A	VHLSS 1998						
1	Upper	2810	28.2	2884	31.2	2821	30.3
2	Upper middle	1479	14.9	1453	15.7	1473	15.8
3	Middle	574	5.8	513	5.5	542	5.8
4	Lower middle	307	3.1	308	3.3	308	3.3
5	Upper lower	216	2.2	205	2.2	208	2.2
6	Lower	99	1.0	92	1.0	93	1.0
	Total	441		210		265	
B	VHLSS 2008						
1	Upper	11,283	38.8	10,018	32.1	10,895	35.0
2	Upper middle	3984	13.7	3867	12.4	3.951	12.7
3	Middle	1737	6.0	1604	5.1	1670	5.4
4	Lower middle	938	3.2	910	2.9	919	3.0
5	Upper lower	575	2.0	585	1.9	584	1.9
6	Lower	291	1.0	312	1.0	311	1.0
	Total	1810		847		1117	
C	VHLSS 2018						
1	Upper	22,009	35.0	26,061	40.5	23,677	36.8
2	Upper middle	8944	14.2	8781	13.6	8891	13.8
3	Middle	4972	7.9	4703	7.3	4833	7.5
4	Lower middle	2809	4.5	2662	4.1	2702	4.2
5	Upper lower	1429	2.3	1360	2.1	1369	2.1
6	Lower	630	1.0	644	1.0	643	1.0
	Total	5229		3133		3837	

Source: Vietnam Household Living Standards Surveys conducted by the General Statistics Office of Vietnam in 1998, 2008 and 2018. Analysed by the authors

Notes: Average income means the income per capita per month (VND1000); income-difference coefficient is the rate compared to the average income of the class which has the lowest average income that is defined as equivalent to 1.0

specifies the threshold for the middle classes as follows: "In our analysis, 'middle-income' Americans are adults whose annual household income is two-thirds to double the national median, after incomes have been adjusted for household size" (Kochhar, 2018). Thus, the classifications of the above-mentioned authors and the categorisation employed in this chapter have certain similarities.

In terms of income disparities, Table 9.2 shows that the income difference between the upper class and the lower class is tremendously high and increased significantly over two decades: 30.3 in 1998, 35.0 in 2008 and 36.8 in 2018. The gap can be observed clearly widening from the upper and the upper middle class to four other classes, but the difference between the upper class and the upper middle class also widened rapidly.

Table 9.2 indicates that in 1998 the monthly average income per capita in urban areas was 2.1 times higher than in rural areas (VND441,000 versus VND210,000). The ratio was still 2.1 in 2008 (VND1,810,000 compared to VND847,000), although it decreased to 1.7 in 2018 (VND5,229,000 compared to VND3,133,000). Thus the average income difference between urban and rural areas did not change in the 2000s and tended to decline in the 2010s.

Regarding the income gaps, in 1998, the income-difference coefficient between the upper and lower classes in urban areas was 28.2, while in rural areas it was higher at 31.2. In 2008, this coefficient was 38.8 in urban areas and 32.1 in rural areas. By 2018, it had increased to 35.5 and 40.5 respectively. The patterns of the coefficient change between these two areas are very different. The coefficient in urban areas surged in the period 1998–2008 (from 28.2 to 38.8) and fell back slightly in between 2008 and 2018 to 35.5, although it was still higher in 2018 than in 1998. In contrast, the coefficient in rural areas did not change much in the period of 1998–2008 (31.2 versus 32.1) but had risen much higher by 2018 (40.5).

In general, the social classes have better income levels in urban areas than in rural areas. Be that as it may, there are some notable exceptions. The monthly income per capita of the urban upper class in 1998 was lower than that of the rural upper class (VND2,810,000 compared with VND2,884,000). On the contrary, by 2008, the average monthly earnings per capita of the upper class in urban areas had exceeded those in rural areas (VND11,283,000 compared with VND10,018,000). By 2018, however, these figures were VND22,009,000 and VND26,061,000 respectively. So, the average monthly income per capita of the upper class in rural areas surpassed that in urban areas by more than VND4,000,000. Not only that, but the average earnings of the upper lower and the lower class in rural areas are generally higher than those in urban areas.

5 Conclusion

This chapter presents the results of a quantitative structural analysis of social classes in Vietnam during the period 1998–2018, taking into account two different dimensions: (i) changes in the ratios of the income-based class structure, and (ii) the degrees of variation in the income gap between income-based classes. These two aspects concern different policies. In terms of changes in the configuration of social stratification, the research results show that there has been significant progress. Yet they also give rise to considerable apprehension in terms of the widening income inequality between classes.

There are some considerable advancements in the shape of stratification over three key points in time. In 1998, the class structure and social strata remained pyramidal. By 2008, the pyramid had appeared to swell up at the top and middle levels while slimming down at the base. By 2018, it had become fully rhombic. All three segments of the middle classes have expanded remarkably while the two lower classes have steadily shrunk over time.

The income-difference coefficient between social classes increased between 1998 and 2018. The disparity is particularly evident for the upper class and the upper middle class compared with the rest. It was low in the 2000s and grew higher in the 2010s. If policies and development contexts remain unchanged in the 2020s, will the gap and the speed of change escalate exponentially?

The income-based class structures have always been plainly different between urban and rural areas. The rural class structure had always been evolving about one decade behind its urban counterpart, yet took a critical turn in the 2010s. Overall, the urban-rural disproportion in average income tended to decrease in the period 1998–2018. Notably, the earnings gap between the upper class and the lower class was higher in rural areas than in urban areas.

Income is a condition and an important resource for an individual or household seeking to pursue their social goals. Income can be converted into assets, creating economic capital, and transformed into other forms of capital (human, social, political), and vice versa. In that sense, the income variable has significant explanatory power and can be used as a criterion to stratify social classes, at least for today's Vietnamese society to date. In other words, income is capable of generating and revealing profound social differences that help to create social classes that are vastly different from one another, with boundaries separating them that are difficult to cross.

Acknowledgement The chapter is based on the findings of the project titled "Structure of Classes and Strata in the Southeastern Region of Viet Nam in the Period 2010–2020" funded by the Vietnamese Academy of Social Sciences.

References

Bui The Cuong. (2015a). *Social Stratification in the Southeast Region of Vietnam* (IAS Working Paper No. 16). , Institute of Asian Studies.

Bui The Cuong. (2015b). Nong dan trong cau truc phan tang xa hoi [Peasantry in social stratification]. *Journal of Sociology, 2*(130), 20–31.

Bui The Cuong. (2015c). Nghien cuu phan tang xa hoi o Nam Bo [Social stratification research in the southern region]. *Review of Social Sciences Ho Chi Minh City, 9*(205), 42–57.

Bui The Cuong. (2016). Canh quan nghien cuu phan tang xa hoi o Viet Nam [The landscape of social stratification research in Vietnam]. *Journal of Sociology, 3*(135), 7–14.

Bui The Cuong. (2017). Mot phan loai giai tang trung luu Vung Kinh te trong diem phia Nam [A classification of the middle classes in the southern key economic region]. *Journal of Sociology, 3*(139), 43–51.

Bui The Cuong. (2019). Étude de la structuration des couches sociales du Vietnam des années 1980. *Revue des sciences sociales de Ho Chi Minh-Ville Vietnam, 1*(1), 10–31.

Bui The Cuong, & Pham Thi Dung. (2016). Chuyen dich co cau nghe tren mot mau khao sat lap lai o Dong Nam Bo [Changes in occupational structure from a longitudinal survey in the southeastern region]. *Review of Social Sciences Ho Chi Minh City, 1*(209), 29–42.

Bui The Cuong, & Vu Manh Loi. (2017a). Khac biet do thi-nong thon va tieu vung trong co cau xa hoi dua tren nghe o Vung Kinh te trong diem phia Nam giai doan 1999–2009 [Differences in occupational structure by urban-rural areas and sub-regions in the southern key economic region in the period of 1999–2009]. In Le Thanh Sang (Ed.), *Quan he nong thon-thanh thi trong phat trien ben vung vung Dong Nam Bo. Ky yeu Hoi thao Khoa hoc quoc gia* [Rural-urban relationship in sustainable development of the southeastern region.

Proceedings of the national science conference] (pp. 252–268). Social Sciences Publishing House, Hanoi.

Bui The Cuong, & Vu Manh Loi. (2017b). Khac biet toc nguoi trong co cau xa hoi dua tren nghe o Vung Kinh te trong diem phia Nam giai doan 1999–2009 [Ethnic differences in occupational structure in the southern key economic region in the period of 1999–2009]. In *Nhung van de co ban, cap bach ve dan toc, toc nguoi o nuoc ta hien nay: Ly luan va thuc tien. Ky yeu Hoi nghi Khoa hoc quoc gia 2016* [Basic and emerging ethnic issues in our country today: Discourses and reality. Proceedings of the National Science Conference 2016] (pp. 345–355). Social Sciences Publishing House, Hanoi.

Do Nguyen Phuong. (1993). *Nhung van de chinh tri-xa hoi cua co cau xa hoi-giai cap o nuoc ta* [Socio-political issues of the social class structure in our country]. National Political Publishing House and Science and Technics Publishing House.

Do Nguyen Phuong. (Ed.). (1994). *Ve su phan tang xa hoi o nuoc ta trong giai doan hien nay* [Social stratification in our contemporary country]. GEOPRICO.

Do Thien Kinh. (1995a). *Thuc trang xu huong bien doi cua phan tang xa hoi o nong thon Dong bang song Hong* [Trends of social stratification change in rural areas of the red river delta]. Vietnam Academy of Social Sciences, Institute of Sociology.

Do Thien Kinh. (1995b). May nhan xet ve su so sanh phan tang muc song giua nong thon dong bang song Hong va nong thon mien nui phia Bac trong thoi ky doi moi [Remarks on living standards stratification comparison between rural areas of the red river delta and that of the northern region during Doi Moi period]. *Journal of Sociology, 1*(49), 62–68.

Do Thien Kinh. (1995c). Su bien doi cua co cau nghe nghiep va phan tang muc song o nong thon dong bang song Hong [Changes in occupational structure and living standards stratification in rural areas of the red river delta]. *Journal of Sociology, 3*(51), 68–74.

Do Thien Kinh. (1996). Su chuyen doi co cau lao dong-nghe nghiep va tac dong cua no den phan tang muc song o mot xa vung dong bang song Hong [Changes in occupational structure and its impact on living standard stratification in a commune of the red river delta]. *Journal of Sociology, 4*(56), 28–34.

Do Thien Kinh. (Ed.). (1999). *Tac dong cua chuyen doi co cau lao dong nghe nghiep xa hoi den phan tang muc song* [The impacts of changes in occupational structure on living standards stratification]. Agriculture Publishing House, .

Do Thien Kinh. (2000). *Nghien cuu dinh luong ve phan hoa giau ngheo va vai tro cua nhan to hoc van trong viec nang cao muc song cho nguoi dan Viet Nam (Qua 2 cuoc khao sat dieu tra muc song dan cu Viet Nam nam 1993 va 1998)* [Quantitative research on rich-poor differences and the role of educational factor in improving living standards for Vietnamese people (From surveys on Vietnam living standards in 1993 and 1998]. Vietnam Academy of Social Sciences, .

Do Thien Kinh. (2003). *Phan hoa giau ngheo va tac dong cua yeu to hoc van den nang cao muc song cho nguoi dan Viet Nam* [Rich-poor differences and the role of education in improving living standards for Vietnamese people]. Social Sciences Publishing House.

Do Thien Kinh. (2005). *The Effects of industrialization upon social stratification and social mobility: Educational inequality, social inequality and social mobility in contemporary Vietnam* (Publication No. UT51-2005-B956) [PhD Dissertation, Kwansei Gakuin University]. NDL Search.

Do Thien Kinh. (2012). *He thong phan tang xa hoi o Viet Nam hien nay (Qua nhung cuoc dieu tra muc song ho gia dinh Viet Nam 2002–2004–2006–2008)* [Social stratification system in Vietnam today (From the Vietnam household living standards surveys 2002–2004–2006–2008)]. Social Sciences Publishing House.

Do Thien Kinh. (2015). Xu huong bien doi cau truc cac tang lop xa hoi o vung kinh te trong diem phia Nam trong thoi ky doi moi [Trends of changes in social structure in the southern key economic region during Doi Moi period]. *Review of Social Sciences Ho Chi Minh City, 4*(200), 29–40.

Do Thien Kinh. (2018). *Phan tang xa hoi va di dong xa hoi o Viet Nam hien nay* [Social stratification and social mobility in Vietnam today]. Social Sciences Publishing House.

General Statistical Office. (1994). *Khao sat muc song dan cu Viet Nam 1992–1993* [Vietnam living standards survey 1992–1993]. Statistical Publishing House.

General Statistical Office. (1999). *Phan tich ket qua dieu tra doi song, kinh te ho gia dinh nam 1999* [Analysis of survey results on household life and economy in 1999]. Statistical Publishing House.

General Statistical Office. (2000). *Dieu tra muc song dan cu Viet Nam 1997–1998* [Vietnam living standards survey 1997–1998]. Statistical Publishing House.

General Statistical Office. (2004). *Ket qua dieu tra muc song ho gia dinh nam 2002* [Results of household living standards survey 2002]. Statistical Publishing House.

General Statistical Office. (2006). *Ket qua khao sat muc song ho gia dinh nam 2004* [Results of household living standards survey 2004]. Statistical Publishing House.

General Statistical Office. (2007). *Ket qua khao sat muc song ho gia dinh nam 2006* [Results of household living standards survey 2006]. Statistical Publishing House.

General Statistical Office. (2010). *Ket qua khao sat muc song ho gia dinh nam 2008* [Results of household living standards survey 2008]. Statistical Publishing House.

General Statistical Office. (2011). *Ket qua khao sat muc song dan cu Viet Nam nam 2010* [Results of Vietnam living standards survey 2010]. Statistical Publishing House.

General Statistical Office. (2014). *Ket qua khao sat muc song dan cu Viet Nam nam 2012* [Results of Vietnam living standards survey 2012]. Statistical Publishing House.

General Statistical Office. (2016). *Ket qua khao sat muc song dan cu Viet Nam nam 2014* [Results of Vietnam living standards survey 2014]. Statistical Publishing House.

General Statistical Office. (2018). *Ket qua khao sat muc song dan cu Viet Nam nam 2016* [Results of Vietnam living standards survey 2016]. Statistical Publishing House.

Kochhar, R. (2018). The American middle class is stable in size, but losing ground financially to upper-income families. *Pew Research Center*. https://www.pewresearch.org/fact-tank/2018/09/06/the-american-middle-class-is-stable-in-size-but-losing-ground-financially-to-upper-income-families

Le Huu Nghia, Nguyen Dinh Tan, & Le Ngoc Hung. (2010). *Co cau xa hoi va phan tang xa hoi (Qua khao sat mot so tinh, thanh pho o Viet Nam)* [Social structure and social stratification (From survey in some provinces and cities in Vietnam]. Vietnam National University Press.

Le Kim Sa. (2016). Nhan dien tang lop trung luu o Viet Nam qua cach tiep can da chieu [Identifying Vietnam middle class from a multi-dimensional approach]. *Journal of Economics and Development, 228*, 24–32.

Le Kim Sa, & Vu Hoang Dat. (2014). Nhan dien tang lop trung luu o Viet Nam qua cach tiep can da chieu [Identifying Vietnam middle class from a multi-dimensional approach]. *Journal of World Economics and Politics Issues, 10*, 68–80.

Le Thanh Sang, & Nguyen Thi Minh Chau. (2013). Co cau phan tang xa hoi o Dong Nam Bo trong tam nhin so sanh voi Thanh pho Ho Chi Minh va Tay Nam Bo [Social stratification structure in the southeastern region in comparison with Ho Chi Minh city and the southwestern region]. *Review of Social Sciences Ho Chi Minh City, 2*(174), 20–32.

Luu Hong Minh. (2001). *Thuc trang phan tang xa hoi theo muc song o nong thon Dong bang song Hong—Du bao va nhung kien nghi* [Living standard stratification in rural areas of the red river delta—Forecasts and recommendations] (Publication No. LA01.0398.3) [Doctoral thesis, Ho Chi Minh National Academy of Politics]. National Library of Vietnam.

Ly, C. (2018). The quest for research on social class in contemporary Vietnam: Overview of current approaches and suggestions for considering Pierre Bourdieu's theoretical framework. *Journal of Vietnamese Studies, 13*(1), 42–79.

MacQueen, J. B. (1967). Some methods for classification and analysis of multivariate observations. *Proceedings of the Berkeley Symposium on Mathematical Statistics and Probability*, 5(1): 281–297. University of California Press.

Nguyen Tran Lam, & Nguyen Viet Cuong. (2017). *Intragenerational and intergenerational mobility in Vietnam* (ADBI Working Paper No. 722). Asian Development Bank Institute.

Noll, H. (1997). Class, stratification and beyond: The German Case. *The Tocqueville Review, 18*(2), 103–128.

Oxfam. (2018). *Dich chuyen xa hoi va binh dang co hoi tai Viet Nam: Xu huong va cac yeu to tac dong* [Social mobility and equality of opportunity in Vietnam: Trends and impact factors]. Hong Duc Publishing House.

Pham Bich San. (1992). Mot so van de nghien cuu Ha Noi va nhung nhan xet so khoi qua nghien cuu giai doan II [Issues in Hanoi research and preliminary remarks on phase II research]. *Journal of Sociology, 4*(40), 29–34.

Savage, M., Devine, F., Cunningham, N., Friedman, S., Laurison, D., Miles, A., Snee, H., & Taylor, M. (2015). On social class, Ano 2014. *Sociology, 49*(6), 1011–1030.

Savage, M., Devine, F., Cunningham, N., Taylor, M., Li, Y., Hjellbrekke, J., Roux, B. L., Friedman, S., & Miles, A. (2013). A new model of class analysis? Findings from the BBC's great British class survey experiment. *Sociology, 47*(2), 219–250.

Ta Ngoc Tan (Ed.). (2013). *Xu huong bien doi co cau xa hoi Viet Nam* [Trends of changes in social structure in Vietnam]. National Political Publishing House.

Tan Ern Ser. (2015). *Class and social orientations: Key findings from the social stratification survey 2011* (IPS Exchange Series 4). National University of Singapore.

Trinh Duy Luan. (1992). Su phan tang xa hoi theo muc song tai thu do Ha Noi trong nhung nam dau thuc hien Doi Moi [Living standards stratification in Hanoi during the early years of Doi Moi]. *Journal of Sociology, 4*(90), 16–28.

Le Van Toan. (2012). *Phan tang xa hoi o Viet Nam trong qua trinh chuyen doi sang nen kinh te thi truong va hoi nhap quoc te* [Social stratification in Vietnam during the transition toward market economy and international integration]. National Political Publishing House.

World Bank. (1995). *Vietnam: Poverty assessment and strategy* (Report No. 13442-VN). World Bank.

World Bank. (1999). *Vietnam development report* 2000 *attacking poverty* (Report No. 19914-VN). World Bank.

World Bank. (2003). *Vietnam development report 2004 poverty* (Report No. 27130-VN). World Bank.

World Bank. (2007). *Vietnam development report 2008 social protection* (Working Paper No. 43653). World Bank.

World Bank. (2019). *Vietnam development report 2019: Connecting Vietnam for growth and shared prosperity*. World Bank.

World Bank and Ministry of Planning and Investment of Vietnam. (2016). *Vietnam 2035 towards prosperity, creativity, equity, and democracy*. World Bank.

Wright, E. O. (2005). Foundations of a neo-Marxist class analysis. In E. O. Wright (Ed.), *Approaches to class analysis* (pp. 4–30). Cambridge University Press.

PART III

Vietnam in the Regional and Global Settings

CHAPTER 10

Vietnam's WTO Accession and the Pathway to a Global Playing Field: A Critical Perspective

Elodie Mania, Arsène Rieber, and Thi Anh-Dao Tran

1 Introduction

The involvement of developing countries (DCs) in international trade has increased sharply over the last three decades. Since the beginning of the 1990s, they have been engaged in processes of integration that are both regional and multilateral. Indeed, one of the key vehicles of economic integration is the ongoing process of internationalisation of production

This chapter is part of a research study that was presented at the 2nd Workshop of the Growth Models in the Global South Studies Network, *Implications of Post-Keynesian Economics for the Study of Growth Models in the Global North and South: Theoretical and Methodological Challenges* (9 September 2021). The authors are grateful to the participants for helpful comments. All remaining errors or omissions are ours.

E. Mania
Paris Dauphine University, Paris, France
e-mail: elodie.mania@dauphine.psl.eu

T. A.-D. Tran (ed.), *Rethinking Asian Capitalism*,
https://doi.org/10.1007/978-3-030-98104-4_10

through the entry of transnational corporations (TNCs) into manufacturing activities and financial services. Moreover, the rapid growth of the newly industrialising countries (NICs) and the emergence of China in the world economy have added weight to the idea of waves of industrial development spreading across the Asian area. This regional pattern of industrialisation has been likened to the "flying geese" paradigm originally formulated by Akamatsu (1932). Devised to analyse Japan's catch-up process, it describes the change in industrial structure over time, starting with labour-intensive industries and shifting gradually to more capital-intensive industries. As successive stages are described as inverted V-shaped curves (depending on shifts in industry competitiveness), the author imagined the flying geese metaphor.

This paradigm provides a description of the life cycle of various industries in the course of economic development; but more prominently, it involves a division of labour on the basis of industrial and locational hierarchy that contemporary globalisation has shaped. In this process, trade and foreign direct investment (FDI) are the main mechanisms by which development is transmitted from one country to another through "spread effects". The development process results from waves of industry spread, which are dictated by market relations (i.e. corporate strategies) rather than by any country specialisation.

The early performance of the first-tier NICs suggested that outward orientation and reliance on exports became a model for promoting long-run growth. However, the depth of the economic devastation that hit Asian countries in July 1997 caused analysts to wonder whether a trade-led growth regime could be resilient to unpredictable shocks.[1] The very marked decline in imports and the absence of export vigour in the crisis

[1] Economic vulnerability is the exposure of an economy to exogenous adverse shocks while economic resilience is defined as the ability of an economy to withstand or minimise the effects of such shocks.

A. Rieber
University of Rouen Normandy, Paris, France
e-mail: arsene.rieber@univ-rouen.fr

T. A.-D. Tran (✉)
LASTA (University of Rouen Normandy), Faculty of Law, Economics and Management, Rouen, France

IRASEC-CNRS, Bangkok, Thailand
e-mail: thianh-dao.tran@irasec.com

countries confirmed the importance of trade in the spread and amplification of real shocks, both through a traditional multiplier effect linked to the decline in economic activity and domestic demand (the worst afflicted countries being South Korea, Indonesia and Thailand) and, more particularly, through another multiplier effect relying on the trade between supplying and vertically linked industries. This is the consequence of both the rapid spread of industrialisation within the region and the successful integration of these countries into the international production networks of TNCs.

In fact, the trade-FDI *nexus* aimed at accelerating the industrialisation process has made most Asian countries strongly interdependent and competitors as they have become embedded in complex subcontracting networks. The related division of labour creates a strong link between imports and exports, so that any fluctuation of one country's exports immediately affects its imports. This strong sensitivity of imports to GDP, together with the geographical concentration of trade, amplifies the spillover effects of a recession occurring in one country on its trading partners. In the light of growing inter- and intra-regional trade, it appears that export-oriented industrialisation provides active transmission channels to any potential shock in international demand.

Since the early 1990s, integration into the world economy has been the key driver of Vietnam's outstanding economic outcomes by encouraging competition and a market-friendly business environment (World Bank, 2020). The country formally completed World Trade Organization (WTO) accession on 11 January 2007, which marked the culmination of a lengthy series of efforts to integrate the national economy into global markets. Today, the Southeast Asian economy is clearly one of the most open to world trade, with an average ratio to GDP of 61.5% and 66.6% for exports and imports of goods respectively. In 2018, trade in merchandises reached 196% of GDP. Meanwhile, exports and imports grew at an average rate of 4.3% and 3.4%, respectively, per year over the period 1990–2018.[2]

Vietnam is following the successive waves of rapid industrialisation in East Asia by implementing an export-oriented growth strategy. Against this backdrop, the country is deeply integrated into global value chains (GVCs), one of the most prominent features of globalisation. The GVC

[2] Unless otherwise noted, data are taken from the World Bank's World Development Indicators (WDI) database.

participation index provides an estimation of how much an economy is connected to these chains through its foreign trade. According to the OECD-WTO trade in value added (TiVA) database, Vietnam's GVC participation index was 55.6% of total gross exports in 2015 (14 points above the average rate for DCs), with an average growth rate of 16.5% per year over the period 2005–2015 (10 percentage points higher than that for its other developing counterparts). Because export-oriented activity clearly supports the country's growth, further opportunities are expected from the recent adoption of three major free trade agreements (FTAs), namely the Comprehensive and Progressive Agreement for Trans-Pacific Partnership (CPTPP) with 10 of the fastest-growing Pacific Rim economies in December 2018; the European Union-Vietnam Free Trade Agreement (EVFTA) in June 2020; and the Regional Comprehensive Economic Partnership (RCEP) with 14 Asian neighbours in November 2020. Together, these three agreements covered approximately 81% of Vietnam's trade flows in 2019 (World Bank, 2020).

This experience is not unique to Vietnam: for many DCs, export performance has become crucial in order to make international integration an efficient instrument of development. Their involvement in TNC production is expected to boost their export capabilities by attracting FDI on a large scale. In the long term, however, there will be a differentiated impact on countries' export and import growth rates, which suggests that integration into the globalised economy may impact on the indigenous economy through changing patterns of trade and redefine the long-run growth rate accordingly. A key concern, then, is whether Vietnam's trade-led growth is sustainable in the long run and whether it is resilient to any unpredictable shocks.

This chapter examines Vietnam's growth performance over the past years of integration efforts to join the global playing field. To this end, we apply the multi-country specification of Thirlwall's law proposed by Bagnai et al. (2016). Because of cross-country linkages forged by bilateral trade and given Vietnam's heavy reliance on foreign-based determinants, a decomposition of the evolution of the balance-of-payments (BP) constraint (i.e. BP performance) into different factors from different sources is undertaken in order to address the post-WTO outcomes. More specifically, we measure the respective contribution of Vietnam's trading partners to its long-run growth rate. This allows us to analyse how and through which transmission channels the geography of international trade has impacted Vietnam's growth before and after WTO accession.

The remainder of this chapter is organised as follows. Section 2 describes the theoretical framework for this study, while in Sect. 3 we present our database. We begin by analysing how partners' income growth and the structure of trade evolved. We go on to consider Vietnam's trade elasticities. In Sect. 4 we assess the impact of WTO accession on the long-run growth rate as well as the trade position relative to partners. In Sect. 5 our main results are summarised and conclusions drawn.

2 Our Theoretical Framework

2.1 Interdependency in an Open Economy

As globalisation makes nations more interdependent, Vietnam has to address future challenges by considering the potential "international spillovers" to the domestic economy that come from trade integration. In a highly interconnected global system, the spillover effects stemming from trade mean that countries and industries are growingly inter-linked or embedded; this is a permanent, structural feature of contemporary globalisation. A striking example is the extent to which the World Bank (2020) attempts to identify "a trade-oriented connectivity strategy" wherein specific corridors will prove critical to improving Vietnam's trade competitiveness in nine value chains, which together account for over 70% of total exports.[3] According to the report, the country needs to further embrace global markets and actively participate in GVCs.

In our view however, there are two main drawbacks to the current growth literature applied to Vietnam. Firstly, the existing studies on the impacts of trade integration (either through WTO membership or through participation in GVCs) on the long-run growth rate mainly adopt a supply-side approach to various aspects of the economic system, with a focus on the production function aspects such as the supply of productive factors, productivity growth, technology change or technical efficiency. The supply side is obviously essential but these are problems on which most DCs are already focusing their efforts. Secondly, most studies say nothing of the economic consequences emanating from foreign trade; and when they are taken into account, external factors are either given or rather "anonymous". But in the real world, it is impossible to understand the growth

[3] These nine value chains are textile and garments, leather and footwear, electronics, wood products, rice, aquaculture, coffee, rubber, and vegetables and fruits.

rate in an open developing economy without reference to the changing structure of trade or demand-led constraints. For example, Korniyenko et al. (2017) adopt a network approach to their analysis of localised supply shocks in GVCs, but they assume constant demand. Although Vietnam's gross exports are growing, the large differences between exports in the BP (i.e. aggregate trade flows) and value-added exports clearly indicate that the country's exports have a high import content.[4] In heterodox thinking, what changes is the real history under analysis and the theoretical background needs to adapt to this new historical context.

The country has become a favoured destination for export-processing production. Ultimately, however, the changing geography of international trade can shape the evolution of a country's future path through international spillovers, that is, the transmission of any shock or disturbance from one country to the others in a highly interconnected global trading system. An illustrative example was the East Asian financial crisis of 1997, then the global financial crisis of 2008, where exporters and importers facing collapse in external and domestic demand had to adjust their trade flows accordingly. International spillovers reflect the fact that the responsiveness of trade flows to change in demand has been rising over time (Freund, 2009). When any trend emerges, Vietnam could be further affected by the effects produced by the country's trading partners. In the long term, there will be a differentiated impact on export and import growth rates, and that impact will vary across different groups of exporting and importing countries. It is clear then that the external demand-side factors are neither given nor anonymous anymore.

The belief that aggregate demand can have long-lasting effects on economic growth is not new to heterodox economists. Against this backdrop, we propose to examine the macroeconomic determinants of Vietnam's growth by means of a demand-led decomposition on the foreign side. In that respect, the theory of balance-of-payments-constrained growth (BPCG) is particularly well suited to our purpose. Originally proposed by Thirlwall (1979), this theory draws on the BP constraint in order to explain long-run growth. It has two salient features in trying to give demand a prominent role in growth theory.

[4] In 2018, exports in the BP were four times greater than value-added exports; this large difference was attributable largely to intermediate goods imported for export processing (ASEAN-Japan Centre, 2020).

Firstly, the theory questions the profitability of openness for DCs by concentrating attention on the BP aspects of trade. Drawing on structuralist development economics as a school of thought that prevails in Latin America, and whose most important contributions were either Prebisch's (1959) centre-periphery or Chenery and Michael's (1962) two-gap models, Thirlwall's law uses the historical-deductive method in order to understand economic systems and economic development (Bresser-Pereira et al., 2014; Taylor, 2004). For most DCs, the dominant constraint is a shortage of foreign exchange ("external strangulation") associated with BP deficits; BP equilibrium requires that the growth of output be constrained so that imports grow no faster than exports. In other words, the real resource gains from trade may be offset if foreign exchange is the dominant constraint on output.

Secondly, the theory argues that the major constraint on demand in an open economy is its BP position, and that it is the *structure* of exports and imports that determines GDP growth consistent with BP equilibrium working through their income elasticities (Thirlwall, 2013). In a structuralist vision, the role of foreign financing in the development process is to relieve the dual gaps (i.e. either domestic saving or foreign exchange). However: "In the long run, no country can grow faster than that rate consistent with balance of payments equilibrium on current account unless it can finance ever-growing deficits, which, in general, it cannot" Thirlwall, 2011: 310). Because DCs are not allowed to run current account deficits for considerable periods of time, only additional foreign exchange can relieve the BP constraint. Accordingly, a central feature of the BPCG framework is the role of the structure of production and trade in determining the growth of exports and imports, and consequently the BP performance. Any industrial sectors or partnerships likely to enjoy high (low) elastic-income demand for exports (imports) are to be promoted.

Because the BP is a determinant of growth performance, its reliance on foreign-based determinants enables us to analyse how, and through which transmission channels, the changing pattern of production-trade resulting from WTO accession is likely to impact the evolution of Vietnam's external constraint and corresponding growth rates. In that respect, this historical-structural approach to the BP is at odds with the economic orthodoxy that currently prevails in Vietnam. Unlike the neoliberal consensus, which assumes economic growth and trade to be supply oriented, the demand-side view of growth based on the BP constraint is a powerful predictor of inter-country growth differences (Thirlwall, 2013).

2.2 The Balance-of-Payments-Constrained Growth Model

In the basic model assuming constant relative prices, Thirlwall's law postulates that the growth rate of an open economy that is consistent with BP equilibrium (denoted here $\dot{Y}_{BP}$) defines the maximum rate that it can reach in the long run (Thirlwall, 1979). In its original version, this growth rate of domestic income is determined by the growth of its exports in volume ($\dot{X}$) divided by the income elasticity of demand for imports (π). To put it differently, the BP equilibrium growth rate depends on the exogenously given growth of world income ($\dot{Z}$) and the relative size of the income elasticities of demand for exports (ε) and imports (π). This relation can be formulated as follows:

$$\dot{Y}_{BP} = \frac{\dot{X}}{\pi} = \frac{\varepsilon \dot{Z}}{\pi} \tag{10.1}$$

If the actual growth rate is lower than the BPCG rate $\dot{Y}_{BP}$, the country will accumulate trade surpluses and become a net capital exporter. Conversely, if it exceeds $\dot{Y}_{BP}$, the current account worsens and the country will become a net capital importer, but this cannot continue indefinitely. An economy is "BP constrained" whenever its growth rate must adjust downwards to maintain the BP equilibrium. In the long run, therefore, $\dot{Y}_{BP}$ defines a binding constraint on growth in the sense that it cannot exceed this upper limit for prolonged periods because, if it does, it will quickly incur BP difficulties.

In practice however, a country exports to, and imports from, many different destinations. This makes it necessary to disaggregate the BPCG model into a multi-country setting in order to capture trade relations between the individual country and blocks of countries. A "generalised" model was originally developed by Nell (2003), who disaggregates the world income growth variable ($\dot{Z}$) to deal with the income elasticities of exports and imports to/from different partners. However, the author assumes, rather than testing, the irrelevance of relative prices. In view of this, Bagnai et al. (2016) extend the multi-country specification by developing a rigorous decomposition of the BP constraint to highlight asymmetries in relative price changes among partner areas. This allows the authors to identify the role of structural parameters in bilateral trade, such as import and export market shares, price and income elasticities, in predicting growth rates in the long run.

Based on Bagnai et al. (2016), our analytical extension assumes that a given country *i* has *n* trading partners. As a consequence, Eqs. (10.2) and (10.3) feature the conventional demand functions for imports and exports respectively, and Eq. (10.4) sets an equilibrium condition for the current account of BP as follows:

$$M_{ij} = \left(\frac{P_i}{E_{ij} P_j} \right)^{\psi_{ij}} Y_i^{\pi_{ij}} \tag{10.2}$$

$$X_{ij} = \left(\frac{E_{ij} P_j}{P_i} \right)^{\eta_{ij}} Y_j^{\varepsilon_{ij}} \tag{10.3}$$

$$P_i \sum_j X_{ij} = \sum_j E_{ij} P_j M_{ij} \tag{10.4}$$

where X_{ij} is the real demand of partner *j* for country *i* exports, M_{ij} is country *i*'s imports from partner *j* and Y_i (Y_j) denotes income in country *i* (country *j*). The price and income elasticities are denoted by $\psi_{ij} > 0$ and $\pi_{ij} > 0$ respectively for country *i* imports from partner *j*; $\eta_{ij} > 0$ and $\varepsilon_{ij} > 0$ for country *i* exports to *j*. We will define $R_{ij} = P_i/(E_{ij}P_j)$ as the bilateral relative price or real exchange rate (RER, namely the ratio of domestic to foreign prices expressed in domestic currency) where P_i is country *i* export prices, P_j is export prices in *j* and E_{ij} is the bilateral nominal exchange rate (measured as the domestic price of foreign currency).

If we express the BP-equilibrium condition (10.4) in terms of growth rates, we obtain:

$$\dot{P}_i + \sum_j v_{ij} \dot{X}_{ij} = \sum_j \mu_{ij} \left(\dot{E}_{ij} + \dot{P}_j + \dot{M}_{ij} \right) \tag{10.5}$$

where:
$$v_{ij} = \frac{X_{ij}}{\sum_j X_{ij}} \qquad \mu_{ij} = \frac{E_{ij} P_j M_{ij}}{\sum_j E_{ij} P_j M_{ij}}$$

v_{ij} and μ_{ij} are, respectively, the market shares of partner *j* in country *i*'s total exports (in volume) and in country *i*'s total imports (in value).

Solving for the growth rate of country *i*, we obtain a disaggregated version of Thirlwall's law as follows:

$$\dot{Y}_{i,BP} = \frac{\sum_j \dot{R}_{ij} \left[\mu_{ij} \left(1 - \psi_{ij} \right) - v_{ij} \eta_{ij} \right] + \sum_j v_{ij} \varepsilon_{ij} \dot{Y}_j}{\sum_j \mu_{ij} \pi_{ij}} \tag{10.6}$$

where dots on letters stand for the growth rate of variables.

Equation (10.6) defines the maximum growth rate that an economy *i* can reach in the long run and expresses propositions central to the BPCG approach. Firstly, country *i*'s growth rate consistent with BP equilibrium is dependent on other countries' *j* growth rates; however, how fast *i* grows relative to *j* in the long run depends crucially on structural and behavioural parameters. The export volume term in the numerator features a weighted sum of real export growth, where the export market shares intertwine with the income elasticities to magnify trading partners' GDP growth. Secondly, country *i*'s growth rate consistent with BP equilibrium is inversely related to its appetite for imports, which is featured in the denominator by a sum of bilateral income elasticities of imports weighted by the corresponding market shares. At the core of BPCG models are the income elasticities of demand for exports and imports; but the contribution of our multi-country setting is to add market shares on exports and imports, which lie at the heart of the country's competitiveness.

Lastly, the relative price term at the numerator can raise the growth in income consistent with BP equilibrium provided the Marshall-Lerner condition (MLC) for a successful depreciation holds at the bilateral level. A decrease in bilateral relative prices (i.e. a real depreciation, $\dot{R}_{ij} < 0$) has a positive effect on $\dot{Y}_{i,BP}$ if the term in square brackets (whose sign depends on the trade-weighted price elasticities) is negative, that is: $\mu_{ij} - \mu_{ij}\psi_{ij} - v_{ij}\eta_{ij} < 0$.

If relative price changes are assumed constant in the long run, not efficient enough to adjust BP, then Eq. (10.6) becomes:

$$\dot{Y}^{*}_{i,BP} = \frac{\sum_{j=1}^{n} v_{ij}\varepsilon_{ij}\dot{Y}_{j}}{\sum_{j=1}^{n} \mu_{ij}\pi_{ij}} \tag{10.7}$$

While there is a potential channel for the RER to relieve the BP constraint, this Perraton's (2003) "strong" version of Thirlwall's law tells us that patterns of production and trade are critical because the only sure and long-term solution to raising country *i*'s growth rate consistent with BP equilibrium is structural change affiliated to income elasticities. In other words, *structure* matters for the growth rate consistent with BP equilibrium.

To some extent, the BP constraint measures country *i*'s competitiveness *vis-à-vis* each partner *j*, which is expressed jointly in the volume effect (the weighted sum of bilateral exports growth rates from country *i* to its partners using the export volume market shares) and in the appetite for imports (the weighed sum of the income elasticities of bilateral imports of country i from its partners using the import value market shares). Any improvement in bilateral exports growth has a positive effect on long-run growth; conversely, a heavier reliance on bilateral imports has a negative effect that is detrimental to long-run growth.

Another central feature of the multi-country specification is that it cannot be additively disaggregated by partner area; hence, we cannot define something as a "BoP-constrained-by-partner-j-growth rate". In fact, any bilateral deficit could be financed by another bilateral surplus; as a consequence, the aggregate BP constraint cannot be expressed as an additive function of bilateral balances (Bagnai et al., 2016). However, the extended law allows one to assess separately the contribution of each partner j's variable (either in country i''s export market or import demand) to *changes* in the aggregate BP constraint of country i. By relaxing the external constraint, any structural change that positively affects the BPCG rate will reflect improved relative competitiveness. Similarly, any change in the geographic distribution of import and export market shares adds to the structural parameters in determining the BPCG rate.

3 Database and Preliminary Estimations

3.1 Data Analysis

To assess the impact of Vietnam's WTO accession on the country's long-run growth, we need to identify its patterns of trade, that is, the geography of Vietnam''s bilateral imports and exports. Since the economic growth of one country depends on the growth rate of others through the external constraint, this mutual interdependence should be captured. By the same token, the import behaviour should be differentiated in order to assess the critical role of geography in determining Vietnam's foreign dependency.

In the empirical implementation of the BPCG model, we select ten key countries or blocks of countries that are Vietnam''s major trading partners. Appendix A presents the list of countries in each partner area; the 11th group covers the rest of the world. In our trade statistics, these ten partner areas accounted in 2017 for 90% and 91% respectively of Vietnam's exports in volume and imports in value. Because international trade is limited to merchandises, data on the variables of interest were collected from the UN Comtrade statistics and the World Bank WDI database over the period from 1990 to 2017. Descriptions of the data used for the analysis are given in Appendix B.

Before analysing our findings, we need first to examine how ***partners*** matter in Vietnam's external constraint. Because of cross-country linkages, there are three explanatory elements when looking at Eq. (10.6), and without going into trade elasticities at the moment.

First, the role of relative price change among partner areas ($\dot{R}_{ij}$) is plotted in Fig. 10.1, where a decrease in bilateral relative prices corresponds to a real depreciation. For each partner, the average growth rates are constructed for the whole period 1990–2017 and separately for the two sub-periods before and after WTO accession. When looking at the whole period, the figure highlights asymmetries among partners with a favourable evolution of Vietnam's prices relative to China, the rest of Asia, Latin America and to a lesser extent the rest of the world. However, differences emerge when we split the period considered into two sub-periods. In the first sub-period 1990–2007, the *Doi Moi* policy led subsequently to favourable bilateral prices relative to all partner areas except Japan and, to a slight extent, India. But in the sub-period 2008–2017, relative prices were deteriorating with most partners (higher bars) except China. To

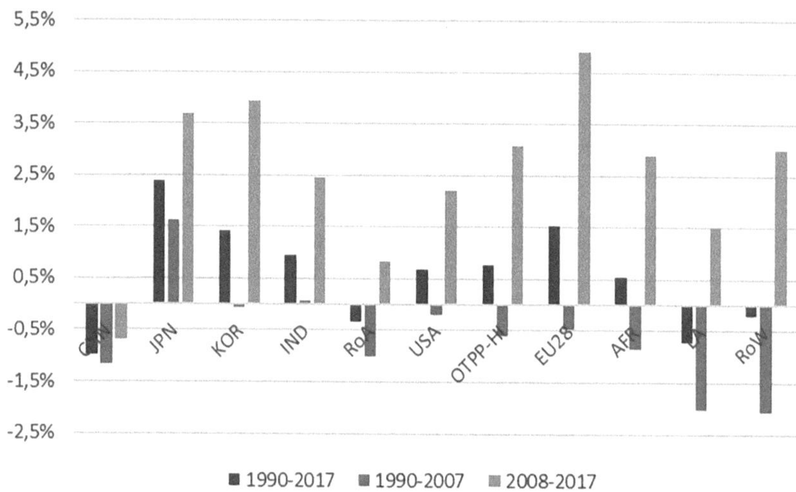

Fig. 10.1 Average annual growth rates of relative prices by trading partner (in %). Source: Comtrade, Authors' calculations

what extent this unfavourable change would affect Vietnam's long-run growth rate after WTO membership depends on whether the bilateral market-share-weighted MLC is fulfilled or not. This provides evidence that the RER variable is only one part of an export-led strategy so long as the effects of export and import market shares both contribute to the evolution of the BP constraint.

Second, the dynamics of partner *j*'s income growth ($\dot{Y}_j$) and the related impact on Vietnam's volume of exports are of major importance (Fig. 10.2). Over the whole period, high average GDP growth for China, and to a lesser extent for India, stands in contrast to the other partners. With the exception of South Korea, the most advanced countries (JPN, USA, OTPPHI, EU28) lag behind with relatively low average growth rates whatever the periods considered. However, all countries show a decline in their growth rates in the second sub-period (lower bars) except for India and the rest of the world. This decline was substantial in China, where the catch-up process was running out of steam: the annual growth rate averaged 10% over the sub-period 1990–2007 and then dropped to 8% during the sub-period 2008–2017. The same trend applies to South Korea, whose average annual growth rates fell from 6% to 3%.

Third, comparison of trade market shares before and after WTO accession gives information about shifts in international trade patterns.

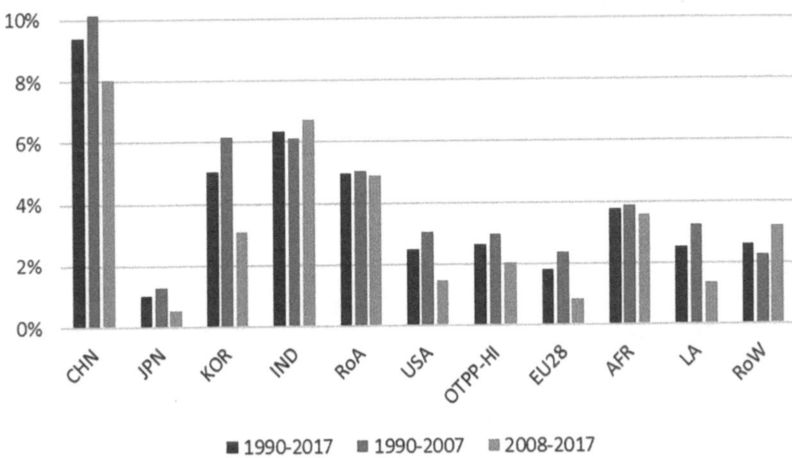

Fig. 10.2 Average annual GDP growth rates for Viet Nam's trading partners (in %). Source: Comtrade, Authors' calculations

Figure 10.3a depicts the evolving shares of Vietnam's total exports in different partner markets. From 2000 to 2017, China and the United States replaced the EU and Japan to become the country's leading export markets. As the former are the two principal trading partners of most countries in Asia and the Pacific Rim, the favourable evolution of this behavioural parameter reveals that Vietnam gained competitiveness *vis-à-vis* its main competitors in the two largest individual markets (China and the United States). Unsurprisingly, the most significant import shares shown in Fig. 10.3b come from regional partners, namely: RoA, CHN, KOR and JPN. In 2000, these partners accounted for 67% of Vietnam's total imports in value; by 2017, China and South Korea captured the largest shares (30% and 21% respectively) at the expense of Japan and the ASEAN members. Trade with these two countries is the most tangible aspect of Vietnam's integration into regional value chains (in electronics for example). As of 2017, Vietnam's trade with other ASEAN members accounted for 25% (just higher than the 23% average for the group) while India was the most important partner in South Asia (World Bank, 2020).

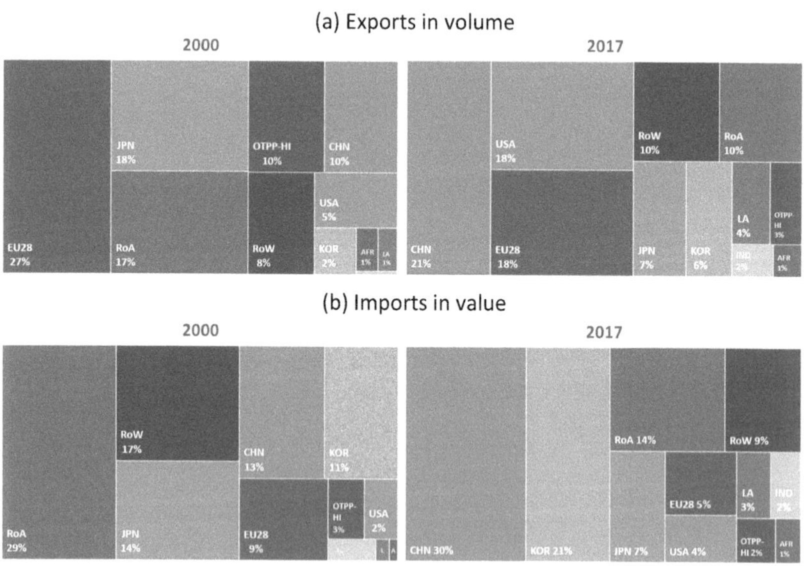

Fig. 10.3 Trade market shares (in %). Source: Comtrade, Authors' calculations

Any change in the shares of total exports (in volume) in different markets and in the sources of total imports (in value) after WTO accession will affect the bilateral MLC. They reflect changes in Vietnam's export ($v_{ij}\varepsilon_{ij}$) and import ($\mu_{ij}\pi_{ij}$) competitiveness relative to partner j. Both terms then play a critical role in summarising the international trade behaviour that is likely to change the country's external constraint.

3.2 Estimation Results on the Long-Run Elasticities

As a starting point, structural parameters (i.e. the long-run elasticities of bilateral exports and imports featuring the BP constraint) are estimated over the period from 1990 to 2017; this will allow us to construct the average growth rates predicted by the BPCG model for Vietnam. Since Thirlwall's law deals with long-run growth, co-integration techniques are used (see Mania et al., 2021). To save space, we report in Table 10.1 the estimation results on the long-run elasticities for import and export demand functions.

On the whole, the income elasticities for both exports and imports are found to be statistically significant with the relevant sign. As usual in open

Table 10.1 A summary of Vietnam's estimated elasticities for the period 1990–2017

	Bilateral Imports		*Bilateral Exports*	
	Income	*Prices*	*Income*	*Prices*
CHN	1.758***	-3.148**	2.521***	1.158*
JPN	2.703***	-0.629***	10.567***	0.860***
KOR	2.756***	*Ns*	3.813***	-0.734***
IND	3.402***	*Ns*	4.566***	*Ns*
RoA	2.370***	*Ns*	2.026***	0.915***
USA	2.647***	*Ns*	11.298***	0.721*
OTPP-HI	2.364***	0.778*	4.054***	1.947**
EU-28	1.891***	*Ns*	8.556***	*Ns*
AFR	3.539***	*Ns*	3.743***	*Ns*
LA	3.839***	*Ns*	6.869***	*Ns*
ROW	1.357***	*Ns*	3.840***	*Ns*

Notes: *ns* stands for not significant. ***, ** and * indicate that coefficients are significant respectively at 1%, 5% and 10%

Source: Mania et al. (2021)

economies, the income elasticities are bigger than one but they are higher on the export than on the import side, with the largest ones featured in the United States, Japan, and the EU (i.e. the North). However, asymmetry in Vietnam's bilateral income elasticities contradicts Dutt's (2003) North-South model of trade with empirical evidence that the Southern export elasticity with respect to Northern income growth is less than the reciprocal elasticity for the North (i.e. the South's import elasticity). Our estimation results imply that, with constant market shares, the GDP growth rates of these key Northern partners will impact strongly on the corresponding bilateral balance. Only in the rest of Asia does an income elasticity of imports bigger than that of exports mean that if both Vietnam and the corresponding partner attempt to grow at the same rate, the situation is clearly not sustainable in the long run because the rate of Vietnam's imports growth will be greater than the rate of exports growth. Bilateral trade with RoA will generate a growing and perpetual deficit for Vietnam.

In contrast, bilateral price elasticities are statistically significant only in a few cases, with the largest number on the export side. Interestingly, the price elasticities of Vietnam's imports are statistically significant with a negative sign for China and Japan. Symmetrically, Vietnam's exports to South Korea display a significant, but negative, price elasticity. This counterintuitive sign is consistent with recent findings on a negative value of Vietnam's price elasticities in bilateral trade as a consequence of Asia's vertical integration (Ha et al., 2016; Hooy et al., 2015; Phi & Tran, 2020). It appears that participation in GVCs challenges the price elasticities when gross exports in the BP (i.e. aggregate trade flows) are computed.

Taking into account a structural approach to the BP, Vietnam's long-run predicted growth is based on trading partners' growth, on the one hand, and, on the other, on the country's competitiveness as reflected in trade elasticities. But against the backdrop of GVC participation and greater regional integration, it appears that another line of inquiry (labelled "East-West") has shaped the geography of trade.

To some extent, it is not easy to sell more when external conditions are unfavourable and when price elasticities are low (Thirlwall, 2013). In Vietnam, relative price changes do not work as an adjustment mechanism because the bulk of price elasticities are insignificant and, when significant, they are low as shown here. Table 10.1 implies that, with given market shares, the bilateral MLC is not satisfied in most cases: in the face of price inelasticity, it is primarily income that adjusts to maintain current account equilibrium of BP (Thirlwall, 2013). While introducing a relative price term, the generalised version of Thirlwall's law applied to Vietnam strongly supports the role of structural parameters in determining BPCG rate predictions. In other words, the RER as a development-relevant policy tool is perhaps a necessary, but not sufficient, condition for supporting export-led growth.

4 Empirical Results

4.1 A Global Assessment

We now turn to the main purpose of our empirical investigation, which is to test the model predictions for Vietnam. Moreover, our multi-country version will allow us to break down the overall impact of WTO accession in such a way as to show the evolution of Vietnam's trade position *vis-à-vis* each partner *j*. The objective then is twofold. Firstly, we construct the average growth rates predicted by the BPCG model for Vietnam. Secondly, we examine how, and through which transmission channels, WTO accession explains the evolution of Vietnam's external constraint.

In this subsection, we first compare the two average growth rates predicted by Eqs. (10.6) and (10.7) with the actual rates in order to test whether or not the country's growth was BP constrained over the period from 1990 to 2017 and to distinguish before and after WTO accession. Table 10.2 reports the predicted BPCG rates and the actual rates ($\dot{Y}$ in the last column). We observe that the Vietnamese economy grew at a slightly lower rate (6.8%) than that predicted by the generalised BPCG model (7%). Hence, Vietnam was respecting its BP constraint and our generalised Thirlwall's law aptly predicts its long-run growth path.

What the empirical results by sub-period reveal is that there are two clearly distinct stages: the country was respecting its BP constraint during the sub-period 1990–2007 when the actual growth averaged 7.3%, while

Table 10.2 Viet Nam's BP-constrained and actual growth rates by sub-periods

	$\dot{Y}^*_{BP}$	$\dot{Y}_{BP}$	$\dot{Y}$
1990–2017	7.2%	7.0%	6.8%
1990–2007	8.0%	7.5%	7.3%
2008–2017	5.6%	5.8%	6.0%
08–17/90-07change	**-2.4**	**-1.7**	**-1.3**

it grew above the BPCG rate after 2007 at an actual average rate of 6%. This comparison across time shows that Vietnam's external constraint shifted downward, compelling the country to slow down its actual growth rate in order to maintain the BP equilibrium. The generalised BPCG as well as the actual growth rates both declined from 1990–2007 to 2008–2017, with a spread of 1.7 and 1.3 percentage points respectively. The gap is even worse when we take into account the strong law (first column), meaning that changes in the export volume term and in the appetite for imports were prevailing in the result.[5] This overall impact is reflected in a 22.6% reduction in the average growth rate after joining the WTO; it is consistent with stylised facts as a slight surplus on the current account was registered first, before subsequently turning out to be in turbulence after 2007.

Our results suggest that, in the post-WTO accession era, the BP constraint appeared to be binding. First, relative prices have been considered, as we can see that the strong law defined by Eq. (10.7) overvalues the constrained growth rate by about 0.2 of a percentage point. In fact, there are still difficulties in understanding the exact mechanisms between the RER, trade and growth; more theoretical work is still needed to better understand them. To this end, a neo-structuralist approach is proposed which posits that the RER is not determined outside the system (Bresser-Pereira et al., 2014; Cimoli & Porcile, 2013). In Vietnam, however, relative price changes are not an efficient BP adjustment weapon as the demand for exports and imports is inelastic to prices.

Second, the changing geography of international trade has shaped the BP performance, as the export volume term and the appetite for imports are rooted in different patterns of production-trade. Accordingly, the expected outcomes of Vietnam's accession to WTO should take into account not only export performance but also the imported goods that are used to produce exports. In our view, however, they are worrisome for growth predictions as the increased appetite for imports with export orientation should be interpreted as an obstacle to achieving sustainable growth.

[5] The decline is substantial because, as growth is a cumulative process, the reductions in GDP levels translate into consequent reductions in average annual GDP growth rates over the sub-period.

4.2 A more Detailed Analytical Breakdown

Overall, Vietnam has achieved rapid growth in recent years but it has proved to be unsustainable and macroeconomic stability has deteriorated as a result. What is now interesting is to examine the channels through which the overall impact of WTO accession is transmitted into Vietnam's BP performance. As pointed out already, the generalised law cannot be additively disaggregated by partner area. However, it still makes sense to analyse the contribution of each explanatory variable to the *change* in the BP constraint. The multi-country specification enables us to separately assess the contribution of partner *j*'s variables to the tightening of the BP constraint between the two sub-periods.

Owing to its structure, Eq. (10.6) can be decomposed linearly through a Taylor series expansion as follows:

$$\Delta \dot{Y}_{VN,BP} = \sum_j \left\{ \underbrace{\Delta \dot{Y}_j \frac{\partial \dot{Y}_{VN,BP}}{\partial \dot{Y}_j}}_{\text{partner growth}} + \underbrace{\Delta v_{ij} \frac{\partial \dot{Y}_{VN,BP}}{\partial v_{ij}}}_{\text{export market share}} + \underbrace{\Delta \mu_{i,j} \frac{\partial \dot{Y}_{VN,BP}}{\partial \mu_{i,j}}}_{\text{import market share}} + \underbrace{\Delta \dot{R}_{i,j} \frac{\partial \dot{Y}_{VN,BP}}{\partial \dot{R}_{i,j}}}_{\text{relative price}} \right\} + R \qquad (10.8)$$

Where Δ represents change in the variables between 1990–2007 and 2008–2017 sub-periods and the last term R is the remainder of the approximation.

Because all the derivatives with respect to partner *j*'s variables represent change relative to the 2008–2017 sub-period (i.e. an overall decline of 1.7 percentage points in Vietnam's predicted growth rate), a positive change associated with one component explains the overall decline in the BPCG rate. Conversely, a negative sign means that it mitigates the decrease. The BP constraint development can then be disaggregated into four components (see Mania et al., 2021):

(i) *A partner growth effect.* Partners' income growth, by modifying Vietnam's volume of exports, will subsequently affect the external constraint. A positive sign associated with this component explains the tightening of the BP constraint.

(ii) *An export market share effect.* When WTO accession increases the relative size of Vietnam's volume of exports in partner *j*'s market, it will reflect an improvement in country's competitiveness and soften the constraint tightening. This favourable effect is then associated with a negative sign.

(iii) *An import market share effect.* Symmetrically, when partner *j* increases its share in Vietnam's imports (in value), the unfavourable effect explains the tightening of the BP constraint and is therefore associated with a positive sign.

(iv) *A relative price effect.* In the partial derivative with respect to partner *j*, the effect of the relative price change depends on whether the market-share-weighted MLC is fulfilled or not. If the relative price term is important in determining growth, as argued in the neo-structuralist literature, it is still subject to behavioural parameters.

Table 10.3 presents the result of the linear decomposition of $\Delta \dot{Y}_{VN,BP}$ by effect and by partner area. To get a better understanding of their relative weights, the contributions of each effect and partner are expressed as a percentage of the overall decrease in the predicted growth rate after 2007. The different effects by aggregating over partner *j*'s contribution are depicted in the last column. For example, the contribution of China's income growth to the tightening of Vietnam's BP constraint is equal to 16.8% of the overall decrease (first line, first column), while the total partner growth effect is equal to 183.3% (last column of Table 10.3). The same breakdown is produced when we aggregate over the different effects by partner area (last line of Table 10.3). A positive sign associated with China in the last line (14.4%) means that this partner worsens Vietnam's BP constraint.

By aggregating over partner areas, we get the decomposition by effect of the overall constraint tightening (shown in the last column of Table 10.3), which enables us to gauge the relative importance of the different mechanisms at work. We observe that 183.3% of the deterioration in the BP constraint is explained by foreign income changes and 21% by Vietnam's deteriorating import market shares. As shown in Fig. 10.2, growth in all trading partners declined after 2007, except in India and the rest of the world. But average growth rates remained sluggish in the

Table 10.3 A full breakdown of the total decrease in Vietnam's BPCG rate between 1990–2007 and 2008–2017 by effect and by partner area (in %)

	CHN	*JPN*	*KOR*	*IND*	*RoA*	*USA*	*OTPP*	*EU28*	*AFR*	*LA*	*RoW*	***Total by effect***
Partner growth	16.8	17.9	12.1	-0.8	0.9	75.4	3.7	56.1	0.4	8.4	-7.8	**183.3**
Export market share	-27.8	6.2	-7.2	-3.9	8.4	-34.2	1.2	6.6	-0.8	-2.9	-5.3	**-59.7**
Import market share	36.2	-6.6	4.5	4.2	-18.9	4.9	-0.9	-7.2	1.4	7.4	-3.8	**21.0**
Relative prices	-10.7	-2.6	-15.3	-1.2	-2.8	5.1	6.8	-7.7	-0.7	-1.9	-13.5	**-44.5**
Total by area	**14.4**	**14.9**	**-5.9**	**-1.8**	**-12.3**	**51.1**	**10.8**	**47.8**	**0.4**	**11.0**	**-30.4**	**100.0**

developed economies (JPN, USA, OTPPHI, EU28) and this impacted heavily on Vietnam's BP performance.

With regard to the export market share and relative price effects, a contrasting picture emerges, with a negative sign meaning that they mitigate the decrease in Vietnam's BPCG rate. When the WTO accession came into force, Vietnam benefitted from better access to foreign markets and higher export market shares helped to counterbalance the unfavourable partner growth effect. In addition, Fig. 10.1 plots the unfavourable change in relative prices between the two sub-periods. However, the bilateral MLCs are unfulfilled in most cases, leading unexpectedly to an easing of Vietnam's external constraint.

If instead we aggregate over the three effects, we get the decomposition by partner area reported in the last line of Table 10.3. Another contrasting picture is revealed between the United States and EU28 on one hand, which contributed the most to the overall downward shift, and the rest of the world, the rest of Asia and South Korea, on the other hand, which contributed instead to the opposite. This line of interpretation sheds some light on trade diversification or, conversely, on increased dependence on specific foreign partners as explanations for Vietnam's macro resilience. It enables us to understand how the changing geography of trade has constrained Vietnam's BP performance to a greater or lesser extent.

If the partner/effect levels are combined, it can be observed that the largest positive effects (i.e. the main explanations for the overall tightening of Vietnam's BP constraint) are income changes, with the largest unfavourable effects resulting from GDP growth in the United States (+75.4%) and the EU (+56.1%), and the import market share attributed to China (+36.2%). In other words, Vietnam was hit by sluggish growth in the two Northern partners with the highest income elasticities of exports (USA, EU28) while a heavier reliance on Chinese sales made it difficult to maintain BP equilibrium after 2007. Conversely, a sizeable negative effect (i.e. the main explanation for the mitigation of the overall tightening) is the export market share effect relative to the United States (-34.2%) and China (-27.8%). Put in other words, Vietnam gained relative competitiveness in the two largest individual export markets by joining the WTO (Fig. 10.3a). The rest of Asia helped to alleviate the impact of WTO accession on Vietnam's long-run growth through lower import market shares (-18.9%), but it was counterbalanced by the increased appetite for imports from China (Fig. 10.3b).

The fact that the sign of the relative price effect depends on two elements shows the conditions under which partner j contributes to the evolution of Vietnam's BP constraint after WTO accession. Firstly, the bilateral relative prices consistently decreased only relative to China (Fig. 10.1). Vietnam has gained price competitiveness in exports specifically to China, its first and most important trading partner. However, the lower real depreciation after 2007 is associated with a bilateral MLC that is positive and greater than 1 and explains the favourable relative price contribution (-10.7% in Table 10.3). By the same token, the bilateral MLCs are unfulfilled in South Korea and the rest of the world, leading to an easing of Vietnam's external constraint despite an increase in relative prices against those countries. According to the results presented in Table 10.1, insignificant price elasticities in exports and imports imply that only the bilateral "pure terms of trade" effect (measured by μ_{ij}, i.e. the market share of partner *j* in Vietnam's total imports in value) plays a role in the specific cases of the rest of the world, India, EU28, AFR and LA. That is the reason why the relative price effect evolved favourably here.

All in all, our decomposition exercise clearly shows that WTO accession impacted Vietnam's economy through changing trade patterns. Looking simply at predicted changes in the country's BP constraint, these aggregate outcomes result from a perverse change after 2007, which acted to reduce the export volume term and increase the appetite for imports; in this context, the BPCG rate declined.

Despite a generalised integration into world markets, export orientation is a decisive factor but does not guarantee sustainable growth. The structural characteristics of DCs are thus critical in tightening or loosening the external constraint. The need for the structural change for which Thirlwall (2013) consistently calls provides theoretical insights into phenomena that new or neo-structuralism has highlighted since the 1990s, for example, the fact that global asymmetries are underpinned by the existence of endogenous and structural factors in patterns of production and trade, market structures and the evolving international context (Bresser-Pereira et al., 2014).

5 Conclusion

Vietnam's accession to the WTO paved the way for the country's entry into the global economy, with bilateral and multilateral FTAs. This membership opened a new chapter in which FDI grew, trade relations expanded and integration into the global economic map intensified. Today, Vietnam is one of the fastest growing economies in the world. However, one wonders if this huge step forward explains the build-up of pressures on the country's macro resilience. Because of strong trade linkages within the region and between geographical areas, an export-oriented growth strategy may increase Vietnam's vulnerability through a tighter external constraint related to unfavourable international engagement and asymmetries in the era of globalisation. To some extent, Vietnam's experience is nothing but a case study that echoes neo-structuralist thinking about systemic interdependent growth with a high level of exposure to the global trade system. It questions the relevance of export-led growth strategy in breaking out of economic dependency or subordination and the subsequent need to reformulate development models.

In an attempt to contribute to the literature, our chapter has aimed to identify the impact of WTO accession on Vietnam's long-run growth through the BP aspects of trade. The theory of balance-of-payments-constrained growth is a particularly appropriate approach and constitutes our contribution to the growth literature applied to Vietnam. It enables us to analyse how, and through which transmission channels, the changing patterns of international trade (marked by the country's integration into global markets with WTO accession) are critical in determining growth performance.

Vietnam's BP constraint tightened after joining the WTO. Our linear decomposition of the evolution of the BP constraint shows that the lengthy series of efforts to integrate the national economy into global markets impacted the country's long-run growth rate. A matter of serious concern is the fact that the export volume term and the appetite for imports both worsened. First, because the United States is the second largest individual market for Vietnam's exports, the high income elasticity interacts with sluggish growth to deeply affect the BPCG rate. This shows that the country's macro resilience is heavily dependent on US growth. Second, China's growing share in Vietnam's imports reflects a bilateral dependency which underlies the country's improved market share in exports with respect to this partner. All in all, our findings reveal that China contributes to worsen the BP constraint.

Because the BP is a determinant of growth performance, it is clear that the demand-side factors matter. As Vietnam is much more open than other DCs and is an active participant in GVCs, the domestic economy is highly exposed to shocks in international demand. This implies that an export-led growth with a heavy reliance on foreign goods and services may be detrimental to long-run growth. Moreover, real depreciation cannot raise the country's growth rate on a permanent basis because many of the goods traded are price inelastic.

This chapter illustrates how important the choice of trading partners is in building macro resilience (i.e. the capacity to minimise output losses). By looking simply at predicted changes in country's BP constraint, another line labelled "East-West" has taken place with the existing North-South one to reflect global asymmetries. In tackling this axis, we argue that re-orientating patterns of trade through appropriate efforts to diversify export markets or import suppliers could help to improve the BP performance. This corroborates recent development studies that make a case for appropriate diversification (in export markets or import suppliers) to shift economies onto resilient growth paths.

Appendix A Countries in each Vietnam's Partner Group

CHN China (including Hong-Kong, SAR)

JPN Japan

KOR Rep. of Korea

IND India

USA United States of America

RoA (Rest of Asia) Bangladesh, Bhutan, Brunei Darussalam, Cambodia, Indonesia, Lao PDR, Macao SAR, Malaysia, Mongolia, Myanmar, Nepal, Pakistan, the Philippines, Singapore, Sri Lanka, Thailand.

OTPP-HI (Other Trans-Pacific Partnership-High Income) Australia, Canada, New Zealand.

EU-28 (European Union) Austria, Belgium, Bulgaria, Croatia, Cyprus, Czech Republic, Denmark, Estonia, Finland, France, Germany, Greece, Hungary, Ireland, Italy, Latvia, Lithuania, Luxembourg, Malta, Netherlands, Poland, Portugal, Romania, Slovak Republic, Slovenia, Spain, Sweden, United Kingdom.

AFR (Africa) Algeria, Angola, Burkina Faso, Cameroon, Dem. Rep. of Congo, Rep. of Congo, Cote d'Ivoire, Arab Rep. of Egypt, Ethiopia, Ghana, Guinea, Kenya, Libya, Madagascar, Mali, Morocco, Mozambique, Nigeria, Senegal, South Africa, Sudan, Tanzania, Tunisia, Uganda, Zambia, Zimbabwe

LA (Latin America) Argentina, Bolivia, Brazil, Chile, Colombia, Costa Rica, Cuba, Dominican Republic, Ecuador, El Salvador, Guatemala, Honduras, Mexico, Panama, Paraguay, Peru, Venezuela RB

RoW Rest of the World

Appendix B Data Sources and Definitions

We use Comtrade database to construct Vietnam's bilateral trade flows, namely bilateral exports and bilateral imports in USD current prices. We cover the period 1990–2017 for each partner except for the United States where the period 1994–2017 is selected because the embargo was only lifted in 1994. If data were missing, we reconstruct it from its "mirror". When a trade flow is reported by Vietnam and has at the same time its "mirrored" value, we calculate a weighted average (export flow weights for one third and import flow for two thirds).

The Rest of the World (RoW) series are deducted from difference between the total trade flow and the sum of partners' bilateral trade flows. Thus, to build our database, bilateral import volumes are calculated by deflating import series with partner *j*'s aggregated export deflator and bilateral export volumes are obtained by deflating export series with Vietnam's export deflator. We define the export deflator by the ratio of nominal to real exports in USD which are collected from the World Development Indicators (WDI) database.

Note that all real variables from WDI database are given in constant 2010 USD. Therefore, Vietnam's and its aggregated partners' real GDPs are directly extracted from the WDI database.

Relative prices are constructed as the ratio of domestic prices (expressed by Vietnam's export deflator) to foreign prices (defined by partner *j*'s GDP deflator).

References

Akamatsu, K. (1932). "The synthetic principle of the economic development of our country" (in Japanese).

ASEAN-Japan Centre. (2020). "Global Value Chains. Vietnam". Paper 11, ASEAN Promotion Centre on Trade, Investment and Tourism, May.

Bagnai, A., Rieber, A., & Tran, T. A. D. (2016). Sub-Saharan Africa's growth, south-south trade and the generalized balance-of-payment constraint. *Cambridge Journal of Economics, 40*(3), 797–820.

Bresser-Pereira, L. C., Oreiro, J. L., & Marconi, N. (2014). A theoretical framework for a Structuralist development macroeconomics. In L. C. Bresser-Pereira, J. L. Oreiro, & N. Marconi (Eds.), *Financial stability and growth: Perspectives on financial regulation and new Developmentalism* (pp. 55–73). Routledge.

Chenery, H. B., & Michael, B. (1962). Development alternatives in an open economy: The case of Israel. *Economic Journal, 72*, 79–103.

Cimoli, M., & Porcile, G. (2013). Technology, structural change and bop-constrained growth: A structuralist toolbox. *Cambridge Journal of Economics, 38*(1), 215–237.

Dutt, A. K. (2003). Income elasticities of imports, north-south trade, and uneven development. In A. K. Dutt & J. Ros (Eds.), *Development economics and Structuralist macroeconomics. Essays in honor of lance Taylor* (pp. 307–335). Edward Elgar.

Freund, C. (2009). "The Trade Response to Global Downturns: Historical Evidence". The World Bank, Policy Research Working Paper Series, No. 5015, Washington: World Bank.

Ha, Y. S., Chung, K. J., & Seo, J. S. (2016). An analysis of Korea-ASEAN trade and its implications for the shipping industry in Korea. *Asian Journal of Shipping and Logistics, 32*(2), 63–71.

Hooy, C. W., Law, S. H., & Chan, T. H. (2015). The impact of the renminbi real exchange rate on ASEAN disaggregated exports to China. *Economic Modelling, 47*, 253–259.

Korniyenko, Y., Pinat, M., & Dew, B. (2017). "Assessing the Fragility of Global Trade: The Impact of Localized Supply Shocks Using Network Analysis". *IMF Working Paper WP/17/30.* Washington DC: The International Monetary Fund, February.

Mania, E., Rieber, A., & Tran, T. A. D. (2021). "Vietnam's trade-led growth, balance of payments and macro resilience". Conference paper for the *Second Workshop of the Growth Models in the Global South Studies Network:* "Implications of Post-Keynesian Economics for the Study of Growth Models in the Global North and South: Theoretical and Methodological Challenges", September 9, 2021.

Nell, K. (2003). A generalised version of the balance of payments growth model: An application to neighbouring regions. *International Review of Applied Economics, 17*(3), 249–267.

Perraton, J. (2003). Balance of payments constrained growth and developing countries: An examination of Thirlwall's hypothesis. *International Review of Applied Economics, 17*(1), 1–22.

Phi, M. H., & Tran, T. A. D. (2020). *Should I stay or should I go?* The role of the renminbi in trade partnerships in the Asia-Pacific region. *Post-Communist Economies, 32*(8), 1062–1088.

Prebisch, R. (1959). Commercial policy in the underdeveloped countries. *American Economic Review, 49*, 257–269.

Taylor, L. (2004). *Reconstructing macroeconomics. Structuralist proposals and critiques of the mainstream*. Harvard University Press.

Thirlwall, A. P. (1979). The balance of payments constraint as an explanation of international growth rate differences. *Banca Nazionale del Lavoro Quarterly Review, 128*, 45–53.

Thirlwall, A. P. (2011). Balance of payments constrained growth models: History and overview. *PSL Quarterly Review, 64*(259), 307–351.

Thirlwall, A. P. (2013). *Economic growth in an open developing economy. The role of structure and demand*. Edward Elgar.

World Bank. (2020). *Vietnam development report 2019: Connecting Vietnam for growth and shared prosperity*. World Bank.

CHAPTER 11

Illicit Border Trade in the Borderlands of Thailand and Lao PDR Under Trade Liberalization and AFTA

Natedao Taotawin

1 Introduction

Thailand and the ASEAN countries established the ASEAN Free Trade Area (AFTA) in 1993 in order to promote economic development and the expansion of international and border trade. Against a background of globalization and liberalism, the Thai state has sought to reduce trade barriers and to flexibly implement regulations in support of border trade. Moreover, the state has developed many measures to encourage cross-border traders to move into legal and formal trade (Thailand Board of Investment, 2011).

There are two approaches to international trade policy. The first approach is free trade policy, which puts the emphasis on the reduction of international trade barriers and no government intervention in international trade. The second approach is a protectionist trade policy. Under this approach the government encourages exports and discourages

N. Taotawin (✉)
Ubon Ratchathani University, Ubon Ratchathani, Thailand
e-mail: natedao.t@ubu.ac.th

T. A.-D. Tran (ed.), *Rethinking Asian Capitalism*,
https://doi.org/10.1007/978-3-030-98104-4_11

imports. The government intervenes in international trade through measures such as tariffs, import quotas, export restrictions, dumping and the provision of export subsidies (Srisiri et al., 2011).

Under trade liberalization and AFTA, the role of the state is no longer to act as a governing body that collects taxes for on imports and exports but to be a trade facilitator for imports and exports. The customs checkpoints are still collecting a small tax on some import and export products, and inspecting illegal items, or are engaged in legal control only (Thai Customs, 2016). Nevertheless, informal trade is widespread in the Thai-Laos border areas. This raises the question of why illicit border trade is still prevalent in times of trade liberalization and how such trade takes place.

This research aimed to analyze the complexity of "illegal border trade" by taking the state definition of "illegal border trade" as a starting point. Border trade is trade between two countries that share common borders. "Illegal border trade" as defined by the Thai state means "smuggling goods through the convenience of terrain without customs clearance" (Srisiri et al., 2011).

However, in this research we did not expect to assess how illegal border trade may damage the economy and national security as feared by the state. On the contrary, we sought to understand how some border trade has been transformed into "illegal border trade" and how the laws and regulations are not consistent with some forms of border trade.

Illicit border trade is considered by the state to be a clandestine economy and a threat to national security (Donnan & Wilson, 1999; Office of the National Security Council, 2012). As such, the state is actively trying to eliminate such illegal trade. But in reality informal and illegal border trade is still widespread in the Thai-Laos borderlands.

This chapter is based on a research project conducted in 2017 in the Thai-Lao People's Democratic Republic (PDR) borderlands (Taotawin & Taotawin, 2018). The research raises a question regarding the conditions of illicit border trade in the Thai-Lao PDR borderlands in the context of trade liberalization and AFTA. Additionally, the research examined the interaction and cooperation between licit and illicit border traders in the Thai-Lao PDR borderlands. Finally, the research examined how significant the illicit border trade is to the local economy and local livelihoods in the borderlands.

2 Fieldwork Aspects

2.1 Study Sites

The research study sites were several border checkpoints along the Thai-Lao PDR borderlands. Major study sites were located in the borderlands of Khemmarat District to Natan District of Ubon Ratchathani Province in Thailand. These borderlands are estimated to stretch for around 60 kilometers along the lower Mekong River. Additional study sites were border checkpoints and markets located in Savannakhet Province and Lakhon Peng City and Kong Sedone City in Salavan Province in Lao PDR. The selected study sites included several formal checkpoints established by the state of Thai-Lao and many "natural check points" that were not established by the state of Thai-Lao but remain informal cross-border channels.

Border trade in this area is supervised by the Khemmarat customs checkpoint. The volume of trade supervised by this customs post is not very high when compared to other customs checkpoints such as that at Nong Kai, which is considered to be the highest volume of import and export goods in Northeast Thailand, and the Mukdahan customs checkpoint, which oversees the second highest volume of import and export goods in the Northeast.

This area was selected for various reasons. Firstly, there is a lot of informal border trade. Secondly, there are many border villages along the Mekong River on the Thai and Lao banks. Thirdly, there are two major trade checkpoints for border trade on the Thai side. One border checkpoint is located at Pak Sang Village, Natan District of Ubon Ratchathani Province. It is adjacent to the Laos border checkpoint at Pak Tapan Village in Salavan Province of Lao PDR. Another checkpoint for border trade is located on the edge of Khemmarat municipality, the Khemmarat District of Ubon Ratchathani Province; it is adjacent to a natural checkpoint at Ta Pat Chum Village in Savannakhet Province in Lao PDR. Fourthly, there are many natural border paths in the Thai-Laos border areas. Finally, in Khemmarat District there are many flea markets along the border, including one large market that attracts many Laotians and Laos traders to come to buy goods to take back home. Two to three decades ago, border trade in this border area, which has mixed characteristics, both formal and informal trade, expanded.

2.2 Research Methodologies

The research was qualitative in nature. Sociological and anthropological approaches were adopted in order to examine the diverse meanings and the significant roles of illicit border trade in boosting the local economy and enhancing the livelihoods of local people in the Thai-Lao borderlands. The field research was conducted between May 2017 and May 2018.

Various data collection methods were adopted, including survey, non-participatory observation, semi-structured interviews, in-depth interviews and focus group discussions. The in-depth interviews were conducted with various key informants, including 13 state agencies, 30 Thai entrepreneurs and traders. Moreover, semi-structured interviews with 30 informants were conducted and two meetings with Thai villagers and related organizations for the purpose of "brainstorming" were organized.

Additionally, quantitative data were collected in order to estimate the volume of illicit cross-border trade taking place in the Thai-Lao borderlands. Surveys were conducted of the border trade in four markets in the Lao PDR borderlands. Additionally, informal interviews with 20 Lao government officers, border traders, Laos entrepreneurs and local people were conducted in order to understand the illicit cross-border trade on the Laotian side.

3 Conditions of Illicit Border Trade in the Borderlands of Thai-Lao PDR

In the past, traveling forth and back between Thai-Laos along the Mekong River was a normal way of life for people living in the border villages. "Ports" (*called Tha Kam in Thai*) are one of the important features along the Mekong River. These ports are natural cross-border paths found in various villages on both the Thai and Laos sides. Crossing borders through these ports was a way of connecting with others for various business purposes, visiting relatives, attending traditional merit events, earning a living in a rice field or through animal husbandry, as well as exchanging products or buying goods.

Elderly villagers in the Thai village said that the trade at that time was uncontrolled, as Laotians often crossed over the Mekong River to buy essential items such as salt, hoes, spades, clothes and to sell forest products or trade forest products for Thai products. The items often sold by Laotians included forest products, frogs, wild animals and cattle.

Since a communist regime was established in Laos in 1975, relations between Thailand and Lao PDR became fraught with tension. In the borderlands, villagers said that state officials ordered the Thai village headmen to prevent Laotians from crossing the border.

In 1977 the officials were still stricter in controlling border crossings of both goods and people. This created shortages of essential products in Laos. This situation led in turn to the emergence of smuggling, with traders from Khemmarat District or elsewhere in Ubon Ratchathani Province in Thailand delivering goods to people in the border villages. After that, Laotians began to cross the Mekong River clandestinely in order to pick up goods to take back home to Laos.

The establishment of the Khemmarat customs checkpoint in 1941 was the beginning of the Thai government's efforts to control border trade. The customs post was responsible only for controlling and inspecting goods imported and exported by villagers for compliance with regulations. However, border trade in this period was not a target of state control. Traders did not pay import or export tax as the state considered that trade in everyday goods was a way of life for Thais and Laos living in the borderlands.

Between 1988 and 1990, the Thai government adopted its so-called *Turning the Battlefield to be Trade* policy (*Plean Jak Sa Nam Rob to Sa Nam Kan Ka in Thai*). In 1992, the Greater Mekong Sub-Region (GMS) project was initiated in order to promote economic and social corporations among countries in the Mekong River Basin. This led to the construction of infrastructure such as roads and bridges and the establishment of trade facilitation mechanisms.

At the same time, Lao PDR adopted a policy of reducing state control and emphasizing cooperation with other countries. In 1986 Lao PDR moved from a centralized socialist economic system to a free economy as part of a policy known as the New Economic Mechanism (or NEM). Under this new policy, the Lao government relaxed its control over the economy and began to use market mechanisms to boost economic development. Moreover, the government opened the country up to foreign aid and direct investment (FDI) (Panya, 2015).

In addition, Laos, which joined ASEAN in 1997, gradually reduced product tax to between 0 and 5 percent by 2009 while Thailand reduced tax to the same rate at the same time (Department of Foreign Trade, 2016). Nevertheless, the import and export of goods from Lao PDR is far from trade liberalization, as Lao PDR has a high tax rate and six types of tax collection from Laos and foreign entrepreneurs, resulting in high operating costs for businesses (Department of Foreign Trade, 2010).

The implementation of the Free Trade Agreement and Thai-Lao Cooperation has significantly increased the overall value of Thai-Laos border trade from about 25 billion baht in 2004 to approximately 140 billion baht in 2014, an almost six-fold increase over 11 years (Department of Foreign Trade, 2016).

Since 1987, the Thai government has adopted a policy of encouraging trade liberalization through AFTA. The government has reduced barriers to trade and flexibly implemented regulations in support of cross-border trade between Thailand and neighboring countries. Moreover, the Thai government has developed measures to encourage cross-border traders to move into legal and formal trade. For instance, the Thai government allows exporters who comply with the regulations on export goods to apply for a reduction of 7 percent on their VAT payments (Thailand Board of Investment, 2011).

Two kinds of border trade are found in the Thai-Loa borderlands: formal or legal border trade and informal or illegal border trade. "Legal border trade" refers to imports and exports of goods that cross borders by obtaining clearance at official customs posts; illegal trade, on the other hand, means smuggling by using clandestine trails to evade customs posts (Srisiri et al., 2011).

Border trade between Thai-Lao passes through 36 trade channels. These channels are classified into three categories: (1) border checkpoints (*called Jud-Pan Daen-Tha-Vorn in Thai*); (2) checkpoints for border trade (*called Jud-Pon-Pron-Pua-Karn-Ka in Thai*); and (3) temporary checkpoints (*called Jud-Pan-Dan-Choy-Krao in Thai*).

The border checkpoints (*called Jud-Pan Daen-Tha-Vorn in Thai*) are entrance-exit channels that allow citizens of both countries, tourists and commercial, tourist and private vehicles to cross the border in both directions. There are procedures regarding immigration and customs clearance in accordance with the regulations of both countries. In Thailand, the opening of permanent border crossings must be approved by the Cabinet and the Ministry of the Interior (Office of the National Economic and Social Development Council, 2016).

The establishment of border checkpoint at Pak Sang Village in Na Tan District in 1990 was considered a permanent border crossing. Pak Sang Village was selected as the site of a permanent border crossing, because it is the location of an old village, the old temple of *Pra-To* and of *Pra-Chao-Yai-Ong-Tue*, an important image of Buddha.

Another reason for choosing Pak Sang Village as a border checkpoint was the local infrastructure, and particularly the road network. Highway 2112 was built according to the strategic border plan between 1971 and 1975 as a border security route along the banks of the Mekong River. From Pak Sang Village, the road takes travelers to Khemmarat District, a distance of about 25 kilometers. This road connects with others Ubon Ratchathani City, a distance about 100 kilometers.

On the bank of the Mekong River at Pak Ta Phan Village in Lao PDR, there is a dirt road that runs for a distance of about 18 kilometers to connect with highway No. 13, the main road of Lao PDR. This road starts at the town of Bo Ten in northern Laos and runs to the Chinese border. Moreover, this road is connected to Vientiane, the capital of Laos, and to Luang Prabang in the north of the country, and goes down to the Mekong River, ending at the Cambodian border.

The checkpoints for border trade (*called Jud-Pon-Pron-Pua-Karn-Ka in Thai*) are the channels that the Thai government opens to help neighboring countries in humanitarian affairs and to promote public relations at the local level by allowing relief to trade in essential consumer goods. This is for psychological effect. Checkpoints for border trade are one-sided border openings. Their opening is initiated by the subcommittees at the provincial level, which consider the appropriateness of opening trade relief checkpoints. However, final approval has to be given by the Ministry of Interior (Office of Strategy and Area Development Planning, 2016).

The establishment of a checkpoint for border trade took place in 1992 on the edge of Khemmarat Municipality, in the Khemmarat District of Ubon Ratchathani Province. It is adjacent to a natural checkpoint at Ta Pat Chum Village in Savannakhet Province in Lao PDR. The reason for selecting this location as a checkpoint for border trade was the high volume of border trade between the two banks of the Mekong River.

On the Thai side, trade in Khemmarat District is booming. There are many shops, including wholesale shops that sell goods to traders and consumers in Laos. On the Laos side, along the banks of the Mekong River adjacent to Khemmarat District, there are many villages. From these villages, there are many others reaching deep into the interior of Laos (these villages are administered from Song Khon City, Savannakhet Province in Lao PDR). People from these villages come to buy consumer and other goods from Thailand because it is less far to travel that going to the city in the Laotian interior.

Thus the announcement of this place as a checkpoint for border trade was intended to make the lives of villagers in the border areas easier and to promote the local economy. The establishment of checkpoint for border trade is also a long-term guarantee for border trade.

After the opening of the checkpoint for border trade on the edge of Khemmarat Municipality, trade became livelier. This was reflected in the number of wholesale and retail stores selling various consumer products in Khemmarat District from just a few stores to dozens. One of the largest stores estimated that, at that time, the turnover of his store was not less than 10 million baht per month. In addition, this period saw the emergence of flea markets along the Mekong River and many forms of traders.

A temporary checkpoint (*called Jud-Pan-Dan-Choy-Krao in Thai*) is an entrance-exit channel that opens for a specific purpose for a certain time, whether for economic or other activities. According to the regulation, a temporary checkpoint does not allow people who are not involved in the activity in question to go in and out after the expiration or completion of specific objectives. When the objective has been achieved, the temporary checkpoint will quickly close (Office of Strategy and Area Development Planning, 2016).

While border trade in Khemmarat District increased, one constraint in the eyes of entrepreneurs in Khemmarat District or those who use Khemmarat District as a place for importing and exporting goods was the lack of a bridge over the Mekong River connecting Thailand with Lao PDR. This absence of a bridge meant that goods had to be transported across the border by motorboat, severely restricting the number of goods that could be carried at a time. Later on, there was a plan to open a car ferry operated by two private companies in 2002 at Na Hin Ngon Village, Pha Lan Sub-district, Na Than District of Ubon Ratchathani Province, allowing border traders to carry trucks across the Mekong River.

The opening of a temporary checkpoint at Na Hin Ngon Village, which is about 25 kilometers from Khemmarat District, reflects the superior status of those promoting this temporary checkpoint. This temporary checkpoint is another point of entry and exit for imports and exports; the products exported here are not household consumer goods but include construction materials, fuel and chemical fertilizers, while imports include lumber, cassava and sand. Those who import and export goods through this checkpoint are local and national merchants who are registered with the government. They are large traders who import and export goods legally through customs. Importers and exporters using this temporary checkpoint must request permission for each import and export.

Between November 2016 and August 2017, smuggled products, including narcotics, Siamese rosewood, garlic, motorcycles and cattle, were seized along the Mekong River by the Navy's Peace Keeping Unit in the Khemmarat District of Ubon Ratchathani Province. As a result, the Thai state adopted strict border control policies. The main point of strict border control is to limit the crossing of people and the extent of border trade to certain points only. Military personal and border patrols are deployed at certain crossing points in order to control the access of people and goods. Strict border management not only creates restrictions on people crossing borders but significantly affects border trade between Thai-Laos.

4 Interaction and Cooperation Between Licit and Illicit Border Traders in the Thai-Lao PDR Borderlands

In the context of trade liberalization, it is assumed that informal border trade should be reduced. In reality, at least in the area under investigation, informal border trade is still widespread because border traders do not want to engage in formal border trade.

The state classified illegal border trade by referring to the lack of customs clearance, but trade that does not pass through customs can be either legal or illegal because its status depends on intent and various other relevant factors.

In the area under investigation, the informal border trade consists mainly of consumer goods. Exported consumer products here can be divided into categories as follows: (1) the foodstuffs include fresh food such as chicken, eggs, duck eggs, frozen seafood, vegetables, fruits, meatballs, hot dogs and pork sausage; (2) food ingredients such as sauces, fish sauce, vegetable oil, sugar and wheat flour; (3) soft drinks such as fruit juices, energy drinks, milk boxes, condensed milk and coffee; (4) snacks; (5) personal hygiene and cleaning products such as soap, shampoo, toothpaste and detergent; (6) kitchenware such as pots and pans; (7) clothing, underwear, shoes, hats, jewelry for women or men; (8) construction materials such as nails, wire, sanitary ware, a bag of cement, a box of floor tiles, barbed wire, plumbing pipes and paint; (9) agricultural tools and supplies such as spades, fishing equipment, chemical fertilizer and so on; (10) car parts; (11) carpentry tools; (12) equipment for electricians; (13) fish for raising such as catfish and snakehead fish.

However, informal trade can be either legal or illegal. Legal border trade is trade by people in border areas. Traders buy goods for household use and carry products across the border at various border crossing points, including the border checkpoints, the checkpoints for border trade and the natural cross-border paths leading to border villages.

Illegal border trade also takes place at the same places as legal border trade. In this research, I argue that informal cross-border trade refers to border trade that does not completely comply with state laws. Some trade procedures may be in accordance with the laws, but others may not comply with the laws. Sometimes, informal cross-border trade may be in accordance with the laws of one country but not with those of another country.

In the areas under investigation, illicit border trade can be found in three forms:

1. Cross-border trade that is in accordance with the laws of Thailand but not with those of Lao PDR.

Thai law allows citizens in the borderlands to buy goods for personal consumption that are not to be sold for profit. Products can be taken out without notifying the authorities. Under this law, Lao traders pretend to buy a small amount, but actually buy lot of consumer goods in order to sell, but transporting the products at a time not much. This is illicit and is an informal trade. But the trader is familiar with the officials. In this case, the officer has the power to exercise discretion whether to allow the products to be taken out or not. Removing the products in this way is often done by paying bribes to the officials.

Consequently, the export of consumer goods from Thailand is regarded as "legal" according to the Thai laws. However, when the border traders cross the Mekong River to the port in Lao PDR, the import of consumer goods to Laos is considered "illegal" according to the Laos regulations. Laos traders have to clear goods with state officials in Laos. Usually, they prefer to take the goods to the port under military control because they see it as less expensive and inconvenient than the border crossing controlled by the Laos Customs Department.

2. Trade that is in accordance with Lao laws, but does not comply with Thai laws.

For instance, Thai traders order forest lumber from Lao PDR. Cross-border trade in timber is different from that in consumer goods because wood from natural forests is a valuable natural resource and hence a national security concern. Cross-border timber trade is therefore subject to Thai laws and regulations, and is supervised by various state agencies, such as the Department of Forestry, the Customs Department, Thai Army The Convention on the International Trade in Endangered Species of Wild Fauna and Flora (CITES), the international regulation, also applies.

In Thailand, the importation of timber from neighboring countries is governed by Ministry of Commerce regulation 92 (1992) and Ministry of Commerce regulation on the imposition of customs importation of lumber into the Kingdom 2005, which specify that imported timber must have a certificate of origin (CoO) or evidence of export authorization from the exporting country for the value declared to the Thai customs. Nonetheless, it is important to note that the two Ministry of Commerce regulations do not apply to lumber imported from Lao PDR and Malaysia (Heuch et al., 2011).

Laos Customs Law No. 04/NA, dated 20 December 2011, states that wood is basically not a product for export and needs to be licensed and certified for export by the relevant government agencies. In addition, the import of lumber by ship from Lao PDR must also comply with Lao PDR customs law No. 71, which stipulates that the use of ships carrying goods or passengers must comply with the regulations (Lao PDR Trade Portal, 2011).

The boat's owner must register the boat and must show proof of ownership to the customs post where the boat is registered. Laos custom law also stipulates that before loading goods on to a ship or clearing goods from a ship, a transporter must stop at a customs post in order to allow the customs officers to inspect the vessel ownership documents and the goods to be loaded and to check whether the ship's owner is acting in accordance with the regulations (Lao PDR Trade Portal, 2011).

In Ubon Ratchathani Province, the government permits the import of lumber from Lao PDR into Thailand via three routes.

(a) The Chong Mek Border Checkpoint is located at Chong Mek Customs Checkpoint, Sirindhorn District. This checkpoint is connected with Lao PDR via terra firma, and is opposite Ban Wang Tao Checkpoint, Pak Se Town, Champasak Province of Lao PDR. It is the main channel for importing timber from Lao PDR.

(b) The border checkpoint at Pak Sang Village, Na Tan District of Ubon Ratchathani Province. This channel connects with Lao PDR via the Mekong River and is a sub-division of the Khemmarat customs checkpoint. This permanent border checkpoint is adjacent to Pak Ta Phan Village, La Khon Peng City, Salavan Province in Lao PDR and is a crossing point for imported lumbers from Salavan Province.

(c) Checkpoint for border trade on the edge of Khemmarat Municipality, Khemmarat District of Ubon Ratchathani Province, opposite Tha Pat Chum Village, Song Khon City, Savannakhet Province in Lao PDR. It is a crossing point for imported lumber from Savannakhet Province.

The import of timber from Lao PDR to Thailand has a long history. The import of timber from Lao PDR began after Thai government announced the end of forest concession in the state forest area in 1989. After that, Thailand became an important importer of timber from Lao PDR, which has a lot of forest resources.

In Khemmarat District in Ubon Ratchathani Province, there are 3–4 border traders that have imported timbers from Lao PDR to Thailand. They act as intermediaries, importing Laos timber to resell in Thailand or to make furniture for sale in the country and export to foreign countries. From 1988 to 1990, when the Thai government adopted its policy of "Turning the Battlefield to be Trade", the border traders informed us that the import of timber from Lao PDR was a very prosperous business.

There are approximately ten timber traders in Salavan Province. The major Thai traders usually import timber from big Laos entrepreneurs while small Thai traders buy wood from small Laos entrepreneurs. The timber exported from Lao PDR to Thailand is hardwood from rare and expensive species such as teak, rubber trees, red wood, Maka wood, Takian wood and so on. Timber is exported from Laos in the form of sheet or processed wood. Thai traders will order the timber from Laos entrepreneurs by telephone. It is paid for in cash, after which Laos entrepreneurs will process documents for permission to export the timber and go to customs clearance on the Laos side.

When the timber is sent to a Thai port, Thai entrepreneurs also do the customs clearance and pay the fee on the Thai side themselves as well as paying for the transport costs. Customs and forestry officers inspect the documents, check the imported timber and give permission for the timber to be transported to its destination, usually the wood processing plants.

There are two incidents that have affected the border trade in timbers in the area under investigation. The first incident occurred in 2016. The Laos government officially prohibited the export of timbers from Lao PDR to Thailand (Chareonsuk, 2016). The second incident happened in 2017, when the Khemmarat customs checkpoint prohibited the importation of timber from Laos to Thailand through the Khemmarat customs house in response to the Lao PDR policy mentioned earlier (from the interview of customs officer at Khemmarat District, 2017).

The first incident caused the importation of timber through the Khemmarat customs checkpoints to slow down. In reality, the import of timber through the Khemmarat customs checkpoint continued until July 2017, although the Laos authorities had announced the end of timber exports from Laos in May 2016.

The value of timbers, wood shutters and wood furniture imported from Lao PDR through the Khemmarat customs checkpoint each year from 2014 to 2017 was as follows. In 2014, it was estimated about 1,100,202 baht or approximately US $34,381, making it number 3 in a list of the 10 most imported products from Laos. In 2015, it was estimated about 1,559,313 baht or approximately US $48,728.53, with wood products imported or equivalent to 2nd in a list of 10 products with the most imports from Laos. In 2016, it was estimated about 2,883,885 baht or approximately US $90,121 or equivalent to 3rd in a list of 10 products with the most imports from Laos. In 2017, it was 24,244,422 baht or approximately US $757,638 or equivalent to 2nd in a list of 10 products with the most imports from Laos (Khemmarat Customs Checkpoint, 2017, copy document). The statistics of Khemmarat customs checkpoint indicates that import of lumber continues to grow. The total value was approximately 29,787,822 baht (or approximately US $930,869), and average value of imported timber was approximately 7,446,955.5 million baht (or approximately US $232,717) per year (Khemmarat Customs Checkpoint, 2017, copy document).

From May 2016 to June 2017, when the Laos government announced its policy of stopping timber exports, large quantities of timber were still being exported from Laos to the Thai border. Although the Thai customs officers insisted that the import of timber was legal because they had requested permission and taxation from Laos officials correctly, the continued imports of timber during this period show that there was a conflict between government policies, laws and regulations on both the Thai and Laos sides. And it also reveals a conflict between government officials at national and local levels. This phenomenon raises the question of how it was possible to export timber from Laos at all. What was the status of timber imported from Laos? And what were the reasons for allowing or prohibiting the import of timber from Laos to Thailand?

Despite the legal procedures for importing forest products into Thailand, the mere existence of timber imports from Lao PDR is no guarantee that such imports are legal, since Thai customs officers are responsible only for checking the export documents and the exported timber itself.

The inspection of imported timber from Laos is the only validation of the Thai timber importing process, but it does not extend to verification of the process of exporting timber from Laos because Thai customs officials do not have the authority to carry out inspections outside the kingdom (interview with a Khemmarat customs officer, 30 August 2017).

As such, the trade in timber along the Thai-Laos borderlands is at risk of being "illegal". As long as the inspection processes for exports from Laos and the import of Thai products are not part of the same system, validation of the import and export processes along the Thai-Laos border is far from complete.

3. The third form of illicit border trade is that in which some procedures may be in accordance with the Thai laws but others may not be so compliant.

The Customs Department announcement in 2016 allows the export of small quantities along the border, not exceeding 50,000 baht (or approximately US $1562) in value, provided that Laos traders submit the "outbound products detail notification" (called *Kor Sor Kor 153* in Thai) or hire Thai brokers to process it. According to this Customs Department announcement, the export process can proceed in three ways. The first way is the export of goods according to the value and amount as specified in the outbound products detail notification and is considered a legitimate operation.

The second way is to export more than 50,000 baht's worth of goods by dividing the products into multiple batches. Each batch has a value not exceeding 50,000 baht. This method bypasses the laws and may be regarded as legal or illegal, depending on how officials interpret the legislation.

The third way is false notification. The outbound products detail notification is filled in but the declared amounts and values are not accurate. In this case, Laos border traders are hoping that, when the products are inspected at the customs checkpoints, customs officials may allow them to pass. They may bribe officials to turn a blind eye. This method is certainly illegal and constitutes informal trade.

Both licit and illicit trade are commonly found in the Thai-Lao borderlands, for various reasons. Firstly, border trade is a traditional way of life among the people who live along the Thai-Laos border zone, the trade mostly consisting of everyday consumer goods. People living along the Laos border rely heavily on imported products from Thailand for their daily lives.

Secondly, crossing the border and buying Thai commodities to take back to Laos remains relatively cheaper than buying the same commodities in Lao PDR. Many villages along the border of Lao PDR are located in remote areas and far from the province's center of prosperity and commerce. Consequently, crossing the border of the Mekong River to buy products in the Khemmarat or Na Than District of Thailand is easier and cheaper than traveling to various provinces of Lao PDR.

Finally, the cross-border traders see that the laws and state regulations are not consistent with the trade routes of small cross-border traders and their capability to trade and compete with the large traders.

The border traders use both licit and illicit methods. The trade strategy adopted by border traders is based on the following principle: "Which product is cheaper? We buy there regardless of whether it constitutes formal or informal trade". Border traders use state regulations to benefit themselves. In practice, they use various methods to bypass the laws. In other words, border traders exploit the state regulations for their own benefit and are not above negotiating with and even bribing officials.

The border traders explain that although informal trade is less costly than formal trading, they do run the risk of being arrested, having their goods confiscated or paying fines. Consequently, they have to reduce the risk by "paying under the table", that is, bribing state officials. If such bribery is still cheaper than formal trade, then border traders will use these "informal" trade methods. However, whenever the cost of informal trade increases considerably, they will revert to formal trade. They may subsequently return to informal trade if the cost of importing products changes.

5 Significance of Illicit Border Trade for Local Economy and Livelihoods of Borderlanders

Both licit and illicit border trades are very significant for the local economy and the livelihoods of border people. As illicit border trade is a traditional way of life among the people who live along the Thai-Laos border zone, it is difficult to distinguish from licit border trade. In addition, many groups of people engage in both licit and illicit border trade.

The border checkpoint in Pak Sang Village lies on an important route for travelers and goods between Thailand and Lao PDR. Consequently, this checkpoint is in an important economic area for local people, who engage in many occupations. The main occupation of the villagers here is to transport people and goods across the Mekong River. In addition, about 20 motorcycles and 3–5 pick-up trucks carry passengers to the port in Pak Sang Village. And, about 20 wage laborers carry luggage from the bank on to the boats. Each day, about 50 villagers are engaged in economic activities at the crossing. Each person earns between 200–1000 baht per day.

On Wednesdays there is a flea market at the border crossing where around 20 merchants and street vendors come to sell consumer goods and fresh foods to Thai and Laos people. The illicit border trade value at this permanent checkpoint was estimated to be worth approximately 20 million baht in 2018.

The checkpoint for border trade on the edge of Khemmarat Municipality has become a career-building area for many people. The main occupation is driving a motorboat to transport passengers and carry goods to Lao PDR. Each day there are 15 motorboats to provide services for passengers on the Thai side while there are many motorboats that also provide services for passenger on the Laos side. Consequently, a passenger transportation agreement has been established between the two groups of boats on the Mekong River such that "the Laos boats cross the Mekong River to send passengers to Thailand while the Thai boats carry the passengers back". In this way, the work can be shared more equally. In addition, there are about 30 workers carrying luggage or goods from the boats to the top of the banks. Other workers provide transport services using tricycles and trailers, what local people call "skylab cars". Drivers are grouped together, with about 30 vehicles providing the service.

On Mondays there is a huge flea market at Pra Cha Ka Sem Temple where over 100 merchants and street vendors come to sell consumer goods and fresh foods to Thai and Laos people. The illicit border trade value at the Khemmarat customs checkpoint was estimated to be worth approximately 74 million baht in 2018. Moreover, the value of the illicit border trade at the natural cross-border paths located at all border villages on the Thai side was put at approximately 178 million baht in 2018. Therefore, the total value of illicit border trade at all checkpoints was estimated to be approximately 273 million baht in 2018.

6 Conclusion

The application of the principle of economic liberalism to international trade does not lead to any reduction in the state's role in economic control but rather to a new form of state control. In Lao PDR, state regulations on the import of goods constitute barriers to trade, providing benefits to certain groups and discriminating against others as well as importers and exporters in certain countries. The introduction of import licenses for goods has led to many practical difficulties. The high taxes and fees charged have become a barrier to trade with Thailand. Such barriers make importing legal goods a difficult and lengthy process and increase the cost of managing the importation process to a very high level.

In Thailand, despite tax reductions, trade facilitation measures and tax incentives to attract border traders to enter into formal trade, Laos traders still want products from informal trade because such trade is cheaper and more convenient than formal trade. In this situation, Thai entrepreneurs choose to respond to their Laos partners by using informal channels to reduce the cost of imports and exports, provided that the risk and management costs are not very high.

This research has considered the border trade from the point of view of the border people who bypass the legal/illegal framework of the state. We find that the border traders have a desire; they want to develop a business and raise the status of their families by learning things, improving themselves, and by seeking opportunities for trading channels. Their trading has created a cross-border trade network, composed of retailers in various areas of the border.

Cross-border exporting is an important procedure within cross-border trade. A border checkpoint is the negotiating space used by traders to resist state control. The cross-border traders manipulate the laws and exploit regulations to their own advantage. As the economic value of the informal cross-border trade is significantly high, we propose the use of the phrase "informal border trade" instead of "illegal border trade", as being more appropriate in representing the recognition of the human rights and the local way of living, providing the opportunity to manage the border areas in new ways.

References

Chareonsuk, T. (2016). *Moon light at Chai Khong: When Lao PDR stop exporting wood*. Matichon Online. Retrieved April 5, 2018, from https://www.matichon.co.th/prachachuen/news_148417

Department of Foreign Trade. (2010). *Guide for border trade with neighboring countries*. Department of Foreign Trade, Ministry of Commerce.

Department of Foreign Trade. (2016). *Asean Free Trade Area (AFTA)*. Retrieved November 30, 2017, from http://www.dft.go.th/th-th/DetailHotNews/ArticleId/5079/-AFTA-1-2

Donnan, H., & Wilson, T. M. (1999). *Borders: Frontiers of identity, nation and the state*. BERG.

Heuch, J., Sandom, J., & Sunthornhao, P. (2011). *Timber flows and their control in Thailand*. Report of the Forest Law Enforcement, Governance and Trade Office for Asia Region in 2011. Retrieved July 10, 2018, from http://www.euflegt.efi.int/documents/10180/23308/Timber+Flows+and+t heir+Control+in+Thailand+%28Thai+Translation%29/861f041d-3ea6-4715-a726-f9024f5a9b8c

Khemmarat Customs Checkpoint. (2017). *Total border trade value through the Khemmarat Customs Checkpoint 2013* (Copy Document).

Lao PDR Trade Portal. (2011). Customs law No. 04/NA. Retrieved October 15, 2017, from https://www.laotradeportal.gov.la/index.php?r=site/display&id=247

Office of the National Economic and Social Development Council. (2016). Definitions related to border trade. Retrieved March 18, 2018, from www.nesdb.go.th/ewt_dl_link.php?nid=6211

Office of the National Security Council. (2012). Development strategy for national security (2013–2017). Retrieved October 30, 2013, from http://planning.pn.psu.ac.th/Budget/data/south/strategy_6.pdf

Panya, S. (2015). Chinese capital in Luang Nam Tha District and the adjustment of the Lao government in the post-new imagination. In C. Vaddanaphuti & S. Rungmanee (Eds.), *Yad Yang Kan Pattana and modernity* (pp. 54–80). Asean Studies Center.

Srisiri, A., Panthong, P., & Tierprasert, M. (2011). *Problems of the operation of agencies related to the import and export of Thai-Laos border products: Case study of restricted and unregulated products*. Thailand Research Fund.

Taotawin, N., & Taotawin, P. (2018). *Illicit border trade: Its conditions, mechanisms and management by state agencies*. Thailand Research Fund.

Thai Customs. (2016). *Custom clearance products export by land*. Retrieved February 11, 2016, from http://www.customs.go.th/cont

Thailand Board of Investment. (2011). *Index and guide for investment in Lao People's Democratic Republic*. Thailand Investment Promotion Project in Cambodia, Lao PDR, Myanmar, Vietnam.

CHAPTER 12

Challenging the Concept of "China-World"

Anne Cheng

The well-known paradox of the concept of universality is that it is anything but universal. Even speaking of "universality from a Chinese point of view"—or, more precisely, of "universality *à la chinoise*"—immediately underscores how problematic the concept is. The universality of human rights is ostensibly a product of the philosophy of the Enlightenment, which represents "the triumph of Reason." Chinese universality, by contrast, is linked to a certain idea of civilisation—of Chinese civilisation, of course—with a centre (*zhong*) from which civilisation radiates out to the periphery. One should recall that China designates itself or, more exactly, has been designated by its neighbours as "the Middle Kingdom," *Zhongguo*. The power of a single ruler—the Son of Heaven or the incarnation of the Dao, often transcribed Tao—is represented as both mystical and cosmological in the way it spreads out and transforms the beings who submit to it. The realities of imperial power, based since the third century BCE on an ever more sophisticated system of bureaucracy and administration, have been superimposed onto this representation.

For more than two millennia, "China" had the peculiarity not only of seeing itself as the centre of the world—nothing very special in that—but

A. Cheng (✉)
Collège de France, Paris, France
e-mail: anne.cheng@college-de-france.fr

T. A.-D. Tran (ed.), *Rethinking Asian Capitalism*,
https://doi.org/10.1007/978-3-030-98104-4_12

of *being* the world: until the start of the twentieth century, the Chinese empire readily called itself "all under heaven" (*tianxia*). Numerous common sayings originating in the Confucian canon reinforce this self-image of China-as-world, the centre from which civilisation spreads: "between the four seas, all men are brothers."[1] According to a trope of Confucian political rhetoric, the sovereign is supposed to "pacify those who are closest and attract those who are far away by his benevolence."

Particularly striking is the description in the ancient *Book of Rites* of the Son of Heaven sitting in the centre of a square formed by feudal lords, a cosmological image of the Earth repeated by a second, wider square of the "barbarian" tribes of the four orients, distinguished not by ethnicity but by their ignorance of rites—that is, of civilised manners. The description gives us a visual representation of a hierarchised and centralised space that, without being closed, is in no way equivalent to the strictly political space of the Greek *polis* or of the Roman *civitas*.

However symbolic—perhaps precisely because it was symbolic—this representation was apparently coextensive with imperial ideology during its two-thousand-year history. From the founding Han dynasty (206 BCE-220 CE) onwards, which established a *pax sinica* at the eastern end of the Eurasian continent while the *pax romana* held sway at the other extreme, one omnipresent idea was already being used as a political slogan: "the Han unify all under heaven" (*Han bing tianxia*). The phrase is everywhere, even the most trivial places—on roof tiles, for instance. The Han dynasty, which consolidated the First Emperor Qin Shihuangdi's unification of Chinese territory in 221 BCE, gave Chinese civilisation its name, its language and what is currently categorised (in Stalinist style) as its "dominant ethnic group"—gave it, that is, a form of national identity *avant la lettre*. In the eighteenth century, during the Manchu Qing dynasty—which was to be the final imperial dynasty—we find a visual reference to the idea of *tianxia* in a *Treatise on the Calendar and on Music* sent by the Jesuit missionary Joseph Amiot (1718–1793) to Henri-Léonard Bertin, one of Louis XVI's ministers. Amiot depicts the choreography of ritual dances performed at the Imperial Court. The area of the dance is a symbolic, cosmological representation of the empire, set within the universe: a square, representing the Earth, is inscribed in a circle, representing the sky, split into nine squares corresponding to the Empire's

[1] See Confucius' *Analects*, 12.5. This formula was selected by the authorities as one of the slogans to be chanted during the opening ceremony of the 2008 Olympic Games in Beijing.

nine provinces. Following tradition, the north is placed at the bottom and the west at the right; the image has to be turned upside down to read the characters correctly. There are sixteen dancers at the intersections of the squares, tracing out characters as they progress inwards. (Recall that Chinese characters are often called "square characters.") Their dance delineates the characters that make up the phrase *tianxia taiping* 天下太平: "All under heaven"—that is, the entire empire—"lies in Great Peace."

The so-called Sinicised world is the geopolitical translation of this power of symbolic diffusion, covering all of East Asia around China proper: Korea, Japan, Vietnam, Mongolia and Tibet. Each of these cultures has, to different degrees and at different times, felt China's influence, whether by adopting its writing system, its structures of government, its bureaucratic model, its conceptions of social hierarchy or religious forms born in or assimilated by China, especially Buddhism, which originated in India but was almost totally Sinicised by the seventh and eighth centuries.

Conversely, whenever Chinese space has been encroached upon, invaded and occupied by "barbarians," the idea prevailed that these enemies would ultimately find themselves transformed, adopting Chinese culture—true historically, particularly in the case of the Mongol Yuan dynasty (1264–1368) and the Manchu Qing dynasty (1644–1911). It was not until the mid-nineteenth century that the Chinese empire began sending diplomatic missions to other countries; until then it had relied on the periphery to mark its allegiance to the centre through tribute.

It was only following attacks by Western powers, starting with the Opium Wars of 1840–60, that China was forced to see itself as one country or nation among many. But the Chinese empire's self-image as the "world-civilisation" died hard. In 1898, under one of the last Qing rulers, Kang Youwei (1858–1927) led a group of scholars attempting for the first time in imperial history to set out political reforms. They proposed a constitutional monarchy modelled on Meiji Japan (1868–1912). As a good traditional scholar, though, Kang Youwei still largely based his ideas on canonical Confucian sources and on a universalist utopia rooted in the traditional vision of Chinese universality Kang himself described in the *Book of the Great Unity* (*Datong shu*), whose title evokes the "Great Peace" (*taiping*) mentioned above. These efforts ended in disaster. While Japan had been able to negotiate the Meiji transformation by affirming its national identity largely in explicit contrast to Chinese universality, China missed its opportunity in 1898 by continuing to refer to a canonical tradition that did not allow the establishment of a genuine nation state. This failure of tradition left a political gap that successive twentieth-century revolutions sought to fill, but to no avail. The culturalist option failed to compensate for the absence of a constructive political solution.

Central to the culturalist option is the problematic issue of Confucianism's survival in a modern—or postmodern—society. For two thousand years, Confucianism provided an ideological and institutional foundation for an imperial regime that disappeared definitively only in 1911.[2] (Note that "Confucianism" is a Western neologism; it remains unclear precisely what it means, or at least its meaning should be specified in each occurrence.) The modern era blamed this Confucian heritage for China's backwardness, seeing it as the source of all its woes. Confucianism was a main target for the iconoclastic movement of May 4, 1919, one of whose rallying cries was "Down with Confucius and Co.!" It was systematically destroyed between 1966 and 1976 by the Cultural Revolution, culminating in the 1974 campaign of "criticism of Lin Biao and Confucius." How, then, can one explain Confucianism's role from the late 1970s onwards as the apparent engine of economic growth in Japan and the "four little dragons," South Korea, Taiwan, Hong Kong and Singapore? How can we explain its central place, for some leaders known for their authoritarianism, in talk about "Asian values"?

"Confucius fever" reached the People's Republic in the 1980s as it tried to emerge from the Cultural Revolution and Maoism. The decade was marked by two symbolic dates: 1984, the year a Confucius Foundation was created in Beijing, under the aegis of the highest Party authorities, on the occasion of the 2535th anniversary of the Sage's birth; and 1989, the year of the bloody repression of the student democratic movement in Tian'anmen Square—with the Berlin Wall falling just a few months later and the Soviet Union two years after that. Chinese leaders took the latter as a cautionary tale, opting instead for a neo-authoritarianism justified by the need for political and social stability to guarantee economic development, and endorsed by the new "neo-Confucian" ideology, a symbolic representation of the supposed unity and continuity of Chinese culture. In the early 1990s, citing Lee Kuan Yew's Confucian-authoritarian Singapore as a model, Deng Xiaoping introduced his famous concept of the "socialist market economy" with an equally famous slogan: "Getting rich is glorious!"

[2] On the Chinese intellectual tradition, see my *Histoire de la pensée chinoise*, Paris, Seuil, revised pocket edition 2014.

The most remarkable thing is that culturalist arguments were soon used to explain this economic phenomenon: a set of so-called Confucian values—valorisation of the family, respect for hierarchy, enthusiasm for education, hard work, thrift—were proposed as explanatory factors in an economic model of Asian development. This was a complete, spectacular reversal of how Confucianism had been judged up to that point. Ironically, precisely those factors that Weber and Marx saw as obstacles to capitalist development became factors of growth, ones that would, moreover, spare East Asian societies the problems affecting modern Western ones—too much individualism, too much hedonism, too much selfishness. Such thinking is still present in official discourse in China.

The ideology of "Asian" or "Confucian" values is not limited to the re-Confucianisation of Chinese society (which, as in Singapore, sometimes happened through the medium of English). Its defenders believe it can restore and enlarge the old process of Confucianisation in countries viewed as "Sinicised" satellites of the Chinese empire—and so the concept of a "cultural China" was born. Tu Wei-ming—a Sino-American scholar, a long-time Harvard professor now comfortably retired in Beijing and a proponent of "third-wave" Confucianism—represents this using concentric circles. The centre is composed of mainland China (including Hong Kong), Taiwan and Singapore. Then comes the wider circle of Chinese communities in the global diaspora. Last is the virtual circle of individuals worldwide—intellectuals, academics, journalists, businessmen and so on—who strive to understand China and are responsible for spreading the word in their own linguistic communities.[3] We should look forward to a "cultural China" that will effectively make Confucianism into a system of universal "ethical-spiritual" values, comparable with the other great religions, Christianity, Islam and Buddhism, and able to enter into dialogue with them. Questions of human rights are carefully left to one side.

The instrumentalised version of the Chinese philosophical tradition that gave intellectual backup to discourse about "Confucian values" in the 1980s marks a desire among a portion of the Chinese intellectual elite, present across the English-speaking world and largely in the United States, to regain the guiding role it had in the old Chinese vision of universality,

[3] See Tu Wei-ming, "Cultural China: The Periphery as the Center," in *The Confucian World Observed: A Contemporary Discussion of Confucian Humanism in East Asia* (Honolulu: The East-West Center, 1992); and Tu Wei-ming, ed., *The Living Tree: The Changing Meaning of Being Chinese Today* (Stanford: Stanford University Press, 1994).

preaching Confucian values as universal (or at least universalisable) and suitable, above all, for building a "new globalised humanism."[4] We are witnessing the return of the universality of China-as-world, undermined by Western colonial powers at the end of the nineteenth century, not just as a nostalgic image but more aggressively as a unifying factor in the predominant ideology of "Greater China" and intellectual speculation about "the philosophy of *tianxia*" or "*tianxia*-ism" (*tianxiazhuyi*).[5] The People's Republic is promoting all kinds of forums, conferences, periodicals and books holding forth endlessly on "Confucian ethics and globalisation" and aspiring to an international audience—largely made up, in reality, of Chinese living overseas.

The dream of pan-Confucianism has overtaken another, much more explicitly hegemonic one: that of a People's Republic that is taking up and attempting to dominate discourse within Asia, both through the dream of "Greater China" and by claiming to lead the region. But it can only assert its claim to a non-Western universality by resorting to culturalist strategies, brandishing the banner of "Asian" or "Confucian values" against the "human rights" Westerners champion so enthusiastically. To overcome the bankruptcy of Maoist ideology and to maintain control over society—especially over young people—the so-called Confucian values are wheeled out once more: respect for order, obedience to superiors, devotion to the state and defence of the family. These values favour harmonious development by limiting individual appetites. "Confucianism" is supposed to put group interests above those of the individual, ensuring social stability, chief among the regime's priorities. (Whence the slogan launched by Hu Jintao in 2006: "socialist society of harmony.")

Within this "neo-authoritarianism" dressed up as Confucianism, ex-Marxist ideologues in Beijing and anti-Marxist ones in Taiwan, Seoul and Singapore agree on a crucial point: instead of a utopian image of a socialism without the West, they aspire to a supposedly "post-modern" or "post-Western" economic modernity, also without the West—a convenient excuse for bypassing the work of building democracy. Such Confucianism lets the leadership in Beijing kill three birds with one stone.

[4] See in this regard my article "Confucianisme, post-modernisme et valeurs asiatiques," in Yves Michaud, ed., *Qu'est-ce que la culture?* (Paris: Odile Jacob, 2001), 80–90.

[5] See Zhao Tingyang, "The Philosophy of *Tianxia*," in the issue of *Diogène* (January–March 2008) devoted to current trends in political philosophy in China. Zhao advocates *tianxia-ism* as a way of overcoming the failings of global organisations of nation-states like the United Nations.

First, it gives them the political and moral legitimacy they have been lacking, especially after the Tian'anmen massacre. Society is to be brought together around a new project, a new reason for unity following the failure of the Maoist utopia, which showed its true face in the Cultural Revolution and the suppression of the Beijing Spring. We saw this at work in the wake of the Sichuan earthquakes a few months before the 2008 Olympics, when leaders rushed to the scene to project the highly Confucian image of responsible, compassionate leaders caring for a population in distress. At the same time, they were brutally suppressing demonstrations by Tibetans.

Secondly, it allows them to encourage a sense of national identity fuelled by the belief that China will be the next world superpower. "The Chinese are a great people, with an unbroken, five-thousand-year history of glorious culture and tradition"—a recurring formula in the language of Chinese officials, often former Red Guards who have striven in their youth to demolish the cultural heritage they now lay claim to so loudly, and of which they are so crassly ignorant. Finally, where the conflict between tradition and modernisation has been a major problem for China, and remains one for many developing countries, it allows the leadership to move towards modernisation while still claiming to observe tradition. In other words, China's "culture of millennia" becomes—thanks to the concept or, rather, the oxymoron of "soft power"—one more argument for its supposedly untroubled ascent.

But such excuses only poorly disguise the liberal, capitalist, Anglo-Saxon option that Chinese leaders claim from Western modernity. (It is significant, in this respect, that the word "freedom" was taken up by Japanese and then Chinese modernity, from the translation of John Stuart Mill's *On Liberty*.) It neglects the question of the Rights of Man that the French Revolution posed, choosing once again to take the "all-economy" path rather than embracing a broader, more constructive politics. But for how much longer?

References

Analects (*Lunyu*). (1997). French translation by Anne Cheng, *Entretiens de Confucius*. Editions du Seuil, 1981; English translation by Simon Leys, *The Analects of Confucius*. Norton, 1997.

Cheng, A. (2001). Confucianisme, post-modernisme et valeurs asiatiques. In Y. Michaud (Ed.), *Qu'est-ce que la culture?* (pp. 80–90). Odile Jacob.

Cheng, Anne. (2014). *Histoire de la pensée chinoise*. Editions du Seuil, 1997. Revised pocket edition 2014.

Tu, W.-m. (1992). Cultural China: The periphery as the Center. In *The Confucian world observed: A contemporary discussion of Confucian humanism in East Asia*. The East-West Center.

Tu, W.-m. (Ed.). (1994). *The living tree: The changing meaning of being Chinese today*. Stanford University Press.

Zhao, Tingyang. (2008, January–March). The Philosophy of *Tianxia*. *Diogenes*.

PART IV

Stakes and Uncertainty in a Globalised World

CHAPTER 13

Vietnam's Mode of Development in the Face of Climate Change

Thi Thu-Ha Nguyen and Etienne Espagne

1 Introduction

The Vietnamese Prime Minister Pham Minh Chinh announced in Glasgow on 1 November 2021 that Vietnam would achieve a net-zero emissions target by 2050. This ambitious move seemed to take the international community by surprise, while at the same time highlighting the efficacy of a Vietnamese "environmental state" (Larsen, 2018) that has so far been largely ignored. Vietnam is typically expected to be susceptible to climate change for a number of reasons. With a long coastal line and abundant geological and natural diversity, Vietnam has emerged as one of the most vulnerable countries to climate change in the Asia-Pacific region. The annual average temperature increased by 0.89 °C according to the latest Report on Climate Change and Sea Level Rise scenarios for Vietnam (IMHEN, 2021). Extreme climate events continue to be recorded with

T. T.-H. Nguyen (✉)
LASTA, Université de Rouen Normandie, Rouen, France

E. Espagne
Agence Française de Développement, CERDI, Paris, France
e-mail: espagnee@afd.fr

T. A.-D. Tran (ed.), *Rethinking Asian Capitalism*,
https://doi.org/10.1007/978-3-030-98104-4_13

greater intensity and frequency. The highest and lowest temperatures during the day have become more extreme. The upward trend in sea level was about 3.6 mm/year for the period 1993–2018, while subsidence dynamics in the two major deltas (Red River and Mekong) amplify this effect by a few cm/year. The recent COP26 special assessment report of the GEMMES Vietnam project puts the potential direct costs due to climate change at 1.8% of annual GDP in the case of a 1 °C increase in global temperature, at up to 4.5% in the case of a 1.5 °C increase and at 6.7% for a 2 °C increase (Espagne et al., 2021).

Climate policies aimed at mitigating global warming or adapting to its most detrimental effects are the dynamic result of complex processes involving scientific evidence and the social and economic feasibility of instruments that involve parties with varying interests in taking action. The national socio-political and economic specificities of societies are thus key determinants of the emergence of any form of climate policy regime. The historical and cultural evolution of the people, in particular with regard to their relation to nature, but also most obviously the socio-economic dynamics of recent decades, shape the type of concrete environmental policies that can emerge. If climate change constitutes today a major challenge for the country, its people and the government, the construction of a Vietnamese "environmental state" (Larsen, 2018) has grown through different institutional arrangements that cannot be reduced to the instantaneous picture of the ambitious COP26 announcement made by Prime Minister Pham Minh Chinh.

After a decade of the Indochina war against the French colonizers (1945–1954) and two decades of the American War (1954–1975), the post-1975 period opened on to a landscape of unprecedented human, economic and environmental destruction for Vietnam. In addition to the estimated 3 million casualties and the additional 1 million who emigrated immediately after reunification, the notion of "ecocide" was specifically devised in order to describe the direct implications of the massive bombings and use of Agent Orange during the American War (Zierler, 2011). Against the background of this unprecedented wartime ecocide, the first post-war five-year development plan set ambitious goals for economic development, including a 13–14% aggregate annual growth rate of the economy. "Heavy state-led industrialization was prioritized in government budget allocations and in international collaboration (with foreign assistance flowing in from socialist partners including China, the Soviet Union, and Eastern Europe)" (Tarp, 2018). Some industrial growth did take place but at a very high economic and environmental cost. The Vietnamese intervention in Cambodia in late 1978 and the removal of the Khmer Rouge regime from power led to international isolation and even a Chinese attack along the northern border in early 1979.

After General Secretary Le Duan passed away in July 1986, the subsequent election of Nguyen Van Linh at the Sixth National Congress of the Communist Party of Vietnam in December 1986 coincided with the adoption of the *Doi Moi* ("renovation") program. It also marked the moment when the first official planning documents were drawn up for the conservation of natural resources, notably with the creation in 1985 of a "committee for the rational utilization of natural resources and environmental protection". From that moment on, crop production expanded fast and growth has remained positive ever since. Importantly, the politically sensitive food shortages started to decline quite significantly, alongside the substantial drop in the number of people suffering from undernourishment. A major reason behind this progress lies in the phenomenal progress in rice production. In a short span of 15 years, Vietnam turned itself from heavy dependence on food imports into a major producer and exporter of rice and other agricultural products. As Finn Tarp (2018) puts it, Vietnam really became a "dragon that rose from the ashes".

However, this success was not without significant environmental impacts. The building of a "socialist-oriented market economy" in the 1990s was also characterized by growing pollution. It was mainly the pollutions and environmental degradation caused by a very rapid development process that caught the attention of Vietnamese people and the government during that period. The creation in 1992 of the Ministry of Science, Technology and Environment, followed the next year by the first law on environmental protection, marked the emergence of the environment as a public policy issue, although the new ministry was much less influential than the Ministry of Planning and Investment or the Ministry of Construction. Since the establishment of this first "pollution policy regime", the Vietnamese government has been putting more effort and communication on climate change (and especially climate impacts) and sustainable development at the heart of development policy.

The official creation of the Ministry of Natural Resources and the Environment in 2002 also marked the emergence of the Vietnamese strategy on climate change. The first pillar of the strategy is acknowledgment of the importance of international aid as a key enabler of the country's own climate ambition. Second, most efforts have been focused on the notion of adaptation to impacts, although sometimes without really disentangling the effects of climate from more local anthropogenic drivers, especially in the Mekong delta (Eslami et al., 2021b). The second phase in the evolution of the Vietnamese "environmental state" could be described as a period of "benign neglect", which corresponds to a specific stage in its own socio-economic development process and the mobilization of different social groups in order to embed the climate issue at the margins.

COP26, at least as read through the lens of the official Vietnamese announcements and a wider international trend toward carbon neutrality plans and announcements, may have ended this second phase. It remains to be seen if the new regime can be characterized as one of "benign concern" or one of "ambitious socio-ecological transformation" and which socio-economic forces might lead to one or the other outcome.

In this chapter, therefore, we will aim to analyze how the changes in political and socio-economic conditions impact on the environmental policies. We will consider how climate change and the political discourse on climate change have been progressively institutionalized and have become an integral component of Vietnamese social dynamics. After this introductory section, in Sect. 2, we describe the emergence of an "environmental state" in Vietnam in the decades after *Doi Moi* and its specific position within the country's rapid development process. Section 3 examines how the climate change issue in Vietnam transformed this pre-existing environmental state and the broader political action. We then discuss, in Sect. 4, the prospects for an increased ambition and accelerated action in the global fight against climate change in Vietnam after the COP26 announcements on carbon neutrality.

2 An Environmental *"Doi Moi"*?

2.1 A Successful Structural Transformation

The economic and political reforms under *Doi Moi* in 1986 took Vietnam from a centralized economy to a "socialist oriented market economy". Indeed, the 6th National Congress of the Communist Party of Vietnam in December 1986 defined this model as a multi-sectoral market economy where the state sector plays the decisive role in directing economic development, with the eventual long-term goal of developing socialism. The 1986–1999 period is associated with the *Doi Moi* economic reforms themselves. The *Doi Moi* economic reforms introduced laid the foundations for

Vietnam's remarkable development record, with a growth rate of 2.7% in 1986 rising to 7.3% by 1989 (Fig. 13.1). One of the determinants of national economic development from 1986 onward was an emphasis on widespread de-collectivization, trade liberalization and reform of the agriculture sector. Figure 13.3 shows the composition of exports by type of goods. Vietnam exports mostly heavy industrial/mineral products, light industrial and handicraft goods and agricultural/aquaculture products. As discussed by Tarp et al. (2003), this period also saw an increased reliance on both foreign aid and foreign direct investment (FDI), and the quantity and composition of international trade changed dramatically. Vietnam joined the Association of Southeast Asian Nations (ASEAN) in 1995 as relations with the US normalized and is also a member of the Asia-Pacific Economic Cooperation forum. The key economic and trade program for ASEAN is the ASEAN Free Trade Area (AFTA), and AFTA's core instrument is the Common Effective Preferential Tariff. By joining ASEAN, therefore, Vietnam at an early stage entered into international commitments on trade policy, which have had a profound impact on its productive structure.

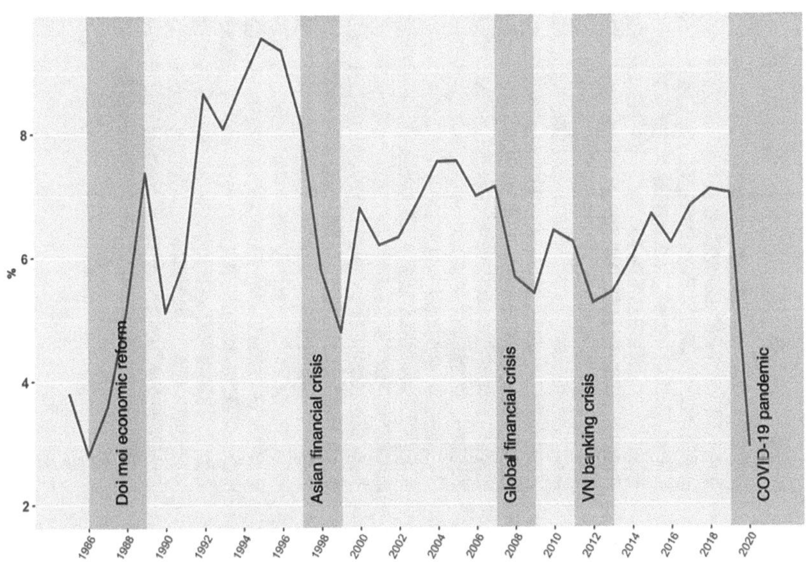

Fig. 13.1 Vietnam's growth rate. (Source: General Statistics Office (GSO))

The second period ran from 2000 to 2009 and saw Vietnam's rapid integration into the global economy (Fig. 13.1). The US–Vietnam Bilateral Trade Agreement was signed in 2000 and Vietnam became a member of the World Trade Organization in 2007. Further agreements followed with China, India, Japan and Korea, the Trans-Pacific Partnership and Europe. Vietnam pursued an export-oriented industrialization strategy and to attract foreign direct investment (FDI). After the great crash due to the Asian financial crisis in 1997, the Vietnamese economy grew at an average of 6–7% per year. The share of manufactured products increased, which might reflect the rapid growth of FDI flows; at the same time the share of agricultural/aquaculture products decreased (Fig. 13.2). Indeed, multinational companies or foreign direct investment firms developed the production and export of higher value-added goods, such as computers, telephones, electronics and machinery.

In many respects, Vietnam is a case of successful structural transformation. Over the past three decades, workers have gradually migrated to urban areas and found employment there. Agriculture is still an important component of national employment and is actively supported by

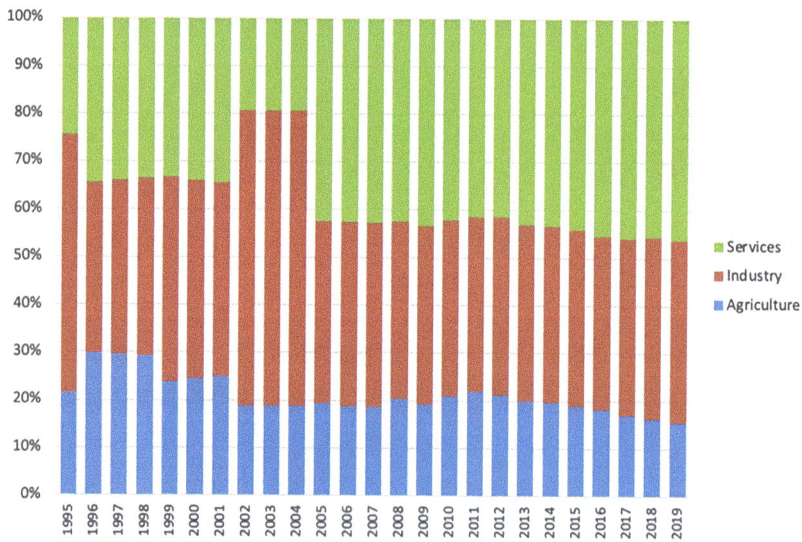

Fig. 13.2 Decomposition of Vietnam's production structure. (Source: General Statistics Office (GSO))

state-coordinated support measures. Consequently, and importantly for the process of structural transformation, agriculture has grown substantially in absolute terms. In sum, the general economic transformation story that emerges from Vietnam includes a combination of labor moving out of agriculture to be absorbed into the expanding higher value-added manufacturing and services sectors (Fig. 13.2). If this structural transformation looks impressive in social and economic terms, we now turn to the environmental effects of this period, which shed light on the missing "environmental *Doi Moi*".

2.2 *But Benign Neglect of Environmental Degradation*

The major political economic changes in Vietnam in the 1980s and 1990s had an impact on the environment. The *Doi Moi* reforms were mainly characterized by four factors: growing diversification of capital investment; land-use rights as commodity; commercialization of the housing sector and slow changes in the planning system. Another implicit factor was the

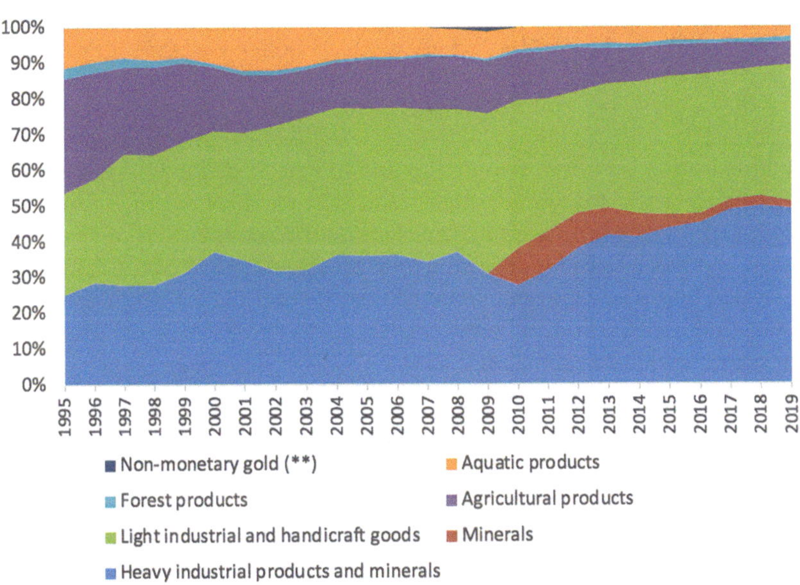

Fig. 13.3 Decomposition of Vietnam's exports by products. (Source: General Statistics Office (GSO))

devolvement of power to local authorities. Many problems resulted from such a rapid and uncontrolled housing market and residential construction boom. The spontaneous housing boom led to chaos in urban development and to drastic changes in the urban landscape of Vietnamese cities. In the early days of the economic reforms, the Vietnamese government did not consider the issue of the greenhouse gases produced by wet rice agriculture, nor did it take the toxic effects of chemicals in agriculture and industrial pollution into account. For the Party, economic growth objectives took priority over environmental concerns.

This priority given to rapid development did not preclude the building of a state environmental department. Indeed, in 1986, the Vietnamese government established a Committee for the Rational Use of Natural Resources and Environmental Protection (CRUNREP) that produced the National Conservation Strategy (NCS). The Council of Ministers Ordinance on the Transfer of Foreign Technology to Vietnam of December 1988 also highlighted the concern with environmental protection. The next important step was the Environmental Protection Law, which was approved in 1993. Vietnam introduced a system of national pollution standards and environmental safeguards and guidelines in the mid-1990s. This framework imposed a system of environmental impact assessments (EIA) for area-based land-use plans and zones. Environmental audits were conducted and environmental management plans imposed on existing plants. The 1993 Environmental Protection Act laid the foundations for Vietnam's legal framework on the environment. It defined basic concepts associated with the environment and environmental protection and included specific provisions on the rights and responsibilities of organizations and individuals for environmental protection. However, the Act also revealed limitations that had to be addressed amid the country's efforts to boost industrialization and modernization and developments in globalization and world economic integration.

2.3 *The Missing Environmental* Doi Moi

Air Pollution

Vietnam is struggling with alarming air pollution levels. According to a study by Greenpeace and AirVisual IQ published in 2021, Hanoi and Ho Chi Minh City, the country's two largest cities, were among the most heavily polluted cities in Southeast Asia in 2020. Dominici et al. (2006)

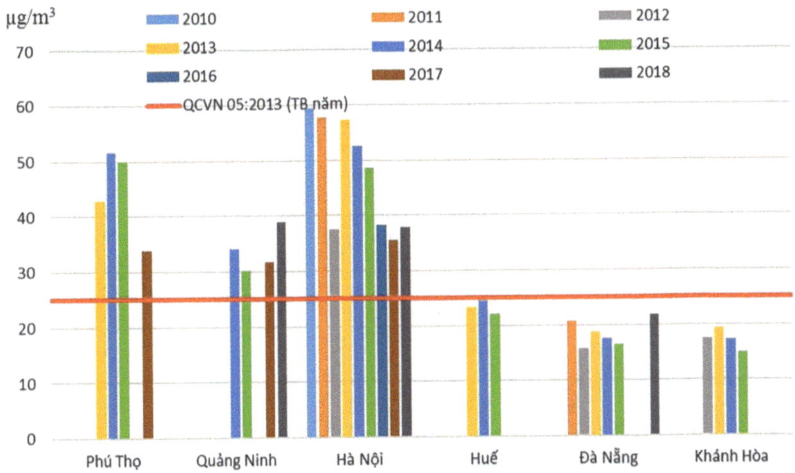

Fig. 13.4 Average PM2.5 at different stations compared to the NAAQ standard. (Source: Le et al. (2018)—Vietnam environment administrator magazine (VEM)—Vietnam Environment Administration (VEA))

demonstrate that the exposure to the fine particulate matter with an aerodynamic diameter ≤ 2.5 μm (called PM2.5) increases the risk of hospital admission for cardiovascular and respiratory diseases. PM2.5 can be directly emitted by physical-chemical transformation processes in the atmosphere. Motor vehicle exhausts, biomass burning and the combustion of fossil fuels are the main anthropogenic sources of PM2.5 (To et al., 2019). Vietnam now has more than 3.6 million automobiles and 58 million motorbikes, many of which are old vehicles that emit large volumes of air pollutants. The PM2.5 concentrations in Vietnam are high, implying that the Vietnamese population is breathing air with a high level of air pollutants (Fig. 13.4). In April 2013, for the first time, the Vietnamese Ministry of Natural Resources and Environment added new limits of PM2.5 concentration to the National Technical Regulation on Ambient Air Quality (NAAQ) (QCVN 05:2013/BTNMT).

Water Pollution

Water pollution is one of the country's biggest problems (Fig. 13.5). It has many causes. The industrialization process led to water polluted by sewage and waste. Industrial waste consists of some kind of chemical

Fig. 13.5 Thi Vai River pollution due to Vedan. (Source: VietNamNetNew)

substance such as sulfur, which is harmful to marine life. Asbestos is known to be highly carcinogenic. Nitrates and phosphates derived from fertilizers can be a risk to the marine environment. Oil discharged from shipping and, in some cases, the illegal exploitation of petroleum resources are possible explanations for the deaths of fish or sea-birds. Currently, there are 348 industrial parks in 61 provinces in Vietnam, 204 of which are located along three major river basins, including the Nhue, Cau and Dong Nai rivers. In the Mekong River delta, there are 33 industrial parks located across the region's 12 provinces.

Wastewater from daily activities is pumped directly into canals, rivers and irrigation canals. There are many hospitals and chemical sites that have not got wastewater treatment. In Hanoi alone, around 350,000–400,000 m^3 of wastewater and more than 1000 m^3 of waste are discharged every day. But only 10% is treated and the rest is discharged directly into rivers, polluting the water and killing fish. In Ho Chi Minh City, water pollution is worst in the Thanh Luong cluster, with about 500,000 m^3 of wastewater per day from washing powder, paper and dyeing factories. Not only in big cities but also in many urban areas, waste is not treated and permeates the soil, which makes the environmental pollution more and more serious. In rural areas, due to farming methods that misuse herbicides, the water in rivers, canals and lakes is extremely polluted.

Deforestation

The increase in Vietnam's forest cover over the last 20 years is remarkable, but the quality of its natural forests has suffered. Between 1943 and 1993, forest cover in Vietnam declined from an estimated 43% to 28% due to the war with the United States. Since 1993, the government has implemented policy reforms and forest programs that have led to an increase in forest cover to 14,415,381 ha (December 2017) or 41.65% of the country's land area (Fig. 13.6). Natural forests account for 10,236,415 ha and plantations account for 4,178,966 ha. While the forest cover continues to increase, due largely to the expansion of forest plantations, the quality of native forests continues to deteriorate. This is also reflected in the forest reference emission levels Vietnam submitted to the United Nations Framework Convention on Climate Change (UNFCCC) in 2016, which

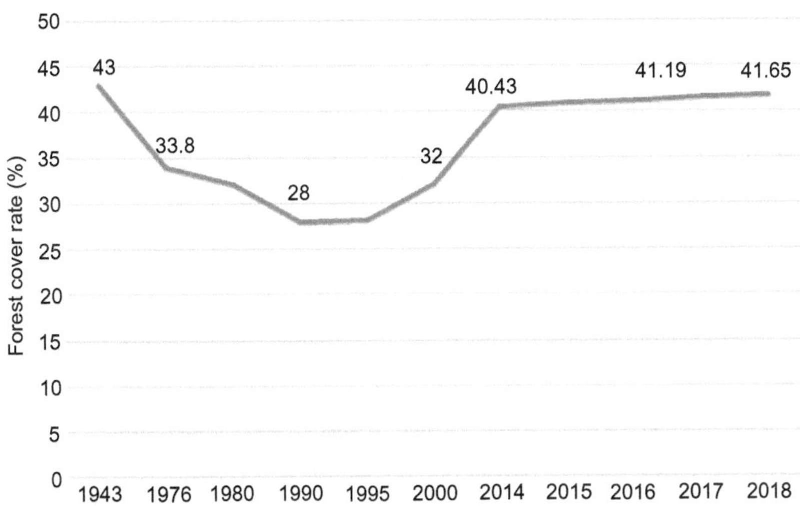

Fig. 13.6 Forest cover change. (Source: FPD (Forest Protection Department). Data on forest changes available on: http://www.kiemlam.org.vn/Desktop.aspx/List/So-lieu-dien-bien-rung-hang-nam/)

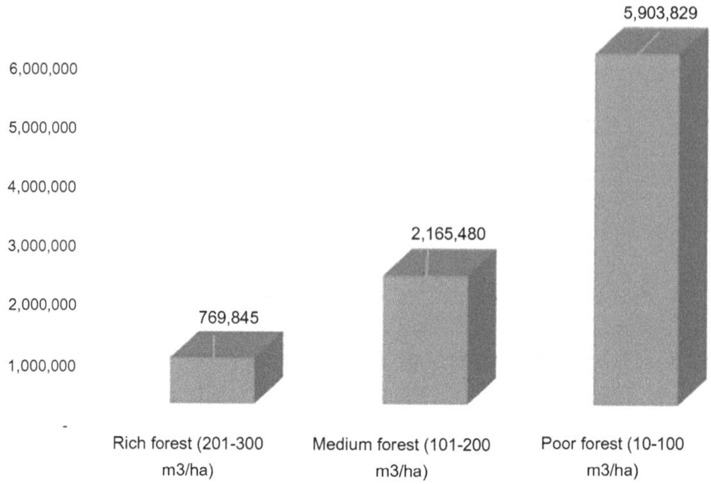

Fig. 13.7 Quality of forest. (Source: VNFOREST.2016. Final Report on National Forest Inventory for the period 2013–2016)

estimated that over two thirds of Vietnam's natural forests are in poor condition or regenerating, while rich and closed-canopy forest constitutes only 5% of the total (Fig. 13.7).

Food Security

The FAO defines food security by reference to four indicators: food availability, food accessibility, food utilization (nutrition) and food safety. Over the 40 years of reform, Vietnam has achieved several successes in food security. However, the country is still facing some challenges in food safety and nutrition, mainly due to a booming population. There has been an increase in cases of food poisoning. The main causes include the widespread use of chemicals, fragmented production and processing, weak food safety control and so on. Food poisoning urges the public sector to address the safety regulations. Vietnam notified the Draft Bill on Food Safety to the World Trade Organization's (WTO) Sanitary and Phytosanitary Committee (SPS) (G/SPS/N/VNM/08) on September 15, 2009. The US Government and a number of US agriculture trade associations provided comments on the Bill. The Vietnamese Food Safety Act was signed by Former President Nguyen Minh Triet on June 28, 2010 and ratified by the National Assembly on June 17, 2012. The Food Safety Act entered into force on July 1, 2011. The Act provides organizations and individuals with rights and obligations to ensure food safety and contains regulations on food safety, food production and trading, food import and export, food advertisement and labeling, food testing, food risk analysis and the prevention and management of food safety incidents, information, education and communication on food safety and the state management of food safety.

3 The Emergence of the Climate Question in Vietnam

3.1 Climate Change as a Driver of Vietnam's Global Integration

In the 2000s, Vietnam ratified most international environmental framework agreements, such as the United Nations Framework Convention on Climate Change (UNFCCC) in 2003, the Paris Climate Agreement (COP21) in 2015, the 2030 Agenda on Sustainable Development that same year and the Nagoya Protocol on Biodiversity and, more recently, the Glasgow Climate Pact at the UN Climate Change Conference (COP26) in Glasgow. This acceleration of Vietnam's participation in the global climate arena is concomitant to its insertion in the globalization process.

The achievement of World Trade Organization membership in 2006 marks a milestone in Vietnam's integration into the world. As a result, the updated Environmental Protection Act of 2005 introduces fundamental and comprehensive amendments in a bid to adapt the country's environmental legislation to a market economy and its integration into the global economy. Other significant environmental legislation include: the 2003 Land Act, the 2004 Act on Forest Protection and Development, the 2007 Act on Chemicals, the 2008 Act on Biodiversity, the 2010 Minerals Act, the 2010 Act on Environmental Protection Tax, the 2010 Act on the Economical and Efficient Use of Energy and the 2012 Act on Water Resources.

The National Target Program to Respond to Climate Change (NTP-RCC), adopted in 2008, sets out legislative, planning and investment priorities in response to climate change but focuses predominantly on adaptation measures, not mitigation. However, it contains few concrete policy commitments and rather constitutes a first step in directing ministries and provinces to formulate specific sector and regional plans of action based on more detailed impact assessments. This program was updated in 2012 for the period up to 2015. In 2016, it became the National Target Program to Respond to Climate Change and Green Growth (NTPRCC-GG). The key adaptation-related tasks focus on developing, updating and implementing national-, sectoral- and provincial-level action plans to respond to climate change, as well as on building capacity and raising awareness about climate change responses.

For some specific sectors, the NTP-RCC contains different plans or programs. Regarding the energy sector, the National Target Program on Energy Efficiency and Conservation for 2006–2015 was the responsibility of the Ministry of Industry and Trade (MOIT), including the formulation and implementation of greenhouse gas (GHG) mitigation options and, above all, providing financial and technical support for energy efficiency improvements in major industries. In the agriculture sector, the Ministry of Agriculture and Rural Development (MARD) Action Plan on Climate Change seeks to mobilize development assistance for climate change mitigation and adaptation in order to minimize its adverse impacts and then ensure sustainable development in the agriculture and rural development sector. It also covers the stability and safety of residents in cities and different zones and regions, especially the Mekong and Red River deltas and the central and mountainous areas. The plan aims to ensure stable agricultural production and food security in an agricultural area; the maintenance of dyke and infrastructure systems to meet disaster prevention and mitigation requirements. International cooperation with regional programs providing technical and financial assistance ensures financial support for the plan's implementation from the government budget and the mobilization of official development assistance, international cooperation support programs and other sources of national and international assistance. The Ministry of Transport enacted a framework for the Transport Action Plan of the NTP-RCC in early 2011 that focuses on assessing the impacts of climate change on the transport infrastructure, identifying suitable mitigation and adaptation options for transport projects and collaborating with ministries, institutes and international agencies. The MOIT has developed the MOIT Climate Change Action Plan, which focuses on adaptation and mitigation planning with appropriate decision support tools.

The National Strategy on Climate Change (NSCC), endorsed in 2011 by the Prime Minister, is one of the most important adaptation policies, as it sets out the key principles, visions and objectives to be followed in other policies. The key principles are strengthening people's and natural systems' adaptability to climate change, and thus developing a low-carbon economy in order to protect and improve quality of life, guarantee national security and sustainable development in the context of global climate change and proactively work with the international community in protecting the earth's climate system. The NSCC found concrete expression in the National Action Plan on Climate Change (NAPCC) with the first approved in 2012 and updated in 2020 for the 2021–2030 period.

After the Paris Agreement at COP21, the National Plan for the Implementation of this Agreement (PIPA) was approved in 2016 with adaptation, which is one of the five main components of the PIPA. The 2020 update of Vietnam's Nationally Determined Contribution (VN's NDC, 2020) was submitted to the Secretariat of the UNFCCC in September 2020. The updated NDC 2020 contains new policies on adaptation and response to climate change: (i) the National Adaptation Plan for the 2021–2030 period, with a vision through to 2050 (NAP) and a focus solely on adaptation; (ii) the post-2020 NSCC and (iii) the National Action Plan to Respond to Climate Change (NAPRCC) for the 2021–2030 period. The latest currently exists in a draft version only, but after approval this plan will give ministries, sectors and localities specific directions to continue developing and implementing climate change adaptation actions, in line with the socio-economic development plan.

3.2 *The Remaining Climate Policy Gap*

In the past decade, the faltering "environmental state" that emerged after *Doi Moi* has been transformed into an all-embracing effort to envisage the potential impacts of climate change and, with the active support of the international community, to put in place adaptation strategies. Most development aid has indeed been targeted at activities and projects intended to contribute to fulfillment of the Paris Agreement, or at least to a green growth strategy. This has transformed the practices of Vietnam's ministries and institutes without completely redirecting the country's development trajectory. Some more immediate anthropological factors that have contributed to environmental degradation may also have been incorporated into the broad "climate adaptation" narrative in order to attract foreign investors.

Indeed, Vietnam is still one of the countries that is most vulnerable to climate change. We summarize here the key results of the COP26 special report on the basic trends in climate change in Vietnam in the recent past produced by the GEMMES Vietnam project (Espagne et al., 2021).

Temperature

The observed trend in Vietnamese temperatures shows an overall increase during the period 1981–2018, with the greatest increases recorded in recent years (2011–2018). The increases vary between regions (Fig. 13.8) but the average annual temperature across the country as a whole increased

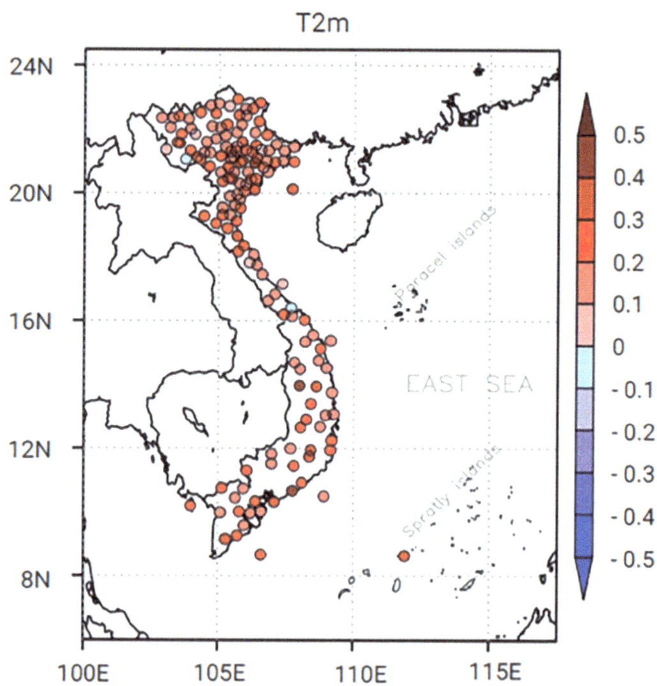

Fig. 13.8 Average annual T2m increase in Vietnam for the period 1981–2018. (Source: GEMMES Vietnam report (2021))

by 0.78 °C over the period 1981–2018. That is equivalent to an increase of around 0.205 °C per decade. The highest increases were recorded in the Central Highlands in autumn and in the North Delta in spring. The lowest increase was in summer in the Northeast and North Central regions.

Regarding the extreme temperatures (Fig. 13.9), the average daily maximum (Tx) and minimum (Tn) temperatures increased across the whole country over the period 1981–2018. High records were set mainly in El Niño years (1987, 1997, 2010, 2017). The general incremental levels were from 0.11 to 0.32 °C/decade in almost all regions. However, the Tx increased relatively faster in the North Delta, southern Northeast, northern North Central and eastern Southern Vietnam. Tx increased relatively more slowly in the South Central and western Central Highlands. Tn recorded its greatest increase in the Central Highlands (0.5 °C/decade), followed by 0.45 °C/decade in the Northwest, 0.29 °C/decade in the South, and ~0.24–0.26 °C/decade in the remaining regions.

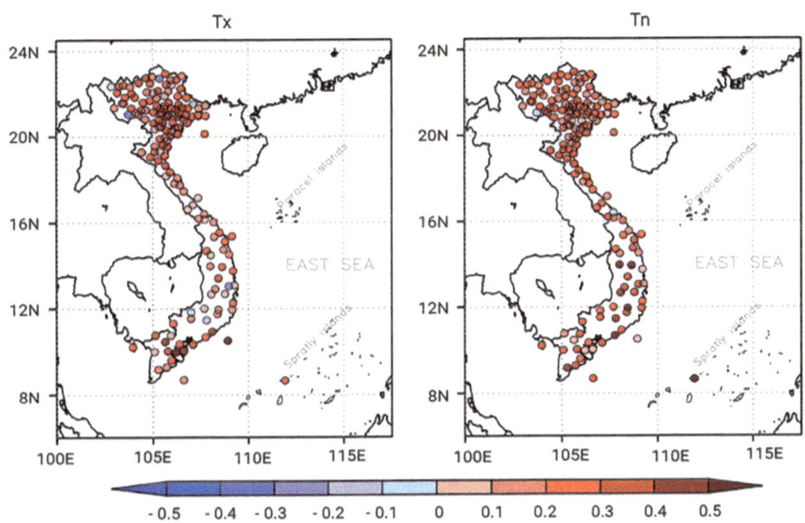

Fig. 13.9 Average daily maximum temperature (Tx) and daily minimum temperature (Tn) changes for the period 1981–2018. (Source: GEMMES Vietnam report (2021))

Rainfall
Average annual precipitation for the whole country increased slightly by 5.5% over the period 1981–2018, albeit with regional variations (Fig. 13.10). Annual precipitation actually declined at several stations in the North and North Central regions and increased at many stations in the Northeast, North Delta, South Central and Central Highlands. However, unlike temperatures, the rainfall trend is statistically significant at only a

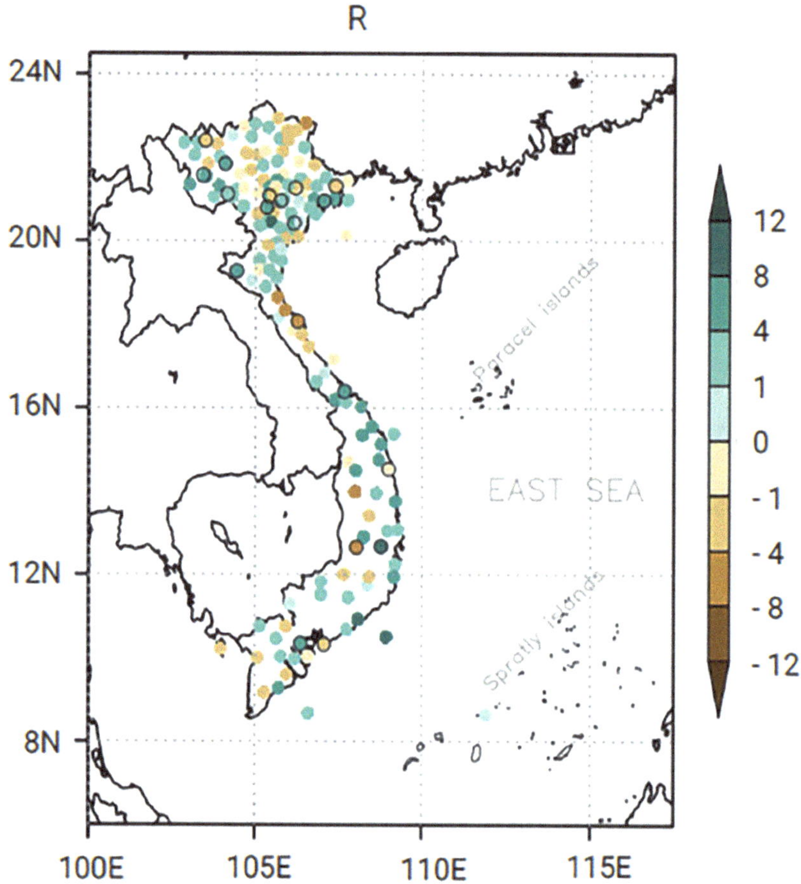

Fig. 13.10 Annual rainfall changes in Vietnam for the period 1981–2018. (Source: GEMMES Vietnam report (2021))

small number of stations. In recent years, heavy rainfall has occurred abnormally in terms of time, place, frequency and intensity (IMHEN, 2021). Such rainfall has occurred not only during the normal rainy seasons but also during the usual dry ones.

Figure 13.11 shows the rainfall trend extremes during the observation period 1981–2018. The trend in maximum 1-day rainfall (Rx1day) was upward in the center of the North East region, some areas of the North and in the northern part of the Southern Central region, with increases of between 5% and 30% (i.e., 1.3–7.9% per decade). In contrast, Rx1day declined in a few provinces in the coastal areas of the North Central region and in most of the Southwest region. The maximum 5-day rainfall (Rx5day) increased more than Rx1day, with typical increases from 1.3% to 15.8% per decade. The highest increases were in some areas of the North and Southern Central regions, while 0.5–5.3% decreases in Rx5day were recorded in parts of the North East, North Central and Southwest regions.

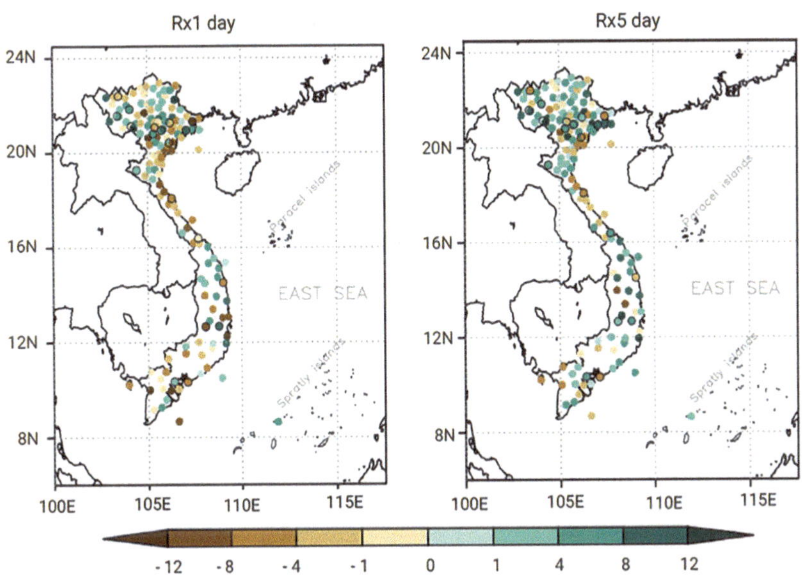

Fig. 13.11 Rx1day and Rx5day changes in Vietnam for the period 1981–2018. (Source: GEMMES Vietnam report (2021))

Sea-Level Rise

According to the Intergovernmental Panel on Climate Change (IPCC)'s Special Report on the Ocean and Cryosphere in a Changing Climate (IPCC, 2019), the global mean sea level (GMSL) rose by 0.16 m (likely range 0.12–0.21 m) between 1902 and 2015, due to ocean thermal expansion and ice loss from glaciers and the Greenland and Antarctic ice sheets. For Vietnam during the period 1993–2014, the trend assessment of the mean sea level at all stations shows an increase of around 3.36 mm per year (Fig. 13.12).

The most important source of the relative sea-level rise in Vietnam, however, is the dynamic of subsidence in the two major deltas, which is mainly local and anthropogenic in origin. The main causes of anthropogenic subsidence are groundwater extraction and sand mining activities (Eslami et al., 2021b).

Extreme Events

The observed trends in tropical cyclones occurring in Vietnam did not change significantly between 1959 and 2014 (Fig. 13.13). However, the number of strong typhoons (over level 12) has increased slightly in recent years (Fig. 13.14).

In addition, throughout its history Vietnam has been constantly hit by violent climatic events, and that far from being exceptional, the alternation of droughts, floods and typhoons is Vietnam's "normal" climatic regime due to its geographic position (intertropical and eastern coastal region of a continent). With one-minute sustained wind speeds that can reach more than 64 knots, typhoons are intense storms accompanied by heavy rainfall. When they make landfall, typhoons cause flooding and trigger landslides.

In addition, the energy sector is responsible for 60% of Vietnam's total greenhouse gas emissions (MoNRE, 2019). Fossil fuels (coal, oil and gas) are the country's main energy source. The contribution of fossil fuel consumption to total energy consumption has been increasing rapidly in Vietnam, from 27.6% in 1990 to 70% in 2016 (computed from British Petroleum (BP), 2018; International Energy Agency (IEA), 2018). Cleaner energy sources are essential for reducing greenhouse gas emissions and climate change mitigation strategies.

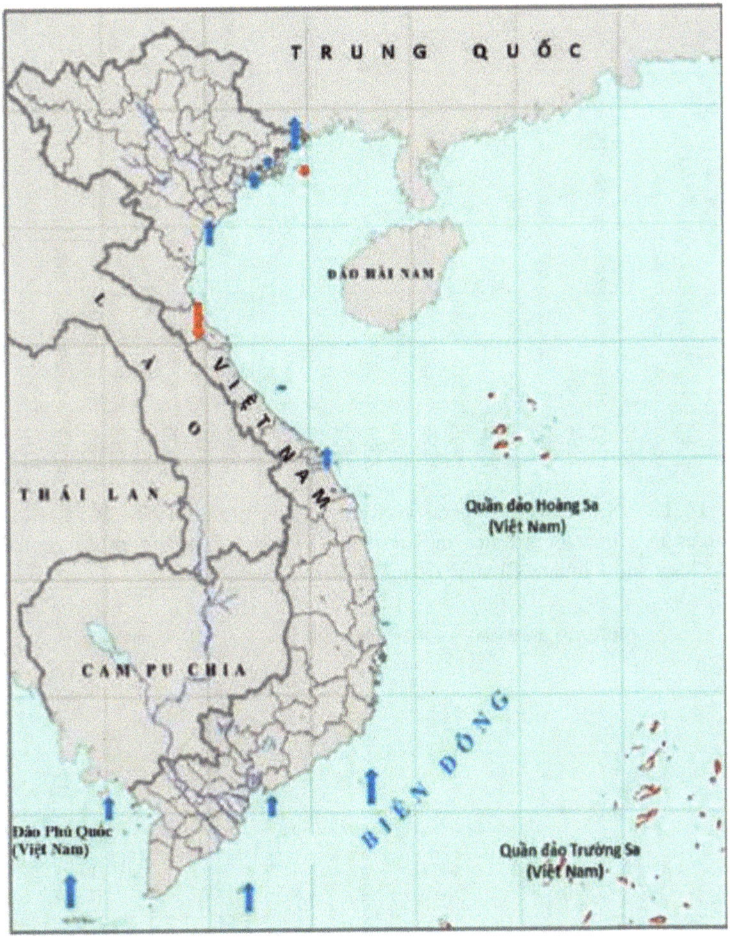

Fig. 13.12 Changes in sea level during the period 1993–2014. (Source: MONRE (2016))

4 After COP26, the Real Ecological Turning Point in Vietnam's Development Path?

4.1 Dire Prospects in the Business-as-usual Scenario

Until now, the most rapid economic development possible remained the highest policy priority. This policy has transformed Vietnam from one of

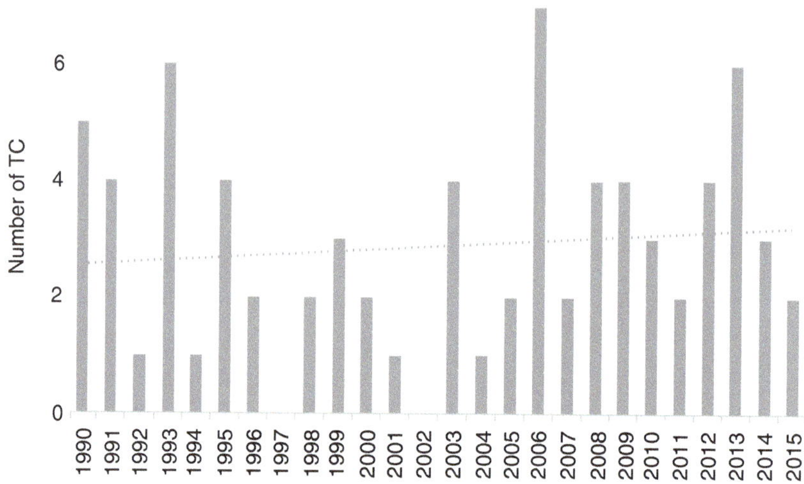

Fig. 13.13 Number of tropical cyclones in the period 1959–2014. (Source: Changes in climate extremes in Vietnam (Vietnam Institute of Meteorology, Hydrology and Climate Change))

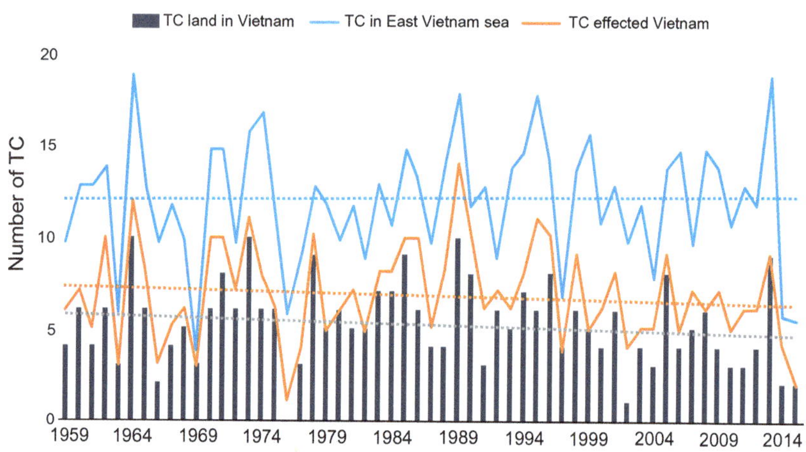

Fig. 13.14 Number of typhoons over level 12 in the East Sea in the period 1990–2015. (Source: Changes in climate extremes in Vietnam (Vietnam Institute of Meteorology, Hydrology and Climate Change))

the poorest nations in the world into a lower middle-income country in 2010. Real GDP per capita reached more than US $2000 in 2019 (Fig. 13.15). The Communist Party is aiming for Vietnam to reach GDP per capita of US $5000 by 2025 and to be a developed country by 2045. However, the recent announcement of the Vietnamese government at COP26 seems to indicate a change in that order of priority. The Vietnamese government has certainly accepted climate change as a vital issue and climate policies as a possible new mode of development.

Vietnam is facing loss and damage from climate change even when climate change adaptation and mitigation measures are effectively applied. According to the climate change projections, increasing loss and damage is inevitable. Vietnam Institute of Meteorology, Hydrology and Climate Change (IMHEN) projection results show that the rate of temperature increase in Vietnam is slightly lower than the global average, particularly for Representative Concentration Pathway—RCP8.5. The average temperature in Vietnam increases by 1.13 ± 0.87 °C under RCP2.6 and by 1.9 ± 0.81 °C under RCP8.5 by the middle of the twenty-first century. At the end of the twenty-first century, temperature in Vietnam increases by 1.34 ± 1.14 °C under RCP2.6 and by 4.18 ± 1.57 °C under RCP8.5. However, projected temperature increases in the North, from Northeast to North Central, are higher than those in the South, from Central Highland to Southern Vietnam.

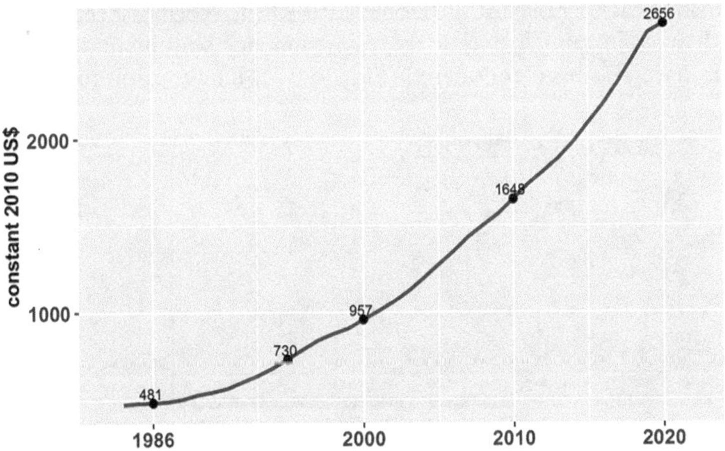

Fig. 13.15 Vietnam's per capita GDP in constant 2010 US$. (Source: World Bank)

Annual daily maximum temperature Tx and annual daily minimum temperature Tn are also projected to increase under RCP4.5 and RCP8.5 but the increase is higher in RCP8.5 than RCP4.5 (Fig. 13.16). In the end-century period 2080–2099 under RCP4.5, Tx is projected to increase by 1.7–2.6 °C; the North increases by 2.0–2.6 °C and the South by 1.7–2.9 °C. Under RCP8.5, much higher increases of 3.2–4.7 °C are projected for Tx, with the highest projected increases of 4.0–4.7 °C observed in the North. Annual daily minimum temperature Tn is projected, in the end-century period and under RCP4.5, to increase by 1.7–2.1 °C, with widespread increases of over 2.0 °C in the North. At the end of the twenty-first century, projected Tn generally increases by 3.3–4.1 °C.

Future projections for rainfall usually contain more uncertainties than those for temperature (Knutti & Sedláček, 2013; Ngo-Duc et al., 2017). One model predicts increased rainfall at a particular location while another shows decreased rainfall. In the case of Vietnam, the rainfall projections certainly vary according to the model, region or scenario chosen. The projected rainfall results obtained with the five dynamic downscaling experiments provided by IMHEN show an increase in annual average rainfall throughout Vietnam under both RCP4.5 and RCP8.5. The increases for the whole country may be 10–20% by the end of the century under RCP4.5. Projected rainfall is lower in Lao Cai and Ha Giang but by a negligible amount, generally less than 5%. At the end of the century under RCP8.5, the increases are typically about 10–25% throughout Vietnam, reaching over 40% in some parts of the Northeast region.

Changes in rainfall during the rainy and dry seasons under the two RCPs have also been considered (Fig. 13.17). Rainy season precipitation

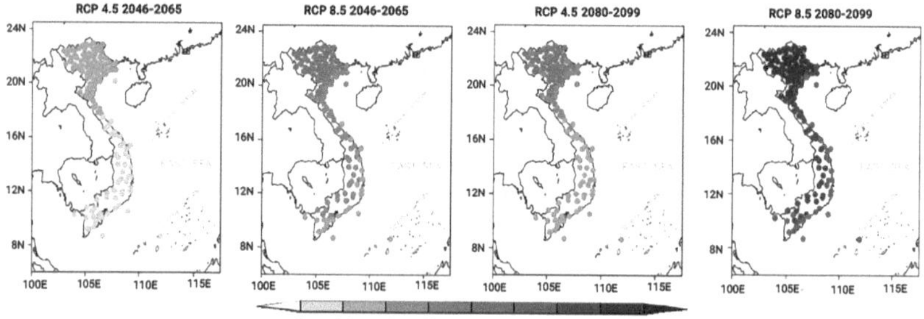

Fig. 13.16 Annual temperature changes under RCP4.5 and RCP8.5. (Source: IMHEN, 2021)

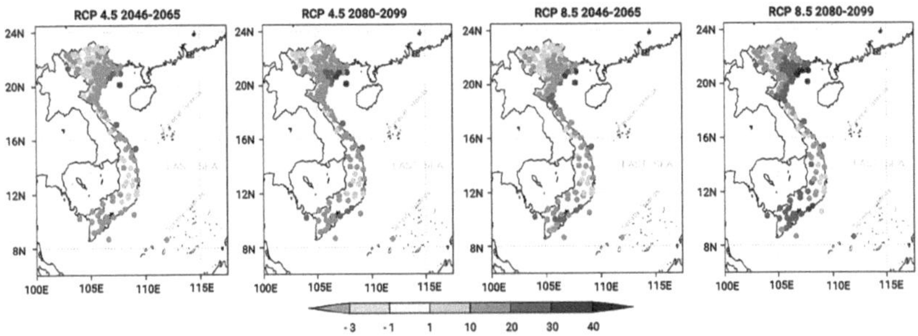

Fig. 13.17 Annual rainfall changes under RCP4.5 and RCP8.5. (Source: IMHEN, 2021)

increases by 10–40% by the end of the century under RCP4.5; under RCP8.5, the increases are 15–30%. Dry season precipitation is projected to increase by 10–25% by the end of the century under RCP4.5, with relatively higher increases in the coastal Northeast region and lower increases in the Central Highlands and the Northern Central region. Under RCP8.5, 5–25% rainfall increases in the dry season are projected over almost all the country by the end of the century, except for some parts in the North Delta, southern Central Highlands and Southeast Vietnam, where decreases of less than 5% are forecast.

Annual maximum 1-day precipitation (RX1day) and annual maximum 5-day consecutive precipitation (RX5day) are projected to increase throughout Vietnam in the twenty-first century under RCP4.5 and RCP8.5. RX1day is generally projected to increase by 24–30% and 25–40% respectively under RCP4.5 and RCP8.5 by the end of the century. Projected RX5day increases by 20–30% and 25–40% by the end of the century under RCP4.5 and RCP8.5 respectively. The North Delta region has the highest increase in both RX1day and RX5day by the end of the century.

According to process-based modeling studies (IPCC, 2019), the GMSL rise will continue in all climate scenarios. Up to 2050, it is argued that uncertainty in future GMSL is relatively small with differences limited to a few centimeters between RCPs. The projections of sea-level rise for Vietnam have been updated following the IPCC Special Report on the Ocean and Cryosphere in a Changing Climate (IMHEN, 2021). Table 13.1 shows the projected sea-level rise in the coastal region of Vietnam for the different RCP scenarios. Note that the regional variations

Table 13.1 Projections of sea-level rise in the coastal regions of Vietnam compared to 1986–2005

	2050	*2100*
RCP2.6	0.24 m (0.13 ÷ 0.32)	0.44 m (0.27 ÷ 0.66)
RCP4.5	0.23 m (0.13 ÷ 0.31)	0.53 m (0.32 ÷ 0.76)
RCP8.5	0.27 m (0.19 ÷ 0.36)	0.73 m (0.49 ÷ 1.03)

Source: IMHEN (2021)

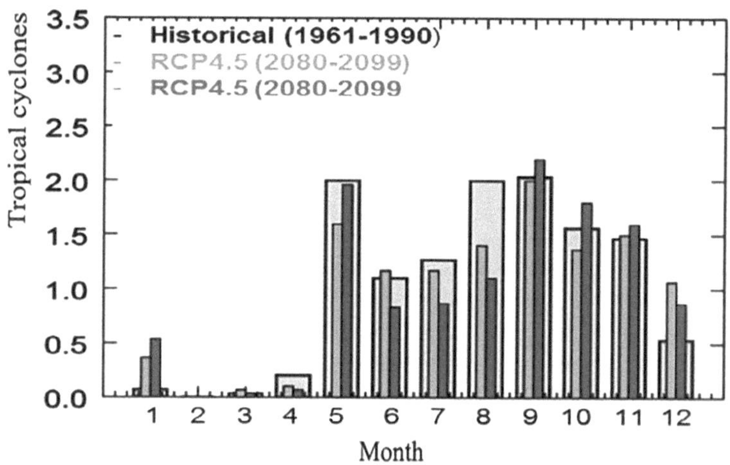

Fig. 13.18 Number of tropical cyclones at the end of the twenty-first century (Providing Regional Climates to Impact Studies (PRECIS) model). (Source: Changes in climate extremes in Vietnam (Vietnam Institute of Meteorology, Hydrology and Climate Change))

along Vietnam coastlines are limited to a few cm. However, it is worth noting that there is only medium confidence in these projections. It is currently estimated that there is a 17% chance that the global mean sea-level rise will exceed 0.59 m by 2100 under RCP2.6 and 1.10 m under RCP8.5 (IPCC, 2019). According to the structured judgment of 22 glaciological and modeling experts (Bamber et al., 2019), there might even be a 5% probability of reaching the extreme forecasts.

Figure 13.18 shows a downward trend for tropical cyclones in the typhoon season (June-August) under both RCP4.5 and RCP8.5 scenarios but an increase in the last typhoon season. Figure 13.19 indicates that the number of weak and normal typhoons will decrease, while the number of

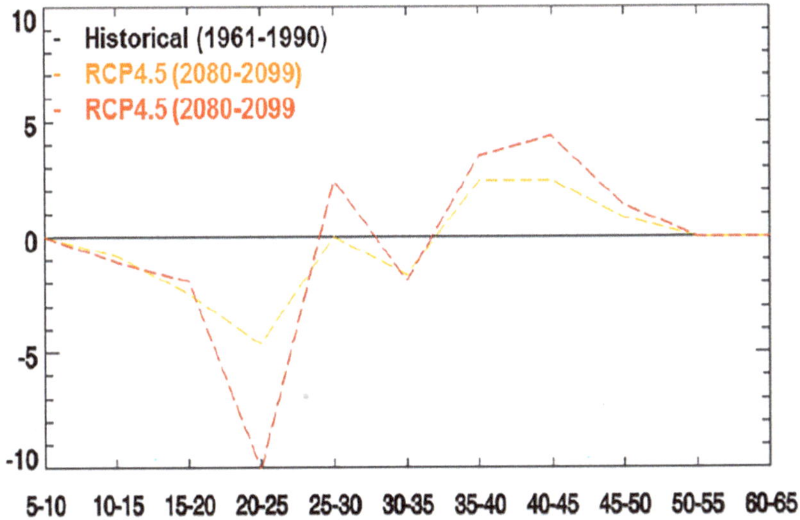

Fig. 13.19 Changes in tropical cyclones of different intensities at the end of the twenty-first century compared to the baseline scenario (PRECIS model). (Source: Changes in climate extremes in Vietnam (Vietnam Institute of Meteorology, Hydrology and Climate Change))

strong typhoons will increase significantly by the end of the twenty-first century.

4.2 *A Real Ecological Turning Point: Prospects and Difficulties*

Recognizing that the revised Environment Protection Act of 2014 has proven too weak to effectively tackle environmental pollution, Vietnam's National Assembly passed a decision on the revision of the Act in June 2019. The new Act represents the most significant modernization of Vietnam's environmental law regime. The aim is to reinforce its impact and to strengthen compliance with the law. Besides improved regulations and permits, better economic instruments, enhanced environmental impact assessments and improved institutional governance, one focus is on updating the chapter on climate change. Indeed, this updated environment law reflects the institutionalization of the key national strategies of developing a low-carbon economy that is resilient to climate change and promoting the circular economy.

As one of the countries in the world hardest hit by climate change, Vietnam needs to make the economy grow green and do so quickly in order to protect against the risk of rising sea levels and increased extreme weather. The Green Growth Strategy was developed in order to accelerate the process of economic restructuring with the aim of making efficient use of natural resources, reducing greenhouse gas emissions through research and the application of green technologies, developing the infrastructure order to improve the overall economic efficiency, coping with climate change, contributing to poverty reduction and creating the momentum for sustainable economic development. The technological level of the world and of Vietnam is increasingly being raised with the fourth industrial revolution (Industry 4.0). The technology that can promote energy efficiency and enable the circular economy to be more productive through eco-innovation and technology transfer will contribute to sustainable development and the mitigation of greenhouse gas emissions. Indeed, technological advances can indirectly reduce pollution levels through the more efficient use of inputs, while filters or waste cleaning devices directly reduce pollution levels. The amounts of polluting waste from industries can drop while production goes up if such a rise is induced by clean and advanced technologies.

In addition, the updated Nationally Determined Contribution (NDC), approved in 2020, confirms Vietnam's utmost commitment to cut greenhouse gas emission—the primary cause of the earth's rapid climate change. The target is to reduce greenhouse gas emissions by 9% by 2030, 1 percentage point higher than the target set in 2015. This could be further increased to 27% with international support through bilateral and multilateral cooperation and mechanisms under the Paris Agreement. This updated NDC included not only mitigation and adaptation policies but also the impacts, advantages and challenges of NDC implementation and a plan for NDC implementation and for the monitoring and evaluation of implementation. Indeed, mitigation measures are identified for the period 2021–2030 in the following sectors: energy, agriculture, waste, land use and industrial processes (IP). The possible measures in the energy sector consist of improving energy-saving and energy efficiency and reducing energy consumption; changing the fuel and energy structure in industry and transportation; shifting passenger and cargo transportation models; promoting the efficient exploitation of renewable energy sources and increasing their proportion in energy production and consumption. In agriculture, reducing GHG emissions can be achieved through sustainable agricultural development, and improving the effectiveness and competitiveness of agricultural production; managing and developing sustainable forests, enhancing carbon sequestration and environmental services; conservation of biodiversity associated with economic development and increasing incomes for forest-dependent communities and people. Waste needs to be managed. The industrial process must replace construction materials and improve cement and chemical production processes together with reducing the consumption of hydrofluorocarbons (HFCs). Improving adaptive capacity, enhancing resilience and reducing the risks caused by climate change are the main objectives of the adaptation component which contributes to achievement of the country's sustainable development goals. It involves strengthening state management and resources, increasing the resilience and adaptive capacity of communities, economic sectors and ecological systems and reducing disaster risks and minimizing damages and preparing to cope with increased natural disasters and climate extremes due to climate change. These strategic tasks are consolidated in the National Adaptation Plan (NAP), and the National Action Plan on Climate Change.

Recently, at the 26th United Nations Climate Change Conference of the Parties (COP26), held in Glasgow, Scotland, Vietnam declared its commitment to achieving net zero by 2050 and to phasing out coal power between 2030 and 2040. A National Steering Committee was established to direct programs, projects and prioritized tasks in response to climate change and to promote the energy transformation required to fulfill Vietnam's commitments. The current daft of the Power Development Plan VIII (PDP8) is expected to be significantly overhauled in order to create much more room for renewable energy and sustainable energy solutions. However, Vietnam needs to work more on concrete strategies, plans and actions, such as reducing the use of fossil fuels (and especially coal) and pushing the future development of renewable energy, green finance and carbon market. Finance and technology will be decisive in the coming years, with international support in both bilateral and multilateral collaborations crucial if Vietnam is to reach its ambitious but essential objective.

References

Bamber, J. L., Oppenheimer, M., Kopp, R. E., Aspinall, W. P., & Cooke, R. M. (2019). Ice sheet contributions to future sea level rise from structured expert judgment. *Proceedings of the National Academy of Sciences, 116*(23), 11195–11200. https://doi.org/10.1073/pnas.1817205116

British Petroleum (2018). Statistical Review of World Energy 2018.

Dominici, F., Peng, R. D., Bell, M. L., Pham, L., McDermott, A., Zeger, S. L., & Samet, J. M. (2006). Fine particulate air pollution and hospital admission for cardiovascular and respiratory diseases. *Journal of Medical American Association, 295*, 1127–1134.

Eslami, S., Hoekstra, P., Kernkamp, H. W. J., Nguyen Trung, N., Do Duc, D., Nguyen Nghia, H., Tran Guang, T., van Dam, A., Darby, S. E., Parsons, D. R., Vasilopoulos, G., Braat, L., & van der Vegt, M. (2021a). Dynamics of salt intrusion in the Mekong Delta; results of field observations and integrated coastal-inland modelling. *Earth Surface Dynamics Discussions*, 1–36. https://doi.org/10.5194/esurf-2020-109

Eslami, S., Hoekstra, P., Minderhoud, P. S. J., Trung, N. N., Hoch, J. M., Sutanudjaja, E., Dung, D. D., Tran Quang, T., Voepel, H. E., Woillez, M.-N., & van der Vegt, M. (2021b). Projections of salt intrusion in a mega-delta under climatic and anthropogenic stressors. *Nature Communications Earth & Environment, 2*(1), 1–11. https://doi.org/10.1038/s43247-021-00208-5

Espagne E., Ngo-Duc, T., Nguyen, M-H., Pannier, E., Woillez, M-N., Drogoul, A., Huynh, T. P. L., Le, T. T., Nguyen, T. T. H., Nguyen, T. T., Nguyen, T. A., Thomas, F., Truong, C. Q., Vo, Q. T., & Vu, C. T. (ed.). (2021). *Climate change in Viet Nam; Impacts and adaptation*. A COP26 assessment report of the GEMMES Viet Nam project. Agence Française de Développement.

IEA. (2018), World Energy Outlook 2018, IEA, Paris. https://www.iea.org/reports/world-energy-outlook-2018

IMHEN. (2021). *Technical report on Climate change, sea level rise scenarios for Viet Nam* (p. 141). Institute of Meteorology, Hydrology and Climate Change, Ministry of Natural Resources and Environment.

IPCC. (2019). IPCC Special Report on the Ocean and Cryosphere in a Changing Climate [H.-O. Pörtner, D.C. Roberts, V. Masson-Delmotte, P. Zhai, M. Tignor, E. Poloczanska, K. Mintenbeck, A. Alegría, M. Nicolai, A. Okem, J. Petzold, B. Rama, N.M. Weyer (eds.)]. In press.

Knutti, R., & Sedláček, J. (2013). Robustness and uncertainties in the new CMIP5 climate model projections. *Nature Climate Change, 3*, 369–373.

Larsen, P. B. (2018). L'environnement. In B. De Tréglodé (Ed.), *Histoire du Vietnam de la colonisation à nos jours*. Editions de la Sorbonne.

Le, H. A, Duong, N., & Vuong L. (2018). Particulate matter pollution in some cities in Vietnam—Temporal variations and spatial distribution of ambient PM10 and PM2.5 concentrations. *Vietnam Environmental Administration Magazine* (VEM), IV.

MoNRE. (2016). *Climate change, sea level rise scenarios for Viet Nam: Summary for policy makers*. Ministry of Natural Resources and Environment.

MoNRE. (2019). *The Second Biennial Updated Report (BUR2) of Vietnam to the United Nations Framework Convention on Climate Change (UNFCCC)*. Ministry of Natural Resources and Environment, Socialist Republic of Vietnam.

Ngo-Duc, T., Tangang, F. T., Santisirisomboon, J., Cruz, F., Trinh-Tuan, L., Nguyen-Xuan, T., Phan-Van, T., Juneng, L., Narisma, G., Singhruck, P., Gunawan, D., & Aldrian, E. (2017). Performance evaluation of RegCM4 in simulating Extreme Rainfall and Temperature Indices over the CORDEX-Southeast Asia Region. *International Journal of Climatology, 37*, 1634–1647.

Tarp, F. (2018). *Vietnam: The dragon that rose from the ashes*. WIDER Working Paper 2018/126. Helsinki: UNU-WIDER.

Tarp, F., Roland-Holst, D., & Rand, J. (2003). Economic structure and development in an emergent Asian economy: Evidence from a social accounting matrix for Vietnam. *Journal of Asian Economics, 13*, 847–871.

To, H., Nguyen, C., Nguyen, N., Le, V., Norimichi, T., & Huy, D. (2019). Current status of fine particulate matter (PM2.5) in Vietnam's most populous city, Ho Chi Minh City. *Aerosol and Air Quality Research*, 19. https://doi.org/10.4209/aaqr.2018.12.0471.

Vietnam, T. S. (2020). Updated nationally determined contribution of Vietnam (INDC). https://www4.unfcc.int

Zierler, D. (2011). *Invention of ecocide: Agent orange, Vietnam, and the scientists who changed the way we think about the environment*. University of Georgia Press.

CHAPTER 14

From Global to National: Manufacturing Strategies in the US, China, Germany and Japan in Comparative Perspective

Wei Zhao

1 Introduction

At national level, manufacturing strategy can be regarded as the result of a State policy designed to ensure that industrial production is competitive and sufficient to meet a country's internal and external needs. The 2008 financial crisis triggered a global trend toward reindustrialization in developed countries and industrial upgrading in developing countries. Almost all the major industrial nations in the world devised and implemented specific policies and programs to develop, maintain or reinforce their manufacturing activities. For example, the US passed the American Recovery and Reinvestment Act (2009), the Advanced Manufacturing Partnership AMP (2011), the National Strategic Plan for Advanced Manufacturing (2012), the Revitalize American Manufacturing and Innovation Act (2014), the National Innovation Strategy (National Economic Council

W. Zhao (✉)
ESSCA School of Management, Angers, France
e-mail: wei.zhao@essca.fr

T. A.-D. Tran (ed.), *Rethinking Asian Capitalism*,
https://doi.org/10.1007/978-3-030-98104-4_14

and Office of Science and Technology Policy 2015), etc. with the aim of reindustrializing the economy (Office of Science and Technology Policy, 2012). China announced a series of policies, such as the National Medium- and Long-Term Program for Science and Technology Development (2006–2020), the 12th/13th Five-Year Plan, the Plan for Science and Technology Development (2011), the Plan for National Strategic Emerging Industries (2012), the Strategy of Innovation-driven Development (2013), Made in China 2025 (2015), a massive, 30-year program for advancing manufacturing technology, the "Internet plus" Strategy (2015) the Made in China 2025's Guide for Provinces and Cities (2017), etc., in order to lead into the next-generation manufacturing. Germany had the federal government's High-Tech Strategy 2020 Action Plan (2013) and the Digital Strategy 2025 (2016) by BMWi. Its Industry 4.0 model, which is not even an official policy, was one of the future-oriented projects that had emerged since 2011 and became a learning target for China. Japan came out with the Ministry of the Economy, Trade and Industry (METI) industrial policy plan (METI, 2010), the White Paper on Manufacturing Industries, the METI 4th Industrial Revolution Strategy (2015), the Japan Revitalization Strategy (2016), the Future Investment Strategy (2017) etc. South Korea unveiled its "Manufacturing Innovation 3.0" strategy in 2013. The aim was to digitize production facilities and create innovative products, including devices for the Internet of Things (IoT), which would require expenditure of $1 billion to build 10,000 smart factories. Though manufacturing accounted for only 15 percent of Indian GDP, the government had a goal to raise that to 25 percent by 2022 and create 100 million jobs under the "Make in India" program.

Since 2018, the US-China trade war, which is in fact a clash of manufacturing supply chains between the two economies, has intensified the international competition based on manufacturing strategies. Recently, in 2021, the US passed the 1400 page long American Innovation and Competition Act, which allocates approximately US$250 billion to key areas such as R&D and semiconductors in response to China's technological competition. If the outbreak of Covid-19 has woken countries up to the vitality of manufacturing sectors related to personal protection products, the post-Covid 19 world is witnessing a restructuring of global chains, which is pushing nations to go further in manufacturing strategy design and implementation. Renewed global competition around manufacturing activities is imminent.

To gain a deeper understanding of national priorities while highlighting divergent responses to the challenges of global manufacturing competition, this chapter examines the manufacturing strategies of the US, China, Germany and Japan through the analytical lens of the varieties of capitalism and developmental state theories in order to compare their design, implementation mechanisms and institutional complementarity. According to data published by the United Nations Statistics Division, in 2019, China accounted for 28.7 percent of global manufacturing output, US for 16.8 percent, Japan for 7.5 percent and Germany for 5.3 percent. The four countries together counted for 58.3 percent of global manufacturing output. While the developmental state approach highlights the key role played by the State and its policies in making and designing manufacturing strategies, the varieties of capitalism approach suggest that the overall economic outcome will be very much dependent on the "fitness" or "compatibility" between the strategy itself and other relevant institutions. As the times when the US acted as a benign hegemon in the international economic order seem long gone, China is trying to assume the mantle of leadership to become the most competitive export and manufacturing nation. At the same time, various other nations are pursuing a "better deal" for themselves and the world's industrial powers are located somewhere on a spectrum between the two extreme models of the American liberal market economy and Chinese state-dominated developmentalism, but are converging toward the similar developmental state strategies and policy tools.

The chapter is organized as follows. Section 2 reviews and combines the theoretical varieties of capitalism and developmental state approaches and in doing so outlines the analytical framework to be adopted in the chapter. Section 3 gives a detailed qualitative assessment of the manufacturing strategies of the four nations, covering strategy planning and design, governance and execution mechanisms, and their institutional complementarities in each country. Section 4 concludes by briefly discussing implications.

2 Approaching National Manufacturing Strategies: The Analytical Framework

Traditionally, manufacturing strategy refers to the structural positioning of business firms' production function and their strategic decisions on the geographical location of production units, production technology and product range. However, a manufacturing strategy can also be the result of a policy implemented by a nation. In fact, since the 2008 global crisis, many policy makers around the world have already transformed their industrial policy by focusing more closely on manufacturing strategy. Industrial policy can be divided into two types: selective (strategic or defensive) and horizontal (environmental or functional). In the past, there was no lack of experience with targeted industrial policies. Countries including Japan, France, Germany, Britain and the US had all at times targeted individual sectors. Governments used subsidies or tariffs, as well as a variety of hard-to-measure instruments such as tax incentives, credit allocation, procurement policies, recession cartels, red-tape barriers to imports, etc., in order to promote targeted industries (Krugman, 1983). These vertical measures were revived after 2008 (Eder & Schneider, 2018). Manufacturing strategy is by its nature the renaissance of strategic industrial policy in a broader sense. However, it encompasses the horizontal and selective dimensions of industrial policy, draws on all kinds of policy tools and instruments and is more finely calibrated or targeted at a nation's manufacturing activities and technological capacities. For example, having recognized the threat and opportunities in the shift to an all-digital global manufacturing industry, many governments have now established programs and policy plans to make their nations more competitive. Industry groups such as the Industrial Internet Consortium have been established to help advance the technologies needed, and governments have created long-range initiatives to support their manufacturing sectors in the transition to Industry 4.0. In the literature, the US and Germany belong to different varieties of capitalism, while Japan and China are regarded as examples of developmental states. These two theories bring some general observations on the institutional background and operational instruments of manufacturing strategy.

2.1 *The Varieties of Capitalism Approach*

The variety or diversity of capitalism literature argues that capitalism comes in more than one form and depicts the scope of possibilities for the governance of market economies, economic institutions and relations between economic actors (Kalinowski, 2013). It draws a distinction between two forms of capitalism: liberal market economies (typically, the Anglo-American model) and coordinated market economies (typically, the German and continental European model). Liberal market economies rely upon hierarchies within firms and competitive markets. Economic actors have only arms-length relationships with each other, mediated by markets, and coordination takes place in response to price signals. This capitalist model is characterized by flexible labor markets, highly developed financial markets and highly competitive product markets. By contrast, coordinated market economies are based on different forms of non-market coordination, including negotiation, bargaining and collaboration. They are characterized by "a high degree of coordination among employers, inter-firm networks, long-term, bank-based finance, and a system of corporate governance that encourages 'patient capital'" (Hall & Soskice, 2001; Hall, 2003). Germany and Japan are cited as the most prominent examples of coordinated capitalism (Yamamura & Streeck, 2001). In the German "social market economy", the government largely limits its industrial policy to establishing a variety of conditions for innovation and production in a broad spectrum of economic sectors, including R&D; education, training and skills development; taxes, social insurance contributions and bureaucracy; energy and raw materials; the environment; foreign trade and investment; and infrastructure. The social conditions include social cohesion with corporatist arrangements in the labor market and industrial consensus. The conditions on the labor supply side include an excellent secondary school education system, the dual apprenticeship training system for skilled workers, short-time work subsidies during recessions and early retirement subsidies if an unemployed or young person is hired.

Against the backdrop of different models of capitalism, manufacturing strategy can be regarded as an operationalized mode of regulation, that is, a set of means of action that reproduce the fundamental social relations through the conjunction of historically determined mechanisms of adjustment in the markets, support and control the current accumulation regime and ensure the dynamic compatibility of a decentralized set of decisions (Boyer, 1988, 2005). The mode of regulation can have three institutional forms: the law, the rule or the formal regulation; the search for a compromise resulting from negotiations among private agents or groups; and the existence of a system of values or representations sufficient to ensure that routine replaces the spontaneity and diversity of private initiatives (religion, rules of good conduct, conventional views on the future according to Keynes, etc.).

As a specific institutional arrangement, the effectiveness of manufacturing strategy is also influenced by the institutional complementarity provided by the country. It needs to be supported by institutional arrangements in different spheres (for instance, labor markets, competition, foreign trade, technology and financial systems). The notion of institutional complementarity deals with the idea that there exist mutually reinforcing effects among distinct institutional forms (Amable, 2016). The coexistence of two institutions can increase the performance of the economic system compared to the existence of just a single institution. A manufacturing strategy's degree of complementarity depends on its interconnections and integration with other institutional forms or existing modes of regulation that produce system-level coherence. As an outcome at the level of the economic system, each model of capitalism is characterized by specific institutional complementarities and the differences between the various models appear to persist. From a dynamic perspective, hierarchically superior institutions are those whose alteration would imply challenges to the existence of the dominant social bloc or the political leadership (Amable, 2016). New institutions or regulations with political priority in the institutional hierarchy will require other institutions subordinate to them to adapt and make themselves compatible.

However, the real world of competing national capitalisms may be seen to depart from conceptions of the above two categories. Each national capitalism is a distinct historical formation with distinct historical inheritances and regulations (Desai, 2010). In East Asia, development policies and institutions are characterized as "late development" with strong intervention by the "developmental State" (Chang, 2002; Reinert, 2007; Amsden, 2007).

2.2 *The Developmental State Approach*

The developmental state is a particular variant of capitalism in Asia that falls outside the binary opposition between the liberal- and coordinated-market models. The commonality that binds the Asian capitalist economies is the strong degree of government intervention and leadership in export-driven industrialization or the promotion of heavy industry for economic growth. The State is committed to developmentalism, or the "strengthening of the nation" through the economic growth attained by industrialization. The central government itself leads the industrialization drive and makes a robust commitment to dirigisme, often typified as "industrial policy" in terms of standard economics (Amsden, 1989; Haggard, 1986; Johnson, 1982, 1984; Wade, 1990; Weiss, 1998; Woo-Cumings, 1999). In fact, the features of the Asian developmental state are reflected not only in the strategic and selective industrial policy, which should properly be categorized as manufacturing strategy, but to an even greater extent in the powerful strategy governance structure and implementation mechanism, which are well matched to the situation of each Asian society.

At the level of strategy planning and design, Asian industrial policymakers select and promote specific industries, including their international expansion, with strategic finance. Based on the "controlled competition" environment created by protecting domestic markets from export subsidies, providing tax reductions, prohibiting the entry and exit of firms and financially supporting firms, states develop and promote new industries. By selectively supporting business entities and by targeting strategic industries, the policy planning and governance structure are closely interwoven to allocate resources to selected national champions.

At the level of strategy governance and implementation, a group of competent bureaucrats is empowered with sufficient embedded autonomy to coordinate policy (Evans, 1995). The role of the "leading organization" in economic policy planning and implementation is essential. For example, during 1960s and 1970s, the Korean Economic Planning Board took charge of the planning process in heavy chemical industries with highly hierarchical mechanisms and functions as a "control tower" that planned and facilitated the consensus-making process among ministries, providing government subsidies and emphasizing export performance (Amsden, 1989; Wade, 1990).

The developmental state also establishes control mechanisms or a set of institutions that imposes discipline on firms' economic behavior. Firms in receipt of subsidies are subjected to monitorable performance standards that are redistributive in nature and results-oriented. According to Amsden (2001), this control mechanism involves several key government institutions: (1) a sensor, to detect the "givens" in the process to be controlled;

(2) an assessor, to compare what is happening with what should happen; (3) an effector, to change behavior; and (4) a communications network, to transmit information between all functions. Moreover, the industrial policymakers are economic engineers whose job is to make manufacturing industry profitable and to circumvent any obstacle to industrialization created by prevailing prices, whether they are politically, technocratically or market determined. Over time, greater subsidies can be offered to more diversified industries and prospective mid- and high-technology manufacturers. For example, Chinese "science and technology enterprises" are granted a special legal status in exchange for performance standards related to technically trained employment and the share of new products in total sales. Small Taiwanese firms are "cherry-picked" to locate in science parks that oblige them to spend a certain percentage of their sales on R&D and employ advanced production techniques. Made in China 2025 is now following exactly this strategic rationale.

Whether the performance standards are low-technology manufacturing process or patented technologies based on intensive research and development, the control mechanism of strategy implementation always revolves around the key principle of reciprocity: a subsidy (such as duty-free imports) is to be tied to a performance standard (such as 100 percent exporting). Thus, a close network between State and big business conglomerate is established. The relationship between private and public entities can be characterized by hierarchical and centralized State policy planning and implementation, with selective resource allocation procedures that operate as an effective institutional mechanism for unprecedented manufacturing expansion during and after the catch-up period in East Asia.

Although the classic developmental state economies are Japan, South Korea, Taiwan, etc., China and Singapore constitute a new variant of the developmental state, since the latter two countries are largely synonymous with capitalism, meaning they have developed into a form of state capitalism. China goes beyond the traditional developmental state, not only because it maintains an authoritarian regime and a state-centered system that has a huge capacity to mobilize and control all production factors, but also due to the diffusion of developmentalism to local regions, thereby creating many local developmental states within the economy, the operational units for implementing the national manufacturing strategy.

3 Comparing National Manufacturing Strategies: The US, Germany, Japan and China

Although their political and economic models are still diverse, these four nations—the US as a liberal market economy, Germany as a coordinated market economy, Japan as an Asian coordinated market economy regarded as a developmental state and China as a kind of state capitalism beyond the traditional developmental state—they converge in all having own manufacturing strategy now. Our framework for assessing their manufacturing strategy is composed of three parts (Table 14.1). First, their strategy planning and design, including goals, target sectors, focus technologies, etc., will be examined. Second, more attention will be paid to comparing their respective strategy governance and implementation, including leading organizations, policy programs, policy instruments, administration system, etc. According to the developmental state approach, government planning and the implementation mechanism are important for a successful industrial policy. And thirdly, if there is any comparative institutional advantage for the manufacturing sector, the institutional complementarity of a country's manufacturing strategy will play an essential role. According

Table 14.1 National manufacturing strategies: an analytical framework

Strategy plan and design	Strategic goals Targeted sectors Technological focus Key tasks and missions Supporting structures and measures
Strategy governance and implementation mechanism	Governance and administration organization National programs and projects Local programs and implementation mechanism Mobilization and coalitions of relevant actors Policy tools and instruments Government internal management system
Complementarity with other institutional forms in the economy	Macroeconomic policy adaptation National innovation system Country's industrial structure and technological specialization Dominant modes of production and capital accumulation

to the varieties of capitalism approach, economic policy and regulation are deeply embedded in existing policies, institutions and socio-economic structures, policy implementation is path-dependent and the institutional arrangements reinforce each other in helping to sustain the political economic model. Thus, institutional complementarity exerts a wide-ranging influence on strategy performance.

3.1 *Comparing the Strategy Plan and Design*

In terms of strategic goals, the four countries are all targeting the same advanced industries and high-tech areas with the aim of becoming the most powerful industrial economy in the world. The US intends to remain the dominant country in technological advancement on earth, spur investment and position itself for long-term leadership in advanced manufacturing. China wants to make use of all kinds of manufacturing policies to build global production networks under Chinese leadership and occupy all the segments of each industrial sector's value chain. Its goal to become a "real Great Power" has at least three aspects: (1) developing China from a "large manufacturing nation" to a "strong" one, equal to the leading industrial countries in the world and having the most complete manufacturing system; (2) reducing the country's dependence on foreign technology and transforming China from a global center of low-tech manufacturing into a major center of innovation; (3) shifting its economic structure to focus on high value-added industries such as robotics and aerospace equipment in which China is not currently competitive on world markets, but which will be or can be changed in the future (European Union Chamber of Commerce in China, 2017). Germany's "High-Tech Strategy 2020", announced in 2010, involves ten initiatives including an Industry 4.0 program to promote the digitalization of manufacturing. The goal is not only to maintain German leadership in manufacturing but also to ensure that Germany is a major exporter of advanced manufacturing technologies. Germany also wants to maintain its position as a leading manufacturing country, as well as in the 4th industrial revolution as a major socio-economic change. The German Industry 4.0 program seems to be the model for all advanced industries and the country aims to retain its position as a leading technology supplier of industry 4.0 in the world by 2025. Similarly, Japan has the goal of keeping the country among the leaders in high-end manufacturing and assuring unique leading advantages.

The targeted sectors of the four countries mostly overlap with each other. The US is targeting up to 50 sectors, including 35 advanced manufacturing sectors, 3 advanced energy sectors and 12 advanced service sectors. In the US, advanced industries are identified by two criteria: (1) the industry's R&D spending per worker must fall in the 80th percentile of all industries or even higher, exceeding $450 per worker; and (2) the share of workers in the industry whose occupations require a high degree of STEM knowledge must also be above the national average, or 21 percent of all workers. Made in China 2025 has identified 10 key sectors, namely next-generation IT, high-end numerical control machinery and robotics, aerospace and aviation equipment, maritime engineering equipment and high-tech maritime vessel manufacturing, advanced rail equipment, energy-saving vehicles and new energy vehicles, electrical equipment, agricultural machinery and equipment, new materials, and biopharmaceuticals and high-performance medical devices. Japan is targeting five strategic sectors: infrastructure-related and infrastructure system exports; environmental/energy problem-solving industries, including green vehicles; culture, including fashion, food & tourism; medical and healthcare; and the advanced sectors that Japan traditionally has, including automobile, robotics and equipment, aviation, aerospace, etc. As for Germany, automobiles, machinery, chemistry and electronics are the sectors in which it has traditional advantages and are now being targeted by other countries for higher added value and intensive capital investment. Countries aim to compete in technology sectors.

Accordingly, the countries all have industry 4.0-related technologies in their sights as the focus of their technological development. The German Industry 4.0 has become the central element of the new technology cluster. The US is emphasizing the development of Information and Communication Technology (ICT) infrastructure, education and public services, together with a number of vertical priorities, particularly clean energy technologies, biotechnology, nanotechnology, space and advanced manufacturing. China is giving priority to intelligent manufacturing technologies, including AI, big data, cloud computing, IIoT, new generation chips and new materials. Japan is also focusing on IoT, big data, AI, robotics, the sharing economy, automatic driving, healthcare automation and information infrastructure. Germany has its own focus related to the Industry 4.0 model, for example, the ubiquitous connectivity—using internet of things sensors and tags on virtually all machinery and products to enable computer supervision and control. Its Industry 4.0 also involves data analytics and smart systems that can coordinate and optimize all stages of the production and distribution processes; advanced robotics and intuitive man/machine interfaces; new digitally driven production processes, such as 3D printing; new business models—among them are "as a service" approaches that allow mass customization to meet fast-changing demand efficiently; and other new technical systems, such as the Cyber-Physical System, IT and communications technology, IIoT, virtual reality and enhanced reality, intelligent manufacturing, 3D printing, automation, technology fusion, etc.

In planning the corresponding mission priorities and key tasks for sector and technology development, China made innovation, quality development, digitalization and environment its top priorities. It defines the main tasks of manufacturing strategy as (1) improving manufacturing innovation; (2) integrating IT and industry; (3) strengthening the industrial base; (4) fostering Chinese brands; (5) enforcing green manufacturing; (6) promoting breakthroughs in the above 10 key sectors; (7) advancing the restructuring of the manufacturing sector; (8) promoting service-oriented manufacturing and manufacturing-related service industries; and (9) internationalizing manufacturing activities. The US and Japan have set their manufacturing sectors similar tasks. In the US, the key tasks include enabling innovation, securing the talent pipeline, improving the business climate and ecosystem, investment by small and medium-sized enterprises, strengthening work force skills, creating government-industry-academia and private-public partnerships, and promoting federal investment in R&D projects. Japan has identified five pillars of action: (1) build Society 5.0 with connected industries; (2) implement an expansionary external economic policy; (3) consolidate the industrial base and ensure industrial safety; (4) accelerate regional investment in small and medium-sized enterprises; and (5) overcome environmental and energy constraints and increase related investment.

The US, China and Germany also plan to support the implementation of the above missions and tasks with some structural measures, including specific institutional reforms, specific leadership and organization, specific budget allocations, human resources, etc., especially committed to budget allocation. For example, the US decided to set up the National Network of Manufacturing Institutes with a budget of USD 1 billion in 2014 and to allocate Advanced Manufacturing Partnership a budget of USD 500 million. A large share of China's budget will come from local governments and state-owned enterprises. One third of the investment will come from state-owned enterprises and will be channeled by the Chinese government toward industries of strategic importance for national security and economic leadership. Apparently, the Chinese structural measures need reforms to improve access to finance and talent, since the question of training, workforce development and the related changes in labor, social security and other relevant laws has not been addressed and is institutionally excluded. Germany plans a funding of only up to EUR 200 million allocated for Industry 4.0 within the German Government's Action Plan, with representatives from numerous industries also committing to spending EUR 2.5 billion in six areas over the ten-year project lifetime. It planned to reach R&D intensity above 3.5 percent from 2018 onwards.

In general, when countries target new technologies and industrial sectors, Germany's Industry 4.0 strategy serves as the main reference point and technical model. The Industry 4.0 model starts with ubiquitous connectivity, and it is estimated that fully digital control of materials, processes, and supply-chain activity can raise productivity by 26 percent. The shift will also disrupt existing value chains and enable the development of new business models. Industry 4.0 levers can also enable mass customization to meet fast-changing demand efficiently (McKinsey Global Institute, 2017). The four countries' strategic plans overlap considerably in the industries they target, putting them in direct competition with each other. China is strong in planning tasks and supporting policies. Its Made in China 2025 is not merely a program to promote robots and factory automation. The aim behind it is to develop entire new industrial sectors and to capture entire value chains. China has the most comprehensive strategy in this field, since it plans to integrate the development of digitalized manufacturing on the shopfloor with large-scale plans to develop advanced communication infrastructures (Mercator Institute for China Studies, 2016).

3.2 *Comparing the Strategy Governance and Implementation Mechanisms*

In all four countries, central government plays an important role in leading and organizing the implementation of the manufacturing strategy, including policy promulgating, appointing lead organizations, forming key projects, setting up key performance indicators, etc. In the US, the lead organizations often include the White House, NASA, the National Science Foundation, the Departments of Commerce, Defense, Education and Energy, etc. To coordinate the federal government's manufacturing policy and programmatic efforts, the US set up the Office of Manufacturing Policy within the White House in 2011 and, in 2012, the inter-agency Advanced Manufacturing National Program Office, hosted by the Department of Commerce. The departments of Defense, Energy, and Commerce, the National Science Foundation and NASA even jointly ran a competitive selection process for the pilot institute. In 2021, the Biden administration set up the Federal Consortium for Advanced Batteries (FCAB), located in the departments of Energy, Commerce, Defense and State, and promulgated the National Blueprint for Lithium Batteries (2021–2030). In China, the State Council centralizes strategy implementation and all ministries (MIIT, NDRC, S&T, Finance, etc.), local governments, academic units and state-owned enterprises are involved. In fact, the Chinese Academy of Sciences, the engineering departments of major universities, the Ministry of Industry and Information Technology (MIIT) and the Ministry of Science and Technology are the main proponents of the technocratic vision of China's role as a strong manufacturing nation. In Germany, the Federal Ministry of Economy and Energy (BMWi), the Federal Ministry of Education and Research (BMBF), and the Expert Council on Research and Innovation oversee research. The Innovations Dialog is in charge of the dialog between technology, industry and academia. The High-Tech Forum was set up in 2015 for consultancy and proposals. In Japan, the manufacturing strategy is administered by the Prime Minister and the Cabinet, jointly with the Ministry of the Economy, Trade and Industry (METI). Japan has announced it will establish a Government-Civil Council of the 4th Industrial Revolution, with functional sub-councils focusing on talent education, the robotization revolution, AI, etc.

The US, China and Germany all established national programs to create innovation institutes or centers to finance and accommodate R&D projects. The general purpose of policy was to use demonstration projects to diffuse new technologies among users. The major national programs or institutes in the US are (1) the National Network of Manufacturing Innovation Institutes (2012), which would provide total funding of 1 billion USD over a period of 10 years from 2012 for 15 public/private centers for manufacturing innovation, each focused on a different aspect of manufacturing, including 45 million USD of federal funds for a pilot additive manufacturing institute; (2) increasing investment in advanced manufacturing R&D with a budget of 2.2 billion USD for advanced manufacturing R&D; (3) the Digital Manufacturing and Design

Innovation Institution (2014) initiated by the Department of Defense, with more than 80 members, such as Boeing, GE, Siemens and MS; (4) the National Network of Manufacturing Institutes (2015); (5) the creation in 2012 of an 8 billion USD Community College to Career Fund to help create an economy built to last by training two million workers with skills leading directly to a job; (6) launching a Military Credentialing and Licensing Task Force in 2012 to connect veterans to high-skilled advanced manufacturing jobs. The Chinese national programs include (1) the establishment of state-sponsored research projects in intelligent manufacturing, green manufacturing, and other disciplines; (2) the establishment of 15 manufacturing innovation centers by 2020, with a plan to raise the total number to 40 by 2025; (3) demonstration projects to prove the viability of new technologies and approaches that were expected to cut production costs and lead times by half and improve yields by 50 percent. In 2015, the Ministry of Industry and Information Technology singled out 94 projects as Intelligent Manufacturing Special Projects under the umbrella of Made in China 2025. For 2016, there were 64 new pilot projects. The list of participants was an across-the-board selection of manufacturing companies and research institutes from all parts of China, including companies from fields such as dairy production, traditional Chinese medicine pharmaceutics, shipbuilding and steel production. The demonstration scheme emphasized providers of IT, robotics and industrial services, but the selection demonstrated the ambitions of a comprehensive program of product- and process-related upgrades. (4) In following the principle of "promoting a differentiated development and a deep cooperation between ministries and provinces based on comparative advantages", the government nominated 30 pilot demonstration cities across the country by the end of 2017, after having selected them from a list of candidate cities that had previously submitted their application. The Germany programs were mainly the Digital Agenda 2014–2017 (BMWi), the Industry 4.0 From Research to Enterprise Implementation Program (2015, BMBF) that financed 325 projects and the BMBF program to promote R&D in small and medium-sized enterprises. Germany also opened its Industry 4.0 to other countries, so the relevant programs were rather internationalized. More than 30 national action plans are related to Industry 4.0 in the EU, within the EU "Factories of the Future" program.

At local or regional level, only China had implementation details of programs or projects. Since China is geographically very large, the national program for establishing and supporting emerging industries was often coordinated jointly by governments at all levels, research institutions and industrial firms. Local governments played a vital role in financing much of the program, mainly by providing infrastructure and subsidies for land use, infrastructure or research and training facilities. Provincial and local governments provided a large proportion of the resources but at the same time, they had to compete for research projects and recognition from the central authorities. In 2017, local governments in coastal provinces shifted investment from infrastructure to industrial development projects in the fields of smart manufacturing development, robotics and industries related to "Internet +" plan (Yu, 2017). Eastern provinces like Zhejiang, Jiangsu, Shandong and Guangdong developed industries such as high-end shipbuilding, new power equipment and aerospace. The central and northern provinces focused on upgrading the mining, agriculture and related sectors, mainly in terms of new energy sources, new materials, machinery and equipment for coal, chemical and agriculture, phasing out energy-intensive and highly polluting industries. Western and Northeastern China had projects to eliminate outdated production capacity. Sichuan and Chongqing developed their aerospace, cloud computing and big data industries. The provinces of Liaoning, Jilin and Heilongjiang continued their reliance on heavy industry through the state-owned enterprises reform and upgrading program. Guizhou province, in particular Guiyang city, emerged with investment in cloud computing, big data and data storage.

When it came to mobilizing the relevant actors to participate in national programs, the four countries all gave incentives to non-governmental actors such as universities, institutes and associations to engage in strategy implementation and project execution. The US established the American Manufacturing Partnership to encourage companies and universities to submit joint projects. The Smart Manufacturing Leadership Coalition, a nonprofit organization of manufacturers, suppliers, technology companies, manufacturing consortia, universities and government agencies, was formed in 2012. A group of leading American technology firms established the Industrial Internet Consortium in 2014. China gave the rising new multinational companies a large measure of responsibility for implementing the national program. The Made in China 2025 gave a major role to China's rising new multinationals in mid- and high-technology sectors such as solar systems, wind turbines, LED, household appliances or, most prominently, in telecommunications and advanced internet services, reflecting the increased importance of large enterprises, such as Huawei,

Haier and BYD. Germany stuck to its corporatist tradition of getting trade unions involved and adopted an open approach in which a wide range of partners could participate. There were in-depth exchanges between the German government, industry, think tanks and trade unions, with government focusing on facilitating exchanges and supporting relevant R&D. Since 2013, Platform Industry 4.0 has been the platform connecting government, industry, academia and trade unions. In 2014, the Netzallianz was established by the Federal Ministry of Transportation and Digital Infrastructure. Until 2017, 22 SME 4.0 Competence Centers (Mittelstand 4.0-Kompetenzzentren) were built. Japan also launched the Robot Revolution Initiative and IoT Promotion Alliance.

As for the choice of policy instruments, Japan was relatively weak in implementation for macroeconomic and structural reasons and lacked specific policy tools. The US and Germany both mainly used horizontal policy tools such as tax-cutting, tax credits, business environment improvement and energy promoting to implement their strategies. The US reformed the tax code to encourage investment in domestic manufacturing and to repatriate jobs. The Obama and Trump administrations both lowered rates for manufacturers, required companies to pay a minimum tax on overseas profits and expanded, simplified and made permanent the R&D Credit. The federal government also increased the tax deduction for advanced manufacturing, supported investment in next-generation energy manufacturing, abolished deductions for companies that shipped jobs overseas, and provided tax credits for companies that bring jobs home. During the Obama Administration, the US promoted the safe, responsible development of natural gas resources to tap America's large natural gas reserves and support investment in industries that use natural gas. Germany was typical in using horizontal measures. It established strong institutions to protect intellectual property and support for R&D in universities and public research centers. In Germany, the Industry 4.0 initiative only provided support in the form of R&D tax credits, with no subsidies for actual manufacturing or sales of products. Being a highly demanding customer in government procurement, Germany also took measures to ensure that SMEs had an opportunity to participate.

China, for its part, adopted all kinds of horizontal policy tools. In fact, it had almost the fullest list of possible industrial policies to promote industrial upgrading. For example, the concrete policies in Made in China 2025 covered various means of policy implementation, such as technology transfers in exchange for market access, market access and government procurement restrictions for foreign investors, national standards, subsidies, financial policy, government-backed investment funds, support from local government, technology-seeking investments abroad, merger and restructuring of state-owned firms, public-private partnership, etc. China was also the only country that put in place very detailed key performance indicators to be used by government officials monitoring and evaluating implementation. At all administrative levels, strategic goals were translated into quantitative targets under the five-year plan. For example, the central government fixed some key performance indicators, such as raising manufacturing sector R&D spending from 0.88 percent of revenue (in 2013) to 1.68 percent by 2025 (compared with 5.3 percent in the United States), raising labor productivity by 7.5 percent per year by 2020 and by 6.5 percent per year from 2020 to 2025 (compared with 9.5 percent per year between 2010 and 2014), increasing the growth rate of value added in the Chinese manufacturing sector by 2 percent by 2020 and by 4 percent from 2020 to 2025, and raising the domestic content of core components and materials (which was put at 10 to 25 percent depending on categories) to 40 percent by 2020 and to 70 percent by 2025.

Over and above strategy governance, the US and China share many similarities: central government leadership, national programs and mobilization of stakeholders. But the US and China differ in terms of strategy implementation in two ways: the range of policy tools at their disposal and the mechanisms for monitoring implementation. China used the many policy tools at its disposal, while the US federal government had many fewer instruments in its toolbox. China's implementation of the Made in China 2025 plan has been characterized as top-down, driven by the central government and then pursued by local governments. Similar to earlier national policy initiatives in high-technology industries, such as semiconductors or, more recently, new energy vehicles, Made in China 2025 was initiated by professional engineers and leading science agencies and then put forward in terms of technological evolutionism. Once accepted by the technocrats, the bottom-up dynamics became weak. What is striking about China is that the government, as the main body overseeing implementation of the manufacturing strategy, is in effect a special kind of enterprise, the largest one in the country. This is not only because there are many large state-owned enterprises, but also because the decisions and policies made by the government, its departments and leaders are intended to shape firms' business and technology choices rather than the business environment and macroeconomic conditions. Especially when it comes to selecting the target industries, the Chinese government's decisions, processes and means of strategy implementation are equivalent in essence to the business practices of large corporations. Moreover, senior Chinese officials have sufficient information and power to behave like real business decision makers. Their deliberations go far beyond those of conventional companies' intent solely on maximizing business benefits to include calculation of the likely political and social consequences and their benefits, sometimes even at the expense of economic efficiency in exchange for the acquisition of social and political effects. Thus the Made in China 2025 manufacture strategy is not simply an economic policy, but rather a national political strategy dominating the whole policy hierarchy.

3.3 Comparing the Strategies' Institutional Complementarities

The efficiency and effectiveness of national manufacturing strategies depend very much on their compatibility with and adaptation to economic structures, relevant policies and institutions in other fields. All the four countries have worked out some macroeconomic and even international policies to support implementation of their manufacturing strategies, such as the US trade policy and China's Belt and Road Initiative. The aim of US trade policy is said to ensure that American businesses and workers are competing on a level playing field with their international competitors and the US has taken action to stop unfair trade practices abroad, including in China. Even the Obama Administration doubled the rate of trade cases against China compared to the previous administration. The Trump Administration adopted a series of policies such as tax cuts, deregulation, new energy initiatives, bilateral trade agreements, trade tariffs, domestic procurement and defense industry development to bring the global supply chain back to the US. A trade war was launched against China. The corresponding German and Japanese policies were domestic regulations. Germany passed its Anti-Competition Limitation Act in 2017. Japan's supply-side structural reform focused on employment policies, including wage increases, flexible working time, encouragement of female leaders and the establishment of a transparent and free labor market, as well as education, training and hydrogen energy policies.

Manufacturing strategy implementation needs strong support from national innovation systems. Both the US and Germany are reinforcing the strengths of their innovation systems, that is, their technological dynamism based on strong science and engineering. The US redeveloped industrial ecosystems to provide sustainable and transformative innovation. A complete advanced manufacturing innovation ecosystem is composed of government, universities, scientific research institutions, applied research institutions, enterprises and service institutions as the main actors (Berger, 2013). Enhanced US leadership has its roots in science- and engineering-based innovation as well as in its customer-focused innovation. The US continued its commitment to basic research ($80 billion per year, about 60 percent of which is funded by government), while letting markets develop with minimum state intervention. The US innovation system also has a traditionally strong entrepreneurial culture that encourages risk-taking, access to venture funding and ties between business and academia that have led to the formation of thousands of companies. The innovation system has a strong talent pool that includes immigrants from around the world and the US is home to 83 of the world's top 100 universities (Muro et al., 2015). Taking advantage of the close links established between manufacturing and digitalization, Germany has also reinforced its technical and engineering prowess as well as its science- and engineering-based industries. The education system has traditionally turned out scientists and engineers as well as technical workers with intermediate skills trained in apprenticeship programs. The German innovation system is gradually diffusing the Industry 4.0 model among small and medium-sized enterprises, reinforcing digitalization from the manufacturing side.

The Made in China 2025 plan emphasizes an increasing reliance on the country's own technology and taking advantage of the nation's efficiency-driven and customer-driven innovation system. The Chinese manufacturing strategy implies that the Chinese leadership's export-driven model of innovation (climbing the ladder from OEM (Original Equipment Manufacturing; the mode that firm produce products for other firm's brand) to ODM (Original Design Manufacturing; the mode that firm product and design products for other firm's brand) and to OBM (Original Brand Manufacturing; the mode that firm produce products of its own brand)) has exhausted its potential for further industrial development. The basis of the Chinese manufacturing strategy is shifting from integration into the global value chains of certain flagship companies or industrial sectors toward the development of a relatively integrated system led by Chinese companies and industries. Thus, it intends to reinforce its state-led innovation system and consolidate the Chinese manufacturing system as a highly organized whole, while supplementing efficiency- and customer-driven innovations with more developed engineering-based innovations. Japan, on the contrary, has not seen any significant change in its innovation trajectory. However, the Made in China 2025 plan also reflects the weaknesses of a former planned economy that remains a command, economy, that is, a lack of incentives to innovate at firm level, curbs on private companies, and a tendency to become a self-circulating closed system. In Japan, Abenomics was so contrary to the country's own long-established national innovation system that it seems to have become an impediment to successful implementation of a new manufacturing strategy.

The implementation of these national manufacturing strategies has changed each country's industrial structure and technological specialization, thereby creating the new economic and institutional environment within which current manufacturing strategies are evolving. Even before Covid-19, both the US and Japan had seen parts of their supply chains repatriated from developing countries. This is due in part to the rising costs in developing countries such as China but also to the adoption of intelligent manufacturing systems that can reduce the number of workers on production lines. With the shale gas revolution, the United States even became self-sufficient in energy and an energy exporter, resulting in a sharp decline in the cost of power generation. During the Trump period, the average electricity price in the United States was only half that of China. Major companies such as Apple, Caterpillar, Ford, Intel, etc. moved some of their supply chains back to the home country. US spending on information technology as a share of total investment grew to more than 50 percent after 2010. The United States placed greater emphasis on software, research, development, publicity, management and training, and the proportion of intangible assets investment continues to increase. The digital and informatization spheres, including intelligent robot technology, 3D printing, IoT and digital design, became hot investment targets. In the field of advanced digital manufacturing technology, the United States has strong technological and market advantages. In 3D printing, the US accounted for more than one-third of the global market. With the development of intelligent manufacturing systems, the efficiency of American automobile, high-end precision instruments and other industries will be increased by 40 percent. A BCG survey in 2014 showed that 72 percent of US manufacturers with sales of more than 100 million USD had begun to invest in additional automation and advanced manufacturing technologies. The so-called amphibious enterprises emerged in the United States. These are hardware system integration enterprises that vigorously develop software and software system integration enterprises that vigorously develop hardware. For example, some internet companies have found that manufacturing was an opportunity to create value. Google has invested in intelligent robots, unmanned vehicles, drones, the smart home and other new technologies. GE employed 10,000 software engineers in industrial internet development in a drive to accelerate its move from the machine end to the internet end. Japanese companies, such as Toyota, Nissan, Honda, Mazda, Mitsubishi and Suzuki, have also relocated their production lines back to Japan. Japan is fighting to become more specialized in automatic driving and the automation of healthcare, challenging Germany's advantage in intelligent manufacturing.

The application of technologies in new fields, such as digital and the Internet, enabled China to boom in E-commerce, the sharing economy, mobile payment and high-speed trains. However, the consequences also include increased excess capacity expansion and wasteful competition. Almost every province has already declared it is developing most of the 10 core sectors identified in Made in China 2025. China now has more than 40 industrial parks specializing in the production of industrial robots and nearly 2000 suppliers of robotics and components. On the one hand, targeted advanced sectors are emerging across the country with a solid industrial base and dense suppliers' networks already in place; on the other hand, the overall upgrading of industrial sectors is not yet completely achieved.

On a larger scale, since the current manufacturing strategy is based on a new generation of technology, its implementation has to be associated with changes in work organization and face up to the financialization tendency within the existing techno-economic paradigm. As the US embarks on another round of reindustrialization, the country is embracing the Wintelist production mode while at the same time resuming the old modes of production such as post-Fordism in some regions. Reindustrialization is a counterattack against the excessively finance-led regime of accumulation. Germany continues its export-led regime of accumulation based on flexible specialization, especially in equipment and machinery. Without much substantial implementation, Japan maintains to a large degree its regime of accumulation based on the principles of the Toyota production system. In China, firms have adopted various modes of work organization, from Taylorism, Fordism and Toyotism to Wintelism, with over-investment creating excess production capacity, resource misallocation and duplication of projects in different regions. As mentioned before, the Chinese manufacturing strategy has a dominant position within the institutional hierarchy and the Chinese leadership expects that its strategy, once fully implemented, will replace the export-led regime of accumulation with a real economy based on intelligent manufacturing systems and technological innovation. The Chinese leadership is sticking to its plan to build the strongest real economy in the world and recently began to regulate the powerful consumer-end digital platform business, which is dominated by more asset-based and finance-led regimes of accumulation.

4 Concluding Discussion

Despite the interruption caused by the Covid-19 pandemic, the strategic changes in manufacturing activities in the US, China, Germany and Japan represent an on-going transformation of capitalist economic models and the world-wide popularity of the developmental state. Before the pandemic, the international scene had seen the rise of nationalist rhetoric in the Western world and in emerging countries, which was followed by policies favoring protectionism and domestic firms, boosted by the Trump Administration and the Brexit campaign (Rodrik, 2018). After many decades of liberalization, deregulation and globalization based on free trade policies, economic nationalism is now on the rise. The major manufacturing countries are still competing on the basis of their different varieties of capitalism, while their national manufacturing strategies are converging quickly toward the developmental state approach in terms of goals, planning, governance structure and even control mechanisms. If the American liberal market economy and Chinese state developmentalism represent two extreme poles of a continuum, Germany, Japan and many others are hesitant about which path to follow. Nevertheless, their manufacturing strategy is pulling more countries toward the coordinated market economy and developmental state capitalism, if not socialism.

The short-term consequence of pursuing a national manufacturing strategy is an intensification of international competition. The US-China trade war is part of the clash of manufacturing strategies. The 2017 US Trade Policy Agenda singled out China as one of the major sources of the decline of US manufacturing and jobs and announced its intention to strengthen the national manufacturing base. The competition among different manufacturing powers will be based in the long term on the domestic and international institutions that a country faces, especially the degree of complementarity between a country's national institutions and its manufacturing strategy. This historic change of perspective has been made clear by the Chinese leadership, but it is not well understood in Western debates. At implementation level, manufacturing strategy is deeply embedded in a country's existing institutions and economic structure. In the US and Germany, implementation is essentially a bottom-up process led by firms, while the Chinese approach is primarily top-down. China now has a distinctive and aggressive approach to competition, not only because it has a "whole-nation" approach but also because it puts manufacturing strategy hierarchically above all other institutions and policies and implements it vigorously in order to adapt the whole national economy to a new techno-economic paradigm. Under a super developmental state, the country's domestic institutional complementarity with its manufacturing strategy seems to be the greatest contribution to China's competitive advantage in the world.

References

Amable, B. (2016). Institutional complementarities in the dynamic comparative analysis of capitalism. *Journal of Institutional Economics, 12*(1), 79–103.

Amsden, A. (1989). *Asia's next Giant: South Korea and late industrialization.* Oxford University Press.

Amsden, A. (2001). *The rise of the rest: Challenges to the west from late-industrializing economies* (p. 405p). Oxford University Press.

Amsden, A. (2007). *Escape from empire: The developing World's journey through heaven and hell* (p. 197). MIT Press.

Berger, S. (2013). *Making in America: From innovation to market.* MIT Press.

Boyer, R. (1988). Technical change and the theory of 'regulation'. In G. Dosi, C. Freeman, R. Nelson, G. Silverberg, & L. Soete (Eds.), *Technical change and economic theory.* Pinter Publishers.

Boyer, R. (2005). How and why capitalisms differ. *Economy and Society, 34*(4), 509–557.

Chang, H.-J. (2002). *Kicking away the ladder: Development strategy in historical perspective.* Anthem.

Desai, R. (2010). The absent geopolitics of pure capitalism. *World Review of Political Economy, 1*(3, Fall), 463–484.

Eder, J., & Schneider, E. (2018). Progressive industrial policy – A remedy for Europe. *Journal für Entwicklungspolitik, XXXIV*(3/4), S. 108–142.

European Union Chamber of Commerce in China. (2017). *China Manufacturing 2025 Putting Industrial Policy Ahead of Market Force* (p. 68). Research Report.

Evans, P. (1995). *Embedded autonomy: States and industrial transformation.* Princeton University Press.

Haggard, S. (1986). The newly industrializing countries in the international system. *World Politics, 38*, 343–370.

Hall, P. (2003). Varieties of capitalism: And then there was one? *Comparative Politics, 36*(1), 103–124.

Hall, P., & Soskice, D. W. (2001). *Varieties of capitalism, the institutional foundations of competitive Advantage*. Oxford University Press.

Johnson, C. (1982). *MITI and the Japanese miracle: The growth of industrial policy, 1925–75*. Stanford University Press.

Johnson, C. (1984). Introduction: The idea of industrial policy. In C. Johnson (Ed.), *The industrial policy debate* (pp. 3–26). Institute of Contemporary Studies Press.

Kalinowski, T. (2013). Regulating international finance and the diversity of capitalism. *Socio-Economic Review, 11*, 471–496.

Krugman, P. (1983). Targeted industrial policies: Theory and evidence. In *Proceedings of economic policy symposium* (pp. 123–176). Federal Reserve Bank of Kansas City.

McKinsey Global Institute. (2017). *Digital China: Powering the economy to global competitiveness* (p. 163). *MGI Report*.

Mercator Institute for China Studies. (2016, December). *Made in China 2025: The making of a high-tech superpower and consequences for industrial countries* (p. 73). MERICS Papers on China, No. 2.

Muro, M., Rothwell, J., Andes, S., Fikri, K., & Kulkarni, S. (2015). *America's advanced industries* (p. 84). The Brookings Institution report.

National Economic Council, & Office of Science and Technology Policy. (2015). *A Strategy for American Innovation* (p. 120p). The White House.

Office of Science and Technology Policy. (2012). *A National Strategic Plan for Advanced Manufacturing* (p. 38). Report of Interagency working group on Advanced Manufacturing.

Reinert, E. (2007). *How rich countries got rich... And why poor countries stay poor*. Constable.

Rodrik, D. (2018). Populism and the economics of globalization. *Journal of International Business Policy, 1–2*, 12–33.

Wade, R. (1990). *Governing the market: Economic theory and the role of the government in east Asian industrialization*. Princeton University Press.

Weiss, L. (1998). *The myth of the powerless state: Governing the economy in a global era*. Polity Press.

Woo-Cumings, M. (Ed.). (1999). *The developmental state*. Cornell University Press.

Yamamura, K., & Streeck, W. (Eds.). (2001). *The origins of nonliberal capitalism: Germany and Japan in comparison*. Cornell University Press.

Yu, H. (2017). Pivot to internet plus: Molding China's digital economy for economic restructuring? *International Journal of Communication, 11*(2017), 1486–1506.

CHAPTER 15

Time for Another Kind of Globalization: Challenges for Theory and Proposals

Finance Capital—Its Power and Logic—Is the Common Adversary

Frédéric Boccara

The question of a different kind of globalization is crucial for our societies. It constitutes a challenge for heterodoxy.

Economic heterodoxy refuses to consider the market as natural, as impossible to surpass and as the "end of history". But heterodoxy also has to face the conjunction of the profound changes taking place in today's economic reality—the informational revolution, monetary revolution, ecological revolution and "anthroponomical" revolution[1]—and the

Many thanks to Stephen Chalk for his precious help with English translation.

[1] Revolutions in demography, culture, values, etc. "Anthroponomy" is the domain of the generation and "re-generation" of human beings i.e. the relationships between humans, since the economy is the domain of the production and reproduction of goods and services,

F. Boccara (✉)
Economie & Politique Review, CEPN, Sorbonne Paris Nord University, Paris, France

T. A.-D. Tran (ed.), *Rethinking Asian Capitalism*,
https://doi.org/10.1007/978-3-030-98104-4_15

growing risks, such as a new catastrophic financial episode of the systemic crisis or an ecological catastrophe.

There is a need for debate in order to make advances together in the common core of heterodox economics, taking seriously the "new" and "past" challenges of the reality of which globalization is a decisive nexus. We need to go beyond the past "common core", but without regressing.

1 The Common Core of Heterodox Economics and the Need for Debate

The current relevance of the common core needs to be stressed.

(a) The automatic self-balancing of the market has to be rejected
(b) We know that crises necessarily return
(c) The "fanaticism" of supply-side economics does not work (Stiglitz, 2003); the insufficiency of global demand must be stressed (Keynes, 1936). That fanaticism conceals a fanaticism for profit and capital accumulation above all else (Marx, 1867 and 1894).

I add: we have to link demand and supply. Behind the insufficiency of demand, there is the contradiction between capital and workers, and the insufficiency of workers' development, with the domination of capital and the criteria and culture of profitability. Behind the market and the fictitious commodity of labor power characterizing capitalism (Marx, 1867, and also Polanyi, 1944), we must see the person of the worker him/herself. The workers are on both sides: the demand side (through their wages and consumption) and the supply side (as producers, whose capacities have a growing influence on the efficiency of production).

(d) The excess of capital and goods, on which Keynes insisted, and the increase in the capital/output ratio (Kalecki), or the diminution of capital efficiency (Marxist approach), is an important part of the common core of the heterodox tradition in the explanation of crises. Interest in this common core is reawakening due to the finan-

that is, the relationships between humans and nature for humans' vital needs (Boccara, 2017). The "re-generation" of human beings (Boccara) is a different conception than the "economicist" and rough material notion of "reproduction" (on which Boyer, 2020 and Veltz, 2021 are focused).

cial crisis and the increasing debate on the excessive "cost of capital" thanks to several schools of heterodox thought, which highlight excess dividends and interest payments.

In this light we question the evolution of the capital/output ratio (index of the organic composition of capital) and of the aggregate profit rate. Indeed, the role of capital and the profit rate is still crucial in our economies and a factor in crises. It must be radically incriminated, with the aim not of limiting its role in economic regulation, but of implementing alternative efficiency criteria for use of funds and for firms' management, that is, new social, ecological and economic criteria. At the heart of these alternative efficiency criteria is the saving of capital (e.g. VA/K criterion as opposed to profit rate, P/K).

We must re-investigate this in the light of Marx's theory of the overaccumulation of capital (over-investment for Keynesians) and its development in P. Boccara's theory of capitalism's regulation by overaccumulation/devalorization, including the new systemic vicious circles during the systemic crisis of state monopoly capitalism (SMC).[2] It includes the theory of "catching up state socialism" (CSS). For societies in which capitalism has not been sufficiently developed, this means catching up with the level of development of capitalism by a socialist state, combining the capitalist kind of total productivity growth (primary priority of capital accumulation) ***and*** high levels of correction of social inequalities by the state, particularly with a large influential mass of state-controlled firms.

This brings the question of firms and banks to the top of the agenda.

(e) Firms have not always been part of the common core of heterodox economics, which has sometimes been too preoccupied with the aggregate approach. Yet there are important strands of heterodox economics willing to deal not only with the "distribution side" but also with the "production side". There are also important heterodox approaches that emphasize the power of the firm, whether it be market power and necessarily imperfect markets, or powers in the

[2] There are three different French "regulation schools" (cf. Jessop & Sum, 2006). P. Boccara founded the first of these, from which came Aglietta, who later founded the third (the Parisian school) with Boyer, transforming the meaning of "devalorization" into loss of value (although it denotes a lower profit rate), and emphasizing "wage regulation" and "Fordism", the profit rate regulator having disappeared. The second is that of De Bernis.

economy as part of the economic field itself (e.g. approaches dealing with financial capital or the "economic sociology" school developed by Granovetter (2005) or the Marxist tradition, or the issues of "imperialism" and "neo-colonialism"). The question of economic powers is related to the (not exclusively economic) question of democracy and liberty.

Firms are active units (F. Perroux), transforming the economy itself by their own reactions, especially multinational enterprises (MNEs). Their role in three main radical transformations has to be stressed: technological transformations tending toward the informational revolution, financial transformations tending toward financial globalization and ecological transformations meaning that the economy is threatening humanity's ecological niche. The role of firms, and the general pattern of their behavior, is crucial not only in these past transformations but also for the future.

(f) Finance and monetary creation is a growing element of the common core of heterodoxy (see Giraud 2014a, b, Galbraith, 2014, and Kelton, 2020). It is central to Keynes' analysis (and to Minsky's after him). It is also crucial to Marx's analysis (especially in Volume 3 of Capital), and was developed by Hilferding and Lenin, but denied in Trotskyist approaches, for which financial capital is only "fictitious capital", a passive veil.

Nowadays, banks, as active and fundamental units, with credit and monetary creation, are becoming a kind of new common decisive sphere, a "new frontier" to be reached by Keynesians, ecologists and Marxists, especially with regard to the question of a *new selectivity* with positive *new financing criteria* (see Durand, 2005).

(g) Ecology. The content of production has always been a crucial point common to many heterodox approaches, but for a long time it was not related to the "capital/labor" content of growth, or to the issue of public and collective services versus private and market services. Now, the ecological challenge is extending the need for a genuine radical view of the content of production, and of growth (Boccara, 2010, 2011), and even of technology itself ("capital saving" versus "direct labor saving").

It reinforces the role of enterprises and production, but also the challenge of working on a positive logic to replace the logic of profit and capital accumulation as the driver of the economy and technological change. Combining this challenge with (1) the issue of money creation, (2) questions of power and (3) the crucial role of firms should highlight debates on the criteria for the use of funds and on mastering enterprises' action. Criteria are at the center of economic and democratic challenges, with new democratic institutions and powers over enterprises and banks.

(h) Two major issues are now emerging for heterodoxy: technology (behind the labor/capital relationship and beyond it) and public services (beyond public intervention), including the issue of common goods. Note that public services have no existence in economic analysis, although they have shown their crucial importance in dealing with the health crisis.

Technology and public services call into question the link between economics and social values, including democracy and liberty ("anthropogenetic development", Boyer, 2020, "humano-centered economy", Veltz, 2021, common good, Coriat, 2021). Again, the point at issue is the link between the dominance of capital, existing institutions and the organization of powers, but without omitting the crucial point of relating political liberties to domination at work (or without work, through poverty), ultimately pointing toward "a new civilization of sharing for the whole of humanity" (Boccara, 2017).

2 Novelties Within Today's Reality: Needs and Elements for a New Common Core

Technological transformations are fundamental. We interpret them using the concept of the "informational revolution". As we explain below, this revolution places human capabilities at the center of a new efficiency, radically calling into question the dominance of capital bias. Yet, at present, these technologies are mainly used and shaped by capital in order to reinforce its domination.

This is a challenge for heterodoxy.

The challenge of constructing a different kind of globalization is also crucial given the role of markets and the twin—ecological and financial—crisis. MNEs and international institutions are at the heart of the challenge. The agenda is the development of a cooperative globalization for the sharing of resources and costs, and the development of common goods for the benefit of all humanity.

For our theory of MNEs, information now tends to be a global factor, thus invaliding the comparative *national* advantages theory and the Heckscher-Ohlin-Samuelson (HOS) paradigm. MNEs could be viewed as institutions of sharing for international co-production, though at the same time dominated by the profit logic of financial capital.

Taking the new supply-side conditions (technological revolution and ecological revolution) as a starting point, we outline the need to rethink both demand and supply in order to stimulate another kind of *total* productivity growth. But instead of the "creative destruction" of Schumpeter (1947)—the other heterodox economist to whom many economists turn their attention in order to take into account technology and supply-side factors—we insist on the necessity, to which these new conditions give rise, of changing the capital bias toward a human-and-capabilities-bias, in order to avoid the "destruction" and waste of human capabilities by unemployment and the depressive effect of unemployment on overall demand.[3]

This new thinking concerns not only internationalization but also public services, social protection and employment, ecology, and the conception of firms and monetary issues. We need to think of "overcoming" the four markets: the labor/products/money and finance/and international markets (Boccara, 2011).

We need new advances in the debates on theory and ideas, but also on programs and proposals, and subsequent international dialog between intellectuals and social forces in our societies. The need for a new positive core is expressed by a wave of different recent works, against neoclassical

[3] Indeed, there are two symmetrical **blind spots** in the two important non-Marxist heterodox schools of thought: for **Keynes** it is technology and for **Schumpeter** global demand. Keynes's denunciation of the profitability criterion and his demand for the limitation of profit exigencies places him in a better and less unilateral position. But both underestimate the **decisive role of human capabilities *inside* the production process** (employment is not only a demand-side but also a supply-side issue). This is particularly misleading in the new technological conditions created by the current informational revolution.

Hence, we plead for "**security of employment, training and income**" and not for fixed and rigid lifelong employment. We need to allow new economic activities, new firms and productivity increases, even if some activities and firms have to disappear in the process ("creation", not Schumpeter's "destruction").

orthodoxy, that seek to go beyond Keynes (see, notably, Ekstedt, 2019, Guerrien, 2016, Keen, 2013, Lavoie, 2015, Morin, 2017, and Shaikh, 2016). There is also insufficient debate engaging with Marx's most advanced findings and the main twentieth-twenty-first century developments by Marxists. Marxism is almost always reduced to a vulgate or a kind of old "ABC" and/or rejected without discussion by naming it "orthodox Marxism".

3 Some Words About Marx' Radical Legacy for Developing a Common Positive Heterodoxy: The Central Debate on "Regulation" of the System

Marx wrote *"Capital"*, and not "*Labor*" ...

In saying that, I would like to stress that he showed the central role of capital in the logic of capitalism and crises. The logic of capitalism has produced enormous progress compared to feudalism, but capital is also its own "barrier" to accumulation (according to Marx's own words) and to real social development during crises of overaccumulation. Marx particularly stressed the role of the profit rate (in Volume 3 of *Capital*), the profit rate being what we call the central regulator of the system (we = the French Marxist school founded by Paul Boccara). A regulator is not a person. A regulator tends to impose its logic, level, etc., through institutions, powers and culture.

Roughly speaking, regulation of a system can be defined as the process of corrective adjustments conditioned by a regulator (here, the profit rate) through a feedback effect on the inputs and/or their structure (including the technology implemented) relative to the discrepancy observed between the actual output and the expected output of the system's fundamental operation viewed in terms of the regulator (here, production viewed in terms of the resulting profit rate), including through reinforcement of the system's "bias" (here: more capital accumulation or more market) or possibly through transformation of the operation itself (during systemic crises).[4] Institutions play a key role in this process, either through feedforward (prevention) or by resisting changes. We distinguish between regulators, rules and regulative measures. The profit rate dominates capitalist regulation. Capitalist regulation occurs through "normal" economic life as well

[4] See P. Boccara, 2018, pp. 122–125

as through catastrophic crises, in which, going further than Marx, we have to distinguish short-and-medium-run cycles from long-run waves; in other words, between short-term crises and systemic crises. The latter occurs when the development of the social productive forces comes into conflict with the social relations of production, consumption, circulation and distribution, and their structure.

However, the regulation approach is also viewed by other economic analysts as simply a limitation and correction of the excesses of the system.

Yet, in the light of the system's current radically new elements, the role of capital and the profit rate must be comprehensively reexamined, with the aim of not only limiting their role but also establishing alternative social, ecological and economic criteria.

Regulation encompasses three aspects: regulators (i.e. actual profitability, interest rates, etc.), rules (i.e. trade rules, capital flow rules, etc.) and "regulative measures" (or governance, i.e. government, firms' management, etc.).

In Marx's findings, the question of the "regulation" of the system and the changes therein has been too neglected.[5] By contrast, after Marx (and partly contrary to his more advanced findings) too much importance has been attached to the question of the State and the **ownership of capital**— with a structuralist vision. The profit rate logic is the question. Capital ownership and State planning are important *only insofar as* they help to impose a different logic from that of the profit rate.

Our task is neither to think about how to limit the profit rate nor to compensate for its consequences (on inequalities, on prices, etc.). We need another *positive* logic.

Similarly, the **monopoly** question is not only a question of market competition, but should be understood as **a monopoly on the use of financial means**, thereby ensuring a monopoly on economic decisions, with regard to production, employment and the development of technology, whether at national or world level.

Hence, at the heart of Marx's main message, there is the idea that **capital and money *are* political** (compare to J. Tobin: "monetary policy *is* policy"). This must be clearly understood. It implies not only that existing institutions must be called into question but also that new ones must be

[5] Yet see chapter 51 of Capital, volume 3.

created in order to gain control over financial resources and channel them, with the aim of fostering an alternative logic and making it dominant, instead of compensating for or supporting the dominant logic.[6]

4 A New World: Problems and Characteristics—Going Beyond Marx, Keynes and Schumpeter

4.1 The Informational Revolution, Capitalism and MNEs

Two centuries after Marx's Capital (1867, 1885 and 1894), and 80 years after Keynes' *General Theory* (1936), the profit rate is still dominating and driving the regulation of developed capitalist countries all around the world. But it is encountering radically new conditions. I want to emphasize technology: the context of the objective radical transformation in technology that we analyze as an ***informational revolution*** in contrast to the ***industrial*** revolution.[7]

In the face of this *objective* revolution—revolution in the social productive forces—the social structure has remained fundamentally unchanged (relationships of production, consumption, product distribution and income distribution) as has the mode of regulation. That conservation of the social structure is at the heart of the systemic crisis and of its persistence.

The informational revolution can be defined and characterized by contrasting it with the Industrial Revolution. The Industrial Revolution was based on the replacement of the worker's ***hand*** manipulating a tool by a tool-operating machine; the informational revolution is based on the replacement of certain activities of the human ***brain*** (informational activities) by informational machines, such as computers. In other words, the transfer of information, its reproduction and its transformation, can be embodied in machines and hence "separated" or dissociated from human beings in a new way.

Information is not simply a quantity (contrary to Shannon's definition). In Wiener's words, information is what is neither material nor

[6] Of course, in Marx there is also dialectics, historical materialism, class struggle, alienation and exploitation, analysis of the commodity and value, labor power as a commodity which is specific to capitalism, the discovery of surplus-value and so on.

[7] There are at the same time several other objective revolutions: the ecological revolution, demographic revolution, monetary revolution and parental revolution (see also Easterlin, 2019).

energy. Information is, for example, the formula for a pharmaceutical drug. Nowadays it can take the form of a computer program with the operating specifications for the machine (or a set of machines) that will manufacture the drug.

The novelty is very profound, although it is denied by the domination of capital, which is using and shaping the beginnings of the informational revolution in an attempt to impose its own logic. *Firstly*, information has the fundamental characteristic of being capable of being *shared*, in contrast to material products, whose exclusive appropriation structures the logic of capitalism and markets. *Secondly*, expenditures devoted to human beings tend to become decisive for economic efficiency itself, because information, and the creation, development and interpretation thereof, is becoming decisive. This is opposed to the normal capitalist logic of giving priority to capital expenditures. Hence, the necessity of the predominance of human expenditures begins to be imposed by reality itself. But the old structure (criteria, powers, institutions and culture) resists.

Thirdly, the logic of cost embodied, in principle, in the informational revolution is also profoundly different from that of capital and machines. (a) Contrary to a machine, information is not consumed by its utilization. (b) The cost of creating information (R&D, etc.) can be very high. (c) But once it has been created the cost of use tends to be negligible and past expenditures to create it, such as R&D, tend to be a fixed cost that can be divided. This creates a powerful incentive to develop a new type of MNEs, worldwide MNEs of the most extensive possible kind: MNEs based on cost sharing inside their private network, but a cost sharing at the service of profits and the MNEs' capital.

It is not a process of dematerialization, but the construction of different relationships between human beings, material means and information. Here we describe a potential, but the novelty is repressed, distorted, even perverted, as the drive to maximize profitability remains dominant.

This revolution also impacts on culture and life outside work. It tends to disrupt the division between work and nonwork, and work itself. It also requires us to address the human person in all of its capacities, beyond its reduction to a fictitious commodity (labor power, Marx, Polanyi) and beyond the production process and production sphere.

It gives rise to the necessity of developing human beings for themselves, their creativity, both underlying and beyond labor power, hence the development of their knowledge and education as a goal in itself, which invests public services with a key role. This arises from inside the productive system itself—from its exigencies of efficiency—and not only from the "reproduction sphere". But this necessity contradicts the dominant orientation of institutions, firms and policies, which prioritizes capital (Plihon & Mouhoud, 2009 and Weinstein, 2010 insist on the crucial link between finance capital and informational technologies). It is becoming less and less possible to reconcile these two opposing aims.

The contradictions tend to be more radical and systemic than during the previous structural crises (e.g. during the 1930s–1940s). This is because sharing is inherent to the very nature of information, and to give priority to the development of human capabilities runs counter to the essential logic of capitalism, with its appropriation and monopolies, and its capital bias, historically developed from the Industrial Revolution and based on the predominance of material means (in the form of equipment and tool-operating machines). In particular, it encourages large-scale mergers with the aim of lowering costs by sharing informational outcomes (such as R&D results). However, such mergers increase capital expenditure and lead to financial inflation of capital, thus arrogating more profit in opposition to the need to develop human expenditure and public services at the global level.

4.2 *The Opening of a Long-Run Kondratiev Difficulties Phase in the Early 1970s*

In the long-run phase of a systemic crisis of overaccumulation that started with the 1967–73 cycle, the so-called financial crisis of 2008–2009 was an explosion of overaccumulation, in line with Marx's analysis showing that the profit rate is at the heart of the capitalist mode of "regulation" through crisis and unemployment. And now, another explosion of overaccumulation is approaching, during the epidemic, though initially concealed by it and then, in a certain sense, delayed by the exceptional monetary conditions made possible by the specific climate of the pandemic itself (see Fig. 15.8).

The profit rate is at the heart of capitalism itself, as a specific kind of total work productivity growth, prioritizing the growth of—material and financial—capital.

But there are growing contradictions between (1) the profit rate (Profit/Capital) and capital efficiency (Value Added/Capital); and a second set of contradictions (2) between the mass of profit and what we call 'disposable value added' for a population and a territory (dVA). These contradictions tend to call into question the social conditions and even the ecological durability of our economic system. It could be a basis for an ambitious new kind of social alliances (between "social" motives and "ecological" motives", between the "interior" and the "exterior" of firms).

The current crisis is taking place within a long-term depressive trend that started at the beginning of the 1970s. Indeed, beyond Marx's analysis of crisis, our Marxist analysis (P. Boccara) recognizes both medium-run overaccumulation (Juglar cycles) and long-run crises of overaccumulation (Kondratiev). These long-term overaccumulation phases were solved in the past by several transformations of the system: the systemic devalorization of capital[8] together with the creation of new institutions imposed by social struggles (e.g. after World War II: in the USA public utilities, and in Europe: public enterprises and social security) in interaction with the new objective conditions in technology and in demography.

Thus, after WWII, the new institutions led to:

- *on the one hand,* limitation of the profit rate logic inside public enterprises, systematic stimulation of demand by public expenditure and, in several sectors of economic life (health, education), elements of a different kind of logic than that of capital;
- and, *on the other hand,* the domination of the profit rate was maintained as the regulator of the activity of private enterprises and banks.

During the financial globalization phase, the domination of the profit rate was reinforced, not only over banks and firms but over the whole economy.

The economic system reacted to the economic difficulties through the acceleration of technological change, driving the informational revolution, financialization (in a second phase), attacks against public and social expenditure, and pressure on wages and on apparent labor productivity.

As an indicator of the persistence of the difficulties, in the case of France, at aggregate level, the profit rate started to decrease again, as did capital efficiency. This occurred after a certain improvement of the aggregate profit rate during the 1980s due to an increase in the profit/wage ratio in reaction to the profit rate decrease of the 1970s (cf. Figs. 15.1, 15.2, 15.3, 15.4, 15.5, 15.6 and 15.7, capital efficiency is the inverse of the capital-output ratio).

[8] Devalorization means the opposite of valorization: a lower rate of profit than normal, even zero or negative profit rate. It includes destruction of capital and losses of value but it is a wider concept.

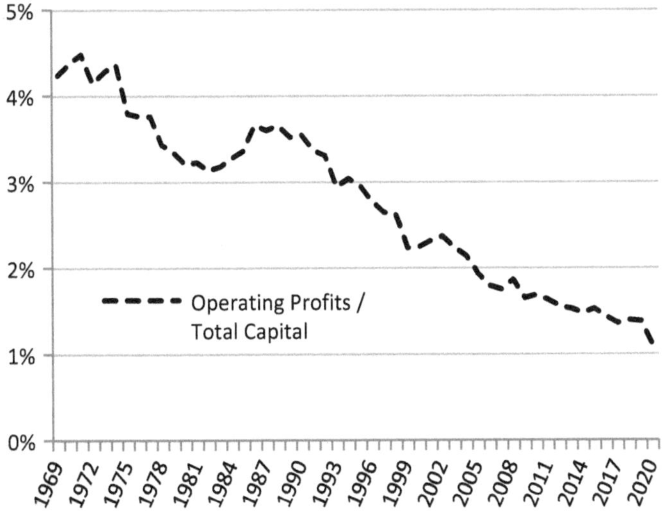

Fig. 15.1 Corporate <u>Total Capital</u> Profitability. (Non-financial <u>and</u> financial corporations, Fi. and non-Fi. Capital Insee and Roll (2019) + author's update, current €)

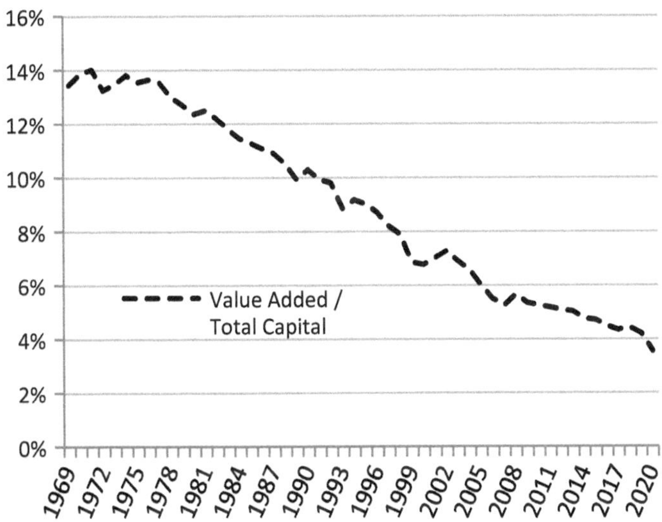

Fig. 15.2 Corporate <u>Total Capital</u> Efficiency. (Non-financial <u>and</u> financial corporations, Fi. and non-Fi. Capital Insee and Roll (2019) + author's update, current €)

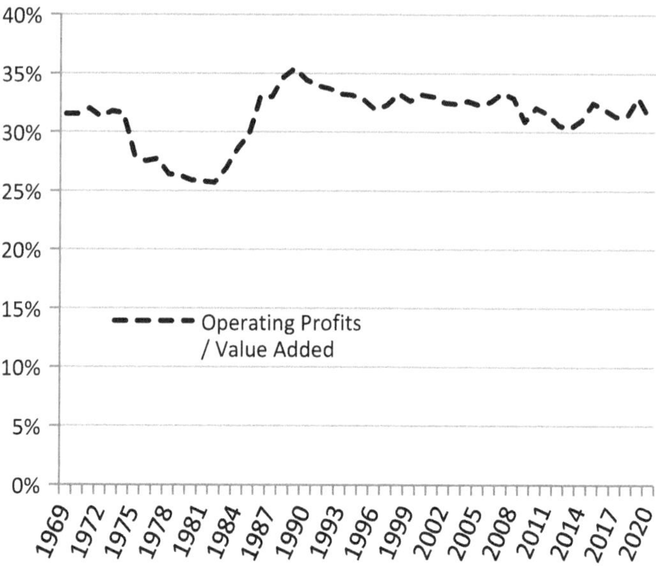

Fig. 15.3 Share of Profits in Value Added. (Non-financial and financial corporations Insee and Roll (2019) + author's update, current €)

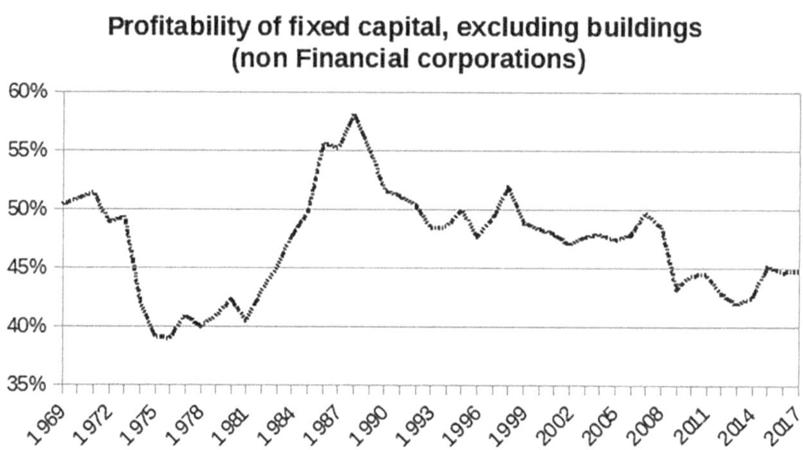

Fig. 15.4 Corporate Fixed Capital Profitability. (Non-financial corporations, Fixed Capital, excluding buildings Insee and Roll (2019))

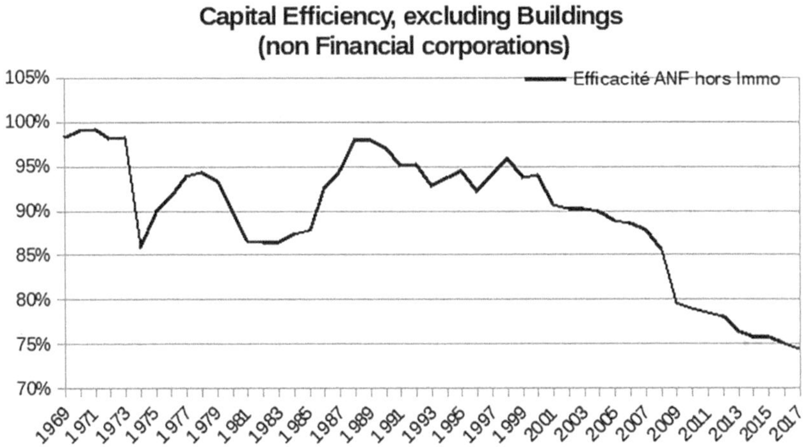

Fig. 15.5 Corporate Fixed Capital Efficiency. (Non-financial corporations, Fixed Capital, excluding buildings Insee and Roll (2019))

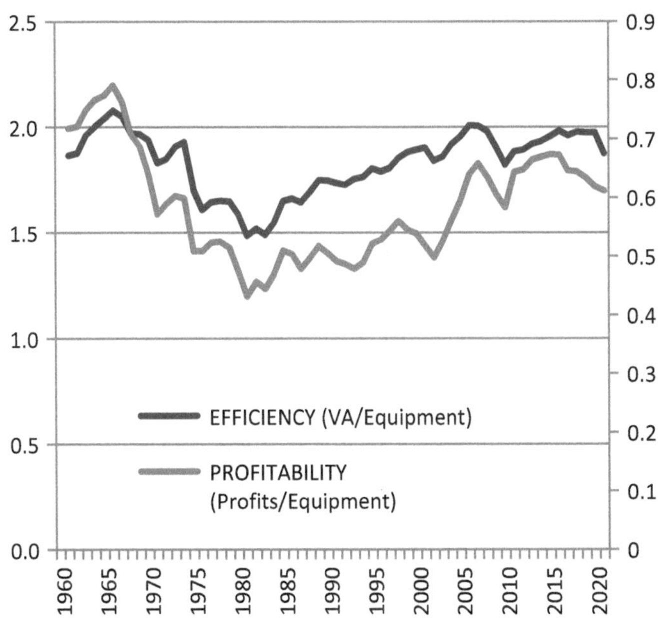

Fig. 15.6 Equipment Efficiency and Profitability. (Business corporations (non-financial and financial), current $. Source: BEA of the US Department of Commerce, author's calculations)

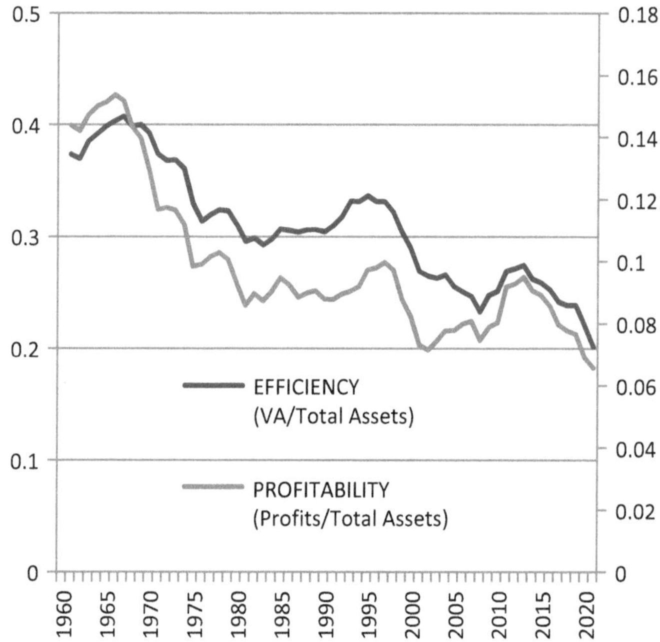

Fig. 15.7 Total Capital Efficiency and Profitability. (Business corporations (non-financial <u>and</u> financial), current \$. Source: BEA of the US Department of Commerce, author's calculations)

In the USA, we can also observe a diminution of the profit rate (at the end of the 1960s) and difficulties in redressing it because of lasting difficulties in total capital efficiency, despite a real improvement in equipment efficiency.

But the novelties are radical (technological revolution, demographic revolution, monetary revolution, etc.) and concern the central "operation" of the system (production). Hence, the Kondratiev cycle is no longer valid, in duration, and its downswing phase seems to last indefinitely.

4.3 *Wrong Answers to Financial Crisis: "More", Rather than "What Kind", of Public Intervention*

After the 2008–2009 crisis, the dominant answer was massive public intervention... but in favor of profits and capital. Especially through central banks (1) providing assistance to the banking system without imposing any conditions, (2) but imposing anti-social conditions on government expenditures.

The debate was focused on "more public intervention" and not on "another kind" of public and state intervention. It was focused on "regulating banks and the financial system", and not on "what kind" of regulation and what criteria. Public intervention thus expanded once again, but in line with the dominant existing incentives: in favor of profit, without laying down any new conditions. And the regulation imposed on banks and the financial system was of a Malthusian and "Hayekian" type: imposing prior saving. It has reinforced the existing selectivity in favor of profit and capital instead of imposing a new kind of selectivity: effects in terms of value added, employment and CO_2 as conditions for loans and for the lowering of interest rates.

The progressive forces in capitalist countries did not succeed in placing the conditions *and the aim* of public intervention—the criteria—at the center of the debate. For the peoples the reasons for the evident failure of the capitalist answers are thus unclear, as are the political stakes. This is the common responsibility of progressive forces and intellectuals. This question has to be addressed for a revival of progressive politics, which is an absolute necessity.

Hence, in 2019, ten years after the deep-seated collapse of 2008–2009, and after the public debt crisis in Europe, we have new signs of a new explosion of overaccumulation (Fig. 15.8).

This time, these signs are also observable in emerging countries, and the IMF has produced some interesting graphs of them, particularly with regard to China (IMF et al., 2018). They show certain pressures of overaccumulation in China itself, with high levels of indebtedness among private firms and their international expansion (FDI). On the other hand, they also show a high level of expansion of spending on public services and infrastructure and a global rebalancing of activity toward internal growth and services. And, after a diminution of capital efficiency, recent years show a new increase (see Figs. 15.9, 15.10 and 15.11).

4.4 *Toward a New Phase of Globalization: Imperialism, Neocolonialism and the Dollar Called into Question*

The present moment also seems to mark a search by imperialist countries for a new phase in the process of globalization. Especially:

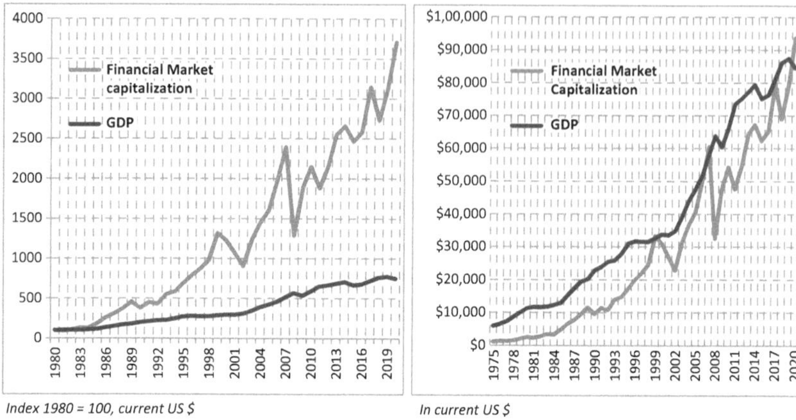

Fig. 15.8 World GDP and Total Market Capitalization value. (Financial Market Capitalization of listed companies (i.e. excluding public debts papers). Source = World Bank)

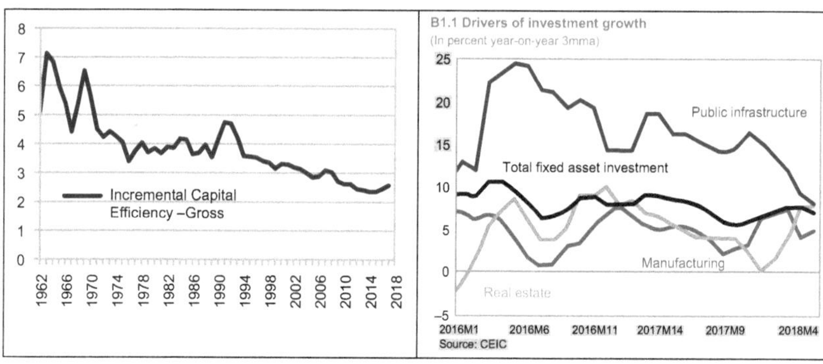

Fig. 15.9 China: Capital Efficiency (incremental). (Explanation: Incremental capital efficiency = Variation of GDP/Investment of the previous year. Source = World Bank, calculations by the author. Extract from IMF et al. (2018))

1. in the US: renewed efforts to attract capital, using the dollar privilege;
2. in other capitalist countries: despite the pandemic, continuation and expansion of systematic attacks against social expenditure, public services, pensions, wages and the status of labor;
3. throughout the world: increasing questioning of international treaties on investment and trade (such as TAFTA, TTIP, TPP) in the search for a post-WTO configuration;

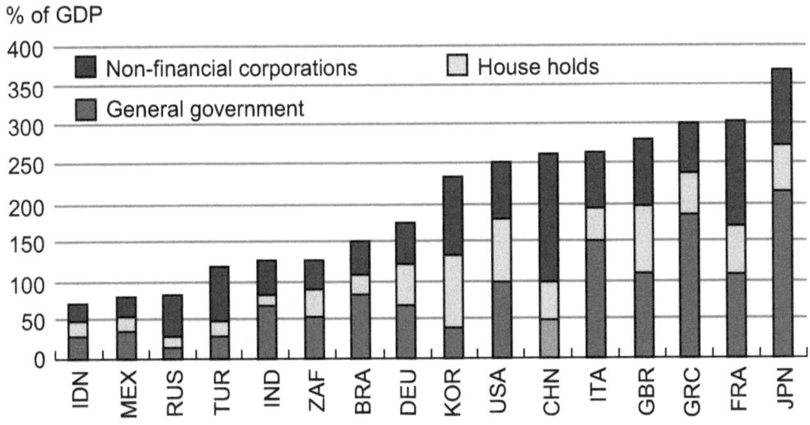

Fig. 15.10 Debt of Main Countries (2018.Q1). (Source: OECD Economic Study. Data: International Settlements Bank)

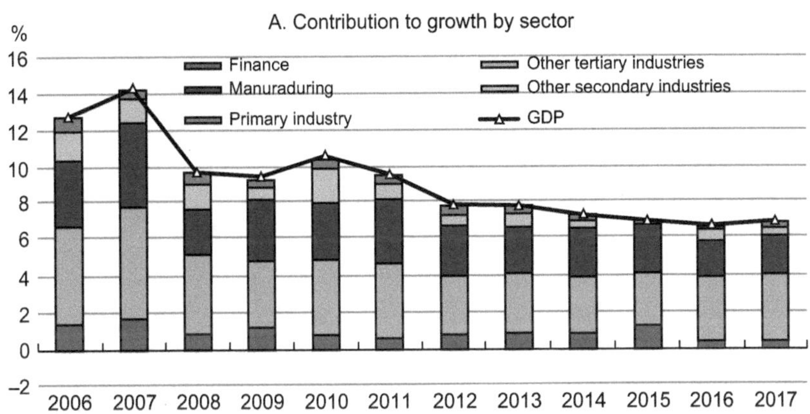

Fig. 15.11 Sectors' Contribution to Growth. (Source: OECD, 2019. Data: China Statistical Yearbook; Calculations OCDE)

4. financial mergers by MNEs aimed at building informational or industrial oligopolies to share costs and control markets in order to obtain efficiency gains and to make transfers in favor of capital (informational efficiency gains and appropriation of rent);
5. more generally, huge efforts by the dominant capitals (of which USA capital and USA-MNEs) to recover their own profit rate, reinforce their technological advance and gain a new lead.

Some statistics on the USA, France, Brazil, China, Vietnam, Egypt, Tunisia, etc. show a clear movement in this direction. That is to say: higher value-added draining from other countries to the USA and the other G7 countries in the form of payments for technology use, fees, dividends and outflows of profits through MNEs' affiliates (see Figs. 15.12, 15.13, 15.14, 15.15, 15.16, 15.17, 15.18, 15.19 and 15.20) since 2009–2010.

These new efforts by financial capital are coming up against peoples' aspirations for development all around the world. They include huge efforts to integrate emerging countries into the logic of financial capital, and even to make some of their sectors "collaborate" with it. Integration efforts are also underway within developed countries, with specific social groups being targeted. For example, in France we have a banker from the Rothschild bank as president...

Financial capital is at the heart of this logic, interconnected with the US dollar and its circuit. Financial capital constitutes a kind of interconnection with the so-called "production" capital. It is the highest stage of the capital form, as "pure" capital; it combines a twofold logic of (1) "money for

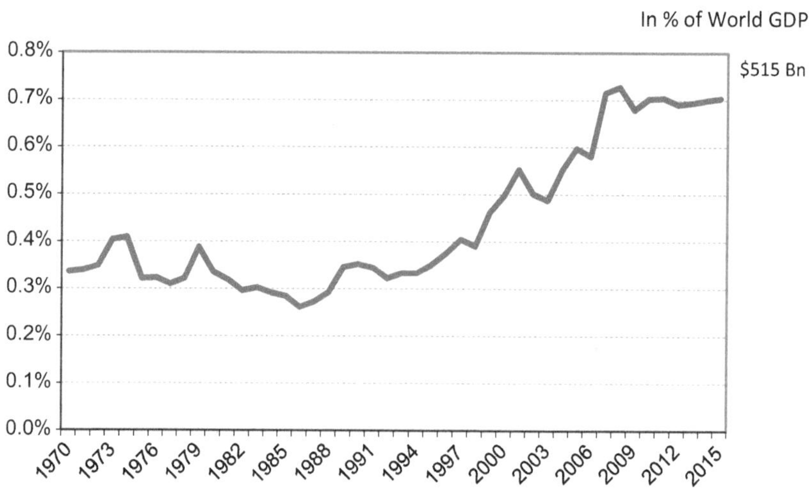

Fig. 15.12 Draining of value by US Multinationals toward the US from the rest of the world. (<u>Source</u>: Balance of payments of countries, from CEPII (Boccara, Nayman, work in progress). Positive sign for funds entering in the USA)

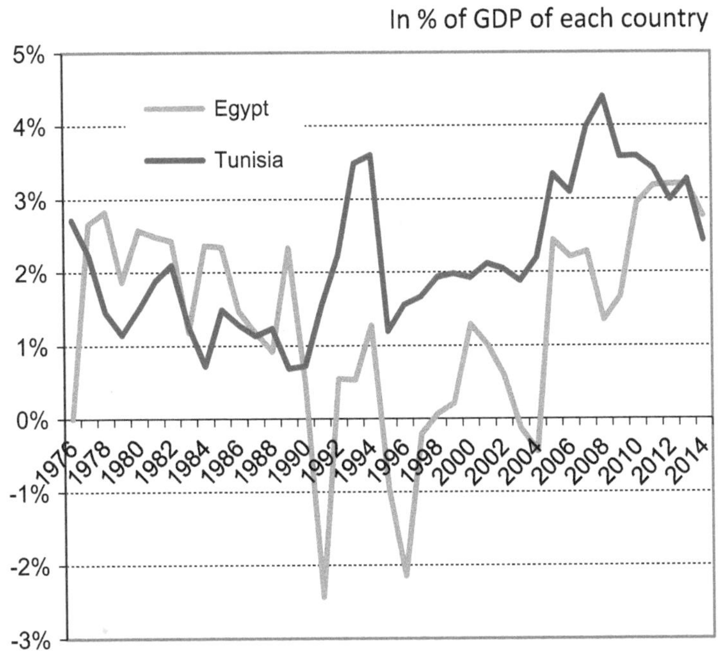

Fig. 15.13 Draining of value from Egypt and Tunisia by Multinationals. (Source: Balance of payments of countries, from CEPII (Boccara, Nayman, work in progress). BoP Sign inversed: positive = draining of value from the GDP out of the country)

money" and (2) distant power over production, acting simultaneously in different places and countries.

Financial capital appears as our common "enemy" (or "adversary") all around the world. It is our common adversary against employment (especially in the North), against social security in all countries, against public services, against security of life, against health and ecology, and against common goods, despite the fact that the underlying production needs all these expenditures.[9]

[9] Financial capital (as defined by Hilferding and by Lenin) must not be confused with equipment, any form of money, or merely financing: in Marxist analysis, capital is a value which is seeking more value, its surplus value. K is seeking $K' = K + \Delta K$. Financial capital is a specific form of it.

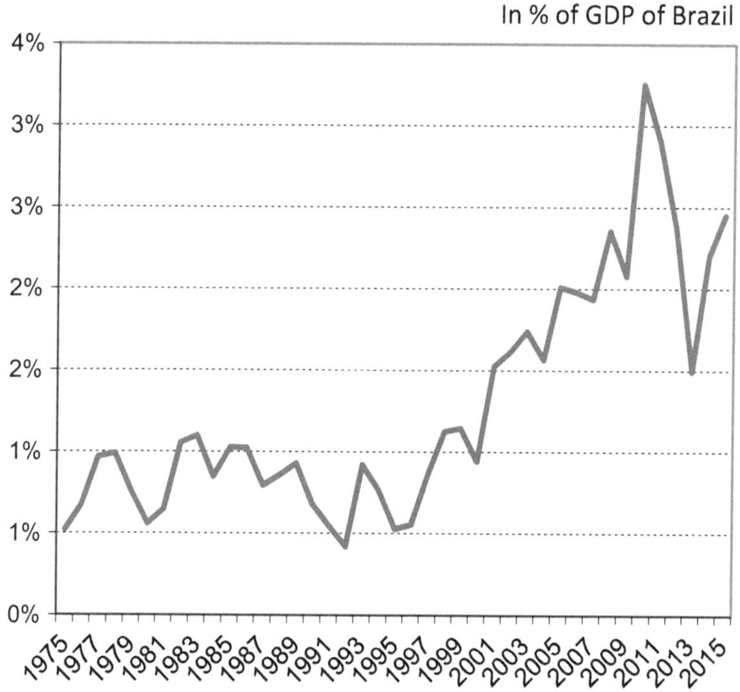

Fig. 15.14 Draining of value from Brazil by Multinationals. (Source: Balance of payments of countries, from CEPII (Boccara, Nayman, work in progress). BoP Sign inversed: positive = draining of value from the GDP out of the country)

5 The Task Before Us

Given the capital logic, our task cannot be to limit it or offset its consequences. We need to implement a different logic. This is also necessary because of the exigencies created by the considerable changes brought by the informational, ecological, anthroponomic and monetary revolutions.

Without a change in the logic itself, we will be affected by a new explosion of overaccumulation, with its terrible social consequences for the peoples.

This could cause deep turmoil and disarray with serious political consequences …

Public services, social protection and employment, interconnected with other efficiency criteria than those of profitability for firms' management,

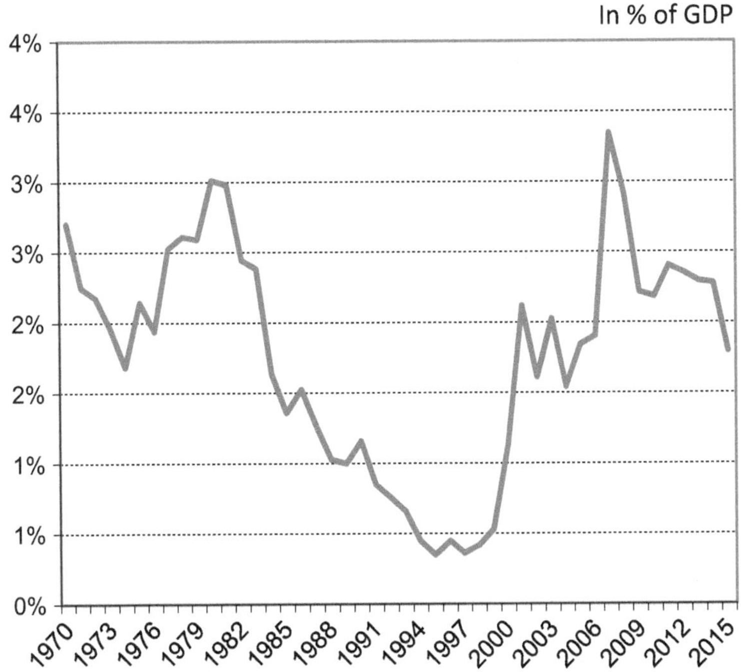

Fig. 15.15 Draining of value from South Africa by Multinationals. (Source: Balance of payments of countries, from CEPII (Boccara, Nayman, work in progress). BoP Sign inversed: positive = draining of value from the GDP out of the country)

are at the center of this alternative logic, acting on both sides: *demand*—for a new kind of demand (more ecological, less material, less market-oriented)—and *supply*—transformation and improvement of production. It would engage our societies in another kind of growth of total labor productivity.

Successful abolition of capitalist logic does not mean mechanically eliminating what exists in a capitalist society. This could be a regression. Rather than regressing in relation to the logic of markets, it makes it necessary to answer the objective problems that capitalism tries to answer. For example, successful abolition of labor markets does not simply mean the legal prohibition of unemployment; it needs to answer the problems of total cost diminution and redistributions of jobs between sectors and industries. In

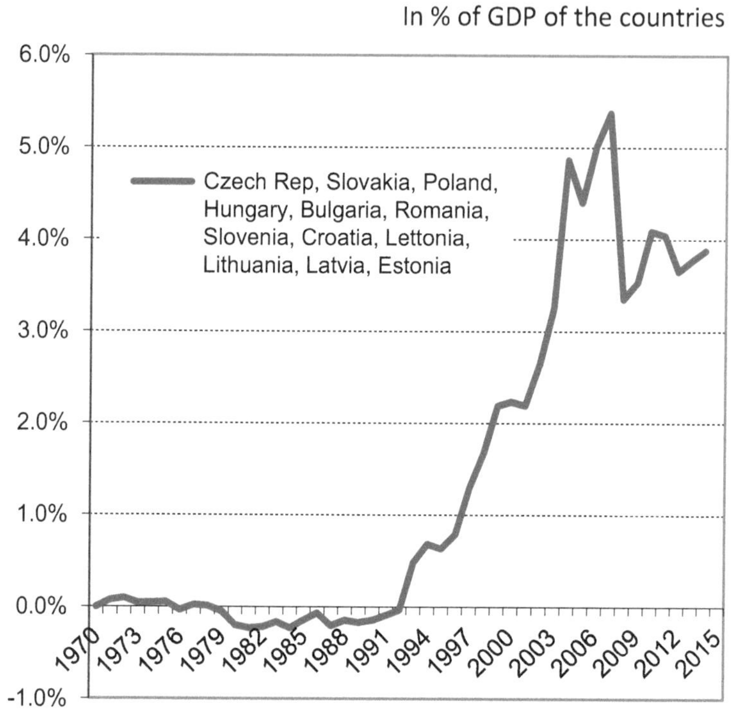

Fig. 15.16 Draining of value from East European EU Members by Multinationals. (Source: Balance of payments of countries, from CEPII (Boccara, Nayman, work in progress). BoP Sign inversed: positive = draining of value from the GDP out of the country)

other words, we need to go beyond the markets, to "overcome" them, to surpass, keeping the adaptability of markets but without their destructive power on people.

Boccara (2012) draws a coherent perspective of "overcoming", "surpassing" and abolition of "the 4 markets" for a new civilization:

- the labor market (unemployment, bad jobs, insecure jobs, and pressure against wages and against training);
- the product market (concerning firms and their management criteria);
- the money and finance market;
- the international market which is transversal to the other three.

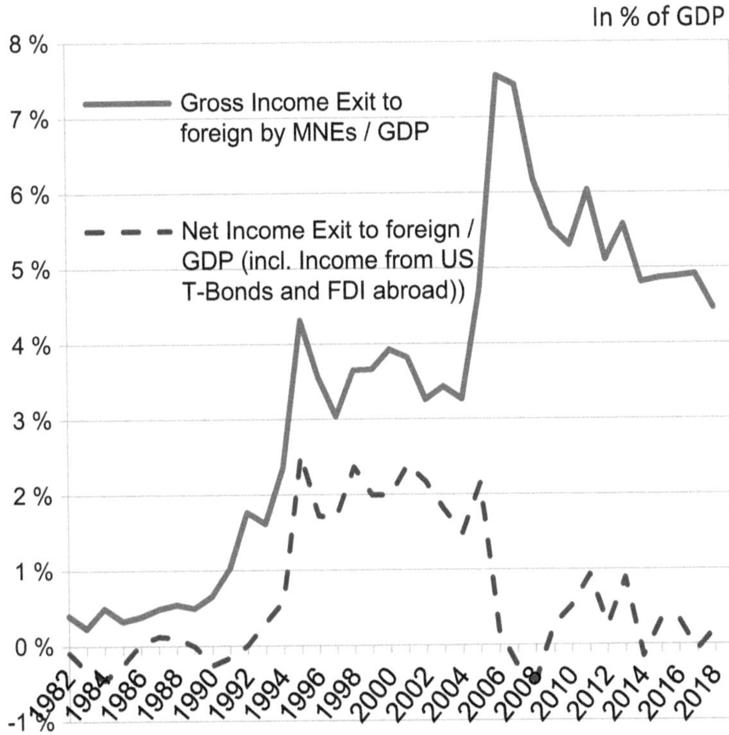

Fig. 15.17 Draining of value from China by MNEs. (Source: Balance of payments of countries, from People's Bank of China + World Bank. *Field:* Mainland + Hong-Kong + Macao. BoP Sign inversed: positive = draining of value from the GDP out of the country = Outflow or Exit. Net Income includes China's income from US Treasury Bonds and from Outward Chinese FDI)

6 Transforming Globalization—Guiding Lines of Alternatives

The question of transforming internationalization is a priority, for reasons of health and ecology, as well as for class and human reasons, and also for civilizational reasons and peace (see F. Boccara, 2020).

Re-appraisal of nationalism is a way in which the people themselves place "a different globalization" at the top of the agenda, especially the working class and the most oppressed.

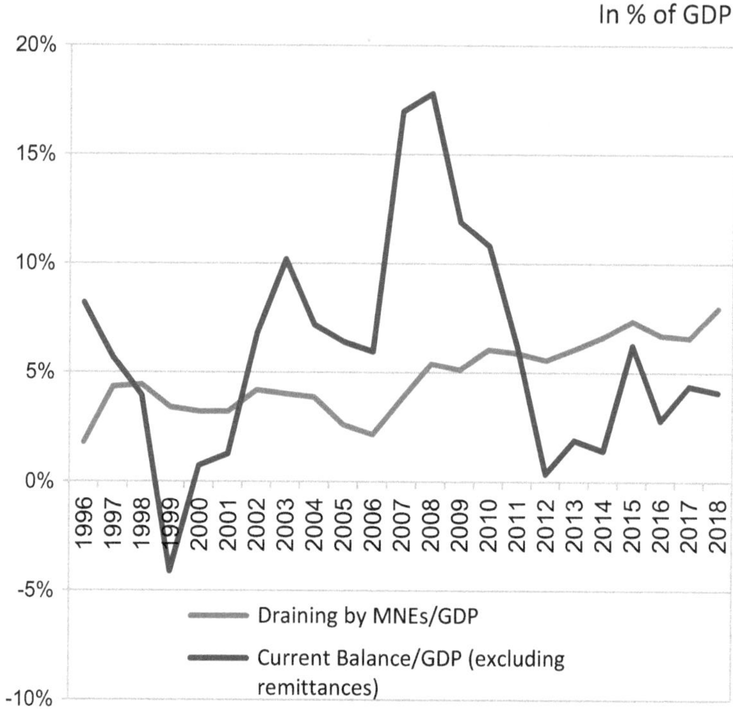

Fig. 15.18 Draining of value from Vietnam by MNEs. (Source: Balance of payments of countries, from People's Bank of China + World Bank. *Field:* Mainland + Hong-Kong + Macao. BoP Sign inversed: positive = draining of value from the GDP out of the country = Outflow or Exit. Net Income includes China's income from US Treasury Bonds and from Outward Chinese FDI)

In Europe, we have both sides: (1) growth of nationalism, including so-called "left-populism" and (2) a still-existing majority of people in favor of developing a progressive European construction, but a majority that is very diverse tending to be silent or paralyzed. Nevertheless, the seduction of false solutions is present, the seduction of facile answers and opportunism, the seduction of the false binary opposition—"open or closed"—whereas the question is *the content* of the openness.

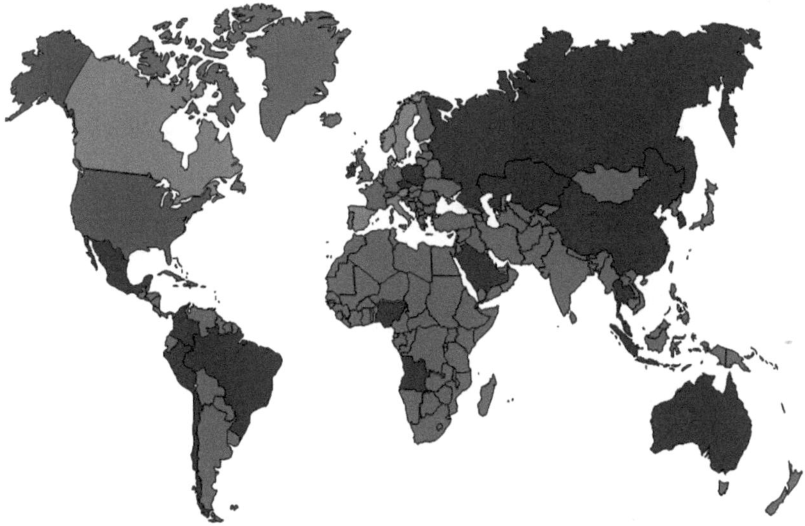

Fig. 15.19 Map of MNEs' Draining. (*Source*: Boccara, Nayman (work in progress, CEPII DataBase, Authors' calculations). In blue: negative transfers from MNEs (draining *from*); In red: positive transfers to MNEs (draining *to*))

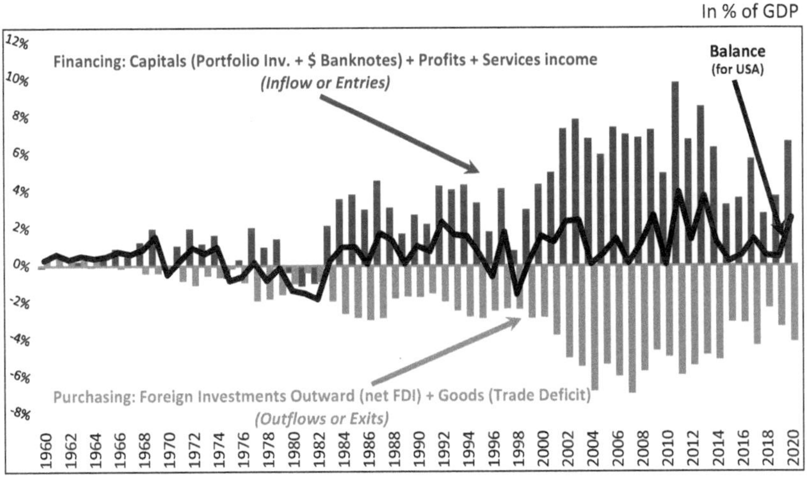

Fig. 15.20 The Dollar and External Financing of the USA. (Source: US Balance of Payments (BEA))

6.1 *Principles*

We must act on the three complementary points of the systemic triangle (objectives of society, financial means, powers and institutions) and promote different efficiency criteria from those of profit rate (criteria structure the links between the three points of the systemic triangle, see Chart 15.1).

This meets the needs of the cultural development of society and the peoples, their demand all around the world for real and efficient democracy, their capacity to intervene with their knowledge with regard to their work and society and their aspiration for self-management.

6.2 *Financial Globalization and MNEs: Toward a New Theory*

The "informational revolution" is at the basis of the development of a new kind of multinational enterprises. This brings radical new challenges for MNEs, because information is similar to a global factor traversing all countries.

In the MNE theory that I have developed, I particularly propose to distinguish between **the function** of the MNE—sharing of resources and

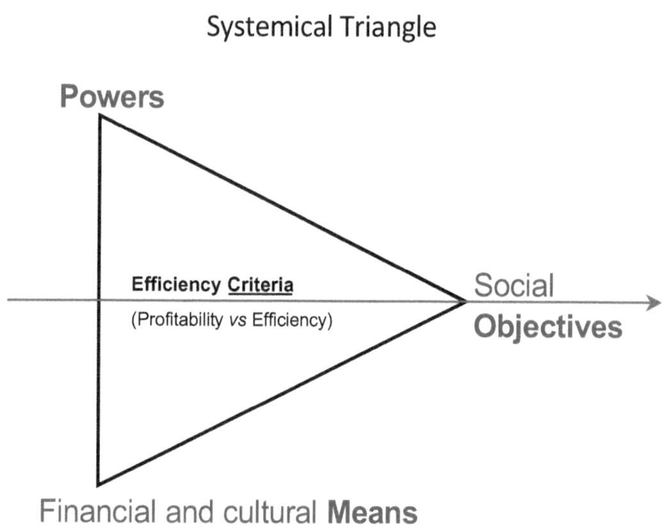

Chart 15.1 Corporate total capital profitability

capacities for international co-production—which needs to be ensured, and **its present form**—a network of affiliates controlled and driven by financial capital. This determines the way MNEs currently carry out their function—by transfers and monopoly in favor of the profit rate of their dominant capital—which needs to be fought. But the sharing is a factor that enables an unprecedented cost reduction. This is at the basis of a new type of MNE. MNEs share their resources (especially informational resources) globally inside the limited boundaries of each MNE, and transfer values thanks to the informational revolution and the rules of the world financial system. This (global factor + global transfers) calls into question the HOS framework and the *national* comparative (or absolute) advantage theory of the *national* benefits of international trade.

In the financial globalization system, value transfers between countries enable the draining of values from countries, which essentially takes place inside MNEs, for their own benefit and for the capital dominating them. This increasingly comes into conflict with territories and global human development, including ecological exigencies. Capital control—at the basis of MNEs' networks of affiliates—is the means to "privatize the sharing" of informational resources (see Boccara, 2013a). Because of the importance of these transfers and the use of a global factor (information, which cannot be allocated to one country or another), we have to conceptually distinguish the "value chain" from the "activity chain". Generally speaking, this difference it is not distinguished with sufficient care (Gereffi et al., 2005 make this kind of confusion).

To give an idea of the value chains, and hence of the draining of values between countries, we can approximate those transfers with certain payments recorded by national balances of payments (BoP) (see **Text Box** for explanation and Figs. 15.12, 15.13, 15.14, 15.15, 15.16, 15.17, 15.18, 15.19 and 15.20 for results, for another vision of geographical international transfers of wealth, see Gourinchas et al., 2011).

Text Box: "Transfers" and Draining by MNEs
MNEs use different means to transfer value from one country to another. Among them, there may be "services" recorded in national balances of payments. But not all services are transfers. So we use several coefficients (calibrated on the example of some known countries) to take a share of each service's line in the BoP (royalties,

(*continued*)

(continued)
license fees, financial services, internal business services, dividends paid, etc.). There are other ways of transferring values: transfer price of exports and imports of goods, capital movements, especially loans and borrowing inside MNEs. Here, we restrict ourselves to services only. We apply it to a world database of countries' BoP (constructed with L. Nayman and based on CEPII data collection). Out of 200 countries, only 19 have positive overall transfers (i.e. in their favor).[10] In 2015, the total of transfers was almost US$1100 billion (of which G7+Switzerland accounted for US$875 billion equivalent and the USA alone for US$550 billion). These figures provide a clear illustration of imperialism and its neo-colonial structuration. For the remaining 181 countries, the draining of values is positive (i.e. it represents negative transfers).

The globalized international financial system developed under the aegis of the IMF, the USA and the WTO, with support from the other dominant capitalist states, allows MNEs to "freely" **transfer** their values (money and capitals), share information and other resources, and control them through FDI.

Using this international financial system of transfers, MNEs play on and develop the opposition between global factors of production—with *global costs*, such as information—and local factors of production—with *local costs*, such as labor and local wages and local public services (including social protection). Our Marxist theory of new MNEs analyzes this opposition (Boccara, 2013).

Hence the intellectual property rules, the contents of international investment agreements, and the rules for transfer prices,[11] in parallel with human capabilities and regional development, tend to come to the top of the agenda in all the countries. This is the case with workers' struggles as

[10] Austria, Belgium, Bermuda Islands, Cyprus, Denmark, France, Germany, Israel, Italy, Japan, Kuwait, Lebanon, the Netherlands, Norway, Spain, Sweden, Switzerland, United Kingdom and the USA.

[11] Transfer prices—*inside* the MNES—are different from market rules but dominated by a "super" market rule for relations *outside* the MNEs: the financial market rule of profitability.

well as with public opinion (e.g. through concerns over tax evasion). It should also be the case for ecological concerns. There are common needs for new international relationships, links between civil society or organizations, not only between governments or states alone. There is a need for a new kind of internationalization.

6.3 For a New Kind of International Economic Treaties

International co-production and transfers by MNEs enable sharing of resources within each MNE. Sharing is a factor in reducing costs and increasing efficiency gains. It is monopolized and driven by capital, and transferred to several specific territories (tax havens, USA, etc.). It is affected through high-cost financial takeovers, which absorb a significant share of the efficiency gains, and are used to intensify the competition against so-called "labor costs" and public and social expenditures. This is destructive for workers, public services, social rights and the environment. This competition tends to depress global demand and reinforces inequalities (Galbraith, 2014). It promotes financial accumulation, which threatens the environment and is creating the conditions for a new explosion of overaccumulation.

A new kind of international economic treaties are needed to enable efficiency and cost gains while avoiding the reinforcement of anti-social and anti-ecological competition. Indeed, we need to enable and promote efficiency gains, but in accordance with another logic than that of financial capital gains.

This new kind of treaties would be **treaties for cooperation and the mastering of trade and investments for the co-development of common goods** (health, environment and public services, including social protection)**, jobs and value added**. It would invert the ends and the means of the current treaties.

The goal of the current treaties (such as transatlantic free trade agreement (TAFTA) and comprehensive economic and trade agreement (CETA)) is "foreign trade and FDI above all", even in opposition to employment, health and the environment. Instead, new kinds of treaties would establish the goals of development of employment, health and environment in the different countries involved. This would invert the legal hierarchy of norms, with international trade and FDI becoming means, conditional upon their effect on the ends. The logic for the evaluation of FDI and trade would be: does this FDI or foreign trade develop employment, health and the environment in both countries?

In the same way as the present treaties include institutional elements and powers (supranational arbitrage courts, for example), these new treaties should include new institutions and democratic rights for the purpose of assessing whether common goods are indeed actually developed by foreign trade and FDI. These institutions would have financial means enabling action to be taken (establishing sanctions and incentives, financed both by taxation and central bank credit lines). These institutions would include workers' representatives from the signatory countries.

In the same way as the present treaties accurately define the "income of the investor" (i.e. its profit) as the main object to be protected by the treaties, the new treaties would define, protect and promote the production of real wealth (value added) and jobs in the different countries, on the condition of meeting social, ecological and health criteria.

Instead of universal rules of competition, we also need to promote rules of cooperation for co-production and co-design, engineering and development—with employment and value-added criteria—between multinationals, between their affiliates or between multinationals and public services: not through capital acquisition. For cooperation between firms, we should be inspired by the existing rules for "apportionment" of activity and work adopted by successful industrial cooperative ventures (such as Airbus in its early days, without financial capital) with the principle of (re-)equilibration of trade and economic activity between countries. For relations between firms and public services (transport industry, energy industry, etc.) the possibility of partnerships for co-design and development driven by public services *including* production must be authorized, instead of the systematic prohibition of relationships of this kind on the grounds of their being considered equivalent to subsidies, and instead of authorization for R&D or the "pre-design" stage alone, forcing the partner firms to enter into competition with other firms (calls for tender) when the projects shift to the production stage. With these current European rules, France's TGV program would not have been possible, for it is the result of constant cooperation between SNCF (French public railways) and a private company (the predecessor of Alstom) from design and development to production.

Thus the aim is to enable genuine international sharing of resources and means, with a different orientation, and not to close frontiers or enter into an economic war against labor, social security and public services. For this new kind of sharing, we need to redefine the financial transfers associated with FDI and foreign trade (including transfer prices and royalties) insisting on cost sharing and cooperation and change the rules of intellectual property rights (currently established by the WTO).

Financial means such as bank credit, monetary policy, taxation on foreign trade and penalties can be used as incentives to drive shared goals in the different countries involved. Our aim is social protections and not protectionism.

To sum up, we could act on MNEs by three means: different rules, effective financial means and new international democratic institutions to monitor them.

More generally, we would aim to establish new world institutions and organizations: organizations for mastering trade and investment (instead of the WTO), organizations for protecting the environment, new deals with MNEs driven by the development of common and public goods. And we would need to fill the gap between these kinds of organizations and the IMF, especially by organizing regular and mandatory dialog between these organizations, the IMF, workers and representatives of civil society and its organizations.

6.4 *Money Creation, Central Banks, the Dollar*

The social mastering of money creation is a decisive alternative to financial capital, if we promote it with alternative criteria for the use of the money and with new democratic powers for citizens and workers over banks and firms that use bank credit, and over governments.

In Europe, people were implicitly fighting for the social mastery of money creation when they protested against the actions of the European central bank and the anti-social conditionalities that the latter imposed when the so-called "troïka" granted its loans.[12] Now the "debt question" is permanently used as a justification of austerity. Yet, the problem is not debt but the *use* of debt (for financial capital or for the development of human beings and natural resources?) and the *conditions* of debt—who holds it and at what interest rate?—together with the power exerted by the holders.

A vast amount of money has been created by central banks, but with a Lilliputian effect on growth and employment. This leads conservative and Hayekian forces (defending the anti-Keynesian idea of *ex ante* saving) to claim that we must restrict money creation and leave its allocation to financial markets. Even now, when the COVID pandemic continues to

[12] European Central Bank (ECB), European commission and International Monetary Fund (IMF).

necessitate further issuance of money, they still put forward the same arguments. At the same time it is a kind of "poisonous addiction" to financial markets, which thus regularly threaten economic stability when monetary authorities try to diminish money creation. But the missing piece of the puzzle today is the domain in which this money creation should be used: speculation versus real ecological production, capital accumulation versus jobs and human resources. It means the criteria of use, and the need for democratic power through institutions to direct the use of money by firms and governments. But the new technological conditions are making human resources (jobs and skills) and public services become the key to efficiency. This is the reason why stimulating (material) investment alone does not work. It is necessary to promote a mix of investment (equipment + R&D) and human resource expenditures (jobs + training+ public services). This implies far-reaching change in the criteria for use of money, not only an *addenda* to or a limitation of the existing capital logic.

6.5 *The US Dollar*

The question of the dollar is central, intertwining money creation and international dominations.

The dollar is a major tool for the USA to attract capital and control the world economy. With the dollar, the USA attracts portfolio investments (treasury bonds + minority shareholders of firms), central bank reserves of banknotes, MNEs' revenues and payments (of services, royalties, technology, financial services and repatriation of profits) (all in blue in the graph). It uses them to buy products (net imports of goods), make loans to its MNEs' affiliates and control world productive chains with outward FDI (net outward FDI from the USA, except for the last two years). The difference between inflows and outflows of funds is a surplus of some US$100 billion, available to finance the USA's informational advance and public services (except during several specific crisis years). It is represented on Fig. 15.20 (inflows in blue and positive, outflows in red and negative, the difference in black).

An alternative to the dollar as the de facto world-common-currency is necessary, through a radical reform of the IMF and development of the special drawing rights (SDR): issuance of SDR for the co-development of peoples (development of social protection and public services, including ecology) and a new selective credit oriented to efficient investment, that is, developing value added and employment in firms and ecological production.

7 Going Beyond the Tradition to Cope with the New Coming Crisis

We need to combine radical and immediate proposals. In parallel, and partly in contradiction, we need clear debates on ideas, to progress on common points and to identify differences in order to build broad and effective alliances in several capitalist countries.

The situation requires radical and coherent changes, of a positive kind not solely aimed at limiting the current logic. This leads us to avoid going back to so-called "Keynesianism" or, conversely, to authoritarian socialism. For example, if we were to advocate more inflation and more credit alone, following Joseph Stiglitz, without further clarifications or changes with regard to the utilization of the credit, this policy would lead to "more" ... but more for capital, as we have seen during the pandemic. It has resulted in exceptional financial market inflation, a worse situation for peoples.

Mastering the use of money, its criteria and the contents of production is a profound democratic challenge. It constitutes a new frontier, beyond traditional Keynesianism and traditional Marxism!

We must demand policies and approaches whose content is of a different kind, especially the introduction of new criteria for the use of money and for democracy. These two questions are not separate. The dominant explanation for the current economic difficulties is the pandemic and the so-called **"trade war"** between USA and China. On the contrary, we have to insist on the real cause which is a kind of **anti-social and anti-ecological war waged by financial capital against public services, workers' rights and social security, against the environment and against all peoples,** exerted from the USA, as the base of world financial capital, even against the American people itself (see analysis, including the rebalancing of global value and activity chains and Chinese rebalancing, in Dimicoli, 2019). The hospital crisis is a symbol of this.

Progressive forces can establish new and common tasks in order to face up to the new coming crisis. New convergences must be promoted at the international level as well as at the national level, convergences in terms of the policies denounced and the demands (or proposals) put forward.

Given the diversity of our theoretical approaches, we need exchanges in order to move toward several fundamental common objectives, aiming to overcome the present fragmentation.

A major common issue at stake is the question of "a different globalization".

8 Conclusion

A decisive agenda for theoretical works and political initiatives is the alliances and the **common demands needed in order to face up to the global domination of financial capital.**

We need to affirm the need to free ourselves from the logic of financial capital if we want to respond to human social needs as a priority. We must sound the alarm about the growing risks of a catastrophic new economic crisis and increasing risks for ecology and health.

The task could be aided by common or convergent work and reflection for a different kind of globalization, directed against capital costs—instead of labor costs, see for example Cordonnier et al., 2013—and against the domination of the world by capital.

The agenda could be the co-development of the people of each country, through the securance of life for each person, with another kind of democracy and another use of money, aimed at the development of world common goods and a different kind of internationalization. World sharing of patents and the development of public services are the first point placed at the top of the agenda by life itself.

Nevertheless, the dull economic issues cannot be avoided. Three common pillars could be:

- A genuine world common currency for a new kind of credit and money creation, against the domination of the US dollar;
- Mastering of MNEs with a new kind of foreign trade and investment treaties;
- New international institutions based on real democracy and with a new role.

References

Boccara, F. (2011 and 2010). « Economie et écologie (1) : où en est-on » « Economie et écologie (2) : pour une vraie alternative », La Pensée, 363 *and* 365, 53–69 and 47–61.

Boccara, F. (2013a). *Firmes multinationales et balance des paiements dans la globalisation financière et la révolution technologique informationnelle—une analyse théorique et appliquée.* Thèse de doctorat de l'Université de Paris 13, tomes 1 et 2, p. 608.

Boccara, F. (2020), « Rapport introductif des rencontres internationales 'Face la mondialisation capitaliste, quelle révolution pour un monde de coopération et de partage ?' », Economie et Politique, n° 786-787, 40–52.
Boccara, P. (2013b). *Théories sur les crises—La suraccumulation et la dévalorisation du capital* (p. 557). éditions Delga.
Boccara, P. (2017). *Neufs leçons sur l'anthroponomie systémique* (p. 230). éditions Delga.
Boccara, P. (2011). We must incriminate the basic rules of capitalism. In P. Herrmann (Ed.), *All the same—All being new. Basic rules of capitalism in a world of change* (p. 61–68, 198). Europäischer Hochschulverlag.
Boccara, P. (2012). *Le Capital de Marx, son apport, son dépassement au-delà de l'économie* (p. 174). Le Temps des Cerises.
Boccara, P. (2018). *Passion et patience de la créativité révolutionnaire* (p. 272). éditions Delga.
Boyer, R. (2020). *Les capitalismes à l'épreuve de la pandémie* (p. 200). La Découverte.
Cordonnier, L., Dallery, T., Dewicquet, V., Melmièes, J., & Vandevelde, F. (2013). *Le coût du capital et son surcoût—Sens de la notion, mesure et évolution, conséquences économiques* (p. 160). Clersé, Université de Lille.
Coriat, B. (2021). *La pandémie, l'anthropocène et le bien commun* (p. 220). Les liens qui libèrent.
Dimicoli, Y. (2019). Mondialisation : fin ou besoin d'une nouvelle phase ? *Economie et Politique, 780-781*, 26–35.
Durand, D. (2005). *Un autre crédit est possible* (p. 367). Le Temps des Cerises.
Easterlin, R. (2019). Three revolutions of the modern era. *Comparative Economic Study*, 10.
Ekstedt, H. (2019). *Developing heterodox theory: Musts and possibilities* (p. 27). mimeo.
Galbraith, James (2014), The end of Normal: The great crisis and the future of growth.
Gereffi, G., Humphrey, J., & Sturgeon, T. (2005). The governance of global value chains. *Review of International Political Economy, 12*(1), 78–104.
Giraud, G. (2014a). *L'illusion financière* (p. 231). Les éditions de l'Atelier.
Giraud, G. (2014b). What understanding of Capital for Tomorrow? In *Documents de travail du centre d'économie de la Sorbonne* (p. 28). Université Paris 1 et CNRS.
Gourinchas, Pierre-Olivier, Rey, Hélène, Truempler, Kai (2011), "The financial crisis and the geography of wealth transfers", NBER-Working Paper, n° 17353, 58.
Granovetter, M. (2005). The impact of social structure on economic outcomes. *Journal of Economic Perspectives, 19*, 33–50.

Guerrien, Bernard (2016), « Une nouvelle « Théorie Générale » ? A propos de *Capitalism, Competition, Conflict, Crises*, d'Anwar Shaikh », Revue de la Régulation, n° 20 Autumn, 13.

IMF (International Monetary Fund), Mano, Rui C., Zhang, Jiayi (2018), "China's rebalancing: Recent progress, prospects and policies", IMF Working papers, n° 243, 17.

Jessop, B., & Sum, N.-L. (2006). *Beyond the regulation approach—Putting capitalist economies in their place* (p. 456). Edward Elgar.

Keen, S. (2013). *Debunking economics-the naked emperor dethroned?* (p. 496). Zed Books.

Kelton, S. (2020). *Le mythe du déficit. La Théorie moderne de la monnaie et la naissance de l'économie du peuple, traduction française de the deficit myth: Modern monetary theory and the birth of the People's economy* (p. 368). Les Liens qui libèrent.

Keynes, JohnMaynard (1936), General theory of employment, interest and money.

Lavoie, M. (2015). *Post-Keynesian economics-new foundations* (p. 680). Edward Elgar Publishing.

Marx, K. (1867, 1885 et 1894). *Le Capital*, Editions sociales, Livres 1, 2 et 3.

Morin, F. (2017). *L'économie politique du 21ème siècle—De la valeur-capital à la valeur-travail* (p. 312). Lux-Humanités.

OECD. (2019). China. *Economic Studies of OECD*, p. 81.

Plihon, D., & Mouhoud, E. M. (2009). *Le savoir et la finance—Liaisons dangereuses au sein du capitalisme contemporain* (p. 238). La Découverte.

Polanyi, K. (1944). *The great transformation* (p. 319). Farrar and Rinehart.

Roll, C. (2019). *« La rentabilité du capital en France », Mémoire de recherche* (p. 52). ENS-Université Paris 1.

Schumpeter, J. A. (1947). The creative response in economic history. *The Journal of Economic History, 7*(2), 149–159.

Shaikh, A. (2016). *Capitalism, competition, conflict, crises* (p. 1024). Oxford University Press.

Stiglitz, J. (2003). *Globalization and its discontent* (p. 304). Norton.

Veltz, P. (2021). *L'Économie désirable : Sortir du monde thermo-fossile, Le Seuil, coll* (p. 128). La république des idées.

Weinstein, O. (2010). *Pouvoir, finance et connaissance—Les transformations de l'entreprise capitaliste entre XXe et XXIe siècle* (p. 200). La Découverte.

CHAPTER 16

Epilogue: The Lessons from Covid-19 Management in Vietnam and Post-pandemic Prospects

Yves Tiberghien

1 Introduction

When Covid-19 appeared in Wuhan in late 2019, Vietnam was right on the frontline. Warned by the SARS pandemic in 2003 that also started in China and quickly landed in Hanoi, Vietnam lost no time in reacting to the situation. On January 23, China announced the full lockdown of Wuhan and the first case was identified in Vietnam. On January 30, within just seven days and similarly to Taiwan, Korea, and Singapore, Vietnam activated its integrated Public Health Emergency Operation Center to discuss and organize its response (Tiberghien, 2021). Vietnam shut down its border with China and organized a national coordinated response and stringent lockdown. It worked. By the end of 2020, Vietnam had suffered only 35 total deaths from Covid-19 and scored the lowest mortality score per million in the whole world (0.36, equal to Taiwan) and was praised by

Y. Tiberghien (✉)
The University of British Columbia, Vancouver, BC, Canada
e-mail: yves.tiberghien@ubc.ca

T. A.-D. Tran (ed.), *Rethinking Asian Capitalism*,
https://doi.org/10.1007/978-3-030-98104-4_16

the World Health Organization (WHO) and the World Economic Reform (WEF). Amazingly, Vietnam also managed to finish 2020 with a positive economic growth rate (+2.9%), just behind Taiwan (3.1%) and ahead of China (+2.3%). Every other country in East Asia (including the whole of South East Asia) finished the year with negative growth.

Vietnam upheld this high performance until June 2021. Then, the Delta variant hit very hard, just as the country and the economy were stretched to the limit and had reached lockdown fatigue. Vietnam started July with a very low vaccination rate (0.2% full vaccination, 4% one dose), due to vaccine supply issues and a strategy that favored developing a Vietnamese vaccine. July, August, and September 2021 turned out to be very painful for Vietnam. In these three months alone, 19,220 people died. The mortality per million reached 200 per million. Vietnam did manage to vaccinate the population and to reach a 70% double vaccination rate by December 31, 2021. But Vietnam has kept struggling between its national priority for political stability and health on the one hand, and its economic positioning as an Asia-Pacific hub in global value chains on the other hand. The growth rate estimate for 2021 was downgraded by 4% by the Asian Development Bank (ADB) between June and December.

This concluding chapter focuses on three questions. First, what were the drivers for Vietnam's initial success in 2020 (phase 1 of Covid-19)? Second, why was the Vietnam response put under so much pressure in the second half of 2021? And third, what are some larger implications of the pandemic for the Vietnamese Doi Moi model?

Building on my East Asian Covid-19 study (Tiberghien, 2021), I argue that Vietnam represented an exemplary case of the East Asian model in response to the Covid-19 crisis. Vietnam's response relied on well-mobilized institutional capacity, rooted in its political system, and on very strong levels of social cohesion and trust. However, in its extraordinary outcomes of 2020, Vietnam relied on extreme levels of mobilization of its party cells and society that could not be sustained for years. Vietnam essentially punched above the structural constraints of its level of development and of its health care system.

In essence, the Covid-19 experience represents the hybrid situation of Vietnam as a combined centralized political system and globalized market-economy in the wake of *Đổi Mới* reforms (Tran Thi Anh-Dao, Introduction page 2 in this volume). Its newly acquired position as lower middle-income economy, its global connections and the organizational power of its one-party system enabled Vietnam to mount a surprisingly effective response.

But the long duration and multiple channels of the Covid-19 shock partially wore Vietnam down over time.

Part I of this chapter presents data on Covid-19 and economic outcomes in Vietnam, in comparison to other countries in East Asia and beyond. Part II focuses on the causal factors explaining this response in the first phase of the pandemic. Part III discusses the remarkable moment of Vietnam leading the completion of the Regional Comprehensive Economic Partnership (RCEP) in November 2020. Vietnam's central role in RCEP is a good illustration of the argument made by Tran Thi Anh-Dao in the introduction: "this economic vitality has allowed Vietnam to play a growing and decisive role in the region through a multilateral policy in which Asia has its rightful place" (Introduction page 2). Part IV focuses on the crisis of Summer and Fall 2021, when the Delta variant took advantage of trade integration to have a big impact on Vietnam. The conclusion draws larger implications from Vietnam's position in the global economy and on its reform pathway.

2 Covid-19 Outcomes in Vietnam—Overview of a Surprising Success

In January, Vietnam reacted immediately and effectively to the Covid-19 pandemic. Surprised by the absence of Covid-19 in such a populated country and near-zero death, international observers and foreign media alike were quick to praise Vietnam. For example, on March 30, 2020, the World Economic Forum published a piece titled "Viet Nam shows how you can contain COVID-19 with limited resources.[1]"

To measure outcomes, we choose here to rely on measures of Covid-19 mortality per million people. These measures are more reliable and comparable than case reporting data, given that cases are massively underreported in most countries and highly depend on the availability and deployment of testing. Mortality data remain undercounted in many countries, but are closer to the actual outcomes and to the human cost from the pandemic. We rely here on data aggregated by Oxford University's Our World in Data (OWID).

[1] Fleming, Sean. 2020. "Viet Nam shows how you can contain COVID-19 with limited resources." https://www.weforum.org/agenda/2020/03/vietnam-contain-covid-19-limited-resources/

Table 16.1 Tracking Covid-19 Outcomes in Vietnam (Oxford OWID data)

Date	*Deaths per Million*	*New Cases per M-7D*	*Full Vaccination Rate*
December 31, 2020	0.36	0.05	0
June 30, 2021	0.8	4.5	0.2% (4% 1 dose)
July 31, 2021 (**Delta**)	13	80	0.6% (6% 1 dose)
August 31, 2021	**113**	135	3% (18% 1 dose)
September 30, 2021	**197**	91	10% (34% 1 dose)
October 31, 2021	225	47	21%+ (58% 1 dose)
November 30, 2021	257	137	54% (74% 1 dose)
December 15, 2021 (**Omicron**)	291	156	57% (76% 1 dose) December 10
December 31, 2021	330	161	70% (79% 1 dose)
January 22, 2022	373	173	73% (80% 1 dose)—January 14

Source: Hannah Ritchie, Edouard Mathieu, Lucas Rodés-Guirao, Cameron Appel, Charlie Giattino, Esteban Ortiz-Ospina, Joe Hasell, Bobbie Macdonald, Diana Beltekian and Max Roser (2020)—. "Coronavirus Pandemic (COVID-19)." Published online at ourworldindata.org. Retrieved from: 'https://ourworldindata.org/coronavirus' [Online Resource]

Table 16.1 measures deaths per million at key moments in the pandemic. We also include a measure of new cases per million (smoothed over seven days) as reported, and vaccination rates.

Table 16.1 shows the extraordinary health outcomes obtained by Vietnam for 18 months from January 2020 to June 2021. These results are particularly striking in comparison to Table 16.2, which integrates similar data for comparable countries in Asia, as well as data for selected countries in North America, Europe, and South America. Vietnam's response to Covid-19 was nothing short of amazing.

Second, Table 16.1 also shows how Delta overwhelmed Vietnam's defenses in July, August, and September 2021. Things improved after October 2021 with high degrees of vaccination. But Vietnam never returned to a full control and zero deaths. Deaths continued to increase at a lower pace and a further acceleration took place in December 2021 and January 2022 with the Omicron variant.

Table 16.2 shows that Vietnam was the best performer in the world and East Asia, along with Taiwan (and to some extent, Thailand) in 2020. In 2021, Vietnam fell behind, but its mortality rates remain almost ten times lower than those of the US and lower than the rest of South East Asia, except for Singapore and Thailand.

Table 16.2 Comparative Mortality per Million Outcomes (as of January 22, 2022)

Cases	*Deaths Per M February 06, 2021 Year 1-Classic*	*Deaths Per M September 26, 2021 Delta*	*Deaths per M January 22, 2022 Omicron*
Brazil	1082	2778	2912
USA	1396	2067	2601
UK	1654	2002	2257
France	1209	1734	1907
Germany	735	1113	1391
Malaysia	26	776	973
Canada	548	728	848
WORLD Avg	296	603	710
Indonesia	115	512	522
Philippines	101	337	481
Vietnam	**0.4**	**189**	**373**
India	112	321	351
Thailand	1	233	315
Singapore	5	13	155
Japan	50	139	147
Korea	29	48	127
Australia	36	48	121
Taiwan	0.4	35	36
HK	25	28	28
New-Z	5	5	10
China	3.2	3.2	3.2

Source: Hannah Ritchie, Edouard Mathieu, Lucas Rodés-Guirao, Cameron Appel, Charlie Giattino, Esteban Ortiz-Ospina, Joe Hasell, Bobbie Macdonald, Diana Beltekian and Max Roser (2020).—"Coronavirus Pandemic (COVID-19)." Published online at ourworldindata.org. Retrieved from: 'https://ourworldindata.org/coronavirus' [Online Resource]

Interestingly, just prior to the Covid-19 outbreak, three large private organizations, the Nuclear Threat Initiative (NTI), the Johns Hopkins Center for Health Security (JHU), and the Economist Intelligence Unit (EIU) launched the first "comprehensive assessment and benchmarking of health security and related capabilities across the 195 countries."[2] Their Global Health Security (GHS) Index sought to measure "national health security" capabilities in dealing with some of "the world's most omnipresent risks: infectious disease outbreaks that can lead to international epidemics and pandemics." The rankings were released in October 2019.

[2] Source: https://www.ghsindex.org/about/ Accessed last on 11/29/2020.

The top five countries were the US (index of 84), the UK (78), the Netherlands (76), Australia (76), and Canada (75). Vietnam was far behind with a score of 49 among the low category, almost equal to the Philippines (48). The fact that Vietnam's human outcome with Covid far outstripped this prediction and positioning reveals surprising strengths in Vietnam's capacity to deal with pandemics.

In terms of economic outcomes, Vietnam managed to finish 2020 with positive growth of 2.9% (after 7.0% in 2019). Its 2021 growth rates, however, fell during the disruptions caused by the Delta variant in Summer and Fall. In its December 2021, Asian Development Outlook Update, the Asian Development Bank lowered the growth estimate for Vietnam in 2021 by a full 4%, from 6.6% to 2.6%.[3] The ADB noted that growth actually contracted by a whopping -6.2% in the third quarter due to Covid-19, as the lockdowns created major labor shortages in and around Ho Chi Minh City. There was some improvement in the fourth quarter, but not to the level initially expected. Inflation remained contained at 2.2% in 2021, but faces risks of increase in 2022 and beyond. Table 16.3 positions Vietnam's economic outcomes relative to other selected countries.

Table 16.3 Comparative Growth Outcomes During Covid-19

	2019	*2020 (WB)*	*2021 (WB GEP)*
USA	2.3	-3.4	+5.6
Canada	1.9	-5.3 (IMF)	+5.7 (IMF est)
Euro zone	1.6	-6.4	+ 5.2
UK	1.4	-9.8 (IMF)	+6.8 (IMF est)
Japan	-0.2	-4.5	+1.7
India	4.0	-7.3	+8.3
China	6.0	+2.3	+8.0
Korea	2.0	-0.9 (ADB)	+4.0 (ADB)
Taiwan	2.0	+3.1 (ADB)	+6.2 (ADB)
Indonesia	5.0	-2.1	+3.7
Vietnam	**7.0**	**+2.9 (ADB)**	**+2.6 (ADB)**

Sources: World Bank. January 22. Global Economic Prospects Report; and Asian Development. December 2021. Asian Development Outlook

[3] Asian Development Bank. December 2021. Asia Development Outlook Supplement. https://www.adb.org/publications/ado-supplement-december-2021

3 The Sources of Vietnam's Strengths During Covid-19 (Phase 1)

Following its experience with SARS in 2003 and in collaboration over recent years with both Japan and the American Center for Disease Control (CDC), Vietnam was better prepared and better organized than appeared based on its level of development and health care spending.

In its own way and with its own methods, Vietnam relied on two pillars: institutional capacity and social resilience. Institutionally, Vietnam relied on all eight pillars of the East Asian Model identified in my book, the *East Asian Covid-19 Paradox*:

- Legal tools in place for pandemic response;
- Rapid mobilization of centralized government pandemic Headquarters (Public Health Emergency Operation Center, activated on January 30, 2020);
- Reliance on empowered health centers and health scientists; lack of politicization;
- Rapid border response (quarantine, isolation, with enough staff);
- Rapid provision of tests, masks and personal protection equipment;
- Contact-tracing capacity (both APP and SMS used in Vietnam);
- Rapid generalized mask-wearing and social distancing: Vietnam reaches 87% by the end of April; and
- Clear, precise, empowering, and effective health communication.

The centralized steering committee (Public Health Emergency Operation Center) formed on January 30 organized much of the response coordination in 2020 (Willoughby, 2021). It incorporated all 23 relevant ministers.

The government rapidly shut down the border to China. By March, they put in place strict 14-day quarantine requirements for all foreigners entering Vietnam (as Vietnam faced inflows from Europe and the US). Contact-tracing was implemented widely, both with an APP launched on February 8, 2020, and with the use of SMS. Contact-tracing became mandatory for all suspected cases, including the release of personal information such as age, occupation, place of residence, and recent activities for infected cases.[4] It was backed up by effective mobilization of staff.

[4] Source: Nikkei Asia. 1/6/2021. "Asian trio of Taiwan, Vietnam and Singapore keep COVID near zero." https://asia.nikkei.com/Spotlight/Coronavirus/Asian-trio-of-Taiwan-Vietnam-and-Singapore-keep-COVID-near-zero. Last accessed 1/23/2021.

After the Tet National holidays in February, schools remained shut down for weeks (Willoughby, 2021). In April, the government organized a strict 22-day lockdown across the country that was ranked among the strictest in the region, as measured by the Oxford stringency index (Hale et al., 2020). This index includes "school closures; workplace closures; cancellation of public events; restrictions on public gatherings; closures of public transport; stay-at-home requirements; public information campaigns; restrictions on internal movements; and international travel controls.[5]" As of April 1, 2020, only Vietnam reached the maximum stringency on that index in Asia.

Apart from the early lockdown and some restrictions on bars in August 2020, Vietnam managed to maintain social life. Vietnam also launched innovations, such as field hospitals and robots to disinfect rooms (Duong, 2020).

Communication was also effective and well organized. As early as January 27, 2020, the Ministry of Health had set up a hotline. By February 3, they had set up a national SMS information system. Communication also took palace through social media with the spread of a handwashing song ("Jealous Coronavirus") that went viral (Duong, 2020).

This institutional cooperation built on the deeper one-party state capacity. As argued by Willoughby, the Vietnam Communist Party (VCP) saw Covid-19 policy and rapid economic recovery as crucial for its legitimacy. The VCP was able to coordinate actions at the top and rely on grassroots party cells and associated social organizations for campaign-style mobilization, contact-tracing and enforcement of lockdown. The system also includes a degree of delegation to regional leaders who all followed this orchestrated mobilization (Willoughby, 2021: 134–135).

The second pillar explaining Vietnam's initial success is the high degree of social cohesion and social trust within Vietnam's society. Reviewing recent data from the 2014 World Value Survey, Ortiz-Ospina and Roser observed that Vietnam was an outlier to the expected relationship between high social trust and high GDP per capita (Ortiz-Ospina & Roser, 2016). Indeed, despite its low GDP per capita, Vietnam showed one of the highest findings in social trust. With its low GDP per capita, Vietnam, he argued, had a level of social trust equivalent to that of Switzerland.

[5] Source: Our World in Data. Oxford. https://ourworldindata.org/covid-government-stringency-index

In the 2017–2020 World Value Survey, Vietnam scores even higher. On the question of Trust your Neighborhood (Fully and Somewhat), Vietnam has the highest score at 91.4. Iceland follows with 91.3.[6] In the same survey, Vietnam also scores extremely high on the question of Trust in the Government with a 92.9 (second only to China at 94.6).

These results are indicated of a populace that is read to act for its neighbors in the name of the collective good and in response to communication from the government.

4 Vietnam at the Heart of Reinforced Multilateralism in East Asia (RCEP)

It is hard to understate the gains made by Vietnam in 2020: it chaired ASEAN (including the signing ceremony for RCEP) and experienced continued large-scale supply chain relocation from China.

In November 2020, Vietnam remotely hosted the leaders of ASEAN (10 countries), China, Japan, Korea, Australia and New Zealand in the signature of RCEP. This represented the largest free trade agreement in the world, in terms of GDP, population and trade covered. It also signified a counter-intuitive acceleration of regional trade and economic integration, a strengthening of regional production value chains in the midst of a disruptive pandemic and a US-China confrontation.

This very important event also featured Vietnam at the heart of Asia-Pacific supply chains, at the very moment when many Japanese, Korean, American, and European firms were in the midst of shifting some of their export-oriented production factories from China to Vietnam.

RCEP appears counter-intuitive in the midst of trends of fragmentation and confrontation. However, the regional response by East Asian countries to the pandemic was enhanced by situational convergence around a sense of heightened vulnerability in 2020. Not only did the pandemic originate in China, at the heart of the region, but the region is also the frontline zone for current trade and security disputes between the US and China. It is also most vulnerable to the erosion of globalization and of the liberal international order. Leaders from most countries have expressed that sense of shared vulnerability in one way or another. This vulnerability is not unique to East Asia and is not sufficient to drive regional institution-building, but it generated an added boost to the process and a sense of

[6] Source: https://www.worldvaluessurvey.org/WVSOnline.jsp

gravitas around it. The consequence of shared narratives, collective practices of mutual toleration, and heightened sense of vulnerability in East Asia was to reinforce Asian soft institutionalism.

5 Tensions Between Health Outcomes and the Model of Global Economic Integration in 2021

By the Spring of 2021, tensions were present throughout Southeast Asia between the strategies of zero-Covid and economic and social pressures. It is one thing to maintain lockdowns or social and trade restrictions when the state can spend 20% of its GDP on social compensation measures funded by debt, as in North America, Europe, and Japan. But socio-economic restrictions are unsustainable in low and middle-income societies with no livelihood support. In addition, the suppression of cultural and family celebrations was hard to endure across South East Asia.

As a booming supply chain hub in the context of the US-China trade war, the situation was particularly unbearable for Vietnam. These growing pressures coincided with the surge of the more transmissible and deadly Delta Variant in May–June 2021.

But Vietnam suffered from a third weakness in 2021: the vaccination question. In the context of its masterful control of Covid-19 in 2020 and the extremely competitive free-for-all competition for the few global vaccines available on the global market, Vietnam decided to wait and seek to develop its own vaccine. The government invested in four Vietnamese vaccine projects. As Flower puts it:

> The government baulked at the cost and the length of the queue and went on record to say it would be better to produce vaccines domestically. Seeing an opportunity to establish a valuable foothold in the biotech sector, Vietnam invested in four indigenous vaccines. Tran Van Phuc, a medical commentator for one government newspaper, wrote in December 2020 that 'it might come out much more slowly than its international peers, but if we can do it, waiting for a homemade vaccine is not a bad option' (Flower, 2021).

Eventually, one of the four vaccines (Nanocovax) started phase I trials in December 2020. Unfortunately, the vaccine was not ready in Spring and Summer 2021, and Vietnam had to scramble for cover in front of the virulent Delta variant without vaccine coverage (see Table 16.1). By that point, Vietnam had only approved Astra-Zeneca and could not procure large quantities. Changing tack, Vietnam quickly approved Moderna, Pfizer-BioNTech, but also Sputnik V, Sinopharm, and Johnson & Johnson for emergency use (Flower, 2021). Vietnam started offering a diverse range of vaccines to its population.

Vietnam went on overdrive negotiated aid and contracts with key partners and COVAX. The vaccination campaign eventually really took off in September to November 2021. Remarkably, Vietnam managed to engage both in a production agreement with Sputnik V of Russia[7] and into technology transfer agreements with the US and Japan.[8] It also accelerated the process of testing Nanocovax (phase 3 trials).

As a result, Vietnam may emerge from this misfortune as a real hub in pharmaceutical and vaccine development in South East Asia.

However, the Summer of 2021 was miserable. As cases multiplied and the death toll escalated (as shown in Table 16.1), Vietnam responded with crippling lockdowns in the Mekong Delta and factory shutdowns ensued, with ripple effects across the world. The health care was stretched beyond capacity, and contact-tracing was swamped. The only realistic strategic became to massively accelerate the vaccination campaign.

By January 22, 2022, the vaccination rate was among the highest in the world at 80% (one dose) and 73% (two doses), a remarkable comeback that even beat its initial target of 70% vaccination by May 2022.

The crisis of Summer 2021 signified the larger issue of finding suitable exit strategies from zero-Covid elimination strategies in the face of waves of variants knocking at the door. This is particularly true in authoritarian regimes such as Vietnam where the government and the party are initially reinforced by successful management of Covid. This gain in legitimacy makes it harder to relax the policy in the face of economic pressures and inevitable social pressures. Living with Covid-19 over the long term is a real challenge.

The Delta (and the Omicron) variants have brought to the fore the real tension between enduring political objectives, such as national unity, national pride, and collective achievement on the one hand and the new

[7] Source: Reuters. https://www.eastasiaforum.org/2021/08/01/delta-variant-sets-off-alarm-bells-in-vietnam/

[8] Source:https://e.vnexpress.net/news/news/vietnam-reaches-tech-transfer-agreement--on-us-covid-19-vaccines-minister-4330367.html

positioning of the country as a globalized hub in the international economic system. It is a struggle between global integration and national control that many countries struggle with. This is particularly hard for a lower middle-income country without all the slack, tools and stabilizers to mediate that tension.

Vietnam's Covid-19 policy was also hit in late December 2021 by a corruption scandal leading to the arrest of the CEO of medical company Viet A, Phan Quoc Viet (Bui, 2022). Viet A is one of the leading companies engaged in providing the mandatory tests in Vietnam.

Despite its successes, the Covid-19 sequence in Vietnam led to social and human costs, revealing some of the gaps in human development analyzed by Tran in the introduction of this book (page 2).

6 Conclusion and Implications

Relying on both exceptional institutional capacity and social cohesion, Vietnam was able to pull together a very effective response to Covid-19 in 2020. This response contained deaths and even cushioned the economic shock that hit the whole region and the world at the same time.

However, as low middle-income country with limited health care capacities, Vietnam was not able to hold such a massive counter-Covid-19 mobilization beyond the first 18 months and in the face of repeated waves of new variants. Vietnam also tried to develop its own vaccine and leapfrog the technological frontier in order to gain more autonomy and a better positioning within the global economy. This bold bet did not bear fruits fast enough to have a vaccinated population in time for the arrival of the Delta variant in July 2021. As a key hub in the global production chains (e.g., producing most of Samsung's smartphones), Vietnam was forced to balance harsh closure with economic reality. The Summer and Fall 2021 hit Vietnam hard and hit migrant workers, the poor, and women the most. It will leave lasting memories.

Vietnam has sought to emerge from this challenge as an able new center for vaccine production in South East Asia, and it may well have succeeded.

Covid-19 has also greatly accelerated the digital transition worldwide. This digital moment presents new opportunities for a country like Vietnam. Vietnam is seeking to capitalize on this new moment by leapfrogging into the digital age, through smarter grid development, mobile payments, smart social media APPS, and remote technologies. There are however pitfalls in this transition, as the digital transition is bound to generate losers and greater inequality. It is also bound to increase social demands on the government and to test the governance system of Vietnam. As well, because of the weak global governance of data and its winner-take-all nature, as well as the gradual fragmentation of the Internet in the context of Sino-US tensions (Tiberghien et al., 2021), Vietnam will have hard choices to make.

References

Bui, Thiem. "Vietnam's COVID-19 testing scandal goes viral." *East Asia Forum* (2022). Published electronically 01/21/2022. https://www.eastasiaforum.org/2022/01/21/vietnams-covid-19-testing-scandal-goes-viral/.

Duong, Minh Cuong. "Lessons from Vietnam's COVID-19 victories." *East Asia Forum* (2020). Published electronically 04/21/2020. https://www.eastasiaforum.org/2020/04/21/lessons-from-vietnams-covid-19-victories/.

Flower, Barnaby. "Delta variant sets off alarm bells in Vietnam." *East Asia Forum* (2021). https://www.eastasiaforum.org/2021/08/01/delta-variant-sets-off-alarm-bells-in-vietnam/.

Hale, T., Webster, S., Petherick, A., Phillips, T., & Kira, B. (2020). *Oxford COVID-19 Government Response Tracker*. Blavatnik School of Government.

Ortiz-Ospina, Esteban, & Max Roser. "Trust." *OurWorldInData.org* (2016). https://ourworldindata.org/trust.

Tiberghien, Y. (2021). *The East Asian Covid-19 Paradox*. Cambridge University Press.

Tiberghien, Yves, Danielle Luo, & Panthea Pourmalek. (2021). Existential gap: Digital/AI acceleration and the missing global governance capacity. *CIGI working paper*. Published electronically 12/6/2021. https://www.peacefulcompetition.org/pub/85cu1r9n/release/1.

Willoughby, E. (2021). Unified, Preventive, Low-cost Government Response to Covid-19 in Viet Nam. In S. L. Greer, E. J. King, E. M. da Fonseca, & A. Peralta-Santos (Eds.), *Coronavirus Politics: the Comparative Politics and Policy of COVID-19* (pp. 127–145). University of Michigan Press.

Index[1]

[1] Note: Page numbers followed by 'n' refer to notes.

T. A.-D. Tran (ed.), *Rethinking Asian Capitalism*,
https://doi.org/10.1007/978-3-030-98104-4

Kolibri 360 GmbH
Ferdinand-Jühlke-Straße 7
99095 Erfurt, Deutschland
produktsicherheit@kolibri360.de